CLASSICAL CONDITIONING AND OPERANT CONDITIONING
A Response Pattern Analysis

CLASSICAL CONDITIONING AND OPERANT CONDITIONING
A Response Pattern Analysis

Wendon W. Henton
Iver H. Iversen

With 106 illustrations

Springer–Verlag　　**New York　Heidelberg　Berlin**

Wendon W. Henton
Senior Research Scientist–Psychology
Dept. of Health, Education, and Welfare
12709 Twinbrook Parkway
HFX-120
Rockville, Maryland 20857

Iver H. Iversen
Research Psychologist
University of Copenhagen
Ryesgade 34A
2200 Copenhagen N
Denmark

Library of Congress Cataloging in Publication Data

Henton, Wendon W., 1941–
    Classical conditioning and operant conditioning.

    Bibliography: p.
    Includes index.
    1. Operant conditioning. 2. Conditioned
response. I. Iversen, Iver H., 1948–   joint
author. II. Title.
BF319.5.06H46   150   78-16542

Printed in the United States of America.

9 8 7 6 5 4 3 2 1

ISBN 0-387-**90326**-7   Springer–Verlag New York Heidelberg Berlin
ISBN 3-540-**90326**-7   Springer–Verlag Berlin Heidelberg New York

FOREWORD

Since the appearance of the treatise on "Schedules of Reinforcement" by Ferster and Skinner over two decades ago, the literature in behavior analysis, both experimental and applied, has been dominated by a range of studies dedicated to providing ever more systematic and refined accounts of these "mainsprings of behavior control." For the most part, the analysis has been pursued in the best traditions of "scientific methodology" with careful attention to the isolation of controlling variables in unitary form. Of late, relatively simple interaction effects have provided an important additional focus for more sophisticated analyses. It is clear, however, from even a cursory survey of the monumental research and conceptual analysis which is represented in this scholarly volume by Henton and Iversen that the surface of this complex "behavioral interactions" domain has barely been scratched.

The primary focus of this pioneering effort extends the competing response analysis across all experimental schedules, both classical and instrumental, as well as the interactions between the two. Appropriately, the analysis emphasizes overt behavioral interactions, beginning with the simplest case of one operant and one respondent, and inevitably implicating more diverse and subtle interactions. As the analysis expands to include interactions between multiple recorded responses, increasingly more precise empirical specifications of reciprocal interactions in response probabilities are revealed independently of conventional procedural labels (i.e., operants, respondents, collaterals, adjunctives, etc.) and traditional theoretical distinctions. Overt responses are treated not as measures of "other things" but rather as behavioral interactions to be explained by an analysis of functional relationships rather than by attribution to hypothetical constructs or intervening abstractions.

From a methodological vantage point, the analysis described in this treatise is advantaged by an imaginative and innovative procedural approach. Unfettered by slavish conventions involving "dependent" and "independent" variable assumptions, this dedicated molecular analysis focuses upon specific sets of events and interactions as multiple determinants of behavior. Of particular interest in this regard is the unique treatment of concurrent classical-operant conditioning schedules and the ingenious experimental manipulations which provide the foundation for a novel interpretive departure from the usual "baseline disruption" account of such interactions. Virtually all combinations and permutations of classical-operant "superimposition" procedures are explored systematically in a series of original experiments which emphasize the significance not of the "baseline disruption," which occurs across procedures, but of the concurrent and competing response characteristics which are usually unobserved and unrecorded.

Of at least as great conceptual import would seem to be the frontal experimental attack by Henton and Iversen upon the myth of "response independence" which continues to dominate contemporary views of operant schedule interactions. In this regard, for example, the data presented on increased rates of orienting behaviors in concurrent response-independent and signaled reinforcement schedule experiments constitute a serious challenge to traditional accounts of reinforcer interaction effects based upon assumptions of negligible competing response influences. Similarly, this molecular analysis of response interactions in multiple operant schedules reveals the critical role of interacting collateral and competing responses which has all too often been obscured by current labeling practices (e.g., "contrast effects," etc.). Even conventionally mislabeled "post-reinforcement pause" and "inter-response time" phenomena observed in simple operant schedules are shown to be influenced directly by the temporal characteristics of collateral competing responses. Indeed, a telling point is made with reference to the issue of response versus reinforcement interactions in the analysis of operant schedules, by directing attention away from a molar analysis based upon data averaged over sessions and focusing upon the molecular effects of real behaviors in the form of local response rate changes which occur and interact frequently in the absence of any local change in reinforcement.

A special place of importance is reserved in the final chapter of this book for a somewhat unconventional but characteristically innovative treatment of both simple and complex classical conditioning paradigms within the empirical framework of the well-developed and demonstrably productive competing response analysis. Here again, the authors present a convincing challenge to one of the more widely held misconceptions regarding the absence of overt responses and the resultant misguided theoretical interpretations of classical conditioning effects. Not only is the data on acquisition of delay conditioning, extinction, external inhibition, and conditioned inhibition persuasively marshaled to document a veritable mosaic of response interactions, but the long-neglected analysis of concurrent classical conditioning effects, suggested in the early writings of Pavlov, is creatively exposed to experimental scrutiny.

This singular empirical analysis with its focus upon the broadly based response interactions which characterize behavioral transactions at all conceptual levels can be seen to represent a "paradigm revolution" in the truest sense. The novelty and comprehensiveness of its integrative features are impressive, the gaps in knowledge which it reveals are critical, and the new directions of experimental inquiry which it suggests are the stuff of which progress in science has traditionally been made.

J. V. Brady

PREFACE

This volume attempts to organize a ten-year experimental analysis of interacting response patterns in behavioral conditioning. The research program actually began at the Walter Reed laboratories in 1968, as an extension of Brady's "competing response" analysis of conditioned emotions. The scope of this work is the development of the "competing response" analysis into a "concurrent response" analysis applicable to many of the common experimental techniques used in behavioral psychology today. More specifically, the present analysis concerns the concurrent and sequential response interactions generated by Pavlovian as well as Skinnerian conditioning procedures.

This book, written specifically for laboratory psychologists and students, is divided into three sections corresponding to the developing conceptual and experimental analysis of interactions in classical–operant schedules ("emotions," Section I), operant schedules (Section II), and classical conditioning (Section III). Section I is the completed analysis of "emotions" as the interaction of Pavlovian and Skinnerian conditioned responses, beginning with a comprehensive parameter by parameter review of the literature. The concurrent response analysis is then developed step by step through an experimental examination, and places Pavlovian–Skinnerian interactions more firmly within the broader framework of concurrent conditioning procedures. Section II expands the analysis into an experimental description of Skinnerian or operant conditioning methods, with chapters devoted to simple operant schedules, concurrent schedules, and multiple schedules, and therefore embraces many of the common Skinnerian procedures. Section III is the current use of the response interaction analysis in the context of Pavlovian or classical conditioning. This latter analysis includes many of the standard classical excitatory and inhibitory procedures, with a further development of Pavlov's work on concurrent classical–classical conditioning. Our continuous concern has been an adherence to the inductive method of direct and systematic replication in the determination of lawful generalizations within and across these popular conditioning techniques.

On the other hand, this empirical approach bumps up against the traditional mentalisms, inferences, and cognitive theories which have gradually evolved into "laws" in each of the three research areas. In our introduction, we reply to the opposing arguments and occasionally heated disproofs of response interactions, with the relevant issues carried forward and specifically illustrated in each of the subsequent sections and chapters.

In all, the volume attempts a systematic position which might have something to offer investigators using either classical conditioning, operant conditioning, or classical–operant combinations. As a new analysis, the work necessarily contains various new procedures, reanalysis of old procedures, and a quantitative analysis of response frequencies and patternings. Our thesis is that behavioral conditioning procedures must control myriad response interactions which are important to the understanding of psychology, but which are nevertheless ignored by typical methodologies which record and analyze but a single response. The concurrent response analysis places these single responses within the ongoing matrix of simultaneous and sequential response interactions.

Lastly, we must express our continuing appreciation to the many individuals who have contributed to the making of this work. Our obvious debts to the science of B. F. Skinner and M. Sidman will be rather apparent. Many portions of the book have immeasurably profited from our personal and professional associations with an ever growing series of colleagues, including A. Brownstein, J. V. Brady, J. P. Huston, M. Lyon, C. L. Salzberg, and J. C. Smith. Significant contributions have also been gratefully received from J. Boren and C. M. Bradshaw. We can only hope that these gentlemen might recognize both their contributions and our deep appreciation.

The statements and opinions expressed in this work represent the views of the authors and may not reflect the views of the Department of Health, Education, and Welfare (HEW), nor any agency of the government of the United States or Denmark.

W. W. H.
I. H. I.

ACKNOWLEDGMENTS

The following journals and publishers have kindly granted permission to reprint previously published figures and illustrations. The appropriate citations are also indicated in the captions of each figure: Almquist and Wiksell, three figures from *Scandanavian Journal of Psychology;* Kenyon College, four figures and one table from *The Psychological Record;* Pergamon Press, one figure from *Physiology and Behavior;* Society for the Experimental Analysis of Behavior, three figures from the *Journal of the Experimental Analysis of Behavior.*

Portions of this work and preparation of the manuscript were supported by grants from the Danish Research Council for the Humanities, Danish Research Council for the Medical Sciences, and a stipend from the University of Copenhagen.

CONTENTS

CLASSICAL CONDITIONING AND OPERANT CONDITIONING
A Response Pattern Analysis

Introduction

Different Views of Psychology

Phrenology, that age old study of the phrenes, continues to be the accepted premise of contemporary psychology—unfortunately. The names and numbers of phrenes have been hotly debated and frequently changed across the decades. The appropriate measuring device is still at issue. Yet, the fundamental concept of physical dimensions as definitive measures of hypothetical entities and causes has not only been unchanged, but assimilated into all current psychologies. In the beginning, mental states were measured by the shape of the skull. More recently, physical behavior has supplanted physical structure as the measuring tool. With some irony, Pavlov's rejection of the "fantastic states" and mentalisms has been ignored, and Pavlovian conditioning is now offered as a premier technique for measuring drives, fears, helplessness, motivation, etc. Similarly, the straightforward assertion by Skinner that behavior is only behavior has also been compromised, with once "radical" behaviorists now promoting overt responses as indices of preferences, memories, inhibitions, values, general emotional states, etc. Within the phrenological systems, behavior as a dependent variable is transformed into behavior as an index or indicant, an intrinsically trivial but convenient epiphenomenon to measure the more interesting workings of the mind (Ebel, 1974).

Phrenology also offers a labor and time-saving alternative to the "thorny Calvinist path" of manipulating independent variables and recording dependent variables (Skinner, 1975). The bypassing or circumvention of an experimental analysis is accomplished by simply reversing the logic of empiricism. Phrenology now begins with behavior and develops a logical regression backward to estimate the necessary characteristics of the imputed cause. The actual efficiency of the system is that the expressed experimental psychologist need not bother with experimentation. In practice, the nominal author of an experimental analysis today does not conduct experiments but provides an editorial evaluation of experiments previously relegated to technicians and students. The "empirical" analysis is in actuality a theoretical interpretation appended to the graphs and data reported from the laboratory. The reasoned analysis usually stops well short of the actual experimental manipulations in favor of a theoretical inference advocated by the author.

Behavior as indicants of underlying causes has been ably described and defended by many authors, and frequently applied with great skill. Thus, Stevens (1951) characterized the larger portion of a handbook of experimental psychology as concerned with behaviors as indicants of various intervening agents. Similarly, Bolles (1967) described the inference of intervening causes from behavioral effects as the "bread and butter of psychological theorizing." Such inferred causal agents may be subdivided into "intervening variables" and "hypothetical constructs" (review by Mac Corquodale and Meehl, 1948). Intervening variables are abstract or metaphorical explanatory devices within particular logic systems and do not have physical attributes (nonspatiotemporal entities; Kantor, 1976). In contrast, hypothetical constructs refer to potentially recordable and verifiable events, frequently within the central nervous system. In both cases, however, the agents are not actually measured or manipulated, but inferred through presumably isomorphic physical effects. Perhaps one fundamental distinction between theoretical and experimental psychology is that inferred explanations may be the food stuff of theory but have proven to be a rather dubious experimental method throughout the history of science (Wallace, 1972, 1974; Bernard, 1957). In particular, the continuing genesis of psychology from philosophy and physiology is such a history of fancied causes, not only promoted as psychical actualities, but also ostensibly measured through physical attribution (phrenology).

Structural Phrenology

The original phrenology is generally attributed to Gall and Spurzheim in the early 1800s, although antecedent traditions may be traced through 17th century philosophers to early Greece (review by Bentley, 1916; Boring, 1957). The term *phrene* comes from early Greek philosophers and quite literally means the diaphragm or lungs, and figuratively means life spirit, will, or faculties. We might speculate that this divergence of literal and figurative meanings prompted Aristotle to warn against the confusion of facts with "reasoned facts" (review by Wallace, 1972). Centuries later, philosophers Reid and Stewart deduced that the mind was a collection of 37 mental states or faculties, differing either quantitatively or qualitatively. The 37 propensities were then individually localized within (conveniently) 37 subdivisions of the brain, with Gall and Spurzheim adding the proposition that the shape of the overlying skull matched and measured the amount of tissue devoted to the localized mental function. This matching law eventually ran afoul of the comparative anatomies of the skull and the brain, and the suggested topographical isomorphism between skull shape and brain function became untenable by 1911 (Boring, 1929).

The physical identification of mental states, however, did not die out with the demise of Gall's system. Phrenology merely fractionated into a multitude of different hypothesis, each advocating a different physical measure or a different measured explanation. The simplist device was to substitute a different overt measure of the inferred faculty. Boring had hardly pronounced phrenology dead when Sheldon and various collaborators proposed that the body was a more precise and appropriate measure of mental propensities. The physical shape of the body replaced the physical shape of the skull in the phrenological analysis (Kretschmer, 1925). Sheldon and associates proposed that the observable physique, characterized as a somatotype, may be used to assess the underlying biological morphogenotype. The somatotype summarized the pattern of three components of the physique: endomorphy (soft and fat), mesomorphy (hard muscle and bone), and ectomorphy (thin and delicate). Next, 650 personality traits were reduced and combined into three categories: visceratonia (glutonous and affectionate), somatonia (athletic), and cerebratonia (inhibited and socially withdrawn). The association between the three types of bodies and temperaments thus suggested that fat people are basically jolly, athletes adventurous, and frail people withdrawn (Sheldon, 1942). Subsequent studies demonstrated that the body somatotype accurately predicted the mental disorders of psychotics and juvenile deliquents as well as the personalities of more normal subjects (Sheldon, 1949). Unlike Gall's system, the constitutional psychology of Sheldon does not seem to have attracted many adherents (Hall and Lindzey, 1957).

Ironically, the progress in neuroanatomy critical of Gall's phrenology gave rise to a different and more severe physiological phrenology. The new phrenology simply eliminated skull shape as the physical measure, while continuing to retain the identity between brain structure and mental function. The later phrenology proposed that regions of the brain with different histological structure necessarily have different psychical functions, and, in extreme form, localized different mental processes in different architectural layers of the cortex (Broadman, 1925). The assertion that isolated, unique functions could be identified with isolated, unique structures was soon criticized as little more than histological phrenology. Franz (1912) argued that such a severe localization was antithetical to the interdependent and integrated activity of the central nervous system. Moreover, Franz questioned the accuracy of operational definitions equating histological and clinical localization with mental localization: "From the anatomical and physiological standpoint, we deal solely with associations of an anatomical and physiological character" (Franz, 1912, p. 327). The stark claim that physiology is solely physiology seems to have been at least as radical in 1912 as in 1970. In spite of the early "radical" physiology of Franz, many predominant theories within psychology continue to identify special attributes with unique structures (e.g., the hippocampus as the center of motivation, learning, memory, information storage, or processing; review by Young, 1976).

Behavioral Phrenology

The early explanatory systems of Gall, Sheldon, and others might be characterized as static phrenology, in that fixed and relatively unchanging physical attributes were employed as the measure of the inner cognitive workings. The
attendant problems of measuring a dynamic function with a static characteristic
resulted in the more sophisticated systems of the twentieth century. The problem has been generally solved by matching a changeable variable rather than a
fixed constant with the presumed dimensions of the conceptual functions.
Within psychology, the physical dimension of choice has been some characteristic of overt behavior, such as response probability, amplitude, or latency. To
be crude, the differences between static and dynamic phrenology are akin to
the differences between palmistry and theoretical psychology. The palmist predicts events by analyzing the fixed lines and features of the hand, where as the
psychologist infers events not from the structure but the movement of the
hand, or forepaw, of the subject. Little doubt is left in both cases, however,
that the real matter of interest and importance lies elsewhere, at other levels
and in other dimensions than the corporeal hand.

An early example of such dynamic phrenology is Fechner's law of psychophysics. Weber, in 1834, had previously observed that the fraction by which a
physical stimulus must be changed to be minimally discriminable is a constant
and is roughly independent of the absolute magnitude of the initial stimulus
($\Delta S/S = C$). Fechner (1860) reformulated the Weber fraction to address the
mind–body problem and substituted the term *sensation* for *stimulus*. Fechner
proposed that mental sensation or perception was a logarithmic function of
stimulus magnitude, and, in result, initiated the physics of the soul. "Psychophysics" remains one of the major areas within contemporary psychology,
with current controversies primarily concerned with the exact relationship between subjective sensation and stimulus magnitude. The underlying assertion
that behaviors are accurate measures of sensations is either ignored or assumed. Only signal-detection theory currently questions the measurement relation between responses and sensations (Swets, 1961). The bulk of data from
signal-detection experiments is rather clear: the distribution of responses is not
a direct measure of stimulus characteristics but is also controlled by the behavioral contingencies scheduled for each response of "Yes, I see it" and "No,
I do not see it." However, signal-detection theory maintains the psychophysics
tradition by subdividing responses into separate estimates of sensation and response bias, and then proposing that physical behavior, corrected for bias,
measures not only sensation but also the "noise" in the sensing system. The
argument between signal-detection and other theories is not whether behaviors
are measures of underlying sensation or perception, but only whether the psychophysical measure is direct or indirect.

The assumption of independent and exclusive sets of stimulus variables and
bias variables critically simplifies the theoretical correction for sensations but is
not wholly consistent with stimulus and schedule interactions noted in conditioning experiments. Relatively recent studies have reported changes in re-

sponse bias with manipulation of stimulus variables within the signal-detection paradigm (Nevin, 1970; review by Dusoir, 1975; Nevin et al., 1975; Molinari et al., 1976). A rather large number of studies, in both the classical and operant conditioning literature, demonstrate that schedule effects are conditional upon the presence and absence of associated stimuli, and that stimulus discrimination is in turn conditional upon differential reinforcement schedules (e.g., Ferster and Skinner, 1957; Sokolov, 1960). As Nevin et al. (1975) suggested, the signal detection procedure is a particular case of discrimination conditioning, and the psychophysical interpretations must eventually be consistent with the related data in animal discrimination experiments. Nevertheless, signal detection has enabled a large step forward in the recognition that behavior cannot be directly reduced to a unidimensional sensory construct.

Additional psychophysical systems offer behavior as an indicant of more central entities and functions rather than afferent sensory processes. For example, changes in operant response rates may be used as measures of emotions, as well as motivation, drive, expectancies, etc. The logical derivation of emotional measurement usually requires a now standard introduction, beginning with a description of operant rates during the presentation of a classical conditioning procedure. The response rate changes are then equated with conditioned emotional responses, which in turn are effects of underlying emotional states. The emotional states are next dependent upon associationistic processes of excitation and inhibition. By appropriate sequential substitution of logical identities, the initial semantic definition of emotion as physical behavior can be transformed into a syntactical relationship between emotions and associationistic states. The initial synonyms of behavior and emotions are simply separated into a causal interpretation, with the conclusion that behavioral changes are dependent upon and a measure of underlying associative processes. Brady (1975) similarly criticized the "use and abuse" of interchangeable definitions and the "host of semantic, linguistic and taxonomic problems" that result in emotion "persistently reified as a substantive 'thing'." In a similar vein, Skinner (1963) suggested that operational definitions have not been especially successful within psychology, in that the defining operations are widely applied as logical equations relating behavior to mental events, but in fact set severe restrictions upon knowledge of subjective events.

Indeed, the current literature abounds with various proofs of specific and general emotional states as actual and substantive things, with diagrams and equations depicting the exact relationship between emotional causes and behavioral effects. The contemporary operational definitions are frequently applied as little more than phrenological assertations. The mental entities are not reduced to the operations of measurement, but the physical measures are offered as indicants and proofs of the mental entities. More generally, matching an actual dimension of behavior and a hypothetical dimension within a mental network is an example of the philosophers "category mistake" (Ryle, 1949) or the "substantialization of abstracta" (Reichenbach, 1958). The advantages and disadvantages of operational definitions are also discussed at length by Bridgeman (1927, 1959) and Stevens (1939).

The behavioral substantialization of cognitive abstracta accepts the double assumptions of both a close correspondence between overt and covert functions, and a further correspondence between covert and cognitive functions. Alternative explanations in physiological psychology emphasize only the first premise and either minimize or disregard the second assumption. The behavioral physiological psychology attempts to isolate and quantify the functions of different portions of the actual brain. One of the more common techniques is the double dissociation procedure described by Teuber (1955) and Rosvold (1959). Double dissociation is an experimental manipulation which demonstrates that lesion of one area of the brain affects behavior A, not behavior B, whereas an injury to a second area only affects behavior B, not behavior A. Mishkin (1972), for example, reported that graded lesions in the anterior inferotemporal area systematically affected simultaneous visual discrimination, not pattern learning. Posterior inferotemporal lesions, however, affected pattern learning, not simultaneous discrimination. The data suggested that the two separate behavioral effects are influenced by different subsystems of the brain.

Double dissociation is a rather powerful technique for determining the influence of specific portions of the brain upon behavior. However, few physiological psychologists apply the same logic of dissociation to the supposed measurement relationship between behavior and central nervous system functions. The conditioning literature again amply demonstrates that behavior can be manipulated across a broad range by altering schedule parameters and contingencies independent of physiological manipulation. The dissociation then suggests that behavior is not necessarily an invarient or direct measure of specific functions of the brain. Similar dissociations have been reported between behavior and the activity of the motor cortex (Fetz and Finnocchio, 1971) and between neural responses and eliciting stimuli in sensory systems (Fox and Ruddell, 1970).

> These observations would suggest some caution in interpreting temporal correlations as final evidence for functional relations . . . Such a consistent temporal correlation under a variety of behavioral conditions would seem to be strong evidence for a functional relation. When cell and muscle activity were simultaneously included in the reinforcement contingency, however, we found that the correlated muscle activity could be readily suppressed. These observations suggest that a possible test of the stability of an observed temporal correlation would be the operant reinforcement of its dissociation. (Fetz and Finnocchio, 1971, pp, 434–435.)

The dissociation of physiological and behavioral responses is comparable to earlier demonstrations that skull shape is not invariantly correlated with brain shape, and equally questions the phrenological assumption that overt attributes are invariant measures of covert functions. The bright prospect of conditional overt–covert response correlations in fact promises a far more comprehensive understanding of behavior and has long been espoused by diverse psychologists (James, 1890; Miller, 1969; Pavlov, 1927; Skinner, 1963). The conditioned modification of covert responses (intereoceptive "feelings," for example, Harris and Brady, 1974; review by Razran, 1961) is of a piece with the variable rather than fixed integration of physiological responses within the total behavioral pattern. This analysis of conditional rather than invariant correlations between behavioral and physiological functions begins to fulfill the promise of a more adequate psychology by considering events within the skin as deterministic responses themselves, rather than mere mediators of behavior.

Reinforcer Value: An Example of a Developing Phrenology

The development of phrenological systems is now difficult to fully appreciate since most contemporary learning theories have developed within the psychological traditions established years ago. The original assertions are either accepted today as traditional and useful truths or rejected as nineteenth century curios. However, at least one currently developing interpretation is verging upon becoming another phrenology. For a decade or more, we have known that rate of reinforcement is one of the independent variables that can control behavior (Herrnstein, 1961). The functional relationship is occasionally reversed, and behavior subsequently offered as an exact measure of reinforcement rate. Next, reinforcement is redefined as obtained reinforcers, in turn equated with the value of the reinforcer. Reinforcer or reinforcement value is further defined to include the effects of parameters other than reinforcement rate. Drugs and deprivation manipulations, for example, are said to affect response rates by means of changes in the "reinforcement context" (Cohen, 1973; Herrnstein and Loveland, 1974). Alternatively, reinforcer matching may involve redefining responses as "other sources of reinforcement" or "inherent reinforcing value" (Rachlin, 1973), as well as incorporating various free-floating constants and exponents. The relative rate of specific behavior can then be argued to match exclusively the computed reinforcer value, which in turn can be inferred from the explained response rate. The explanatory parameter of reinforcement rate has then gradually expanded from a physical variable to a generic value emerging from the organism and assigned to responses (Baum, 1974). (The development of the response–reinforcer value matching law may be found in a variety of theoretical papers: Baum, 1973; Catania, 1963, 1966, 1969, 1973; Herrnstein, 1961, 1970, 1974; Herrnstein and Loveland, 1974, 1975; Mazur, 1975; Rachlin, 1971, 1973; Rachlin and Baum, 1969, 1972.)

Additional semantic problems arise when the matching law is said to demonstrate an independence between responses, with interactions only between values or reinforcement. Catania previously noted that ". . . in order to maintain the independence of two compatible operants, it is necessary to make them incompatible . . ." and ". . . [it] is often necessary to program concurrent schedules in such a way that the operants become even more incompatible . . ." (Catania, 1966, pp. 215–216). However, the term *incompatible responses* is not strictly interchangeable with *independent responses,* since incompatible responses are not independent but temporally dependent. The emission of one response specifically precludes the occurrence of all incompatible responses. Perhaps consistent with the terminological confusion, the matching law seems to demonstrate that rates of independent responses (defined as incompatible responses) match a single dimension of relative reinforcement rate (nevertheless defined as multiple public and nonpublic dimensions), but only by demonstrating that response patterns do not actually match reinforcement patterns (Catania, 1969, 1973, Rachlin and Baum, 1969).

With some irony, the reinforcer matching law is primarily sponsored by the *Journal of the Experimental Analysis of Behavior,* which previously editorialized specifically against the use and abuse of interchanging definitions (e.g., Editors' comments, 1969, vol. 12, pp. 845–846). However, the hegemony of the reinforcer value interpretation has been sufficient to almost oust alternative explanations of operant responses. As with previous phrenologies and matching laws, the interpretive proposition has been that one physical dimension is isomorphic with a second physical dimension (response rate matches reinforcement rate, skull shape matches brain shape), followed by the proposition that one or the other physical dimension is also isomorphic with a more abstract dimension within a particular logic system. The sequence of logical derivations has been to identify a causal relationship, reverse it, relabel dependent measure as an exclusive indicant, and then progressively substitute and interchange definitions until a suitable generality is obtained.

Unidimensional explanations also involve the additional constraint that other previously identified independent variables are actually without effects or can be redefined and subsumed as special cases of the reference parameter. The independent variables known to control behavior, however, are exceedingly diverse and numerous, with no single variable both necessary and sufficient to control response rates. *Psychological Abstracts,* for example, routinely lists several thousand experimental variables. Similarly, Sidman (1960) concluded a general discussion of statistical description and interpretation by noting that:

> A sufficient number of experiments have demonstrated that the behavior of the individual subject is an orderly function of a large number of so-called independent variables. Indeed, we may now presume such orderliness to be the rule rather than the exception . . ." (Sidman, 1960, p. 49).

The more complicated interactions involving three, four, or five variables literally number in the millions. Considering response rate as an exclusive indicant is thus tantamount to entering a matrix of innumerable behavioral functions, and then knowledgably choosing the one function specifying the theoretically "correct" relationship. Indeed, the benefit of response rate as a basic datum lies in it being a generality across many functional relationships rather than uniquely dependent upon reinforcement rate or any other single parameter.

The multiplicity of empirical determining events, however, does not necessarily contradict a unidimensional theory of behavioral causality. The empirical parameters are simply transformed and redefined to converge into an intervening agent, which in turn directly changes the appropriate behavioral indicants. A set of empirical variables may be said to coalesce into an excitation or value or sensation that is in a one-to-one relationship with behavior. More elaborate inferences may be drawn, however, with one set of variables producing a general excitation, and a second set of variables producing a general inhibition, with excitation and inhibition then converging into a single explanatory dimension of "general action potential," "general motivational state," or the "final common path." As a most general scheme, the multitude of independent variables eventually coalesces into a final intervening agent that is isomorphic with and inferable from observed behavior. No other inferential logic would in fact make sense. If the intervening agent is not both necessary and sufficient for the actual behavior, then the proposed explanatory agent could not be unequivocally inferred from the behavioral effects. Most inferential models therefore critically sidestep the possibility of interdependencies between end terms; that is, many "effects" also "feedback" to affect "causes." For example, behavior is said to depend upon reinforcement, but reinforcement also depends upon the occurrence of the behavior. Similarly, the emission of one response may affect the patterning of a second response, but the emission of the second response may as well affect the first response. Such interdependence between end terms ("feedback loops") renders inferential causality as quite difficult if not impossible, even in simple physiological preparations (Horridge, 1969).

More basically, a single event A can only be said to exclusively measure or reflect event B provided observation reveals an ever-existing correspondence between A and B. This is not quite the model attained with the inference of behavioral causality. In no case has a record ever been produced of a covariation between a measuring behavior and an inferentially measured intervening agent. More importantly, an exclusive measurement relationship of "A only if B" is a very strong claim that can only be justified within causal systems that literally prevent interactions with extraneous events.

At this point, the hapless psychologist is in something of a quandary, with little more than three options. First, we might attempt to isolate such an experimental preparation, knowing only full well that any results would have absolutely no generality to other closed systems, or to different systems with interacting variables. Second, we might simply deny the possible existence of any interacting variables, and insist that the A–B function is unconstrained and universally independent of other variables—thus the requirement that sensation is independent of reinforcement schedules, that reinforcement interaction is independent of response interaction, etc. This independence proposition would support exclusive causality and inferential measurement and obviate the need for isolated causal systems; but tends to fly in the face of the interacting relationships accumulated over the years.

Finally, we might forfeit the ghosts of inference and phrenology to first admit and then study the matrix of causal interactions within the phenomenal world. The latter path also suffers disadvantages, by requiring considerable time and effort—occasionally sweatshop effort. One standard and classic scientific method approximates an isolated causal system by determining the relationship between one recorded variable A and one manipulated variable B, while holding constant all other variables (C, D, . . . , N). Next, the A—B function is redetermined again and again when variable C is held constant at different values, only to be redetermined again when variable D is also changed to a different value. As an illustration, we might examine the rate of responding as a function of five different rates of reinforcement, at each of five different deprivation levels, at each of five schedule requirements. Even this relatively simple interaction between only three independent variables would require 125 experimental determinations. At this point, the investigator is quite tempted to retire gracefully from the laboratory and assume a more comfortable inferential rather than experimental analysis. Yet, we are quite fortunate that many previous psychologists have pitched in to at least begin if not finish the empirical analysis of behavior.

Functional Relationships: An Empirical Alternative

On the other hand, a theoretical generality of "A only if B" may be offered as an extreme and starting bargaining position to focus experimental attention upon a particular variable. Almost any relationship between A and B can be systematically manipulated, and indeed most laboratory investigators attempt to do so. In virtually all cases, the initial statement of an unconditional and exclusive relationship is eventually qualified by subsequent experimental effort to "A if B, conditional upon C, D, ..." These empirical functions express the established dependencies between factual events and are neither hypothetical nor refutable. Consequently, functional relationships avoid debate about the possible dimensions, influences, origins, etc. of unrecorded entities, and instead emphasize the observed relationship between actual behavior and actual events. As such, the described relationships enjoy Wittgenstein's (1922) admonition that what can be said can be said clearly, and interobserver agreement must soon flourish.

This direct verification of a behavioral function, followed by a systematic examination of the additional variables previously held constant, will yield a description of the interactions necessary for "positive results" (A if B, given C, D, . . .) and, equally important, the interactions yielding "negative results" (no A if B, given E, F, . . .). The direct and systematic replication techniques generate families of interrelated data that not only define the accuracy of causal statements, but also delineate the additional variables in which a particular behavioral function may or may not be obtained. A general principle is then not so much a universally accurate statement, but a functional relationship that continues to be found across a broad range of additional and interacting functions. Recognition of the limits of any generality in turn serves to focus attention upon the different sets of variables that qualify each general principle. Under the best conditions, a further analysis of the different sets of qualifying variables may then lead to a "paradigm shift" or data revolution (Kuhn, 1970)—a third function that firmly interrelates and merges the formerly disparate generalities. The systematic evaluation of interacting functions has fortunately been successful in psychology (Sidman, 1960) as well as medicine (Bernard, 1957). Rather than some damnable aberration of a science gone wrong, the experimental qualification of one function by additional functions may establish first the reliability and then the generality of any explanatory principle.

An additional consequence of the array of interacting functions is that the behavioral analysis tends to become highly specific or "molecular." The analysis of actual behavior patterns occurring in real time is in fact rather immune to explanation by molar constructs. Accumulated over many subjects or minutes, the averaged rate of one response may be relatively higher than the averaged rate of a second or a third response, with a plausible inference that the first response was generated by a higher value or motivation or expectancy; but the second and third responses may each occur exclusively in any given interval for any given subject. Obviously, this momentary "preference" for another response cannot easily be explained by a higher value assigned to the first response. Such molecular behavioral changes are said to be irregular, chaotic, or indeterminate with respect to the molar analysis of behavior, and are frequently dismissed as trivial or too microscopic.

Some decades ago, momentary behavior oscillations were said to be due to an "oscillatory force" acting upon the "effective reaction potential" (Hull, 1943) or attributed to "fleeting emotions" (Woodworth and Schlosberg, 1954). The local changes in behavior are rather similarly explained today. Thus, Baum has argued:

> From moment to moment, however, the organism engages in one activity or another and switches from one activity to another. These moment-to-moment relationships among activities have little to do with value, because at any moment the organism may be engaging in an activity of any value; it simply engages more often in high-valued activities. The momentary fluctuations in an organisms activities result from momentary fluctuations of variables that have a constant average effect over extended periods of time (e.g., deprivation). (Baum, 1973, p. 150)

The argument proposes that specific changes in behavior are unrelated to the explanatory value, which enters the arena only when the behavioral effects are summed together and statistically averaged. Given the discrepancy between explanation and observation, we might reach an opposite conclusion: the molar explanatory device has little relevance to the control and prediction of the observed changes in behavior. Quite recently, Shimp (1975) also suggested that moment-to-moment behavioral changes are directly controlled by schedule contingencies, and molar results are by-products of more fundamental relations involving local behavioral effects. Shimp more explicitly argued that a molar analysis becomes superfluous to the extent that a molecular analysis is successful.

Historically, the examination of molecular behavioral effects dates back to the beginning formulations of an experimental analysis of behavior (Pavlov, 1927; Skinner, 1938). The early Russian investigations of isolated classical conditioned reflexes soon led to the trial-by-trial analysis of interacting reflex systems (Ukhtomsky, 1954; Anohkin, 1958; Konorski, 1967). Skinner (1938) similarly identified the two principle research tasks within operant psychology as the identification of the laws of isolated responses, and then the analysis of the interactions between responses. "Preference," as one case, may be analyzed as the switching back and forth between responses rather than a construct inferred from statistically averaged response rates (Skinner, 1950). More recently, interacting behavior patterns have also been reported under the general rubric of competing responses, and applied to the investigation of functional interactions within classical and operant schedule combinations ("conditioned emotional responses," Brady, 1975).

The neglect and occasionally heated denial of local behavioral interactions by contemporary theorists is then both surprising and disappointing. The moment-to-moment changes in behavior are simply too apparent and too complex to be ignored or argued into an explanatory limbo. We suspect that a science of behavior might eventually require general principles to explain actual behavioral changes, perhaps in terms of molecular functional relationships, rather than averaged behavioral changes in terms of global logical constructs. The earlier reports of behavioral patterns in classical conditioning schedules, operant conditioning schedules, and classical–operant combinations do in fact seem to require an explicit analysis of interactions and changeovers between responses. This analysis of response patterning and behavioral interactions is then both the purpose and substance of the present work.

In sum, laboratory psychologists are acutely sensitive to assertions that behavior is a "measure" of something else, either hypothetical or actual. We might summarize the objections to both general phrenologies and unidimensional matching laws by paraphrasing Skinner's previous critiques: The objection to general phrenologies is in the use of responses as a measure which appeals to events taking place somewhere else, at some other level of observation, described in different (and contradictory) terms, and measured, if at all, in different dimensions (Skinner's comments on learning theories, 1950, p. 193). The objection to matching laws is that response rates predicted by some hypothesis of sensation or rational utility can be generated by manipulating and balancing a host of variables, but it would be a mistake to regard these as ultimate conditions, or to stop the search for other functional relationships (Skinner's comments on concurrent schedules and matching laws, 1966, p. 26). Reminiscent of the earlier "radical" physiology of Franz and Bernard, Skinner, Sidman, and other "radical" psychologists insist that behavior is solely behavior, and neither a mental nor dimensional measurement.

To this point, the present volume has been something of a harangue—heartfelt and long felt, but a harangue nevertheless. This introduction is also a partial reply to comments over the past decade offered against reporting response patterns in behavioral conditioning ("nonexistant," "trivial," "irrelevant"), and usually arguing for adherence to some explanatory faculty, sensation, state, value, or other preferred psychological construct. Fortunately, conformity to data instead of insistent theory has remained a relatively easy choice year after year. The remainder of the volume is then a rather more positive description of the complex behavioral patterns obtained in classical and operant conditioning.

The work is unabashedly indebted to the continuing influences of J. C. Smith, Aaron Brownstein, and J. V. Brady. Although none of these gentleman would entirely agree with the present analysis, we would nevertheless hope that each would accept some responsibility for the effort and scope of the present work.

The volume is generally arranged in a chronological organization of 10 years of research into the extension of Brady's competing response analysis and includes a variety of classical and operant conditioning combinations (Part I), complex and simple operant schedules (Part II), and simple and concurrent classical conditioning procedures (Part III).

References

Anohkin, P. K.: The role of the orienting-exploratory reflex in the formation of the conditioned reflex. In, L. G. Voronin, A. N. Leontiev, A. R. Luria, E. N. Sokolov, and O. S. Vinogradova (eds.): *Orienting Reflex and Exploratory Behavior*. Moscow, Academy of Pedagogical Sciences, 1958.

Baum, W. M.: The correlation-based law of effect. *J. Exp. Anal. Behav.*, **20**, 137–153, 1973.

Baum, W. M.: Choice in free-ranging wild pigeons. *Science*, **185**, 78–79, 1974.

Bentley, M.: On the psychological antecedents of phrenology. *Psychol. Monogr.*, **21**, 102–115, 1916.

Bernard, C.: *An Introduction to the Study of Experimental Medicine*. New York, Dover, 1957.

Bolles, R. C.: *Theory of Motivation*. New York: Harper & Row, 1967.

Boring, E. G.: *A History of Experimental Psychology*, 1st ed. New York, Appleton-Century, 1929.

Boring, E. G.: *A History of Experimental Psychology*, 2nd ed. New York, Appleton-Century-Crofts, 1957.

Brady, J. V.: Toward a behavioral biology of emotion. In, L. Levi (ed.): *Emotions—their Parameters and Measurement*. New York, Raven Press, 1975.

Bridgeman, P. W.: *The Logic of Modern Physics*. New York, MacMillan, 1927.

Bridgeman, P. W.: *The Way Things Are*. Cambridge, Mass., Harvard University Press, 1959.

Broadman, K.: *Vergleichende Lokalisationslehre der Grosshirnrinde*. Leipzig, Barth, 1925.

Catania, A. C.: Concurrent performances: reinforcement interaction and response independence. *J. Exp. Anal. Behav.*, **6**, 253–263, 1963.

Catania, A. C.: Concurrent operants. In, W. K. Honig (ed.): *Operant Behavior: Areas of Research and Application*. New York, Appleton-Century-Crofts, 1966.

Catania, A. C.: Concurrent performances: inhibition of one response by reinforcement of another. *J. Exp. Anal. Behav.*, **12**, 731–744, 1969.

Catania, A. C.: Self-inhibiting effects of reinforcement. *J. Exp. Anal. Behav.*, **19**, 517–526, 1973.

Cohen, I. L.: A note on Herrnstein's equation. *J. Exp. Anal. Behav.*, **19**, 527–528, 1973.

Dusoir, A. E.: Treatments of bias in detection and recognition models: a review. *Percept. Psychophys.*, **17**, 167–178, 1975.

Ebel, R. L.: And still the dryads linger. *Am. Psychol.*, **29**, 485–492, 1974.

Fechner, G. T.: *Elemente der Psychophysik*. Leipzig, Breitkopf and Hartel, 1860.

Ferster, C. B., and Skinner, B. F.: *Schedules of Reinforcement*. New York, Appleton-Century-Crofts, 1957.

Fetz, E. E., and Finnocchio, D.: Operant conditioning of specific patterns of neural and muscular activity. *Science*, **174**, 431–436, 1971.

Fox, S. S., and Rudell, A. P.: Operant controlled neural events: functional independence in behavioral coding by early and late components of visual cortical evoked responses in cats. *J. Neurophysiol.*, **33**, 548–556, 1970.

Franz, S. I.: New Phrenology. *Science*, **35**, 321–328, 1912.

Hall, C. S., and Lindzey, G.: *Theories of Personality*. New York, Wiley, 1957.

Harris, A. N., and Brady, J. V.: Animal learning: visceral and autonomic conditioning. *Annu. Rev. Psychol.*, **25**, 107–133, 1974.

Herrnstein, R. J.: Relative and absolute strength of response as a function of frequency of reinforcement. *J. Exp. Anal. Behav.*, **4**, 267–272, 1961.

Herrnstein, R. J.: On the law of effect. *J. Exp. Anal. Behav.*, **13**, 243–266, 1970.

Herrnstein, R. J.: Formal properties of the matching law. *J. Exp. Anal. Behav.*, **21**, 159–164, 1974.
Herrnstein, R. J., and Loveland, D. H.: Hunger and contrast in a multiple schedule. *J. Exp. Anal. Behav.*, **21**, 511–517, 1974.
Horridge, G. A.: The interpretation of behavior in terms of interneurons. In, M. A. Brazier (ed.); *The Interneuron.* Los Angeles, University of California Press, 1969.
Hull, C. L.: *Principles of Behavior: an introduction to Behavior Theory.* New York, Appleton-Century-Crofts, 1943.
James, W.: *Prinicples of Psychology.* New York, Holt, 1890.
Kantor, J. R.: Behaviorism, behavior analysis and the career of psychology. *Psychol. Record,* **26**, 305–312, 1976.
Konorski, J.: *Integrative Activity of the Brain.* Chicago, University of Chicago Press, 1967.
Kretschmer, E.: *Physique and Character.* New York, Harcourt, 1925.
Kuhn, T. S.: The structure of scientific revolutions. In: *International Encyclopedia of Unified Science,* vol. 2, no. 2. Chicago, University of Chicago Press, 1970.
Mac Corquodale, K., and Meehl, P. E.: On a distinction between hypothetical constructs and intervening variables. *Psychol. Rev.,* **55**, 95–107, 1958.
Mazur, J. E.: The matching law and quantifications related to Premack's principle. *J. Exp. Psychol.* [*Anim. Behav. Processes*], **1**, 374–386, 1975.
Miller, N. E.: Learning of visceral and glandular responses. *Science,* **163**, 434–448, 1969.
Mishkin, M.: Cortical visual areas and their interactions. In, A. G. Karcymar and J. C. Eccles (eds.): *Brain and Human Behavior.* Heidelberg, Springer-Verlag, 1972.
Molinari, H. H., Rozsa, A. J., and Kenshalo, D. R.: Cool sensitivity measured by signal detection method. *Percept. Psychophys.,* **19**, 246–251, 1976.
Nevin, J. A.: On differential stimulation and differential reinforcement. In, W. C. Stebbins (ed.): *Animal Psychophysics: the Design and Conduct of sensory experiments.* New York, Appleton-Century-Crofts, 1970.
Nevin, J. A., Olson, K., Mandell, C., and Yarensky, P.: Differential reinforcement and signal detection. *J. Exp. Anal. Behav.,* **24**, 355–367, 1975.
Pavlov, I. P.: *Conditioned Reflexes.* London, Oxford University Press, 1927.
Rachlin, H. C.: On the tautology of the matching law. *J. Exp. Anal. Behav.,* **15**, 249–251, 1971.
Rachlin, H. C.: Contrast and matching. *Psychol. Rev.,* **80**, 217–234, 1973.
Rachlin, H. C., and Baum, W. M.: Response rate as a function of amount of reinforcement for a signalled concurrent response. *J. Exp. Anal. Behav.,* **12**, 11–16, 1969.
Rachlin, H. C., and Baum, W. M.: Effects of alternative reinforcement: Does the source matter? *J. Exp. Anal. Behav.,* **18**, 231–241, 1972.
Razran, G.: The observable unconscious and the inferable conscious in current Soviet psychophysiology: interoceptive conditioning, semantic conditioning, and the orienting reflex. *Psychol. Rev.,* **68**, 81–147, 1961.
Reichenbach, H.: *The Rise of Scientific Philosophy.* Berkeley, University of California Press, 1958.
Rosvold, H. N.: Physiological psychology. *Annu. Rev. Psychol.,* **10**, 415–454, 1959.
Ryle, G.: *The Concept of Mind.* New York, University Paperbacks, 1949.
Sheldon, W. H.: *The Varieties of Tempermanent: A Psychology of Constitutional Differences.* New York, Harper, 1942.
Sheldon, W. H.: *Varieties of Delinquent Youth: an Introduction to Constitutional Psychiatry.* New York, Harper, 1949.
Shimp, C. P.: Perspectives on the behavioral unit: choice behavior in animals. In, W. K. Estes (ed.): *Handbook of Learning and Cognitive Processes.* New York, Erlbaum Associates, 1975.
Sidman, M.: *Tactics of Scientific Research: Evaluating Experimental Data in Psychology.* New York, Basic Books, 1960.
Skinner, B. F.: *The Behavior of Organisms.* New York, Appleton-Century, 1938.
Skinner, B. F.: Are theories of learning necessary? *Psychol. Rev.,* **57**, 193–216, 1950.
Skinner, B. F.: Behaviorism at Fifty. *Science,* **140**, 951–958, 1963.
Skinner, B. F.: Operant behavior. In, W. K. Honig (ed.): *Operant Behavior: Areas of Research and Application.* New York, Appleton-Century-Crofts, 1966.
Skinner, B. F.: The steep and thorny way to a science of behavior. *Am. Psychol.,* **43**, 42–49, 1975.

Sokolov, E. N.: Neuronal models and the orienting influence. In, M. A. B. Brazier (ed.): *Central Nervous System and Behavior*. New York, Josiah Macy, 1960.

Stevens, S. S.: Psychology and the science of science. *Psychol. Bull.*, **36**, 221–263, 1939.

Stevens, S. S.: Mathematics, measurement, and psychophysics. In, S. S. Stevens (ed.): *Handbook of Experimental Psychology*. New York, Wiley, 1951.

Swets, J. A.: Is there a sensory threshold? *Science*, **134**, 168–177, 1961.

Teuber, H. L.: Physiological psychology. *Annu. Rev. Psychol.*, **6**, 267–296, 1955.

Ukhtomsky, A. A.: *Complete Works*, vol. 5. Leningrad, State Publishing House, 1954.

Wallace, W. A.: *Causality and Scientific Explanation*, vol. 1. Ann Arbor, University of Michigan Press, 1972.

Wallace, W. A.: *Causality and Scientific Explanation*, vol. 2. Ann Arbor, University of Michigan Press, 1974.

Wittgenstein, L.: *Tractatus Logico-Philosophicus*. London, Routledge and Kegan Paul, 1922.

Woodworth, R. S., and Schlosberg, H.: *Experimental Psychology*. New York, Holt, Reinhart & Winston, 1954.

Young, G. A.: Electrical activity of the dorsal hippocampus in rats operantly trained to lever press and to lick. *J. Comp. Physiol. Psychol.*, **90**, 78–90, 1976.

CONCURRENT CLASSICAL AND OPERANT CONDITIONING PROCEDURES

Chapter 1

Review of Classical–Operant Conditioning, Parameter by Parameter

Wendon W. Henton

History: A Confluence of Three Traditions

The experiments described in this section are concerned with a behavioral analysis of the various permutations and combinations of classical and operant conditioning schedules. For the present purposes, a schedule describes the interrelationship between three primary events: environmental stimuli, responses, and reinforcer delivery. An operant conditioning schedule describes the stimuli in which a reinforcing event is delivered following and contingent upon the occurrence of the recorded response (Ferster and Skinner, 1957). Dependent variables in operant conditioning are the rate, duration, force, and latency of the recorded response (Skinner, 1950; Premack, 1965). A classical conditioning procedure describes the conditional relationship between an environmental stimulus (conditioned stimulus, CS) and the subsequent occurrence of an unconditionally reinforcing stimulus (unconditioned stimulus, UCS) that reliably elicits a recorded response (unconditioned response, UCR) (Pavlov, 1927). The frequency, duration, and latency of responses elicited by the CS, not the UCS, are the primary dependent variables in classical conditioning schedules.

The theoretical and methodological issues involved in defining stimuli, responses, and reinforcers, and the still more subtle distinctions between classical and operant conditioning schedules, have been systematically reviewed by a variety of investigators (Miller and Konorski, 1928; Skinner, 1938; Mowrer, 1960; and especially volume two of *Psychology: A Study of Science,* edited by S. Koch, 1959*). One interpretative issue, for example, is the definition of a

---

* The following definitions are used throughout Part I. A *response* is defined as any environmental change initiated by the organism, either an overt response within the external environment or a covert response within the internal physiological environment. In operant schedules, *reinforcement* refers to the response-contingent delivery of a reinforcer. A *reinforcer* is any contingent

(con't.)

classical conditioning UCS as a stimulus that reliably elicits a dominant reflexive response (Pavlov, 1927), any reflexive response (Konorski, 1967), or any
measurable response (Stolurow, 1973). The divergent definitions of UCS have
somewhat subtle yet pervasive consequences for the distinctions between classical and operant conditioning procedures (Kimble, 1961; Kling and Riggs,
1971). However, in spite of conceptual and linguistic issues, traditional operational distinctions between classical and operant conditioning are rather fundamental. For classical conditioning, the primary characteristic is that the reinforcing event is delivered in a specified temporal relationship to the CS,
independent of all responses. In contrast, reinforcer delivery is explicitly dependent upon the occurrence of a response in operant conditioning. Both classical and operant conditioning schedules may be simple arrangements between
one response, one reinforcer, and one stimulus, or complex programs in which
a variety of responses, reinforcers, and stimuli are combined in simultaneous or
successive components (Pavlov, 1927; Ferster and Skinner, 1957; Findley,
1962). The classical and operant schedule combinations described in this section, for example, are concurrent schedules in which the subject is simultaneously conditioned on (1) a simple classical conditioning schedule and (2) a
simple operant conditioning schedule (Henton and Brady, 1970; Brady, 1971;
Henton, 1972).

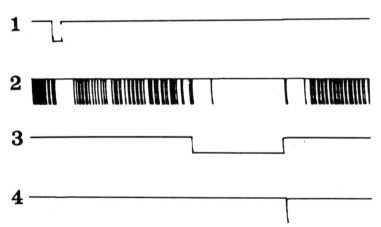

Figure 1.1. Suppression of behavior during Estes-Skinner procedure. Trace 1: delivery of operant
reinforcer on a VI 2-min schedule. Trace 2: operant key-pecking responses by pigeons. Trace 3:
duration of Pavlovian CS. Trace 4: delivery of shock UCS.

event that alters the subsequent probability of the specified response. In classical conditioning, the
unconditioned stimulus (UCS) is any stimulus that reliably and consistently elicits a specified response (UCR). The *conditioned stimulus (CS)* is any stimulus that does not initially elicit the specified UCR but may nevertheless elicit other specific responses. The *conditioned response (CR)* is a
new or acquired behavior during the CS as a result of pairing with the UCS. *Reinforcement* in classical conditioning refers to the presentation of the UCS contingent upon the occurrence of the CS.
Thus, in classical conditioning, reinforcement is stimulus contingent and response independent,
and, in operant conditioning, reinforcement is specifically response contingent. One common feature, however, is that positive and negative operant reinforcers may also be arranged to serve as
positive or negative UCS in classical appetitive and defensive conditioning, respectively.

The explicit history of classical–operant combinations is relatively brief, dating back to an experiment by Estes and Skinner (1941). This report by Estes and Skinner described the rate of lever pressing reinforced with response-contingent food (operant schedule) during the superimposed presentation of a stimulus terminated by response-independent shock (classical conditioning schedule; Figure 1.1). This recent history, however, is firmly imbedded and intermixed within several scientific and philosophical traditions. The confluence of different traditions has now resulted in an occasionally bewildering variety of opinions about classical and operant interactions. However, the writing and verbal behavior of psychologists, like the behavior of all other organisms, may be profitably examined within the context of previous and current training histories (Skinner, 1953). Current formulations of classical and operant schedule combinations might then be viewed as various blends of at least three traditional considerations within psychology—the analysis of emotions, classical conditioning, and the elimination or disruption of behavior.

Emotional States

"Anxiety has at least two defining characteristics; (1) it is an emotional state, somewhat resembling fear . . ." (Estes and Skinner, 1941). Within a fraction of the introductory first sentence, Estes and Skinner acknowledged the status of emotional states, anxiety, and fear. The universal and ageless study of emotions continues to be one of the dominant influences controlling current interpretations of classical–operant schedule effects.

The philosophical interest in feelings and emotions was initially translated into behavioral measures at least as early as the introduction of Darwinian evolution. *The Expression of the Emotions in Man and Animals* (Darwin, 1872) proposed that emotions could be inferred and measured by overt responses across a broad spectrum of organisms. Baring of teeth and curling of lips in man as well as animals were inborn, instinctive, and perhaps archetypical measures of emotions. The analysis of feelings and emotions, as described by Boring (1957), was also a major element within the psychological system of Wundt. Wundt's "conscious contents" and "tridimensional theory of feelings" were both tested and supported by correlations between bodily activity and the three continuums of pleasantness–unpleasantness, excitement–calm, and strain–relaxation.

The interpretation of emotions was profoundly influenced by the simultaneous publications in the early 1880s by James in America and Lange in Denmark. James (1884) attempted a logical simplification by proposing that a special and separate center of emotions did not exist within the brain; rather, emotions corresponded to various combinations of ordinary processes in the sensory and motor centers, and therefore did not require the assumption of special seats and centers. James proposed that the body was a "sort of sounding-board," with emotions the perception of changes in ". . . the bladder and bowels, the glands of the mouth, throat, and skin, and the liver . . . and the continuous co-operation of the voluntary muscles." James further distinguished between the primary "emotions" of rage, fear, and anger, and their pale copies of moral, intellectual, and aesthetic "feelings," in which the bodily sounding board was mute. Overt responses and bodily changes were thus expressions of emotions, but not expressions of feelings (James, 1890). In agreement with James, Lange (1885) suggested that emotions included "vasomotor disturbances, varied dilations of the blood vessels, and consequent excess of blood, in the separate organs." In contrast to James, however, Lange proposed that subjective sensations were indirect, secondary disturbances caused by the cardiovascular changes. Thus, as noted by Wenger (1950), the "James–Lange" theory is a historical misnomer: for James, emotions were the perception of bodily changes; for Lange, emotions were the bodily changes.

The neurophysiology and emotional interpretations of James and Lange promoted harsh criticism, and an alternative theory, by Cannon (1914, 1927, 1931; detailed critique by Fehr and Stern, 1970). In reply to James, Cannon (1927, 1931) proposed that (1) the latency of visceral responses was too slow to account for emotions, (2) experimental induction of peripheral changes does not elicit emotions, (3) the viscera are relatively insensitive, (4) the same visceral changes are found in all emotions, and (5) the elimination of peripheral feedback does not alter emotional behavior (also see Sherrington, 1900; Woodworth and Sherrington, 1904; Cannon et al, 1927). Cannon (1927) instead proposed that afferent stimulation from sense organs reaching the thalamus simultaneously (1) elicit changes in the musculature and viscera, and (2) project to the cortex, which in turn releases the thalamus from cortical inhibition. Emotional experience was primarily described as the cortical experience of the thalamic activation.

Following Cannon, and Woodworth and Sherrington, neurophysiological speculations have related virtually every aspect of the forebrain and brain stem to emotional behaviors (review by Brady, 1970a, 1970b). For example, extirpation and electric stimulation experiments suggest that anterior and dorsomedial thalamic nuclei may be related to anxiety, tension, emotional "alerting" responses, and positive reinforcement (Spiegal and Wycis, 1949; Baird et al, 1951; Olds, 1955, 1956). Other brain tissues implicated in emotional behavior include hypothalamic nuclei (Bard, 1928, 1934; Bard and Rioch, 1937; Rioch, 1938; Bard and Mountcastle, 1948), the limbic system (i.e., the hippocampus, fornix, mammalary bodies of the hypothalamus, anterior thalamic nuclei, and amygdala) (Papez, 1937; Kluver and Bucy, 1937, 1938; MacLean, 1949, 1952) and the brainstem reticular system (Duffy, 1957; Hebb, 1949; Lindsley, 1950, 1957; Malmo, 1957, 1962). Attempts to relate overt behaviors to underlying neurophysiological events have been described in detail by Arnold (1950, 1970), Lindsley (1951), and Miller et al. (1960), among many others (reviews by Grossman, 1967; Young, 1943, 1973).

Classical Conditioning

"Anxiety is here defined as an emotional state arising in response to some current stimulus which in the past has been followed by a disturbing stimulus"

(Estes and Skinner, 1941). The second characteristic defining anxiety offered by Estes and Skinner was that the emotional state is established by classical conditioning, but with the added proviso that the reaction to the CS is not necessarily the same reaction elicited by the UCS.

The association of stimulus pairs, of course, was a major issue throughout the history of philosophy (Boring, 1957). The British philosophers especially analyzed successive and simultaneous associations of objects, sensations, and images in terms of the still current laws of contiguity, similarity, frequency, etc. The experimental analysis of spinal reflexes and classical conditioning by Sherrington (1906), Pavlov (1927) and Sechenov (1935) subsequently provided experimental psychology with a ready behavioral analogy for the study of "higher mental processes."

Watson and Morgan (1917) were among the first theorists to suggest a classical conditioning basis for affective behaviors. Watson and Morgan proposed that the gamut of emotions observed in adults are classical conditioned reflexes based upon three inborn or unconditioned emotional reaction patterns of fear, rage, and love. Watson and Raynor (1920) subsequently reported the first experimental analysis of emotional behavior, based upon the classical conditioning or associationistic model. A white rat was shown to a 1-year-old boy, and reaching toward the rat was paired with striking a steel bar immediately behind the subject's head. After seven trials, presentation of the white rat alone elicited crying and crawling rapidly away. Generalization tests with a rabbit, dog, fur coat, cotton, wool, etc, elicited similar "fear" reactions. Watson and co-workers concluded that reflex factors and classical conditioning thus formed the basis of learned emotional reactions. (Note, however, that the "UCS" of striking the steel bar was an operant punishment procedure and response-contingent, rather than the response-independent UCS of the classical conditioning model.)

One of the first therapeutic treatments of emotions was a behavioral technique also based upon the classical conditioning formulation. Jones (1924a, 1924b) described a series of experiments in which stimuli eliciting emotional responses were carefully paired with eating maintained at a relatively constant rate by bits of candy. In impressive anticipation of subsequent procedures and interpretations, Jones reported that (1) the rate of eating could be disrupted by the responses elicited by the fear stimulus, or, with slightly different procedures, (2) the elicited fear responses could be reduced by eating. Jones (1924a) suggested that both the deleterious and beneficial effects were due to an interaction between two competing response systems controlled by fear objects and craving objects.

Pavlov (1927) also described a series of classical conditioning procedures for the study of affective disturbances and pathological states. In each paradigm, a simple conditioning procedure was made progressively more difficult over successive trials until "the animal became quite crazy, unceasingly and violently moving all parts of its body, howling, barking, and squealing intolerably" (Pavlov, 1927, p. 294). The emotional behaviors were produced by (1) gradually increasing the similarity between a circle paired with food and an elipse not paired with food, (2) systematically increasing the interval between CS and UCS presentation for each of six different stimuli paired with food, or (3) progressively altering the locus and intensity of a weak electric current paired with food. The salivation initially conditioned to the CS was replaced by the violent emotional reactions in each procedure. The more or less prolonged pathological states were thought to result from the gradual alteration of the relative balance between inhibition and excitation past a critical adjustment value.

Classical conditioned fear and acquired drives continue to be central elements in current definitions of emotional concepts. The theoretical importance of conditioned emotions is perhaps best exemplified by the continual analysis and reanalysis of emotional processes in motivation and reinforcement described by Mowrer (1939, 1940, 1950, 1960). More recently, systematic positions emphasizing the role of classical conditioning in the acquisition and maintenance of behavior have been elaborated by many authors (Miller, 1948, 1951, 1959; Brown and Farber, 1951; Brown et al., 1951; Solomon and Wynne, 1953, 1954; Rescorla and Solomon, 1967; McAllister and McAllister, 1971). Moreover, experiments by Wolpe (1952, 1958) and Masserman (1943) have generated treatments of emotions based upon antagonistic classical conditioning responses and processes (Wolpe, 1962; review by Wilson and Davison, 1971).

Classical–Operant Interactions

Estes and Skinner (1941) introduced a third and perhaps predominant influence affecting interpretations of classically conditioned emotions. The unique contribution of the Estes-Skinner experiment, and the primary subject of the present chapter, is the alteration of operant behaviors during the superimposed presentation of a classical conditioning procedure. After discussing conditioning and the concept of emotional states, Estes and Skinner proposed that

> A stimulus giving rise to "fear," for example, may lead to muscular reactions (including facial expressions, startle, and so on) and a widespread autonomic reaction commonly emphasized in the study of emotion; but of greater importance in certain respects is the considerable change in the tendencies of the organism to react in various other ways. Some responses in its current repertoire will be strengthened, others weakened, in varying degrees. Our concern is most often with anxiety observed in this way, as an effect upon the normal behavior of the organism. (Estes and Skinner, 1941, pp. 390–391)

The experiments by Estes and Skinner were then designed to examine this disruptive effect of classically conditioned emotional states. More specifically, responses by rats were regularly reinforced by the response-contingent delivery of food every 4 min. The characteristic rate and pattern of the ongoing operant responses were decreased and disrupted throughout the presentation of a 3-min tone (CS) terminated by electric shock (UCS; Figure 1.1). In a second experiment, the operant lever-pressing response was no longer reinforced with food (operant extinction), and the gradually extinguishing lever-pressing rate was similarly disrupted during the tone–shock pairings. In a final experimental manipulation, lever pressing was once again reinforced with food, but the tone was continuously presented alone and unpaired with shock (extinction of classical conditioning). The ongoing operant response was initially disrupted at tone onset, but progressively increased to the normal rate during the remaining portion of the session.

This experimental disruption and manipulation of behavior reported by Estes and Skinner has developed into a major field of experimental research over the past three decades. Undoubtedly, one of the most comprehensive empirical and conceptual analyses of such classical–operant interactions has been described by Brady and associates (Brady and Hunt, 1955; Brady, 1971, 1975). Extensive programs in a number of other laboratories have also systematically examined the behavioral changes during CS–shock pairings (e.g. Kamin, 1961, 1965; Hoffman and Fleshler, 1962, 1964; Lyon, 1963, 1967; Church, 1969). Until quite recently, the analysis of classical–operant combinations has been primarily concentrated on negative classical conditioning procedures superimposed upon positively reinforced operant responses (reviews by Davis, 1968; Lyon, 1968). The consistency of the experimental analysis is rather strikingly confirmed by the extraordinary control of operant rates obtained with the careful manipulation of classical and operant schedule parameters (Hendricks, 1966; reviews by Rosenberger, 1970; Smith, 1970).

Following the reviews of Davis and Lyon, a variety of experiments have further elaborated the complex interactions between the multitude of variables controlling operant rates during superimposed CS–shock pairings. The success of the experimental analysis of "conditioned emotional responses" (Brady and Hunt, 1955), and influential papers by Rescorla and Solomon (1967), Kamin (1969), and others, have generated considerable experimental interest in the analysis of all possible combinations of classical and operant conditioning procedures. The four-fold analysis of positive and negative classical conditioning procedures superimposed upon positive and negative operant conditioning procedures forms the basis of the present review.

Theoretical Positions Briefly Considered

A rich variety of inductive and deductive theoretical formulations have frequently affected experimental research in classical–operant conditioning schedules. A brief consideration of the more prevalent theories would therefore be appropriate if somewhat tangential to the laboratory analysis of concurrent classical–operant schedules.

The first systematic formulation was proposed by Brady and Hunt (1955). After reviewing 54 experimental reports, Brady and Hunt offered an inductive or "experimental approach to the analysis of emotional behavior." The experimental approach was, in effect, a formalization of Estes and Skinner's previous suggestion that some responses in the subject's repertoire will be strengthened and other responses weakened during classical–operant combinations. A broad program for the analysis of interacting response systems was based upon the interrelationships between internal and external respondents, controlled by the classical conditioning schedule, and internal and external operants, controlled by the operant conditioning schedule (Brady, 1970a, 1971). The "competing response" interpretation has focused upon the variety of interacting yet separable response systems involved in the conditioned emotional response paradigm, including endocrine, autonomic, and cardiovascular processes and the more peripheral muscular systems. For example, changes in baseline operant response rates may be related to increased frequencies of incompatible behaviors, such as crouching and "freezing" elicited by the CS–shock pairings. Heart rate and cardiovascular responses may also be altered, which in turn could function as additional discriminative stimuli maintaining the suppressed operant rate (Brady, 1975). *Feelings* and *emotions* were then used as generic terms summarizing internal and external responses and their appropriate controlling variables. Moreover, the complex interrelationships between response systems are viewed as schedule dependent, with a variety of response interactions determined by specific experimental parameters, behavioral histories, and response topographies (Brady, 1971, 1975).

Kamin (1961, 1963, 1965) proposed a similar incompatible response interpretation, although he emphasized the difficulty of selecting the necessary and/or sufficient competing responses from the diffuse array of potentially incompatible behaviors. Kamin and co-workers have instead suggested that the alteration of operant rates may be an indirect quantification of the superimposed classical conditioning processes. An extensive series of experiments using delayed, trace, and backward conditioning procedures have become standard references in the classical–operant conditioning literature (Annau and Kamin, 1961; Brimer and Kamin, 1963; Kamin and Brimer, 1963; Kamin and Schaub, 1963; Kamin, 1965). The experiments using different intensities and sequences of conditioned and unconditioned stimuli do suggest that operant rates may be sensitive to classical conditioned extinction, inhibition, and disinhibition procedures. More recently, Kamin (1968, 1969) and Kamin and Gaioni (1974) have proposed a more cognitive interpretation which suggests that the effectiveness of classical conditioning may vary directly with the "surprising" nature of the UCS. A UCS preceded by a well-established CS may be more expected, and therefore less disruptive, than a similar UCS preceded by a not as yet conditioned CS. Operant rates during a superimposed CS would then be dependent upon the predictability or surprising characteristics of UCS onset.

A "conditioned suppression" analysis that eschews emotional inferences has been proposed by Lyon (1963. 1968). In the conditioned suppression formulation, the operant rate changes are not offered as measures of emotions but simply accepted as functional or empirical effects. The changes in operant responding during the CS may be partially due to competing responses of crouching and freezing (interference hypothesis), or to punishment of the operant response sequence by the shock UCS (punishment hypothesis). [Weiskrantz (1968) also suggested that the response-independent UCS may in fact function as a response-contingent operant reinforcer, differentially maintaining preparatory or postural responses that reduce the aversive effects of electric shock.]

Lyon (1968) thus concluded that the conditioned emotional response paradigm is an aversive control technique that may share nonemotional effects with other aversive control procedures.

An elegant four-decade series of experiments by Konorski (1967) includes a comprehensive if provocative formulation of the interactions between classical and operant conditioning procedures. For Konorski, classical conditioning involves two distinct sets of unconditioned responses, and therefore simultaneously generates two sets of conditioned responses during the CS. Preparatory responses are conditioned to all situational cues, yielding drive-conditioned responses, and consummatory responses are conditioned to the CS, yielding conditioned consummatory responses. (A more detailed description of Konorski's analysis will be presented in Part III.) In appetitive conditioning, the drive responses are inhibited by consummatory response systems. In a somewhat analogous fashion, instrumental responses are suppressed during a superimposed stimulus paired with food, with a concomitant increase in consummatory salivation and approach to the UCS food cup. Konorski further proposed that the disruptive effects did not reflect an interaction between inhibitory and excitatory processes, but an interaction between two excitatory processes conditioned to mutually antagonistic centers. This, the disruption of all motor acts, such as the suppression of baseline operant responses, occurs by the excitation of groups of neurons eliciting antagonistic motor acts (Konorski, 1972).

An interacting or mediational state interpretation of classical–operant schedules has been offered by Rescorla and Solomon (1967). They proposed that classical conditioning establishes an internal emotional state that may interact with a motivational state maintaining the operant response through a shared mediator state. Thus, changes in operant response rates could be indirect but potentially sensitive measures of classical conditioned emotions. In contrast, the peripheral classical conditioned responses such as salivation and cardiac changes are thought to be only imprecise indicators of the emotional states and do not directly mediate or interfere with operant responses. Rescorla and Solomon then concluded that the concurrent measurement of both operant and classical conditioned responses is not merely inefficient but irrelevant to the analysis of classical–operant interactions. Rescorla and Wagner (1972) proposed a revised model, in which the strength or salience of a CS is dependent upon the total associative strength of all CS elements. The individual elements are collectively rather than independently conditioned to an asymptotic value determined by the strength of the UCS. A well-established CS paired with shock will therefore acquire near asymptotic strength and prevent conditioning of any additional stimuli that are simultaneously paired with the same UCS. An asymptotic conditioned emotional state might then block or prevent the conditioning of a similar associative state (Rescorla and Wagner, 1972) but increment or facilitate an aversive operant motivational state (Rescorla and Solomon, 1967; also see Wagner, 1969; Rescorla, 1970, 1971a, 1971b, 1973).

Hoffman and associates (Hoffman and Fleshler, 1961, 1964, 1965; Hoffman et al, 1963) have also interpreted operant suppression as reflecting emotional reactions elicited by the aversive classical conditioning procedure. Hoffman and co-workers have further argued that the disruptive effects of Pavlovian conditioning cannot be due to an increased frequency of behaviors incompatible with the ongoing operant response; rather, Hoffman and Barrett (1971) and Stein et al. (1971) suggested that "freezing" during the CS is not a specific conditioned response, but the total inhibition of all overt responses caused by internal emotional states. Although the details of the inhibitory processes are unspecified, the emotion-induced behavioral inhibitions are consistent with the use of operant changes to measure or index internal fear reactions.

A general motivational theory of punishment by Estes (1969) also includes an interpretation of classical–operant schedule interactions. The Estes interpretation, influenced by stochastic mathematical models (Estes, 1959), suggests that the probability of an instrumental response is proportional to the facilitative input to amplifier drive elements. Stimuli preceding either response-dependent or response-independent shock acquire the capacity to inhibit the amplifier elements maintaining the baseline operant response. This inhibition in Estes' system is primarily an interaction between drive elements, not direct peripheral response interactions. The conditioned suppression of overt responses is therefore said to be mediated by CS-induced reductions in the operant motivational state.

A "general emotional state" has been described by Azrin and Hake (1969) to account for operant changes during stimuli paired with either positive or negative reinforcers. The general emotional state theory argues that operant responding will be suppressed during a stimulus paired with any strong positive or negative reinforcer. Azrin and Hake proposed that the operant changes may be related to a state of "heightened preparedness" and are closely associated with autonomic and cardiac changes, with both covert and overt responses a product of the same underlying emotional state. The general emotional state interpretation may also be a reinforcer value theory (Hake and Powell, 1970) that proposes that a Pavlovian UCS will reduce the value of the operant reinforcer during the CS, and operant response rates will in turn decrease to match the new reinforcer value, as predicted by the response–reinforcer matching interpretation of Catania (1966) and Herrnstein (1970).

The competing response interpretation of Brady and Hunt (1955) was recently extended to a more general concurrent response–concurrent schedules analysis by Henton and Brady (1970) and Henton (1972). The concurrent response analysis suggested that classical conditioning procedures superimposed upon operant baselines define concurrent schedules in which a classical conditioning schedule and an operant conditioning schedule are programmed simultaneously. In consequence, the conditioned emotional response paradigm may be one of many concurrent schedules that simultaneously control two sets of responses. The pattern of responses controlled by one conditioning schedule may then be dependent upon the concurrent pattern of responses controlled by the second conditioning component. The analysis suggested that the classical conditioned response rate may be disrupted by the operant schedule, in much the same fashion that operant response rates are disrupted by the classical conditioning procedure. Facilitative or suppressive interactions between the concurrent operants and respondents may then be controlled by manipulating the stimulus, response, or reinforcement contingencies of each schedule component (Henton, 1972; Henton and Iversen, 1973; similar interpretations have been independently reported by Lo Lordo et al., 1974; Schwartz, 1976; and Schwartz and Gamzu, 1977).

In summary, the heterogeneity of theoretical formulations over the past 30 years has generated widely divergent research strategies and treatments of classical–operant schedule interactions. The formulations range from inductive and experimental approaches (Lyon, 1968; Brady, 1970a, 1971; Henton and Brady, 1970) to inferential and deductive theoretical models (Rescorla and Solomon, 1967; Estes, 1969; Kamin and Gaioni, 1974). In each system, the alteration of peripheral operant responses may be emotional behavior (Brady, 1975) or indirect indicants of emotional states (Kamin, 1965; Hoffman and Barrett, 1971) or may be partially determined by nonemotional effects (Lyon, 1968). Similarly, freezing may be a classical CR (Brady, 1975), the total inhibition of all responses (Stein et al., 1971), irrelevant responses (Rescorla and Solomon, 1967), or concurrent interacting responses (Henton, 1972). Furthermore, the disruption of operant responses may be due to general emotional states (Azrin and Hake, 1969) or mediational states (Rescorla and Solomon, 1967) shared by the operant and respondent systems, to excitatory interactions between various brain centers eliciting antagonistic responses (Konorski, 1967), or to inhibitory interactions between drive elements (Estes, 1969). Finally, positive and negative classical conditioning superimposed upon operant baselines may have identical suppressive effects (Azrin and Hake, 1969), differential facilitative and suppressive effects independent of peripheral responses (Rescorla and Solomon, 1967), or differential effects conditional upon response topographies (Brady, 1971). The set of theoretical formulations thus contains individual elements that overlap to greater and lesser degrees, are frequently mutually contradictory, and are occasionally internally inconsistent.

Experimental Analysis: General Methods

The following review is an organization and description of the empirical parameters that are used to control response rates during classical–operant schedules. Given the extraordinary number of studies using the Estes–Skinner procedure, many experiments have surely been overlooked—hopefully without prejudice. The research in each section is arranged in chronological order, with at least one and frequently several experiments described in some detail. Reference to other papers has been simply based on a compromise between comprehensive coverage and space limitations. For a more objective presentation, the theoretical opinions of the authors have generally been deleted, except when used to augment the historical setting.

Subjects

A strikingly odd variety of species have been successfully used in the Estes–Skinner procedure, ranging from albino rats (Rosenberger and Ernst, 1971) to vampire bats (Shumake et al., 1977). A more complete listing would include cats (Brady and Conrad, 1960), dogs (Waller and Waller, 1963), fish (Wilson et al., 1970), gerbils (Frey et al., 1972), guinea pigs (Valenstein, 1959), mice (Anderson and Ressler, 1973), monkeys (Sidman, 1960b), and pigeons (Stein et al., 1971). In addition, sensory psychophysical studies have compared suppression to auditory stimuli in the bushbaby, hedgehog, opposum, potto, slow loris, and tree shrew (Masterton et al., 1969; Heffner and Masterton, 1970). The previous experiments unanimously suggest a widespread generality of conditioned suppression across all species, with the singular exception of the subject of primary concern, *homo sapiens* (Sachs and May, 1967, 1969; Rand et al., 1971; Sachs and Keller, 1972; Skinner, 1974; but also see Di Giusto et al., 1974).

Conditioning Procedures

Three general types of training procedures have been used; the most prevalent technique is an "on-the-baseline" procedure. In this procedure, the operant response is first trained to a stable rate, with all CS–UCS pairings subsequently superimposed upon the already established operant baseline (e.g., Lyon and Felton, 1966b). A second technique is an "off-the-baseline" procedure, in which the operant and classical conditioning are conducted in separate sessions, and the two schedule components are subsequently combined into one session (e.g., Geller et al., 1955). The off-the-baseline technique is used to prevent unprogrammed or adventitious reinforcement of the recorded operant response by the CS–UCS pairings. A third arrangement is similar to the off-the-baseline procedure, with the exception that the previously established classical and operant conditioning components are subsequently combined during schedule transitions of (1) extinction of the operant conditioning schedule (Estes and Skinner, 1941), (2) extinction of the classical conditioning schedule (Leaf and Muller, 1965), or (3) simultaneous extinction of both the operant and classical conditioning schedules (Rescorla, 1967a). The various extinction procedures are limited to a relatively brief analysis of a small number of sessions prior to complete extinction.

Dependent Variables

The "suppression ratio" remains the most popular dependent variable. The ratio basically compares the operant response rate during the CS with the response rate during a control period in the absence of the CS. The control response rate is usually, although arbitrarily, recorded during the time period immediately preceding CS onset. The suppression ratio may be calculated with a variety of different mathematical formulas that differentially weight the CS and control response rates. Figure 1.2 presents a comparison of the various sup-

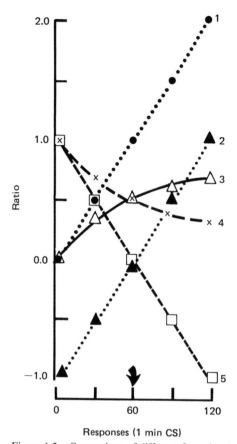

Responses (1 min CS)

Figure 1.2. Comparison of different formulas describing the change in operant responding during superimposed Pavlovian CS. In this graph baseline responding during control periods is arbitrarily defined as 60 responses/min (arrow). 1. CS response rate/control response rate (Stein et al., 1958). 2. CS rate − control rate/control rate (Hunt et al., 1952). 3. CS rate/CS rate + control rate (Annau and Kamin, 1961). 4. Control rate/CS rate + control rate (Goldstein, 1966). 5. Control rate − CS rate/control rate (Hoffman and Fleshler, 1961).

pression ratios as a function of changes in the operant rate during the CS. For each ratio, the duration of the CS and control periods is 1 min, with the response rate fixed at 60 responses/min during the control period. The calculated ratio for a 100% decrease in responding during the CS (relative to control rates) ranges from − 1.00 to + 1.00; for a 100% increase in relative CS rates, the range is − 1.00 to + 2.00. Formulas 1, 2, and 5 yield linear suppression ratios, with equivalent positive and negative changes in CS response rates producing symmetrical alterations in the ratio. Formulas 3 and 4 are curvilinear, negatively accelerated functions, with equivalent positive and negative CS rate changes producing progressively more asymmetrical alterations in the suppression ratio. Formulas 2 and 5 seem to be the most logical, with linear functions symmetrical about a 0.00 suppression ratio for unchanged CS rates. As previously described by Lyon (1968), the logic of formulas 3 and 4 is not especially clear (review of suppression measures by Shimoff, 1972a).

A recovery time measure (not shown in Figure 1.2) developed by Leaf and Muller (1965) and Leaf and Leaf (1966) is becoming increasingly popular (Carlton and Vogel, 1967; Hughes, 1969). The recovery time procedure is a one-trial classical conditioning extinction test in which a previously conditioned CS is superimposed upon licking responses reinforced with water, sucrose, or condensed milk. The dependent recovery time measure is simply the time to complete 10 licking responses during the CS test trial.

The responses controlled by the classical conditioning procedure are generally unrecorded during classical–operant combinations. Preliminary reports of freezing and immobility during conditioned suppression were reported by Brady and Hunt (1955) and Brady and Conrad (1960), and more recently by Hoffman and Barrett (1971) and Stein et al. (1971). Heart rate, systolic and diastolic blood pressure, blood flow, and electromyographic activity have also been reported (Stebbins and Smith, 1964; de Toledo and Black, 1966; Brady et al., 1969, 1970). Alternatively, observational reports by various authors suggest a total absence of behavior, or a failure of classical conditioning to elicit any overt responses when prefood or preshock stimuli are superimposed upon operant schedules (Azrin and Hake, 1969; Seligman et al., 1971). The traditional failure to record the responses elicited by the classical conditioning schedule is especially surprising in view of the heavy explanatory role attributed to classical conditioning processes in the conditioned emotional response procedure. At minimum, respondents should be more direct and at least as sensitive as concurrent operant responses as classical conditioned dependent variables. Moreover, given the well-documented sensitivity of conditioned responses to seemingly trivial and innocuous procedural changes (Pavlov, 1927; Konorski, 1967), no cogent reasoning would suggest any less sensitivity to the effects of superimposed operant conditioning schedules. To invert a previous interpretation by Rescorla and Solomon (1967), any empirical law of operant conditioning may have profound implications for the control of Pavlovian responses when the two procedures are interactively combined. (See, for example, Experiment IX, Chapter 2.)

Negative Classical Conditioning Scheduled with Positive Operant Conditioning

Negative classical conditioning procedures superimposed upon positive operant reinforcement schedules is by far the most studied classical–operant combination. Conditioned suppression of operant responses during stimuli paired with electric shock is in fact frequently accepted as the prototypical model of all classical–operant effects. The independent variables fall rather naturally into three groups: classical conditioning variables, operant conditioning variables, and subject variables (Table 1.1). Guided by theory and tradition, the studies generally emphasize the "emotional" effects of the classical condi-

Table 1.1 Negative classical–positive operant conditioning

Variables	Studies	Results
Classical Conditioning		
UCS Parameters		
intensity	15	suppression as a direct function
duration	1	suppression as a direct function
probability	18	divergent results
random presentation	14	suppression, conditional upon schedules
CS Parameters		
duration	15	suppression as an inverse function
intensity	33	conditional upon other variables
generalization	12	graded suppression
preexposure	16	attenuation of suppression
sensory preconditioning	8	suppression during preconditioned CS
second-order stimuli	8	transient suppression
compound stimuli		
summation tests	7	increased suppression
inhibition tests	23	usually attenuation of suppression
backward conditioning	9	divergent results
spontaneous recovery and retention	7	increased suppression, maintenance of suppression over years
Total	186	
Operant Conditioning		
Reinforcer Parameters		
type of reinforcer	8	conditional upon reinforcer
magnitude of reinforcer	4	divergent results
Reinforcement Schedules		
response rate measures	12	function of reinforcer proximity
response accuracy	9	generally unchanged during CS
operant vs. consummatory responses	2	differentially suppressed
Conditioning History	7	suppression conditional upon history
Adventitious Punishment by UCS	13	increases suppression
Operant S^d compared to CS	5	generally equivalent effects
Concurrent Behaviors	7	inversely related to operant rate
Pre-schedule change stimuli	11	divergent results
Total	78	
Subject		
Age	11	conditional upon procedures
Central Nervous System		
lesions	16	divergent results
stimulation	14	divergent results
electroconvulsive shock	17	transient attenuation of suppression
drugs	45	divergent and conditional effects
Cardiovascular Responses	15	no close correlation with behavior
Total	118	

tioning procedure upon the operant responses, rather than the effects of the operant procedure upon the classical conditioned "emotions." Consequently, the procedures are most frequently selected to optimize the classical conditioning variables relative to the operant conditioning parameters. The procedural bias has therefore resulted in a far more thorough analysis of the variables within the classical conditioning component. In addition, the "conditioned emotional response" (CER) paradigm has generated numerous experiments on the effects of drugs and other subject variables. As summarized in Table 1.1, experimental results suggest consistent behavioral changes as a function of the more powerful independent variables, with the effects of many variables more markedly conditional upon other parameters, or seemingly inconsistent and divergent within and across experiments.

Classical Conditioning Variables

UCS Parameters

UCS Intensity. With few exceptions, electric shock has been the only aversive UCS used in conditioned suppression. The intensity of the shock is one of the most powerful variables determining operant response rates during the CS, with consistent reports of suppression as a direct function of shock intensity (Brady and Sulsa, 1955). Annau and Kamin (1961), for example, used a group design in which a 3-min CS was paired with a 0.5-sec shock of either 0.28, 0.49, 0.85, 1.55, or 2.91 ma. Conditioned suppression was a direct function of UCS intensity across experimental groups. Response rates were (1) relatively unchanged by the lowest shock intensity, (2) moderately suppressed, with individual differences, by the 0.49-ma shock, and (3) completely suppressed at the three higher intensities. Extinction of suppression was an inverse function of UCS intensity during the initial acquisition training (also see Brophy and Tremblay, 1971; James and Mostoway, 1968; Kamin and Brimer, 1963).

Conditioned suppression is also a monotonic function of UCS intensity within individual subjects as well as across experimental groups. Henton and Jordan (1970) superimposed different stimuli paired with 0.0, 0.1, 0.3, 1.0, and 3.0 ma upon a random ratio (RR) operant schedule (Figure 1.3). Initially, suppression during each CS was a direct function of the shock intensity terminating the immediately preceding trial. Asymptotic suppression over the final sessions was a direct function of the shock intensity terminating that trial (also see Ayres, 1968; and Experiment IX, Chapter 2).

Related experiments have examined the effects of sequential changes in shock intensity upon conditioned suppression. Hendry and Van Toller (1965), for example, reported that lever pressing was substantially less suppressed by a 2.0-ma shock for subjects pretrained with a lower 1.0-ma shock. Conversely, Rescorla (1974) reported that the unsignalled presentation of relatively higher shock intensities may facilitate or increase conditioned suppression. Hoffman et al. (1963) and Quinsey and Ayres (1969a, 1969b) similarly reported increased suppression following interpolated unsignaled shock during extinction trials (see also Rohrbaugh et al., 1972; Rescorla and Heth, 1975).

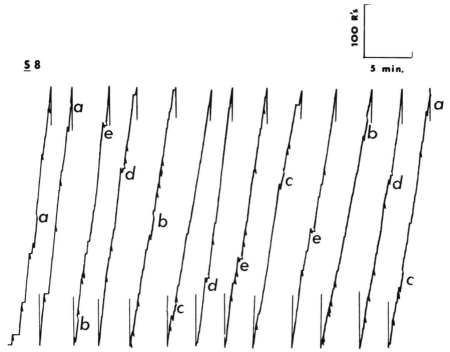

Figure 1.3. Cumulative record of lever pressing by monkey during a session with five different superimposed CSs paired with shock. Each 30-sec stimulus is presented three times per session and paired with shock intensity of 0.0 (a), 0.1 (b), 0.3 (c), 1.0 (d), and 3.0 ma (e). CS presentation is indicated by downward displacement of recording pen. The recording pen moves one unit vertically with each operant response and horizontally with time. A brief displacement of the pen indicates delivery of the operant reinforcer. Data from Henton and Jordan (1970).

UCS Duration. Only one study has examined the relationship between suppression and UCS duration. Using a 0.5-ma shock, Riess and Farrar (1973a) found that response rates were unchanged during the CS when the shock duration was 0.05 sec, but were completely suppressed when shock duration was 1.0 and 3.0 sec. The rate of extinction of suppression was an inverse function of the shock duration used in acquisition.

UCS Probability. Previous studies of the "partial reinforcement effect" have resulted in rather divergent and seemingly inconsistent results. The divergent results have been obtained with acquisition/extinction rates as well as the magnitude of conditioned suppression as the dependent variable. Geller (1964) initially reported that suppression by goldfish conditioned more rapidly and extinguished more slowly in groups trained with 100% CS–UCS pairings. Geller, however, described two unpublished studies with rats in which suppression extinguished more rapidly following 100% CS–UCS pairings relative to groups trained with either 50% or 25% pairings. Geller suggested that the opposite partial reinforcement effects with fish and rats may be a species difference. Brimer and Dockrill (1966) also reported faster acquisition of suppression by rats with

100% pairings relative to 50% and 25% groups. Wagner et al. (1967), however, found no difference between 50% and 100% CS–UCS pairings. Equally divergent results have been reported with an extinction measure of suppression in rats. Scheuer (1969) reported greater resistance to extinction with a 100% shock schedule, whereas Hilton (1969) reported more resistance to extinction with a 50% partial reinforcement schedule (also see Brimer and Wickson, 1971).

Suppression is also determined by the shock probability during the intertrial interval as well as during the CS. Rescorla (1968b) reported suppression as an inverse function of the probability of shock during the intertrial interval. CS response rates are unchanged relative to baseline rates, however, when the probability of shock is equal during the CS and intertrial interval.

Using a within-subject design, Willis and Lundin (1966) reported differential suppression as a direct function of the percentage of CS–UCS pairings. However, using a group design, Willis (1969) reported no difference in suppression with CS–UCS pairings of 100%, 90%, 70%, 50%, and 30%, with differential suppression only in a 10% pairing group. The results of the group design study thus contrasted with the within-subject function reported by Willis and Lundin (1966). Willis (1969) suggested that the divergent partial reinforcement effects in the literature may be partially determined by the experimental design of between-group or within-subject comparisons (also see Homzie et al., 1969).

The results of within-subject experiments are even more inconsistent when the comparison is expanded to include data from related areas. For example, several investigators have reported accelerated response rates during a CS with a zero shock probability when a second CS is paired with shock in the same session ("inhibition of fear," discussed by Hammond, 1966, 1967; Rescorla, 1969a, 1969c). However, a rather large number of experiments routinely use the same Pavlovian discrimination procedures in psychophysical investigations, with unchanged operant rates during the CS associated with the zero shock probability (review by Smith, 1970). Similarly unchanged response rates during the nonshock stimulus have been reported in a variety of other procedures (de Toledo and Black, 1966; Nathan and Smith, 1968; Henton and Jordan, 1970). The surprising divergence suggests that the effects of UCS probability must be highly conditional upon specific boundary conditions, training procedures, and other variables.

Random Presentation of CS and UCS. A special case of UCS probability is the random and independent presentations of the CS and the UCS. A theoretical paper by Rescorla (1967b) proposed that random CS and UCS pairings was the "proper" control procedure in classical conditioning experiments (also see Rescorla, 1966; 1969b). Seligman (1968) subsequently reported a rather complex, multistage experiment that compared predictable or signaled shock and unpredictable or random shock. Lever pressing by rats was completely suppressed during both the CS and the intertrial interval with the random shock procedure. Moreover, the random CS and UCS presentations in one conditioning cycle retarded the acquisition of suppression to a different stimulus paired with shock in the next experimental phase. Seligman suggested that unpredictable shock procedures may condition a "learned fear" or "learned helplessness," and therefore would not be appropriate as neutral conditioning techniques (Seligman et al., 1971).

Davis and McIntire (1969) also compared stimuli paired, unpaired, or randomly presented with shock, and similarly reported suppression during both the intertrial interval and the CS with random CS and UCS delivery. Additional studies show that suppression during stimuli randomly associated with shock is a function of the average interval between random CS and UCS presentations (Kremer and Kamin, 1971) or the relative density of the CS and UCS schedules (Kremer, 1971). Suppression may also be dependent upon sequential effects within the random CS–UCS pairings. Benedict and Ayres (1972) reported suppression during the CS only if chance pairings of CS and UCS occurred prior to nonpairings during initial exposure to the random schedule (also see Ayres and De Costa, 1971; Kremer, 1974; Nageishi and Imada, 1974; Witcher and Ayres, 1975; Baker, 1976).

CS Parameters

CS Duration. The first parameter of conditioned suppression to be extensively studied was the relative duration of the CS (Libby, 1951), with functional relationships subsequently determined for both trace and delay classical conditioning procedures. One standard reference is the study by Stein et al. (1958). Using a delay conditioning procedure, Stein et al. established that suppression was determined by the ratio of CS on-time to CS off-time (i.e., the intertrial interval). Response rates were completely suppressed during relatively brief stimuli when the CS ratio approached 0.00, with higher response rates with increasing CS on/off ratios. However, absolute CS duration per se was not significantly related to response rate across a broad range of CS on/off ratios. Stein et al. proposed that response rates will be reduced during the CS only to the extent that suppression does not markedly reduce the operant reinforcement probability.

Carlton and Didamo (1960) varied the CS on/off ratio by using a fixed duration CS of 3 min and varying intertrial intervals of 4, 6, or 60 min. As in the study by Stein et al., response rates were completely suppressed during the CS with the long intertrial interval, and substantially less suppressed with the two shorter intertrial intervals (also see Davis et al., 1969; Kling, 1972; Yeo, 1974, 1976).

In a related experiment, Shipley (1974) manipulated CS duration during extinction rather than acquisition, and reported that suppression was an inverse function of the total CS on-time during the extinction test. The effect of CS exposure was independent of the number and duration of CS presentations used to generate the total exposure duration.

In a finely detailed series of experiments, Kamin (1961) reported that conditioned suppression was also dependent upon the temporal characteristics of trace conditioning procedures. Suppression was an inverse function of the trace interval between CS termination and UCS onset, as well as the interval between CS onset and UCS onset (also see Leaf and Leaf, 1966; Strouthes, 1965).

A seemingly paradoxical facilitation effect has been reported for low response rates maintained by differential reinforcement of low rate (DRL) schedules.

Finnocchio (1963) reported that the low response rate was relatively increased during a 5-min CS alternating with a 5-min intertrial interval. The DRL rate was suppressed, however, when a 2-min CS alternated with an 8-min intertrial interval (also see Migler and Brady, 1964; Leaf and Muller, 1964; Blackman, 1968a).

CS Intensity. The effects of CS intensity have been reported in a series of papers by Kamin and associates. In the Kamin and Schaub (1963) experiment, three different groups of rats were exposed to 3-min periods of white noise paired with shock. The intensity of the white noise was either 49, 63, or 81 db, and acquisition of suppression was a direct function of CS intensity. Kamin (1965) further compared the effects of stimulus intensity per se against the effects of stimulus discriminability, or change from background noise. For different groups of rats, the CS was a reduction in the white noise from 80 db to either 0, 45, 50, 60, or 70 db. The acquisition and asymptotic level of conditioned suppression was a direct function of the magnitude of stimulus change. In a companion experiment, the direction of stimulus change was reversed, with CS intensity always 80 db, and the background noise level either 0, 45, 50, 60, or 70 db. In contrast to the differential suppression with intensity reduction as the CS, the acquisition and asymptotic level of suppression was equal in all groups with various increases in noise as the CS. The data thus suggest that suppression is not simply related to stimulus intensity per se, but is also determined by the direction and magnitude of stimulus change from background (also see Zielinski, 1965; Dubin and Levis, 1973).

The effects of CS intensity are further complicated by the choice of UCS intensity. Kamin and Brimer (1963) reported a 3×3 factorial study of the interactions between three CS intensities (47, 60, and 81 db) and three UCS intensities (0.25, 0.50, and 0.80 ma). Response rates were unchanged and high during all CS intensities paired with a low shock, equally suppressed during all CS intensities paired with a high shock, but a direct function of CS intensity for groups trained with a medium shock. The series of studies by Kamin provide clear examples of the diverse effects generated by interacting parameters commonly found in all classical–operant schedule combinations. The results would underscore the marked dependence of functional relationships upon the choice of constants and other boundary variables (also see Testa, 1975).

A variety of psychophysical experiments have used the Estes-Skinner procedure and manipulated CS intensity as the major independent variable (Hendricks, 1966; Sidman et al., 1966; Shaber et al. 1967; reviews by Rosenberger, 1970; Smith, 1970). In the Hendricks (1966) experiment, key pecking by pigeons was reinforced on a variable interval (VI) 2-min schedule, with a 20-sec

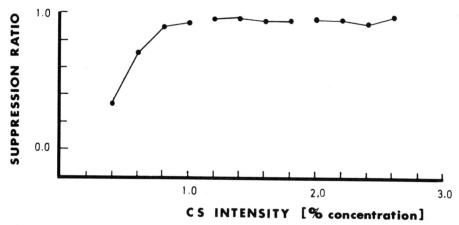

Figure 1.4. Conditioned suppression by pigeons as a function of the intensity of the odor used as the CS. Each data point is the mean of three conditioning trials. Data from Henton (1966).

CS of light flickering at 10 cycles/sec. The CS flicker rate was gradually changed in increments of 1 or 2 cycles/sec, until response rates during the CS were 50% of the rates during continuous illumination (i.e., threshold). The flicker fusion threshold was thus determined for eight different light intensities, yielding critical flicker fusion frequencies as a function of stimulus intensity. The Hendricks procedure has subsequently been used in ascending, descending, and constant stimuli psychophysical methods (Figure 1.4), as well as titration procedures (Rosenberger, 1970). Furthermore, conditioned suppression has been used to determine absolute and difference thresholds in vision (Powell, 1967; Powell and Smith, 1968; Shumake et al., 1968, 1977; Rosenberger and Ernst, 1971; La Vail et al., 1974), audition (Dalton, 1967; Price et al. 1967; Rivizza et al, 1969; Heffner and Masterton, 1970; Heffner et al., 1971), olfaction (Henton, 1969; Henton et al, 1966, 1969; Davis, 1973; Pierson, 1974; Oley et al., 1975), temperature sensitivity (Kenshalo and Hall, 1974), microwave detection (King et al., 1971), and x-ray detection (Morris, 1966; Smith and Tucker, 1969; Chaddock, 1972).

CS Generalization. Conditioned suppression will also generalize to nonshock test stimuli as a function of the physical similarity of the test stimulus to the CS. In a study by Ray and Stein (1959), an 1800-Hz tone was paired with shock, and a 200-Hz tone was simply presented unpaired with shock in the same session. The generalization test consisted of the occasional presentation of four tones with intermediate frequencies between the stimuli paired and unpaired with shock. Conditioned suppression during the test stimuli increased as the tone frequencies approached the 1800-Hz CS.

A number of generalization experiments have been reported by Hoffman and Fleshler (Fleshler and Hoffman, 1961; Hoffman and Fleshler, 1961, 1964, 1965; Hoffman et al., 1963; review by Hoffman, 1969). For example, Hoffman et al. (1963), presented test stimuli of 300, 450, 670, 2250, and 3400 Hz during the extinction of suppression previously conditioned to a 1000-Hz tone. Response rates were most suppressed during the 1000-Hz tone, with diminishing suppression at test stimuli of progressively higher or lower frequencies. The inverted U-shaped generalization gradient became steeper and sharper over successive extinction sessions as the response rates gradually returned to previous baseline rates during each tone. Bimodal generalization gradients around two different tones paired with shock have been reported by Hoffman et al. (1966b) and Desiderato (1964).

In contrast to the previously reported symmetrical gradients around the CS, Winograd (1965) observed asymmetrical gradients to click frequencies in rats. The divergent effects were apparently dependent upon unconditioned effects of the auditory test stimuli, with high click rates unconditionally eliciting more activity and subsequently higher response rates. As a result, response rates were less suppressed during test stimuli of high click rates compared to low click rates, with a resultant asymmetrical gradient skewed by the higher frequencies.

Hendry et al. (1969) replicated the Ray and Stein discrimination procedures but added more test stimuli to determine the generalization of suppression at frequencies beyond the training stimuli paired and unpaired with shock. In general, the maximal lever-pressing rate by rats shifted from the nonshock training stimulus to adjacent stimuli away from the shock CS; conversely, the maximal suppression shifted from the shock CS in the opposite direction away from the nonshock CS (i.e., positive and negative peak shift; Hanson, 1959). The authors noted a variety of individual differences in the shifted generalization functions, however, and discussed the previous contradictory data reported by Ray and Stein (1959), Winograd (1965), and Hoffman, 1967).

CS Preexposure (Latent Inhibition). The alteration of suppression by prior habituation of the to-be-conditioned stimulus was initially reported by Carlton and Vogel (1967) and May et al. (1967). In the Carlton and Vogel study, a 10-sec tone was simply presented without shock during six habituation sessions, and then paired with shock on a single conditioning trial. In subsequent nonshock test trials, licking responses were less disrupted in the group of rats previously habituated to the CS relative to groups trained without tone preexposure or given comparable preexposure to a different auditory stimulus. May et al. (1967) further reported that conditioned suppression was an inverse function of the number of stimulus preexposure trials (also see Leaf et al, 1968; Lubow and Siebart, 1969; James, 1971b; Domjan and Siegal, 1971, Reiss and Wagner, 1972; and Lantz, 1973).

In addition to the above studies using simple delay classical conditioning, latent inhibition of suppression has also been reported during compound conditioning procedures. Schnur (1971), for example, exposed groups of rats to a tone or a light, with subsequent classical conditioning with either light, tone, or light plus tone paired with shock. Suppression was attenuated in the compound conditioning procedure for subjects preexposed to one of the elements of the compound CS. The suppression was not attenuated, however, in control groups preexposed to one CS but tested with the alternative stimulus (also see Anderson et al., 1968, 1969a, 1969b; Dexter and Merrill, 1969; Kremer, 1972).

In a rather complicated experiment, Carr (1974) used a compound conditioning procedure to study the latent inhibition of the "overshadowing" effect described by Kamin (1969). The overshadowing of one stimulus by another is found when subjects conditioned to a compound CS, such as light plus tone, subsequently show less suppression on test trials with one CS element compared to the second CS element (such as overshadowing of noise by light during the compound conditioning). Carr reported that the overshadowing effect was eliminated by preexposure to the light CS. Response rates were relatively more suppressed during the noise test trials for subjects habituated to the potentially overshadowing light. The inhibition of overshadowing by latent inhibition exemplifies further complex stimulus interactions in the conditioned suppression procedure (Kumar, 1970; general review of latent inhibition by Lubow, 1973).

Sensory Preconditioning.   Sensory preconditioning is a second stimulus preexposure technique in which two neutral stimuli are sequentially paired (CS 1– CS 2), with CS 2 subsequently paired with a UCS of food or shock. The sensory preconditioning is an increase in the probability of conditioned responses during test trials with CS 1 (Brogden, 1939). In 1967, Prewitt reported sensory preconditioning of conditioned suppression in rats, Initially, a 10-sec tone was paired with a 10-sec light on 1, 4, 16, or 64 preconditioning trials. The light was then paired with shock in phase 2, with suppression during the sensory preconditioned tone recorded during phase 3. Response rates were unchanged during the tone for subjects receiving random light and tone presentations in the first preconditioning phase, but were suppressed as a direct function of the number of preconditioning trials for the paired tone–light groups (also see Parkinson, 1968; Rogers, 1973).

Experiments elaborating the sensory preconditioning of suppression have been reported by Tait, Suboski, and associates. As one instance, Tait et al. (1969) reported that suppression during a sensory preconditioned tone was an inverse function of the number of interposed preconditioning extinction trials. Subsequent experiments indicated (1) partial reinforcement effects in sensory preconditioning, with greater suppression on CS 1 test trials as a direct function of the percentage of CS 1–CS 2 pairings (Tait et al., 1971), (2) sensory preconditioning in curarized rats (Cousins et al., 1971), (3) discriminative sensory preconditioning, with different tone frequencies paired and unpaired with a light CS 2 (Tait et al., 1972), and (4) sensory preconditioning as a function of the intensity of CS 1 and CS 2 (Tait and Suboski, 1972).

Second-order Conditioned Suppression.   Second-order procedures and sensory preconditioning techniques are quite similar, but with a reversed order of classical conditioning and stimulus pairing phases. In second-order conditioning, the CS–UCS pairings are conducted first, with subsequent sequential pairings of a neutral stimulus with the CS. Preliminary reports of second-order conditioned suppression were described by Davenport (1966) and Kamil (1968, 1969).

Kamil (1969), for example, described two experiments on second-order conditioned suppression in rats. In experiment 1, a 10- or 100-sec tone was terminated by shock, and second-order conditioning consisted of a 30-sec light terminated by the onset of the tone (unpaired with shock). Response rates during the second-order light CS were transiently suppressed as the conditioned suppression progressively extinquished during the first-order tone formerly paired with shock. Kamil's second experiment compared the suppression during a light terminated by tones formerly used in delay and trace classical conditioning. Response rates were equally suppressed during the second-order light in all procedures, in spite of the differential rate of extinction of suppression during the delay and trace conditioned tones. Rizley and Rescorla (1972) also reported that second-order conditioned suppression is independent of the suppression during the first-order CS (also see Byrum and Jackson, 1971). Thus, second-order suppression does not seem to be a classical conditioned association between the first and second-order stimuli. As noted by Kamil, the divergent suppression during the first- and second-order CS is not consistent with classical conditioning formulations of either second-order conditioning or conditioned suppression (also see Holland and Rescorla, 1975; Rescorla, 1976; Rescorla and Furrow, 1977).

Compound CS. A number of interesting experiments have used the simultaneous presentation of two conditioned stimuli within the conditioned suppression paradigm. An early investigation (Ayres, 1966) was designed to examine the information hypothesis of Egger and Miller (1962). In very brief outline, the information hypothesis would predict that if two stimuli were paired with shock, then (1) more suppression would be conditioned to the stimulus whose onset is first (stimulus 2 being redundant), but (2) more suppression would occur to stimulus 2 if stimulus 1 were also occasionally presented alone and without shock (stimulus 1 being an unreliable predictor of shock). However, Ayres found equal suppression on test trials with CS 1 or CS 2, with equal rates of extinction of suppression across testing sessions. Ayres then concluded that redundant and unreliable conditioned stimuli generate as much suppression as more informative stimuli (but also see Scheuer and Keeter, 1969; Seger and Scheuer, 1977).

Summation of Conditioned Suppression. The summation of conditioned suppression during compounding of two CS elements was described by Miller (1969). Initially, a light or a tone was individually paired with shock intensities selected to generate 20% to 40% suppression during each CS. Compound trials with light plus tone were then added to each on-the-baseline session, and operant responses were more suppressed during the compound than during trials with each individual CS element. In a second experiment, response rates were again relatively more suppressed during compound trials, with the compound suppression dependent upon the magnitude of suppression controlled by each CS element. Furthermore, the compound CS continued to suppress responding even when the suppression was completely extinguished during the individual CS elements. More recent experiments have replicated the data of Miller, with reports of (1) increased suppression during a compound CS relative to individual CS elements (Weiss and Emurian, 1970; Van Houton et al., 1970; Booth and Hammond, 1971), (2) continued suppression during a compound CS after extinction of suppression during the individual CS elements (Reberg, 1972), (3) summation of suppression during compound trials with CS elements previously paired with different shock intensities (Hendersen, 1975), and (4) summation of suppression during compounding of stimuli paired with shock onset ("fear" conditioning) and shock offset ("hope" or "relief" conditioning, Zelhard, 1972).

Attenuation of Conditioned Suppression. The attenuation of conditioned suppression by external inhibitors and conditioned inhibitors has also been reported in compound conditioned suppression. Hammond (1967) reported an attenuation of suppression during compound trials with a CS formerly paired with shock and a conditioned inhibitory stimulus previously unpaired with shock. In 1969, Rescorla further reported that the conditioned inhibition of suppression was a direct function of the shock frequency scheduled in the absence of the inhibitory CS (Rescorla, 1969a, 1969b). Reberg and Black (1969) replicated the summation of suppression by stimuli paired with shock and the conditioned inhibition of suppression by stimuli previously unpaired with shock, but reported unchanged suppression during compound trials with an experimentally neutral stimulus (also see Hendry, 1967; Rescorla, 1969c; Cappel et al., 1970). The external inhibition of suppression by an added neutral stimulus has been reported, however, by Brimer and Wickson (1971; Brimer, 1971). The different effects of compounding with neutral stimuli may be partially determined by unconditioned reflexive properties of the added neutral stimulus (Hendersen, 1973). In addition, the attenuation of suppression may be related to the number of suppression trials completed prior to the introduction of the inhibitory stimulus (Brodigan and Trapold, 1974).

A last group of studies using compound CS dealt with the overshadowing effect (Carr, 1974). The overshadowing procedure was originally reported by Kamin (1969); a white noise and a light were separately paired with a 1.0-ma shock, with the two CS subsequently combined during compound conditioning trials. Later test trials with each CS element revealed that responding was less suppressed during the noise CS than during the light CS. The results imply that the compound conditioning phase resulted in suppression primarily conditioned to the light element of the compound CS (overshadowing of noise by light). However, when the UCS intensity was increased from 1.0 to 4.0 ma, conditioned suppression was equivalent during test trials with the noise and light, with apparently equal suppression conditioned to each CS element during the compound light plus noise conditioning trials (additional studies by Rescorla, 1971b; Rescorla and Wagner, 1972; Wagner and Rescorla, 1972; Baker, 1974; and Kamin and Gaioni, 1974). Related experiments described above appear under CS preexposure (latent inhibition).

Gray and Appignanesi (1973) similarly reported that prior conditioning of CS paired with shock blocked the acquisition of suppression to a second CS when the two stimuli were subsequently compounded. In contrast, St. Claire-Smith and Mackintosh (1974) found that the effects of compound stimulus trials may be rather conditional. Compound trials produced clear increments in suppression to each CS element if the separate CSs were previously paired with shock on only a few trials. Alternatively, the compound trials had no consistent effect upon suppression during individual CS elements that had been frequently paired with shock prior to compound conditioning. In the St. Claire-Smith and Mackintosh study, compound trials thus did not produce a decrement in suppression to one or the other stimulus element (also see Mackintosh, 1975, 1976; Donegan et al., 1977).

In summary, experiments using compound conditioned stimuli consistently describe summation of suppression during compound trials with CS elements that individually control moderate suppression. However, the effects of compound trials upon the subsequent suppression elicited by individual CS elements is not yet clear. Similarly, the effect of a neutral stimulus or external inhibitor added to a CS paired with shock has not been consistent across experiments (general review by Weiss, 1972).

Backward Conditioning.   One early report suggested that suppression might also be conditioned by backward (UCS–CS) pairings (Singh, 1959). Kamin (1963), in contrast, failed to replicate the backward conditioning of suppression with either a 0.85- or a 1.5-ma shock terminated by a 3-min CS. Instead, Kamin found a partial suppression of baseline rates during the intertrial interval, and slightly accelerated rates during the backward CS (relative to the suppressed intertrial interval rates). A retardation effect, however, has been reported for the influence of backward UCS–CS conditioning upon the subsequent forward conditioning of suppression to the CS (Siegal and Domjan, 1971). Mahoney and Ayres (1976) also reported that backward conditioning may in fact produce more suppression than random CS and UCS presentation, although less suppression than forward and simultaneous CS–UCS pairings. (also see James, 1971a; Burdick and James, 1973; Heth and Rescorla, 1973; Siegal and Domjan, 1974; Davis et al., 1976.)

Spontaneous Recovery and Retention of Suppression.   Spontaneous recovery, or suppression of responses during postextinction test trials, was described in a paper by Burdick and James (1970). Using a four-phase experiment, the investigators determined the temporal relationship between spontaneous recovery and the length of the postextinction test interval. Following first the acquisition and then the extinction of conditioned suppression, different groups of rats were given a CS test trial at 3.5 min, or 0.5, 1.0, 24.0, or 72.0 hr following the last extinction trial. Suppression during the spontaneous recovery test remained extinquished for the group tested at 3.5 min, with a progressive recovery of suppression across the remaining groups to a maximum at 24 hr. James (1971a) and Kling and Kling (1973) further reported that spontaneous recovery diminished across repeated sets of extinction trials and test trials.

The procedures used to measure the retention of conditioned suppression are basically similar to the spontaneous recovery procedures, with the exception that the retention interval follows acquisition training rather than extinction. The previously cited experiments by Hoffman et al. (1963), and Hoffman et al. (1966a) indicate that conditioned suppression generalization gradients remain relatively intact after 2.5 and 4.0 years in pigeons. Gleitman and Holmes (1967) also reported that suppression by rats is relatively unchanged after a retention interval of 90 days. Hammond and Maser (1970), however, reported that the pattern of suppression may be changed in spite of an unchanged overall suppression during the CS.

Operant Conditioning Variables

Reinforcer Parameters

Types of reinforcers.   Conditioned suppression may be quite dependent upon the specific choice of positive reinforcer selected to maintain the operant baseline. Brady and Conrad (1960) explicitly compared the suppression of responses reinforced by response-contingent stimulation of the limbic system to responses reinforced with water (rats), milk (cats), or sugar pellets (monkeys). In rats, responses reinforced with water were completely suppressed, whereas response rates were virtually unaffected during the CS when the reinforcer was stimulation of the septum or medial forebrain bundle. Similarly, conditioned suppression of monkeys was also attenuated when medial forebrain stimulation was substituted for sugar pellets as the operant reinforcer. Response rates of cats, however, were equally suppressed when the reinforcer was either milk or stimulation of the caudate nucleus. Brady and Conrad suggested that the anatomical location of the electrode seemed to be a critical determinant of the effects of reinforcing brain stimulation upon conditioned suppression (also see Brady, 1957, 1961; McIntire, 1966; Merrill et al., 1970; Haworth, 1971).

Geller (1960) also studied the effects of qualitatively different reinforcers upon suppression. He reported that suppression conditioned more rapidly and extinquished more slowly for subjects reinforced with water relative to subjects reinforced with sweetened milk.

Kruper and Haude (1964) used a rather novel procedure of CS–shock pairings superimposed upon an operant schedule of response-contingent visual exploration. Lever pressing by monkeys was reinforced with a 5-sec view of the external environment, augmented with a panel of 30 colored lights. As with the more conventional operant reinforcers, responses maintained by visual exploration were suppressed during a tone paired with shock.

Reinforcer Magnitude.   An initial study (Vogel and Spear, 1966) suggested that suppression may be partially determined by the quantity or magnitude of the operant reinforcer. Vogel and Spear found that responses reinforced with a 32.0% sucrose solution were less suppressed during CS test trials compared to groups reinforced with 4.0% or 11.5% sucrose. However, Ayres and associates have reported no differential effects of operant reinforcer magnitude upon suppression, either between groups (Ayres, 1966; Ayres and Quinsey, 1970) or within individual subjects (Hancock and Ayres, 1974). In the Ayres and Quinsey study, for example, licking responses reinforced with either 8.0% or 32.0% sucrose solutions were equally suppressed. In reviewing the previous studies, Hancock and Ayres (1974) concluded that incentive and motivational theories of conditioned suppression may be inconsistent with the experimental results.

Reinforcement Schedules

Response Rate Measures. The effects of CS–shock pairings upon response rates generated by different operant schedules was initially described by Brady (1955). The extinction of suppression was differentially dependent upon the baseline reinforcement schedule, with more rapid extinction using variable and fixed ratios (VR and FR), a moderate extinction rate with continuous reinforcement (CRF), and slowest recovery with variable interval (VI) schedules (also see Brady and Hunt, 1955; Goy and Hunt, 1953).

The most detailed analysis of schedule effects is presented in the comprehensive series of papers by Lyon and co-workers. Lyon (1963) compared the magnitude and acquisition/extinction rates of conditioned suppression in VI schedules. Response rates were relatively more suppressed, with faster acquisition and slower extinction, with a VI 4-min schedule compared to a VI 1-min schedule.

In FR schedules, suppression is conditional upon the location of CS onset during the response ratio (Lyon, 1964). Response rates were completely suppressed when the CS was presented early in the ratio, but relatively unaffected by a CS presented later in the ratio immediately prior to reinforcement. Suppression as a function of reinforcement proximity was replicated with FR schedules by Lyon and Felton (1966a) and with FI schedules by Lyon and Millar (1969). In contrast, Lyon and Felton (1966b) reported that suppression of VR responses was independent of the averaged probability of operant reinforcement. Response rates were equally suppressed on VR schedules of 50, 100, or 200 responses per reinforcement. During the CS, response rates tended to have a biphasic pattern and were either completely suppressed or completely unchanged, with no intermediate or graded suppression.

Blackman (1967a), however, criticized the results of Brady and Lyon as a confounding of the different effects of the subject's response rate and the scheduled reinforcement rate. Blackman (1966, 1967b, and 1968b) attempted to separate response rate from reinforcement rate by using response pacing schedules. He reported that suppression may be partially determined by the subject's response rate during the intertrial interval.

Response Accuracy Measures. A derivative question, given the alteration of overall rates during the CS, concerns the effect of the Estes-Skinner procedure upon the proportion of reinforced to total, albeit suppressed, responses. The effects of CS–shock pairings upon the relative distribution of correct versus incorrect responses was described by Migler and Brady (1964). An A–B response chain was reinforced on a DRL schedule, in which the sequence of lever

A and lever B responses was reinforced only if the A–B interresponse time exceeded a minimum of 5 sec. The low overall rate of completed A–B response sequences was suppressed, but the distribution of A to B interresponse times was virtually unchanged during the CS (also see Leaf and Muller, 1964).

In a related experiment, Kruper (1968) also reported overall suppression with relatively unchanged response accuracy in an oddity discrimination task. The rate of choice of the odd stimulus was reduced during a tone paired with a 1.0- to 1.5-ma shock, with further suppression at increased shock intensities of 2.0 to 3.0 ma. However, the proportion of correct responses to the odd stimulus during the CS was identical to the response accuracy during control periods at all shock intensities.

Blackman (1970) subsequently replicated the suppression of A–B response chains using a DRL of 5, 10, or 15 sec. The A to B interresponse times were unchanged with the 5 sec schedule, as previously reported by Migler and Brady. However, the interresponse times were proportionally decreased with the 10- and 15-sec schedules. [Facilitation rather than suppression of DRL response rates has also been reported for various combinations of CS duration and UCS intensity by Finnocchio (1963), and when a limited hold is added to the DRL by Blackman (1968a).]

Response facilitation has also been reported for the low rate of responses in the extinction component of a multiple variable interval: extinction (*mult* VI EXT) schedule. Hearst (1965) reported that CS–shock pairings during the VI component paradoxically increased the near zero rate of responding during the alternate EXT component. However, Weiss (1968) reported three experiments using a similar multiple schedule but was unable to confirm Hearst's results. The VI schedule, shock intensity, and amount of training were manipulated within and across experiments, but the response rates under EXT were reduced rather than increased under all experimental conditions. More recently, Blackman and Scrutton (1973) also reported no "disinhibition" of extinction response rates by CS–shock pairings superimposed upon the VI component of the multiple schedule.

In summary, the current literature consistently demonstrates that the effects of negative classical conditioning procedures are strongly conditional upon operant schedule parameters, ranging from increased to unchanged to decreased operant rates during the same superimposed classically conditioned "fear." The suppression of high response rates tends to be an inverse function of the local probability of response-contingent reinforcement, with the exception of VR schedules. The data for low response rates are markedly inconsistent and range from conditioned suppression to paradoxical facilitation across similar experiments.

Suppression of Operant and Consummatory Behaviors. Studies by DeCosta and Ayres (1971) examined the effects of the Estes-Skinner procedure upon the two different responses involved in an operant contingency—the operant or reinforced response and the consummatory or reinforcing response (Premack, 1965). Licking a 32% sucrose solution was programmed in one session, and bar pressing was reinforced with the sucrose solution on a VI 1-min schedule in alternate sessions. The operant bar-pressing response was suppressed more than the consummatory sucrose-licking response during a 2-min tone paired with a 0.8-ma shock. In addition, bar pressing was again relatively more suppressed when reinforcement density and adventitious punishment effects were equated for both responses. Jackson and Delprato (1974) similarly reported that CS–shock pairings did not suppress the consumption of food pellet reinforcers. The investigators noted that the suppression of operant responses without a suppression of consummatory responses is somewhat inconsistent with contemporary theories of the Estes-Skinner procedure.

Operant Conditioning History

The conditioned suppression of operant responses is conditional upon and indeed may be reversed by manipulating the subject's previous operant training history. In 1958, facilitation rather than suppression of VI responses was reported in subjects with previous histories of avoidance conditioning (Herrnstein and Sidman, 1958). The seemingly aberrant accelerated response rate was converted to the more typical conditioned suppression by interpolating additional sessions of avoidance extinction. Herrnstein and Sidman suggested that the response facilitation may have been dependent upon the operant avoidance history combining with the unavoidable shock to generate adventitious shock avoidance contingencies.

An in-depth analysis of operant conditioning history and conditioned suppression has been reported by Sidman (1958). Responses by monkeys on one lever were reinforced on a VI 4-min schedule, while responses on a second lever had previously avoided a 5.0-ma shock for 20 sec. Responses on both levers were increased, not suppressed, during superimposed CS–shock pairings. However, various schedule manipulations revealed that the responses on the two levers were in fact mutually interdependent, with each response partially controlled by both the avoidance and VI conditioning histories. Separating the concurrent response rates by additional schedule manipulations then resulted in the typical conditioned suppression of food reinforced responses, with an acceleration of shock avoidance responses, during the CS. Thus, the atypical acceleration of VI responding was neither abnormal nor pathological, but rather was determined by an interaction between the normal controlling variables of the two concurrent schedules (Sidman, 1960a, 1960b; also see Kelleher et al., 1963; Waller and Waller, 1963, and Lewis, 1973).

Operant Punishment in Conditioned Suppression

The "response-independent" presentation of a shock UCS is only accurate as a procedural definition, since shock must be temporally contiguous with some aspect of the subject's continuous stream of behavior. This functional nonresponse-independent characteristic of a UCS has prompted an examination of the uncontrolled operant punishment effects of the shock UCS. Hunt and Brady (1951b) found that lever-pressing rates were equally and completely suppressed during stimuli terminated by response-independent shock (conditioned suppression procedure) or associated with response-contingent shock (discriminated punishment procedure). However, subjects in the conditioned suppression group exhibited common behavioral patterns of crouching, freezing, urination, and defecation. In contrast, subjects in the discriminated punishment group simply passively avoided the response lever, while occasionally emitting abortive lever approach sequences.

The Hunt and Brady experiment was further replicated by Hoffman and Fleshler (1965), who specifically equated the frequency of shock during each stimulus. Responding was again equally suppressed by response-independent and response-contingent shock when the shock intensity was 2.0 ma. However, Hoffman and Fleshler reported that the operant punishment procedure produced more suppression when the shock intensity was only 1.0 ma. In contrast, Orme-Johnson and Yarczower (1974) found greater suppression with a conditioned suppression procedure than with an operant punishment procedure, independent of shock intensity and schedule manipulations.

Using different procedures, Gottwald (1967) demonstrated that the effects of conditioned suppression procedures are partially determined by the interval between the operant response and the classical conditioned UCS on the immediatley preceding trial. The adventitious punishment effect across sequential trials was subsequently replicated across four different shock procedures by Gottwald (1969). Church and co-workers have reported an elegant research program comparing the effects of response-independent and response-contingent shock, and also conclude that the unprogrammed operant response–UCS shock correlation is not inconsequential in the Estes-Skinner procedure (review by Church, 1969; Church et al., 1970; also see Herrnstein and Sidman, 1958; Sidman, 1958, 1960a; DeCosta and Ayres, 1971; Desiderato and Newman, 1971; Matthews et al., 1974).

Suppression During Stimuli Associated with Shock Avoidance Responses

A discriminative stimulus that controls operant shock avoidance responses will also function as a conditioned stimulus eliciting suppression of food reinforced responses. In one study (Kamin et al., 1963) a discriminative stimulus formerly used to control shuttle box avoidance responses was presented (without shock) during VI food reinforcement sessions. The VI responding was suppressed, and the magnitude of suppression was an inverted U-shaped function of the amount of previous avoidance conditioning. Kamin et al. therefore concluded that suppression was not simply or linearly related to the efficacy of previous avoidance responses in the shuttle box. Furthermore, conditioned suppression has been reported during a stimulus that controls a concurrent shock avoidance response. Hoffman and Fleshler (1962) reported that the food reinforced response rate was completely suppressed during trials with a successful avoidance response, but only partially suppressed during trials without a concurrent avoidance response. In contrast to the study by Kamin et al., suppression was not attenuated by prolonged shock avoidance training in this concurrent procedure. However, Linden (1969) found that criterion acquisition of shuttle box responses would attenuate conditioned suppression to the CS (also see Tarpy, 1966; Desiderato and Newman, 1971).

Concurrent Behaviors and Conditioned Suppression

A number of investigators (Hunt and Brady, 1951b; Brady, 1953; Davitz, 1953) have described increased crouching, immobility, defecation, and urination concomitant to the suppression of operant responding (review by Brady and Hunt, 1955). More recently, Stein et al. (1971) used a videotape recording system to analyze the subject's behavior, and reported freezing and wing-flapping responses by pigeons during the suppression of key pecking (also see Hoffman and Barrett, 1971). Stein et al. argued that freezing was not a classical conditioned response but a reduction in rate of large classes of overt behaviors during the CS. Alternatively, CS–shock pairings may elicit increased rather than decreased activity in pigeons, with freezing during the Estes-Skinner procedure a paradoxical result of the interaction between CS-elicited activity and baseline operant responses (see Chapter 2).

Time-out from Positive Reinforcement as the Aversive "UCS"

An operant variation of the Estes-Skinner procedure is the substitution of extinction or time-out from positive reinforcement for the shock UCS in the classical conditioning paradigm (Figure 1.5). As a conventional UCS, the alteration of the reinforcement schedule is independent of any specific response but dependent upon the termination of the CS or "warning" signal. Unlike a Pavlovian UCS, the extinction period requires a conditioning history to control a specific response analogous to the UCR. The distinction, however, is somewhat academic and misleading. The response-independent presentation of a food pellet as the UCS also fails to irrevocably elicit approach and consumma-

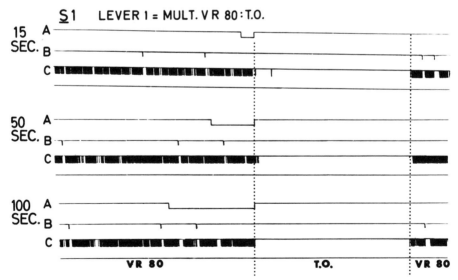

Figure 1.5. Event recordings comparing 15-, 50-, and 100-sec stimuli terminated by 3-min time out from operant reinforcement. A. Duration of pre-schedule change stimulus. B. Delivery of operant reinforcers on variable ratio 80 schedule. C. Lever pressing by monkeys. Data from Henton and Iversen (1973).

tory responses, until the subject is thoroughly apparatus habituated, conditioned to approach the food dispenser, and conditioned to retrieve the UCS from a tray or a bowl (Pavlov, 1927). Similarly, the UCR to electric shock is first conditional upon eliminating a variety of other prepotent responses from the subject's behavioral repertoire. (For example, with rat as subject, escape is prevented by restricting the subject to a box, blatant modification of the shock is prevented by a polarity scrambler across the shock grids, then by a low ceiling to prevent standing on the hind legs, followed by shock added to the walls, food cup, and operant manipulandum, and, if necessary, removal of the insulating fur from the rat's body—only to find that the subject may still minimize the shock by standing awkwardly on its tail, perhaps crouched and balanced against the plastic lens of a chamber light or the Plexiglas door.)

All this merely to suggest that the analogy between electric shock and operant extinction as the UCS may not be as discrepant as cursory examination might dictate. A more fundamental distinction is that the superimposition of stimuli terminated by time-out from reinforcement alters the operant schedule from a simple to a multiple schedule, whereas the addition of a CS-CR–UCS-UCR sequence changes the conditioning procedures from simple to concurrent schedules.

Pliskoff (1961, 1963) first described the operant rate changes during a stimulus terminated by a schedule change to either a lower or a higher density of operant reinforcement. In both experiments, key pecking by pigeons tended to increase during the stimulus paired with the lower reinforcement rate, but to decrease during the stimulus paired with the higher reinforcement rate. The rate changes in both studies, however, were rather variable both within individual subjects and across all subjects. Pliskoff is frequently misreferenced as proposing that baseline rates will be increased during stimuli terminated by a lower reinforcement density but suppressed during stimuli paired with a higher reinforcement density. In view of the data, Pliskoff (1963) explicitly rejected this hypothesis, and instead proposed that response rates would be higher during one stimulus paired with decreased reinforcement compared to a second stimulus paired with increased reinforcement, but not necessarily increased relative to control or baseline rates.

Leitenberg (1966) also reported generally increased response rates by pigeons during a stimulus terminated by time-out from VI reinforcement. The response rates were similarly accelerated when the schedule change to time-out was response independent or response contingent. Leitenberg et al. (1968), however, reported suppression rather than acceleration by rats during a pre–time-out stimulus. Carman (1969) next reported that suppression by rats was "only slight" during a pre–time-out stimulus, and did not occur under some conditions (also see Kaufman, 1969). Calef et al. (1971) subsequently reported substantial response facilitation by rats in early training, but unchanged rates after prolonged training with stimuli paired with time-out (also see Parker et al., 1971; Homes, 1972; and Experiment IV, Chapter 2).

In summary, the effects of stimuli paired with time-out from reinforcement have been inconsistent across different experiments and species, and the controlling variables remain unclear (Coughlin, 1972).

Subject Variables

Age

Relatively recent experiments suggest that conditioned suppression may be an age-dependent phenomenon. Using rats 40, 90, and 354 days of age, Pare (1969) reported that the acquisition of differential suppression during a CS paired with shock and a second CS explicitly unpaired with shock was an inverse function of age. However, the differential effect of age was eliminated in a second experiment by manipulating the auditory stimuli used in the discrimination and also changing the shock intensity. The relative performance of young versus older rats may then be a function of CS and UCS parameters. For example, Frieman et al. (1970) found that conditioned suppression was more broadly generalized across tone stimuli in adult subjects relative to infants. Brunner et al. (1970) and Snedden et al. (1971) have also reported greater suppression with mature rats than infants (also see Campbell and Campbell, 1962; Solyom and Miller; 1965 Frieman et al., 1971; Buchanon et al., 1972; Persinger and Pear, 1972; Wilson and Riccio, 1973; Coulter et al., 1976).

Central Nervous System Effects

Leisons. Neurophysiological investigations have frequently used the CER to analyze the anatomical and physiological parameters of affective behaviors. Brady and Nauta (1953), for example, reported that conditioned suppression was attenuated by placing lesions in the septum. In comparison, neocortical lesions had no detectable effect. Brady and Nauta (1955) replicated the attenuation effects of septal lesions, and further reported that lesions of the thalamic habenular complex had no discernable effect upon the acquisition or retention of suppression but may have produced slightly faster extinction. However, the attenuation of suppression by septal lesions was transient and was paradoxically opposite to the increase in emotional reactivity recorded on a rating scale (also see Brady, 1961, 1962, 1970a; Harvey et al., 1965; Trafton, 1967).

The effect of amygdalectomy on conditioned suppression was described by Kellicut and Schwartzbaum (1963) and Thompson and Schwartzbaum (1964). The acquisition of suppression was blocked by large lesions that included the basolateral and corticomedial nuclei of the amygdala, but was unaffected by lesions of the lateral amygdala and putamen. Thompson and Schwartzbaum proposed that the amygdala may participate in somatomotor inhibition, and therefore lesions would interfere with response inhibition and conditioned suppression. McIntyre and Molino (1972) and Lidsky et al. (1970) also described an attenuation of suppression by large lesions of the amygdala. However, an increased suppression rather than attenuation has also been reported in amygdalectomized rats (Suboski et al., 1970).

Further neurophysiological studies have implicated hippocampal lesions in conditioned suppression. Nadel (1968) reported that dorsal hippocampal lesions facilitated the acquisition of suppression but had no effect upon the rate of extinction. In contrast, ventral hippocampal lesions had an opposite result, with no change in acquisition but a retarded extinction of suppression. The acquisition attenuation effect of dorsal hippocampal lesions, however, may be dependent upon the operant reinforcer (Freeman et al., 1974).

In addition, thalamic lesions also seem to influence conditioned suppression. Lesions of the dorsomedial thalamus may attenuate conditioned suppression, but not the conditioned cardiac responses, during the Estes-Skinner procedure (Nathan and Smith, 1971). A similar attenuation effect has been reported by Dantzer and Delacour (1972), who suggested that the attenuation may be an indirect result mediated by an increase in overall baseline rates.

Amnesiac Effects of Localized Brain Stimulation. The effects of repetitive amygdaloid stimulation following conditioned suppression, shuttle box avoidance, or maze learning was reported by Goddard (1964). Suppression was significantly attenuated by amygdaloid stimulation delivered immediately posttrial or throughout the conditioning session, with no effect of stimulation delivered only during the CS. Goddard proposed that amygdaloid stimulation was functionally equivalent to a lesion and scrambled the orderly flow of neural responses during the consolidation of emotional conditioning (Goddard, 1969). Levine et al. (1970), however, were unable to replicate the effect of posttrial amygdaloid stimulation in monkeys. The retrograde effects were only found with seizures induced by inferotemporal stimulation which propogated the amygdala. A second series of experiments (Lidsky et al., 1970) also failed to replicate the retrograde disruption by low-level amygdaloid stimulation using rats (Experiments 2A,B,C). Anterograde and retrograde attenuation effects were found, however, with high-intensity stimulation that spread diffusely and elicited grand mal type seizure patterns (Experiments 3A,B). Lidsky et al. concluded that the anygdaloid complex does not play an essential role in memory consolidation of aversive processes (also see McIntyre, 1970; McIntyre and Molino, 1972).

Hippocampal stimulation has also been reported to substantially decrement conditioned suppression (Barcik, 1970). The attenuation by localized seizures was in fact comparable to the effects of generalized electroconvulsive seizures. This blocking of suppression by hippocampal stimulation was also described by Shinkman and Kaufman (1972a), and it may be a function of stimulation intensity (Shinkman and Kaufman, 1972b; also see Gustafson et al., 1975). The retention of conditioned suppression may also be disrupted by injection of potassium chloride into the hippocampus (Avis and Carlton, 1968; Hughes, 1969; related experiments by Auerbach and Carlton, 1971; and Avis, 1972).

Generalized Seizures by Electroconvulsive Shock. A long series of experiments using electroconvulsive shock (ECS) has been reported by Brady and co-workers. In the first study (Hunt and Brady, 1951a) ECS was administered three times per day for 7 days following the stabilization of suppression, defecation, and freezing during the CS. The ECS treatments virtually eliminated the suppression of lever pressing, with a concomitant increase in activity and reduction in defecation during the CS. Subsequent experiments demonstrated that the attenuation effects were (1) transient, with a reappearance of complete suppression after 30 days (Brady, 1951), (2) dependent upon the number and temporal distribution of ECS treatments (Brady et al., 1954; Hunt and Brady, 1955), (3) inversely related to the delay between CS–UCS pairings and ECS treatments (Brady, 1952), (4) enhanced by interpolating additional ECS treatments during the retention interval (Brady, Stebbins, and Hunt, 1953), and (5) independent of the temporal order of classical and operant conditioning (Geller et al., 1955) (additional studies by Brady and Hunt, 1951, 1952; Brady, Stebbins, and Galambos, 1953; Hunt et al., 1953).

A similar transient effect of ECS administration has been reported in mice (Kohlenberg and Trabasso, 1968), and the temporal gradient of recovery from ECS effects has been described by Nachman et al. (1969; related experiments by Willi, 1969; Kesner et al., 1970; De Vietti and Holliday, 1972).

The usual ECS methodology was altered in an interesting experiment by Winocur and Mills (1970), who used the ECS as the Pavlovian UCS within the conditioned suppression procedure. The suppression during a stimulus terminated by ECS was equivalent to the typical suppressive effects of CS–shock trials. Suppression during the CS–ECS pairings seemed to be related to elicited convulsive responses rather than retrograde aftereffects during the recovery from the seizure.

Drugs. A host of experiments have assessed the impact of pharmacological agents upon conditioned suppression (reviews by Avis and Pert, 1974; Brady, 1957, 1959; Miczek, 1973). The functional effects of drugs, however, are quite complex, involve divergent effects across behavioral parameters, and also involve a multitude of interacting biochemical parameters (i.e., differential dose–response functions, action time courses, pharmacological metabolic rates, primary and secondary involvement of different neurochemical systems, etc.; reviews by Dews, 1962; Boren, 1966; Fontaine and Richelle, 1969; Kumar et al., 1970; Goodman and Gilman, 1970). For example, Davitz (1953) reported that tetraethylammonium chloride (TEA) altered the extinction rate of emotional freezing responses. Brady (1953) subsequently reported that TEA completely eliminated all activity throughout the conditioning sessions and had no differential or specific effect upon conditioned suppression per se. Similarly, the same drug may have different action times across individual subjects and correspondingly variable effects upon baseline and CS response rates. Brady (1956b), for example, reported that the chronic (daily) administration of reserpine consistently increased response rates and attenuated suppression during the CS but concomitantly decreased response rates during the intertrial interval. The time course of the reserpine effect over sessions was highly variable across subjects, ranging from rapid and abrupt attenuation to slow and gradual transitions in suppression ratios over trials and sessions. In comparison, chronic injection of d-amphetamine, a stimulant, enhanced conditioned suppression but also increased baseline rates during the intertrial interval.

Phenothiazines. Chlorpromazine and other phenothiazines are classified as major tranquilizers, and they are clinically used as antipsychotic agents. Appel

(1963) and Torres (1961) reported attenuation of suppression by chronic administration of phenothiazine compounds (also see Lepore et al., 1974). However, an acute or single injection of phenothiazines apparently has little if any effect (Boren, 1961; Kinnard et al., 1962; Ray, 1964; Cicala and Hartley, 1967; Tenen, 1967; Palfai and Cornell, 1968; but also see Hunt, 1956; and Lauener, 1963).

Reserpine. Reserpine was once used clinically as a major tranquilizer but has now been replaced by more effective drugs (such as butyrophenones or thioxanthenes). The attenuation of suppression by chronic administration of reserpine reported by Brady has been replicated by Weiskrantz and Wilson (1955), Mason and Brady (1956), Appel (1963), Ray (1964), Frey (1967), and Wilson et al. (1970). However, at least one study has found that chronic administration has no effect upon suppression (Yamahiro et al., 1961). Acute injection of reserpine may paradoxically enhance suppression (Valenstein, 1959) or have no discernable effect (Kinnard et al., 1962).

Benzodiazepines. Chronic administration of the minor tranquilizers or antianxiety agents of the benzodiazepine family (e.g., librium) has no apparent effect upon suppression (Stein and Berger, 1969). Other investigators, however, have reported an attenuation by the acute administration of benzodiazepines (Lauener, 1963; Tenen, 1967; Cicala and Hartley, 1967; Holtzman and Villarreal, 1969; Scobie and Garske, 1970; Maser and Hammond, 1972; Miczek, 1973; but also Stein and Berger, 1969).

Meprobamate. Chronic administration of meprobamate seems to attenuate conditioned suppression (Corson and Corson, 1967), whereas acute administration apparently has no clear-cut effect (Hunt, 1957; Lauener, 1963; Ray, 1964).

Barbituates. Current data indicate that suppression is attenuated by barbituates in both chronic (Corson and Corson, 1967) and acute administration (Lauener, 1963; Tennen, 1967; except Stein and Berger, 1969).

d-Amphetamine. The stimulant d-amphetamine has been reported to increase conditioned suppression when used chronically (Brady, 1956a). Glick (1969), using acute administration, also reported increased suppression, whereas Cappel et al. (1972) found an attenuation of suppression as a direct function of d-amphetamine dosage. Miczek (1973), however, found that suppression was unaffected by various dosages (also see Lauener, 1963).

Scopalomine. Scopalomine is an anticholinergic drug that does not seem to affect conditioned suppression in chronic administration (Evans and Patton, 1970). A single injection of scopalomine has been reported to reduce suppression during extinction tests (Avis and Pert, 1974; Pert and Avis, 1974; additional studies by Vogel et al., 1967; Daly, 1968; Berger and Stein, 1969a, 1969b; Goldberg et al., 1971; 1972). Miczek (1973), however, reported no alteration of suppression by scopalomine injections.

5-hydroxytryptamine (5-HTP).   Suppression seems to be increased by acute injection of 5-HTP, which presumably acts indirectly through an increase in brain serotonin (Wise et al., 1970). In a similar vein, Hartmann and Geller (1971) found an attenuation of suppression by p-chlorophenylalanine, which reduces the serotonin level, and a blunting of the attenuation by additionally injecting 5-HTP to increase serotonin (also see Frey, 1967).

Cannabis.   Relatively recent pharmacological studies suggest that suppression may be attenuated by the marihuana homologue pytahexyl (Abel, 1969). Gonzalez et al. (1972) also reported that the acute administration of marihuana extract blocked the acquisition and retention of conditioned suppression, and that chronic injection seemed to disrupt the retention but not the acquisition of suppression.

Drugs as the UCS.   A novel varient of the effect of drugs on conditioned suppression was introduced by Goldberg and Schuster (1967), who used drugs rather than shock as the classical conditioning UCS. Lever pressing by morphine-addicted monkeys was suppressed during a tone paired with nalorphine, a morphine antagonist. The suppression was accompanied by increased salivation, bradycardia, and emesis. Suppression was eliminated by substituting a tone paired with saline in phase 2, and was reconditioned with tone–nalorphine pairings again in phase 3. The nalorphine conditioned suppression then persisted even when the monkeys were no longer physically dependent upon morphine (Goldberg and Schuster, 1970). Suppression during a tone paired with lysergic acid diethylamide (LSD) has also bee reported, with generalization to similar tones during extinction test trials (Cameron and Appel, 1972b). The LSD conditioned suppression was replicated by Cameron and Appel (1972a), who also reported suppression during a light paired with the tranquilizer chlorpromazine. Cameron and Appel pointed out that the conditioned suppression by nonaversive tranquilizers and hallucinogenics does not fit the conditioned fear or emotional state interpretations of classical–operant interactions. Moreover, chlorpromazine apparently has the ironic effect of inducing conditioned suppression when used as a UCS but attenuating suppression when used as a tranquilizer (also see electroconvulsive shock as a UCS; Winocur and Mills, 1970).

Cardiovascular Responses and Conditioned Suppression

Heart rate, blood flow and other cardiovascular responses, like conditioned suppression, have frequently been used as potential indicants and measures of fear. If both lever-pressing rates and cardiovascular responses were equally accurate measures of acquired fear, then elementary logic would suggest that conditioned suppression should be quite closely correlated with heart rate, systolic and diastolic blood pressure, etc. In 1964, Stebbins and Smith compared suppression of operant responses with heart rate and blood flow in monkeys. Lever pressing was suppressed during the CS, with a marked increase in heart rate, blood flow rate, and general activity. (Heart rate and blood flow also in-

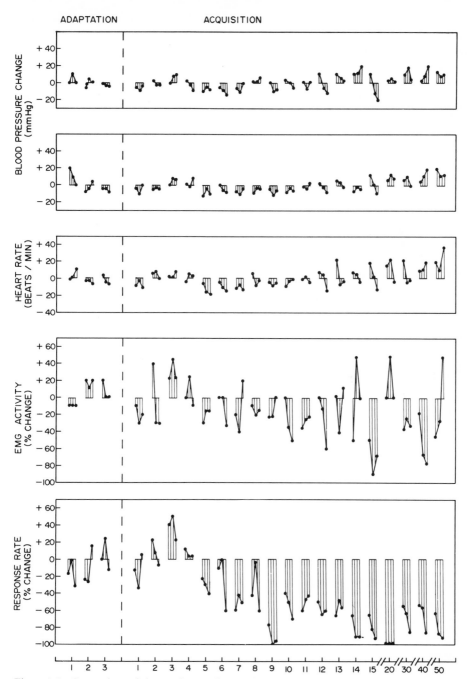

Figure 1.6. Comparison of changes in systolic and diastolic blood pressure, heart rate, EMG activity, and operant suppression in Monkey S-100 during Estes-Skinner procedure. Each data point represents successive 1-min intervals of each 3-min CS. EMG recorded with lumbar paraspinal muscle electrodes, and blood pressure recorded with femoral artery catheter. Data from Brady et al. (1970).

creased during the suppression of avoidance extinction rates during CS–shock pairings.) Stebbins and Smith (1964) therefore proposed an expanded definition of CER to include the large alterations in the autonomic system.

In opposition, de Toledo and Black (1966) reported relatively independent conditioning of heart rate and suppression in rats, and suggested that the divergent effects would pose a problem for the use of responses as measures of fear. Divergent acquisition rates of conditioned suppression and cardiac responses in rats was also reported by Parrish (1967; also see Smith and Nathan, 1967; Nathan and Smith, 1968).

Brady et al. (1969) measured heart rate, blood pressure, and lever-pressing rates during the acquisition, extinction, reconditioning, and reextinction of suppression in monkeys. In general, suppression of lever pressing conditioned and extinquished more rapidly than the cardiovascular responses, with rather divergent patterns of lever pressing, heart rate, and systolic and diastolic blood pressure during the CS. Brady et al. also concluded that the causal independence of physiological and behavioral measures argued against an interdependence of behavioral and physiological events or the theoretical primacy of one or the other response system. The experiment was then replicated with the additional analysis of electromyographic activity (EMG) by Brady et al. (1970; Brady, 1971). Tonic and phasic muscular activity was unrelated to cardiovascular changes in simple classical conditioning or to conditioned suppression and cardiovascular responses in the Estes-Skinner procedure (Figures 1.6 and 1.7). Both EMG acceleration and deceleration were associated with virtually all possible combinations of increased and decreased heart rate, systolic and diastolic

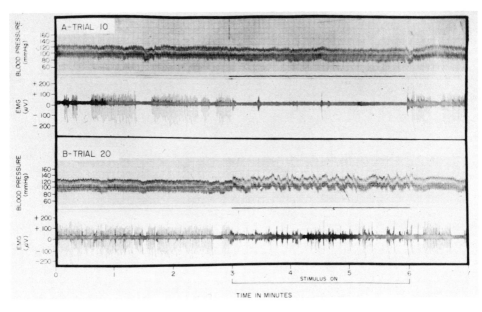

Figure 1.7. Amplified polygraph recordings of blood pressure and EMG activity during the 10th and 20th conditioning trials using a 3-min CS paired with shock superimposed upon operant lever pressing by monkey. Data from Brady et al. (1970).

blood pressure, and conditioned suppression (also see DeVietti and Porter, 1969; Willi, 1969; Zeiner et al., 1969; de Toledo, 1971; Borgealt et al., 1972; Dantzer and Baldwin, 1974; and, in humans, Di Guisto et al., 1974.)

Negative Classical Conditioning Scheduled with Negative Operant Conditioning

The suppression of food reinforced operants by a concurrent negative classical conditioning procedure clearly has been the only classical–operant combination to be studied in some detail. Early investigators pointed out, however, that the original Estes-Skinner procedure was only one of four general methods in which a positive or negative Pavlovian procedure could be superimposed upon positive or negative operant reinforcement schedules (e.g., Estes, 1948; Brady, 1961). The four-fold analysis of classical–operant interactions then progressed to an arithmetic complement. If CS–shock pairings disrupted operant responses maintained by positive reinforcers, then the same classical conditioning procedure might facilitate responses maintained by negative reinforcers. Those of us working with conditioned suppression in the 1960s especially enjoyed the overall simplification and form of such an analysis, with diagrams assigning upward pointing arrows for increased response rates when the operant and classical schedules had the same sign (or the same underlying state, expectancy, motivation, value, etc.), but downward pointing arrows and decreased rates when the two components had dissimilar signs. The results of early studies were quickly generalized, and rather overgeneralized, to support the pleasing symmetry apparent in both the figures and logic of conditioned suppression/acceleration. We might preface the following review section by noting that the initial theoretical symmetry is no longer especially tenable, or at least requires substantial revision in the light of subsequent experimentation.

The earliest study of avoidance rates during superimposed negative classical conditioning was reported by Sidman et al. (1957). In that study, monkeys were trained on a free-operant ("Sidman") avoidance schedule in which each lever press postponed a 1.0-sec, 5.0-ma shock for 20 sec. Lever-pressing rates increased during both control and CS intervals when a clicker was terminated by an unavoidable shock of the same intensity and duration of the avoidable shock. The acceleration gradually declined toward original baseline rates over sessions, with a somewhat slower return to baseline during the CS. In a second phase, CS–shock pairings were combined with extinction of the avoidance response, and again lever-pressing rates increased during both the intertrial interval and the CS. Throughout the study, lever pressing was similarly increased by unsignaled or "free" shock. The initial data then suggested that the effects of negative Pavlovian procedures were not simply restricted to the CS, but also resulted in overall increased responding throughout the session that was not substantially different from the effects of unsignaled shock. Sidman et al. then concluded that the change in avoidance rates was primarily dependent upon the response-independent shock rather than a classically conditioned effect of CS–

UCS pairings (also see Sidman, 1958, 1960a, 1960b; Waller and Waller, 1963; Belleville et al., 1963; Grossen and Bolles, 1968; Kamano, 1968; Rescorla, 1968a).

Table 1.2 summarizes the results of subsequent studies of avoidance behavior during CS–shock pairings. As with the Estes-Skinner procedure, the experiments have predominantly examined the effects of classical conditioning variables rather than operant or subject variables. The results of any one variable are again frequently quite conditional upon the selection of other parameters. Indeed, avoidance rates are either *suppressed* or *accelerated* by CS–shock pairings conditional upon specific parametric interactions, in contrast to the far more consistent conditioned suppression of positively reinforced operants.

Table 1.2   Negative classical–negative operant conditioning

Variables	Studies	Results
Classical Conditioning		
UCS Parameters		
intensity	5	conditional results
duration	4	acceleration as a direct function
probability	2	acceleration/suppression with stimuli paired/ unpaired with shock
type of UCS	4	conditional upon response
CS Parameters		
duration	3	conditional upon other variables
generalization	1	graded acceleration
compound stimuli	1	no effect
backward conditioning	1	suppression a function of UCS–CS interval
Total	21	
Operant Conditioning		
Reinforcement Schedules		
shock intensity	3	conditional upon other variables
response–shock interval	4	perhaps suppression as direct function
partial reinforcement	1	acceleration during CS
Concurrent Behaviors	1	increased during operant suppression
Pre-schedule Change Stimuli	1	acceleration
Total	10	
Subject		
Central Nervous System		
lesions	1	no effect of septal lesions
drugs	3	conditional
Cardiovascular Responses	1	increased during CS
Total	5	

Classical Conditioning Variables

UCS Parameters

UCS Intensity. Avoidance rates are at least partially controlled by the intensity of the Pavlovian UCS. In a study by Martin and Riess (1969), a CS was paired with 0.25, 0.58, 1.90, or 4.90-ma shock and then superimposed without shock upon the extinction of shuttle box avoidance responses. In general, the extinguishing avoidance response was slightly accelerated as a function of the former UCS intensity. A series of papers by Hurwitz and Roberts (1969, 1971) and Roberts and Hurwitz (1970) also indicate that operant avoidance rates during a CS are related to the UCS intensity.

Interactions between the intensity of the UCS and the negative operant reinforcer were studied in a 2 × 3 factorial design by Scobie (1972). First, hurdle jumping avoided either a 0.6- or a 1.3-ma shock in two different groups, with a superimposed CS terminated by a UCS of approximately 50%, 100%, or 200% of the avoidable shock. In the 0.6-ma group, avoidance rates increased when the CS was paired with the relatively lower UCS of 0.3 or 0.6 ma, but were suppressed by the higher UCS of 1.3 ma. In the second group, hurdle jumping maintained by a 1.3-ma shock was only marginally and transiently increased at all UCS intensities. Scobie thus concluded that the behavioral effects were not simply determined by the absolute UCS intensity, but also by the shock intensity relative to the operant reinforcer.

In hindsight, avoidance rates during CS–shock pairings do seem to be affected by UCS intensity. However, the direction of the operant rate change is apparently dependent upon additional variables and has been variously reported to be a direct function (Martin and Riess, 1969) or an inverse function (Scobie, 1972) of UCS intensity.

UCS Duration. The duration as well as the intensity of the UCS has also been reported to determine avoidance rates during the CS; Riess and Farrar (1973b) have reported avoidance acceleration as a direct function of UCS duration. Response latency was an inverse function, and response amplitude and frequency were direct functions of UCS durations of 0.05, 0.30, 1.00, and 3.0 sec. Riess and Farrar also discussed a variety of negative and positive correlations between the different response measures. Related experiments using a "transfer of training" design would also suggest that avoidance responses previously conditioned to a discrete visual stimulus might be elicited by tones previously paired with shock, as a direct function of shock duration Overmeir and Leaf, 1965; Overmeir, 1966a, 1966b).

Probability of the UCS. Rescorla and Lo Lordo (1965) described a group of experiments in which avoidance rates were accelerated during one stimulus paired with shock but suppressed during a second stimulus with a zero shock probability. The differential effects of shock probability were further replicated with a discriminative classical conditioning procedure and a conditioned inhibition procedure. In one experiment, for example, CS 1 was consistently paired with shock, and CS 2 was terminated only by CS 1. The hurdle-jumping responses were initially accelerated during subsequent CS 1 test trials, with a progressive reduction to control rates with continued testing. In contrast, avoidance rates were consistently inhibited or suppressed during test trials with CS 2. This acceleration and suppression of avoidance rates during stimuli paired and unpaired with shock has been replicated by Weisman and Litner (1969) using a wheel turning avoidance response by rats. The pairing of CS 2 with CS 1 in the Rescorla and Lo Lordo experiment is analogous to traditional second-order classical conditioning. The test results for the conditioned inhibition group would then suggest a persistent suppression during the second-order CS 2 but transient acceleration during the first-order CS 1 formerly paired with shock. The avoidance rate changes are then similar to the changes in positively reinforced operants during second-order conditioning, with different rates and patterns of responding during CS 2 and CS 1 in each case.

Type of UCS. A comparison of stimuli terminated by a loud horn and shock was reported by Lo Lordo (1967). Avodance rates were increased during the CS paired with a 108-db Klaxon horn, and also during the CS paired with shock. In comparison, avoidance rates were decreased slightly during a stimulus explicitly unpaired with shock and were unchanged by a stimulus explicitly unpaired with the horn. The increased rates during CS–horn pairings were opposite to the unconditioned freezing responses elicited by the horn UCS. Lo Lordo concluded that the fear elicited by CS–horn conditioning summated with the similar fear motivating the shock avoidance responses.

Studies with rats have also found increased shuttle box avoidance responses (Riess, 1970a, 1970b) but decreased lever-press avoidance rates (Riess, 1971) during a light paired with a buzzer.

Conditioned Stimulus Parameters

Relative Conditioned Stimulus Duration. The divergent reported effects of acceleration and suppression of avoidance rates may be dependent upon the duration of the CS relative to the avoidance response–shock interval. Pomerleau (1970) examined response rate as a function of both CS duration and the response-produced delay of shock in monkeys. Using an accumulating avoidance schedule (Field and Boren, 1963), lever pressing was reinforced by time-out from shocks repeating every 4.7 sec, with each response-produced time-out added to the previously accumulated shock-free time. The procedures were systematically replicated over blocks of sessions using avoidance time-out intervals of 1.0, 2.5, 5.0, and 20.0 sec compared to superimposed CS durations of 12, 48, and 84 sec. With a 1.0-sec time-out, for example, avoidance rates decreased throughout the 12-sec CS but followed a biphasic acceleration–deceleration pattern throughout the longer 48- and 84-sec CSs. Increasing the duration of the response-produced time-out relative to CS duration systematically decreased avoidance response rates, with responding suppressed at all CS durations when the scheduled time-out was 20 sec. As Pomerleau suggested, relative CS duration might then be a fundamental parameter, with analogous effects upon shock avoidance as well as food reinforced response rates.

However, the acceleration of avoidance rates with even relatively long CS durations is also conditional upon the UCS intensity; that is, avoidance rates may be suppressed even when the CS duration is relatively longer than the shock avoidance interval if the UCS intensity is also greater than the intensity of the avoidable shock (Bryant, 1972).

The effects of relative CS duration in superimposed trace classical conditioning have been described by Shimoff (1972b).

CS Generalization. Avoidance generalization gradients about tones explicitly paired and unpaired with shock were reported by Desiderato (1969). In off-the-baseline sessions, an 800-Hz tone or a clicker were explicitly paired or unpaired with shock in a counterbalanced design across groups. A single generalization test session consisted of nonshock presentations of 5-sec tones at 250, 450, 800, 1500, and 2600 Hz during extinction of hurdle jumping responses. The extinquishing avoidance rates were increased for the subjects trained with tone–shock pairings ("excitatory conditioning"), but decreased for subjects trained with the tone explicitly unpaired with shock ("inhibitory conditioning"). The generalization of acceleration and suppression was a U-shaped function across tone frequencies, with a relatively sharper gradient of excitatory acceleration than inhibitory suppression.

Compound CS. A compound stimulus test for external inhibition and disinhibition of avoidance rates was described by Rescorla (1967a). Initially, avoidance rates decreased at the onset of a 30-sec CS ("delay of inhibition") followed by a progressively accelerating rate ("fear conditioning"), which in turn was followed by an abruptly decreased response rate just prior to CS offset (adventitious punishment by the Pavlovian UCS). A 5-sec flashing light was then presented during the early portion of the CS with response suppression or the latter portion with response acceleration. Avoidance rates were relatively unchanged during both compound procedures, with no indication of "disinhibition" of the early "inhibition of delay" or "external inhibition" of the latter "conditioned fear."

Backward conditioning. Suppression or inhibition of Sidman avoidance behavior has recently been reported during a superimposed CS formerly used in backward UCS–CS conditioning. Maier et al. (1976) found that the suppression was dependent upon the duration of the UCS–CS interval; that is, the shock avoidance responses were decreased during the CS when the UCS–CS interval was 3 sec but were unchanged when the interval was 30 sec. These results tentatively suggest at least some conditions in which backward classical conditioning may alter operant avoidance responses.

Operant Conditioning Variables

Avoidance Schedule Parameters

Intensity of the Avoidable Shock. The studies of UCS intensity by Hurwitz and Roberts (1971) and Scobie (1972) also directly manipulated the intensity of the avoidable shock. Hurwitz and Roberts reported that avoidance rates reinforced with a 0.8-, 1.4-, or 2.0-ma shock were, respectively, suppressed, inconsistently changed, and slightly accelerated during the CS. Roberts and Hurwitz (1970) used a similar procedure but "suspended" the operant avoidance schedule during the CS. Response rates were then suppressed at all shock intensities during the CS plus time-out procedure. Scobie (1972) reported that avoidance rates reinforced by a 1.3-ma shock were relatively independent of UCS intensity, whereas avoidance reinforced by a lower 0.6-ma shock was generally increased by low UCS intensities but suppressed by a relatively high-intensity UCS.

Response–shock Interval. The previously cited study by Pomerleau (1970) has shown that avoidance rates during a CS are dependent upon the relative duration of the response-produced delay of shock. The data suggest that avoidance rates may be suppressed when the response–shock interval is long relative to CS duration, but may be facilitated when the shock delay is shorter than the CS. Brady et al. (1967) also reported that avoidance rates during CS–shock pairings were dependent upon the operant response–shock interval (also see Brady and Hunt, 1955). Scobie (1972), however, reported that the influence of the response–shock interval is conditional upon UCS intensity.

Partial Reinforcement of Avoidance Responses. The avoidance rates maintained by partial avoidance reinforcement schedules are also disrupted by negative classical conditioning procedures. Houser (1973) used a procedure in which lever pressing by monkeys was maintained on a response–shock 20-sec shock–shock 2-sec schedule, with only 20% of the due shocks actually delivered. The partially reinforced avoidance rates were substantially increased during superimposed CS–shock pairings. The accelerated CS avoidance rates were subsequently replicated across drug and control treatments.

Concurrent Behaviors and Avoidance Rates

A single paper has examined the changes in concurrent responses as well as operant avoidance responses during classical–operant combinations. Roberts et al. (1977) recorded 10 different behaviors during initial Sidman avoidance conditioning and during a superimposed preshock stimulus. Successful avoidance responding consisted of a variety of different topographical lever-pressing responses, with a reduction in the diverstiy as well as the frequency of avoidance responses during the CS. The changed rates and patterns of avoidance behaviors were associated with an increase in other concurrent responses during the CS. These concurrent response changes seem to be consistent with the suggestion that varients of the Estes-Skinner procedure may control multiple responses within the subject's repertoire.

Operant Avoidance Schedules as the Aversive "UCS"

Avoidance rates during stimuli terminated by schedule changes to higher and lower densities of avoidable shock were examined by Henton (1970). Avoidance responses, maintained by a response–shock = shock–shock = 30 sec schedule, were irregularly increased during 30-sec stimuli terminated with (1) a response–shock = shock–shock = 3 sec schedule, and (2) time-out from avoidance (Figure 1.8). Avoidance rates were equally variable when the duration of each preschedule change stimulus was changed to 15 sec or 60 sec, with averaged avoidance rates tending to be a direct function of stimulus duration.

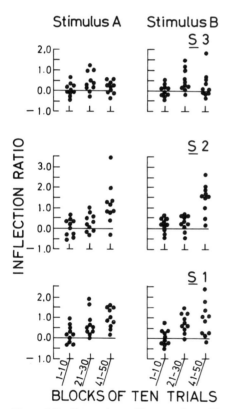

Figure 1.8. Comparison of increase in avoidance response rates by two stimuli terminated by opposite schedule changes. Avoidance responding by monkeys was maintained by a response–shock = shock–shock = 30 sec schedule, stimulus A was terminated by a response–shock = shock–shock = 3 sec schedule; and stimulus B was terminated by time out from avoidance. Data from Henton (1970).

Subject Variables

Central Nervous System

Lesions. A single study by Dickinson and Morriss (1975) indicated that septal lesions in rats have no effect upon the acceleration of wheel-turning avoidance responses during a CS formerly paired with shock.

Drugs. Houser and associates have reported a series of papers analyzing the effects of various pharmacological agents upon avoidance behaviors.

Chlordiazepoxide. Houser et al. (1975) reported that chlordiazepoxide (a minor tranquilizer) had no effect upon avoidance rate, heart rate, and general activity of dogs during the aversive CS. The drug treatments did, however, suppress baseline avoidance rates during the intertrial interval.

d-Amphetamine and α-methyl-p-tyrosine. Chronic administration of the stimulants d-amphetamine and α-methyl-p-tyrosine had no reliable effect upon conditioned acceleration of avoidance in monkeys (Houser, 1973). Again, however, each drug fundamentally altered baseline avoidance rates, with recovery of pre-drug baselines during drug withdrawal sessions.

Scopolamine. A comparison of the central acting scopolamine hydrobromide and the peripheral acting scopolamine methylnitrate was reported by Houser and Houser (1973). Initially, avoidance rates were accelerated (four monkeys) or suppressed (two monkeys) during the CS. The drugging procedure then consisted of daily injection of drug or saline in three-session blocks. The pattern of avoidance responding was reversed by scopolamine hydrobromide: avoidance rates were suppressed in subjects with the former acceleration pattern, and accelerated in subjects with the former suppression pattern. Scopolamine methylnitrate had no reliable effect. The authors suggested that the central acting scopolamine hydrobromide may reduce fear directly by interfering with cholinergic systems, or indirectly through alteration of memory processes.

Cardiovascular Responses

Heart rate, blood flow, and general activity in monkeys were recorded by Stebbins and Smith (1964) during CS–shock pairings superimposed upon avoidance extinction. Heart rate and blood flow consistently increased during all classical conditioning trials. In contrast, lever pressing accelerated during the early trials but was suppressed over the latter conditioning trials. The data thus suggest some independence of cardiovascular and avoidance rates during CS–shock pairings.

Positive Classical Conditioning Scheduled
with Positive Operant Conditioning

The operant changes during CS–shock pairings described by Estes and Skinner were immediatley replicated with CS–food pairings by Estes (1943, 1948). Estes (1943) reported that the "anticipation" of response-independent food would also alter the rate of positively reinforced operant responses. The operant rates were substantially increased during the positive classical conditioning procedure, in striking contrast to the conditioned suppression in the Estes-Skinner experiment. More specifically, bar pressing by rats was reinforced on a fixed interval (FI) 4-min food reinforcement schedule, with off-the-baseline pairings of a 1-min 60-Hz tone with the response-independent delivery of one food pellet. Extinction lever-pressing rates were increased during 10-min test trials when the tone was merely presented without food. Estes (1948) reversed the initial order of training on the operant and classical conditioning components, and reported similar acceleration of extinction operant rates during CS test trials. Estes (1948) therefore suggested that the CS–food pairings may set the occasion for an anticipatory state that could have discriminatory effects upon instrumental responses maintained by the same reinforcer.

European experiments by Konorski and Miller antedated the work of Estes but were largely unknown to Western psychologists until publication of the popular and comprehensive review by Konorski (1967). Konorski and Miller found that an instrumental leg-lifting response was immediately suppressed during a 15-sec CS paired with food, with a concomitant increase in orienting to the UCS feeder and salivation. Suppression invariably occurred in all subjects, despite the loss of available response-contingent reinforcers throughout the CS. In comparison, the instrumental response rates were relatively unchanged during an "inhibitory" stimulus explicitly unpaired with food. The suppression during positive classical conditioned stimuli was systematically replicated across a variety of different experimental procedures. In contrast to Estes, Konorski concluded than an appetitive type I or classical conditioned stimulus not only fails to increase the frequency of an appetitive type II instrumental response, but actively inhibits and decreases the instrumental response rate.

The subsequently reported effects of positive classical conditioning procedures upon positively reinforced operants are summarized in Table 1.3. Although fully as old as the comparable Estes-Skinner procedure, the behavioral effects of superimposed positive classical conditioning procedures have received considerably less experimental examination. The different experimental frequencies are partially due to the traditional negative connotations of emotions such as "fear," "anxiety," and "anger," and hence a greater theoretical interest in negative rather than positive classical conditioned "emotions." Second, positive classical conditioning is more commonly accepted as eliciting specific conditioned responses that may be antagonistic to the recorded operant, and thus complicate and impede the "proper" analysis of underlying associative or emotional states. As with superimposed negative classical conditioning procedures, studies using positive classical conditioning have been predominantly biased toward the analysis of the classical conditioning variables.

Table 1.3   Positive classical–positive operant conditioning

Variables	Studies	Results
Classical Conditioning		
UCS Parameters		
duration	1	no effect
type of UCS	7	conditional upon other variables
CS Parameters		
duration	5	conditional, divergent
Total	13	
Operant Conditioning		
Reinforcement Schedules		
response rate measures	1	conditional upon schedule
response accuracy	2	altered during CS
Concurrent Behaviors	2	inversely related to operant rate
Preschedule Change Stimuli	2	relative suppression
Total	7	
Subject		
Central Nervous System, drugs	1	attenuation of suppression
Cardiovascular Responses	1	unchanged during CS
Total	2	

Finally, the behavioral effects are relatively mixed and conditional, and are more comparable to the operant changes during negative classical–negative operant schedules than to the conditioned suppression in negative classical–positive operant schedule combinations.

Classical Conditioning Variables

UCS Parameters

UCS Duration. UCS duration apparently has little effect upon the food reinforced operants during CS–food pairings. Lo Lordo (1971) reported that key pecking by pigeons on a VI 2-min schedule was slightly increased during a CS paired with either 8-, 4-, or 2-sec access to grain. Response rates were relatively unchanged during a second CS explicitly unpaired with the grain UCS. Lo Lordo concluded that the CS facilitation may be a summation of operant responses plus orienting and approach responses elicited by the CS presented on the operant response key.

Type of UCS. The conditioned facilitation reported by Estes (1943, 1948) was replicated by Brady (1961) using intracranial stimulation (ICS) as the response-independent reinforcer. Operant rates were clearly increased during the CS–ICS interval, with the facilitation effect extinquishing during classical conditioning extinction.

In contrast, the conditioned suppression described by Konorski (1967) was immediately replicated by Azrin and Hake (1969). In that study, lever pressing by rats was reinforced either with food or water, with the subjects then divided into subgroups in which a 10-sec clicker or red light was terminated by food, water, or rewarding intracranial stimulation of the median forebrain bundle and hypothalamus. Operant responses reinforced with food were suppressed during the 10-sec CS paired with food, water, or intracranial stimulation. Water reinforced response rates were also suppressed during the CS paired with food, but were accelerated during the CS paired with water. Azrin and Hake hypothesized that the conditioned suppression must be due to a general emotional state of heigthened preparedness rather than competing body movements, head movements, or freezing during the various CSs. The results were replicated with slightly different procedures by Hake and Powell (1970) and Van Dyne (1971).

The following studies by Meltzer and Brahlek (1970), Henton and Brady (1970), and Miczek and Grossman (1971) also used either qualitatively or quantitatively different response-dependent and response-independent reinforcers.

CS Parameters

CS Duration. The reported suppression and facilitation effects of appetitive Pavlovian procedures seem to be partially determined by the relative CS duration. The first study of CS duration was that of Meltzer and Brahlek (1970), who found that the rate of lever pressing reinforced with food was a direct function of the duration of a CS paired with either 10% or 25% sucrose solutions. Responding was accelerated during a 120-sec CS and suppressed during a 12-sec CS, with intermediate and mixed response rates during a 40-sec CS. Furthermore, the pattern as well as the frequency of responses during the CS was also dependent upon CS duration, with progressively decreasing response rates throughout the 12-sec Cs, constant or slightly decreasing rates during the 40-sec CS, but positively accelerating rates during the 120-sec CS.

The acceleration of DRL response rates is similarly conditional upon the duration of a superimposed CS paired with food (Figure 1.9). Henton and Brady (1970) reported that the low rate of DRL responding maintained with one food pellet was relatively unchanged during a 20- or 40-sec CS paired with five food pellets, but markedly accelerated when the CS was extended to 80 sec. The response facilitation seemed to be related to the response sequences mediating the "temporal inhibition" of DRL responding (see, for example, Chapter 5, Experiment III).

Miczek and Grossman (1971) replicated the Meltzer and Brahlek study and reported a slightly different function relating operant rates to CS duration. Lever pressing by monkeys was suppressed during a 15- or 30-sec CS but relatively unchanged rather than accelerated at longer CS durations of 1, 2, and 3 min. Suppression of lever pressing by monkeys was also an inverse function of CS duration in Experiment VII, Chapter 2.

Using pigeons, Smith (1974) reported a third relationship between CS dura-

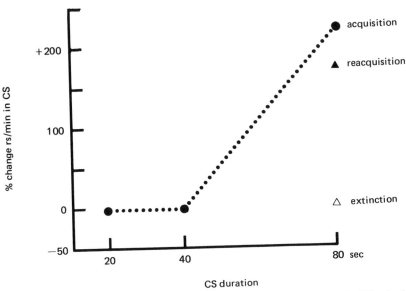

Figure 1.9. Changes in DRL responding as a function of the duration of a CS paired with food. Each data point is the mean of the final 25 conditoning trials in acquisition (filled circles), extinction (open triangles), and reacquisition (filled triangles). Adapted from Henton and Brady: *J. Exp. Anal. Behav.*, **13**, 205–209, 1970.

tion and response rate. Low baseline rates were accelerated, not suppressed, during a 5-sec CS, and relatively unchanged during 30-, 60-, and 120-sec CS–food intervals. In comparison, high baseline rates were slightly accelerated during the 5-sec CS, suppressed during the 30- and 60-sec stimuli, and unchanged during the 120-sec CS.

Thus, the effects of CS duration, like so many other variables, are not totally consistent across experiments and would seem to be conditional upon additional parameters.

Operant Conditioning Variables

Schedule Parameters

Response Rate Measures. The previously cited studies have generally used response rate measures and reported that the same VI or DRL baseline rate may be altered by manipulating CS duration. In addition, Kelly (1973b) compared the effects of CS–food pairings upon the high rate of responses generated by RR schedules and the low response rates maintained by DRL schedules. The high RR response rate was suppressed during the CS, independent of changes in food deprivation or the local intertrial interval response rate. DRL rates were accelerated, however, independent of food deprivation but partially dependent upon local variations in the intertrial baseline rates.

Response Accuracy. Herrnstein and Morse (1957) originally reported the alteration of temporal or spaced responding in DRL schedules during a CS paired
with food. Pecking responses by pigeons were reinforced on a DRL 5-min
schedule, with a 2-min yellow light as the CS projected upon the pecking key.
Response-independent food was delivered 1-min after CS onset. The stimulus–
food pairings produced a generalized increase in responding throughout the experimental sessions, with a further acceleration during the CS by four subjects,
but a relative suppression for two subjects. Herrnstein and Morse proposed
that the initial change in responding must be related to then unknown variables,
with acceleration or suppression adventitiously maintained by correlations between the response-independent reinforcer and either key pecking or incompatible behaviors, respectively.

The Herrnstein and Morse study was later replicated by Henton and Brady
(1970), with an additional analysis of the response distribution as a function of
CS duration. The DRL rates were relatively unchanged during a 20- or 40-sec
CS, but accelerated with a redistribution of interresponse times during the 80-
sec CS. As shown in Figure 1.10, the longer CS generated an increased frequency of unreinforced interresponse times of 0–5 and 25–30 sec. The interresponse time distribution shifted back to control patterns during classical conditioning extinction, with a replication of the accelerated response rate during
CS–UCS pairings in reacquisition.

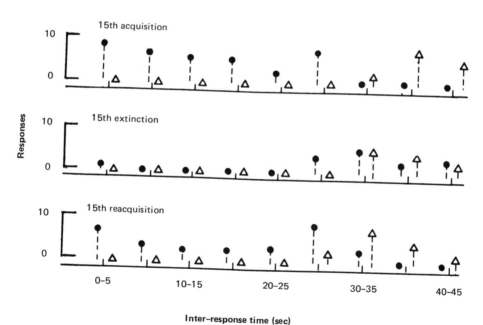

Figure 1.10. Comparison of DRL interresponse times during 80-sec CS paired with food (filled
circles) and equivalent control periods (open triangles). Each data point is the distribution of responses in 5-sec bins over the last five trials of classical conditioning acquisition, extinction, and
reacquisition. Adapted from Henton and Brady: *J. Exp. Anal. Behav.*, **13**, 205–209, 1970.

Concurrent Behaviors

A number of investigators have proposed that the conditioned acceleration and suppression of operant rates may be related to the temporal pattern of concurrent or competing responses elicited by the appetitive classical conditioning (Herrnstein and Morse, 1957; Konorski, 1967; Henton and Brady, 1970; Henton and Iversen, 1973). More recently, Lo Lordo et al. (1974) found that the acceleration of DRL responding by pigeons was related to an increased rate of approach and orienting responses to the visual CS presented on the operant manipulandum. In contrast, a treadle-pressing response reinforced on the same DRL schedule was suppressed along with the increase in orienting responses to the pecking key during the visual CS. By comparison, the key-pecking and treadle-pressing operants were inconsistently affected by a similar 10-sec auditory CS paired with food. The results are consistent with the previous suggestion that conditioned acceleration may be related to the summation of topographically similar responses (Lo Lordo, 1971).

Increased Reinforcement Rate as the Positive "UCS"

The previously described studies by Pliskoff (1961, 1963) reported generally decreased rates during stimuli paired with response-independent schedule changes to higher operant reinforcement rates relative to stimuli terminated by lower reinforcement rates (see p. 51).

Subject Variables

Central Nervous System

A single study (Miczek, 1973) has examined the effects of various pharmacological agents upon operant rates during appetitive classical conditioning in both rats and monkeys. Response rates were suppressed during a 15-sec tone paired with sweetened milk (rats) or food pellets (monkeys); the suppression was attenuated by the stimulant d-amphetamine, but unaffected by benzodiazepines or scopolamine. In contrast, the conditioned suppression during CS–shock pairings was attenuated by the benzodiazepines, but unchanged by d-amphetamine or scopolamine. The divergent drug effects were attributed to a differential susceptibility of the various competing responses elicited by stimuli paired with food and shock.

Cardiovascular Responses

A two-monkey experiment was described by Kelly (1973a) in which heart rate and blood pressure were recorded during a 3-min CS paired with food during operant lever-pressing sessions. Lever pressing was transiently suppressed during the initial trials, but relatively unchanged or slightly accelerated throughout the latter trials of the study; heart rate and blood pressure were unaffected by the CS–UCS pairings throughout the experiment. Kelly proposed that the conditioned suppression may be determined by the monkeys adopting a "why-work-when-you-can-get-it-for-nothing" strategy.

Positive Classical Conditioning Scheduled with Negative Operant Conditioning

The analysis of avoidance behaviors during positive classical conditioning procedures is the most neglected classical–operant schedule. A total of three recent papers have examined shock avoidance rates during superimposed CS–food pairings. In the first study, Coulson and Walsh (1968) reported that a 1-min CS paired with 10 sucrose pellets had no effect upon lever pressing by rats reinforced on a FI or VI shock avoidance schedule. The avoidance rates increased during the CS, however, when the food deprivations were changed from 80% to 70% of normal body weight. Coulson and Walsh concluded that the response-independent food had a behavior energizing or motivational effect that would facilitate ongoing operant behaviors.

In contrast, Davis and Kreuter (1972) found a change in the patterning but not the overall avoidance rate in rats during superimposed appetitive classical conditioning. The lever-pressing rates were suppressed at CS onset, followed by delivery of shock on the programmed avoidance schedule, in turn followed by a postshock burst of avoidance responses in the latter portion of the CS. Davis and Kreuter proposed that the cyclical suppression and acceleration pattern may be most adequately analyzed in terms of interacting schedule contingencies.

Using monkeys, Henton (1972; also see Chapter 2) also reported that conditioned acceleration or suppression of avoidance rates was partially controlled by the CS–food contingencies and the spatial location of the CS and UCS.

Additional studies have used a "transfer of training" design in which a former CS previously paired with food is combined with the extinction of operant avoidance responding. Grossen et al. (1969), for example, reported a suppression of the avoidance extinction rate during tones previously paired with either the response-independent or response-contingent delivery of food. The authors argued that the suppression could not be due to competing food retrieval responses, since the avoidance rates were equally disrupted by tones terminated by food in a classical conditioning box (requiring no retrieval responses) or in an alley runway (requiring a specified retrieval response).

A series of papers from Overmeir's laboratory have also used the transfer of training procedure and similarly describe a suppression of avoidance extinction rates during the stimuli previously paired with an appetitive UCS (Bull, 1970; Overmeir and Bull, 1970; Overmeir et al., 1971). Overmeir and associates interpret the suppressed avoidance rates as an interaction between underlying motivational systems.

Two additional studies have reported accelerated avoidance rates during stimuli terminated by time-out from the operant avoidance schedule in rats (Baron and Trenholme, 1971), and monkeys (Henton, 1970). The avoidance rates were highly variable during the preschedule change stimuli in both studies.

Concluding Remarks

In general summary, the foregoing review would suggest an almost infinite complexity of parametric interactions within the various combinations of classical and operant schedules. Within each major category, consistent behavioral effects have been reported for only the most powerful classical conditioning variables, with the effects of many manipulations conditional upon other parameters, or seemingly inconsistent and divergent within and across experiments. The inconsistent behavioral effects of various parameters would clearly emphasize the still preliminary nature of current behavioral analysis. The obvious disparity in research efforts across the four types of schedule combinations further emphasizes the incomplete and unfinished character of classical–operant schedule analysis. The absence of empirical facts as well as the presence of inconsistent results will hopefully generate a more adequate experimental examination rather than a burgeoning accumulation of "heuristic" and hypothetical opinions. Fortunately, the contemporary literature does indeed provide a number of variables that may be manipulated in concert to purposely control operant rates during superimposed classical conditioning procedures—UCS intensity and CS duration are only two examples. The sheer quantity of controlling variables, and the resultant intricate interactions between variables, however, sharply limit the accuracy of global generalizations and molar explanations of classical–operant effects.

One assumption gone wrong, for instance, is the once firm belief that the Estes-Skinner procedure may be used as a model of classical–operant interactions. Early results could be interpreted as the internalized summation of similar motivational and emotional states, or subtraction of dissimilar states. Classical–operant interactions could then be reduced to a few molar generalizations in the beginning analysis. Conditioned fear would disrupt positive motivations and enhance fear motivation. In a similar manner, positive conditioned emotions would enhance positive operant motivations but disrupt fear motivation. The various internal state doctrines thus neatly prescribed the relationship between emotions and motivations, and, with additional assumptions and operational definitions, could arguably describe the alteration of behavioral and physiological indicants of underlying excitatory and inhibitory processes.

The ensuing years found a number of studies attempting to find the causal functions relating emotional behaviors to underlying states via physiological responses. The expected close correlation between physiological and behavioral measures failed to materialize for virtually all classical–operant combinations, and the conception of behaviors as passive measures of underlying states began to fail. Internal state theories have not been eliminated, however, but merely reinterpreted, perhaps citing Canon's early observations that many physiological and autonomic responses are after all identical in emotional states. Overt behavior might therefore be a true measure of covert mental states if not covert neurophysiological responses. Nevertheless, subsequent investigators have reported similar operant response patterns within different classical–operant schedules, suggesting that overt behavior is as undifferentiated as covert responses across the various "emotional" conditioning procedures.

Additional experiments further question the utility of behaviors as measures of underlying processes. As only one example, the suppression of operant responses during the Estes-Skinner procedure is not associated with corresponding changes in food motivational states as measured by eating (Ayres and Quinsey, 1970; Jackson and Delprato, 1974). Nevertheless, operant suppression has been frequently offered as a measure of the disruption of the motivational value of food by conditioned fear. In reviewing the literature, Hancock and Ayres (1974) simply concluded that motivational state interpretations have little empirical credibility. For this and many additional reasons, it is not clear that a phrenology of states and values is any more accurate when based upon the physical characteristics of behavior than when based upon the physical characteristics of the subject's skull.

Moreover, the rather consistent conditioned suppression during the Estes-Skinner procedure is in fact atypical and the exception rather than the model of acceleration and suppression of operant rates within each of the three remaining schedule combinations. The conditioned suppression and/or acceleration effects pose further problems for underlying state interpretations. The summation of conditioned fear and operant fear motivation might predict acceleration, but not suppression, when a negative classical conditioning procedure is superimposed upon shock avoidance responses. Similarly, the disruption of operant fear motivation by positive conditioned states might predict suppression, but not acceleration, of avoidance rates during superimposed appetitive conditioned stimuli. Although unnecessary, most state and value interpretations assume that the proposed motivational or incentive effects are indifferent to specific response characteristics and topographies. The simplifying assumption does limit the number of necessary explanatory assumptions, but at the cost of categorically specifying equivalent disruption or energizing effects for all behaviors maintained by the same instrumental motivation. In contrast, the multitude of response rates and patterns in classical–operant schedules suggests that changes in behavior must be at least partially determined by physical response characteristics (Brady, 1971; Miczek, 1973; Scobie, 1973). Many years ago, Brady and Hunt discussed much the same point:

> Many attempts have been made to order these diversities in behavior to a single broad principle—i.e., emphasis on the role of conditioned "fear" as a motivational construct mediating the establishment of instrumental responses . . . such monolithic ordering, prematurely embraced, might serve to obscure important differences as well as significant similarities and relationships among behaviors. (Brady and Hunt, 1955, p. 322)

The early warnings of Brady and Hunt are still more relevant to the host of behavioral differences and similarities currently apparent in classical–operant schedules. The diverse interactions between the many known experimental variables continue to preclude a deductive or statistical reduction of response rates to a unidimensional measuring or matching function.

One continuing interpretation, however, has maintained an emphasis upon behavior qua behavior—perhaps not surprisingly, the analysis is the inductive rather than deductive experimental analysis of "emotional" behavior introduced by Brady and Hunt. The experimental analysis has proved to be viable for some 20 years, and in fact is more compelling today than in previous years. Moreover, the experimental analysis not only accepts the role of operant responses, but also classical conditioned responses and interacting behavioral patterns that are commonly denied by deductive models. Admittedly, the analysis of concurrent or competing response patterns is occasionally harshly unpopular—''elliptical and irrelevant to operant-respondent processes,'' ''trivial,'' or ''too quantitative and microscopic.'' The fundamental argument against a response pattern analysis seems to be the cavalier unconcern with academic states, motivations, emotions, general emotions, and whatnot, in favor of observed and recorded behavioral functions. Indeed, the behavioral interactions may be offered as part and parcel of the behavioral effects and are perhaps not elliptical and irrelevant to the analysis of classical and operant schedules—nor trivial.

The experiments presented in Chapter 2 suggest, for example, that avoidance rates may be controlled by the pattern of concurrent UCS approach and retrieval responses during a superimposed appetitive classical conditioning procedure (Experiment IA,B,C). Interdependent response patterns also occur in positive classical–positive operant combinations, with operant rates dependent upon competing response patterns (Experiments II and III). Similarly, discrete trial operant procedures and appetitive classical conditioning procedures control analogous response patterns when superimposed upon a concurrent operant schedule, as a function of stimulus duration (Experiments VI and VII). Importantly, the classical conditioning processes are also disrupted during the Estes-Skinner procedure and are not passively measured by the concurrent operant response rates (Experiment IX). The various concurrent schedule effects do not warrant a collapsing of the diverse independent variables into global constructs, either within or across classical–operant schedules, and the present experimental analysis remains unrepentantly behavioral and quantitative, and occasionally microscopic.

References

Abel, E. L.: Effects of marihuana homologue, pyrahexyl, on a conditioned emotional response. *Psychonomic Sci.,* **16**, 44, 1969.

Anderson, D. C., Merril, H. K., Dexter, W., and Alleman, H.: Contextual effects in emotional learning. *Proc. Am. Psychol. Assoc.* **3**, 147–148, 1968.

Anderson, D. C., O'Farrell, T., Formica, R., and Caponigri, V.: Preconditioning CS exposure: variation in place of conditioning and presentation. *Psychonomic Sci.* **15**, 54–55, 1969a.

Anderson, D. C., Wolf, D., and Sullivan, P.: Pre-conditioning exposures to the CS: variations in place of testing. *Psychonomic Sci.* **14**, 233–234, 1969b.

Anderson, L. T., and Ressler, R. H.: Response to a conditioned aversive event in mice as a function of frequency of premating maternal shock. *Develop. Psychobiol.,* **6**, 113–121, 1973.

Annau, Z., and Kamin, L. J.: The conditioned emotional response as a function of intensity of the US. *J. Comp. Physiol. Psychol.,* **54**, 428–432, 1961.

Appel, J. B.: Drugs, shock intensity and the CER. *Psychopharmacologia,* **4**, 141–153, 1963.

Arnold, M. B.: An excitatory theory of emotion. In, M. L. Reymert (ed.): *Feelings and Emotion.* New York, McGraw-Hill, 1950.

Arnold, M. B. (ed.): *Feelings and Emotion.* New York, Academic Press, 1970.

Auerbach, P., and Carlton, P. L.: Retention deficit correlated with a deficit in the corticoid response to stress. *Science,* **173,** 1148–1149, 1971.

Avis, H.: Hippocampal injections of KCL and shock-induced bradycardia in the rat. *Psychonomic Sci.,* **27,** 283–284, 1972.

Avis, H., and Carlton, P. L.: Retrograde amnesia produced by hippocampal spreading depression. *Science,* **161,** 73–75, 1968.

Avis, H., and Pert, A.: A comparison of the effects of muscarinic and nicotinic anticholingergic drugs on habituation and fear conditioning in rats. *Psychopharmacologia,* **34,** 209–222, 1974.

Ayres, J. J. B.: Conditioned suppression and the information hypothesis. *J. Comp. Physiol. Psychol.,* **62,** 21–25, 1966.

Ayres, J. J. B.: Differentially conditioned suppression as a function of shock intensity and incentive. *J. Comp. Physiol. Psych.,* **66,** 208–210, 1968.

Ayres, J. J. B., and DeCosta, M. J.: The truly random control as an extinction procedure. *Psychonomic Sci.,* **24,** 31–33, 1971.

Ayres, J. J. B., and Quinsey, V. L.: Between-groups incentive effects on conditioned suppression. *Psychonomic Sci.,* **21,** 294–296, 1970.

Azrin, N. H., and Hake, D. F.: Positive conditioned suppression: conditioned suppression using positive reinforcers as the unconditioned stimuli. *J. Exp. Anal. Behav.,* **12,** 167–173, 1969.

Baird, H. N., Gudetti, B., Reyes, V., Wycis, H. T., and Spiegal, E. G.: Stimulation and elimination of anterior thalamic nuclei in man and cat. *Fed. Proc.,* **10,** 8–9. 1951.

Baker, A. G.: Conditioned inhibition is not the symmetrical opposite of conditioned excitation: a test of the Rescorla-Wagner model. *Learning Motivation,* **5,** 369–379, 1974.

Baker, A. G.: Learned irrelevance and learned helplessness: rats learn that stimuli, reinforcers, and responses are uncorrelated. *J. Exp. Psychol. [Anim. Behav. Processes],* **2,** 130–142, 1976.

Barcik, J. D.: Hippocampal after discharges and conditioned emotional responses. *Psychonomic Sci.,* **20,** 297–298, 1970.

Bard, P.: A diencephalic mechanism for the expression of rage with special reference to the sympathetic nervous system. *Am. J. Physiol.,* **84,** 490–515, 1928.

Bard, P.: On emotional expression after decortication with some remarks on certain theoretical views. Parts I and II. *Psycholo. Rev.,* **41,** 309–329, 424–449, 1934.

Bard, P., and Mountcastle, V. B.: Some forebrain mechanisms involved in expression of rage with special reference to suppression of angry behavior. In, J. Fulton (ed.): *The Frontal Lobes.* Baltimore, Williams & Wilkins, 1948.

Bard, P., and Rioch, D. M.: A study of four cats deprived of neocortex and additional portions of the forebrain. *Bull. Johns Hopkins Hosp.,* **60,** 73–147, 1937.

Baron, A., and Trenholme, I. A.: Response-dependent and response-independent timeout from an avoidance schedule. *J. Exp. Anal. Behav.,* **16,** 123–132, 1971.

Belleville, R. E., Rohles, F. H., Grunzke, M. E., and Clark, F. G.: Development of a complex multiple schedule in the chimpanzee. *J. Exp. Anal. Behav.* **6,** 549–556, 1963.

Benedict, J. O., and Ayres, J. J. B.: Factors affecting conditioning in the truly random control procedure. *J. Comp. Physiol. Psychol.,* **78,** 323–330, 1972.

Berger, B. D., and Stein, L.: An analysis of learning deficits produced by scopolamine. *Psychopharmacologia,* **14,** 271–283, 1969a.

Berger, B. D., and Stein, L.: Asymmetrical dissociation of learning produced by scopolamine and W Y 40 36, a new benzodiazepine. *Psychopharmacologia,* **14,** 51–358, 1969b.

Blackman, D. E.: Response rate and conditioned suppression. *Psychol. Rep.,* **19,** 687–693, 1966.

Blackman, D. E.: Conditioned suppression: comments on Lyon's reply. *Psychol. Rep.,* **20,** 909–910, 1967a.

Blackman, D. E.: Effects of response pacing on conditioned suppression. *Q. J. Exp. Psychol.,* **19,** 170–174, 1967b.

Blackman, D. E.: Conditioned suppression or facilitation as a function of the behavioral baseline. *J. Exp. Anal. Behav.,* **11,** 53–61, 1968a.

Blackman, D. E.: Response rate, reinforcement frequency and conditioned suppression. *J. Exp. Anal. Behav.,* **11,** 503–516, 1968b.

Blackman, D. E.: Effects of a pre-shock stimulus on temporal control of behavior. *J. Exp. Anal. Behav.,* **14,** 313–319, 1970.

Blackman, D. E., and Scrutton, P.: Conditioned suppression and discriminative control of behavior. *Anim. Learning Behav.*, **1**, 90–92, 1973.

Booth, J. H., and Hammond, L. J.: Configural conditioning: greater fear in rats to the compound than component through overlapping the compound. *J. Exp. Psychol.*, **87**, 255–262, 1971.

Boren, J. J.: Some effects of adephenine, benactyzine, and chloropromazine upon several operant behaviors. *Psychopharmacologia*, **2**, 416–424, 1961.

Boren, J. J.: The study of drugs with operant techniques. In, W. K. Honig (ed.): *Operant Behavior: Areas of Research and Application.* New York, Appleton-Century-Crofts, 1966.

Boring, E. G.: *A History of Experimental Psychology*, 2nd ed. New York, Appleton-Century-Crofts, 1957.

Borgealt, A. J., Donahoe, J. W., and Weinstein, A.: Effects of delayed and trace components on a compound CS on conditioned suppression and heart rate. *Psychonomic Sci.*, **26**, 13–15, 1972.

Brady, J. V.: The effect of electro-convulsive shock on a conditioned emotional response: the permanence of the effect. *J. Comp. Physiol. Psychol.*, **44**, 507–511, 1951.

Brady, J. V.: The effect of electro-convulsive shock on a conditioned emotional response: the significance of the interval between the emotional conditioning and the electro-convulsive shock. *J. Comp. Physiol. Psychol.*, **45**, 9–13, 1952.

Brady, J. V.: Does tetraethylammonium reduce fear. *J. Comp. Physiol. Psychol.*, **46**, 307–310, 1953.

Brady, J. V.: Extinction of a conditioned "fear" response as a function of reinforcement schedules for competing behaviors. *J. Psychol.*, **40**, 25–34, 1955.

Brady, J. V.: A comparative approach to the evaluation of drug effects upon affective behavior. *Ann. N. Y. Acad. Sci.*, **64**, 632–643, 1956a.

Brady, J. V.: The assessment of drug effects on emotional behavior. *Science*, **123**, 1033–1034, 1956b.

Brady, J. V.: A review of comparative behavioral pharmacology. *Ann. N. Y. Acad. Sci.*, **66**, 719–732, 1957.

Brady, J. V.: Animal experimental evaluation of drug effects upon behavior. *Proc. Assoc. Res. Nerv. Mental Dis.*, **37**, 104–125, 1959.

Brady, J. V.: Motivation–emotional factors and intracranial self-stimulation. In, D. E. Sheer (ed.): *Electrical Stimulation of the Brain.* Austin, University of Texas Press, 1961.

Brady, J. V.: Psychophysiology of emotional behavior. In, A. J. Bachrach (ed.): *Experimental Foundations of Clinical Psychology.* New York, Basic Books, 1962.

Brady, J. V.: Emotion: some conceptual problems and psychophysical experiments. In, M. Arnold (ed.): *Feelings and Emotion.* New York, Academic Press, 1970a.

Brady, J. V.: Endocrine and autonomic correlates of emotional behavior. In, P. Black (ed.): *Physiological Correlates of Emotion.* New York, Academic Press, 1970b.

Brady, J. V.: Emotion revisited. *J. Psychiatr. Res.*, **8**, 363–384, 1971.

Brady, J. V.: Toward a behavioral biology of emotion. In, L. Levi (ed.): *Emotions—their Parameters and Measurement.* New York, Raven Press, 1975.

Brady, J. V., and Conrad, D.: Some effects of limbic system self-stimulation upon conditioned emotional behavior. *J. Comp. Physiol. Psychol.*, **53**, 128–137, 1960.

Brady, J. V., and Hunt, H. F.: A further demonstration of the effects of electro-convulsive shocks on a conditioned emotional response. *J. Comp. Physiol. Psychol.*, **44**, 204–209, 1951.

Brady, J. V., and Hunt, H. F.: The effect of electro-convulsive shock on a conditioned emotional response: a control for impaired hearing. *J. Comp. Physiol. Psychol.*, **45**, 180–182, 1952.

Brady, J. V., and Hunt, H. F.: An experimental approach to the analysis of emotional behavior. *J. Psychol.*, **40**, 313–325, 1955.

Brady, J. V., and Nauta, W. J. H.: Subcortical mechanisms in emotional behavior: affective changes following septal forebrain lesions in the albino rat. *J. Comp. Physiol. Psychol.*, **46**, 339–346, 1953.

Brady, J. V., and Nauta, W. J. H.: Subcortical mechanisms in emotional behavior: the duration of affective changes following septal and habenular lesions in the albino rat. *J. Comp. Physiol. Psychol.*, **48**, 412–420, 1955.

Brady, J. V., and Sulsa, G.: Acquisition and extinction of conditioned "fear" as a function of shock intensity. Paper read at Eastern Psychological Association, Philadelphia, 1955.

Brady, J. V., Stebbins, W. C., and Galambos, R.: The effect of audiogenic convulsions on a conditioned emotinal response. *J. Comp. Physiol. Psychol.*, **46**, 363–367, 1953.

Brady, J. V., Stebbins, W. C., and Hunt, H. F.: The effect of electro-convulsive shock (ECS) on a conditioned emotional response: the effect of additional ECS convulsions. *J. Comp. Physiol. Psychol.*, **46**, 368–372, 1953.

Brady, J. V., Hunt, H. F., and Geller, I.: The effect of electroconvulsive shock on a conditioned emotional response as a function of the temporal distribution of the treatments. *J. Comp. Physiol. Psychol.*, **47**, 454–457, 1954.

Brady, J. V., Libber, S., and Dardano, J.: Some effects of a pre-aversive stimulus on avoidance behavior. Tech. Rep. 67-14, Space Research Lab, University of Maryland, 1967.

Brady, J. V., Kelly, D. D., and Plumlee, L.: Autonomic and behavioral responses of the rhesus monkey to emotional conditioning. *Ann. N. Y. Acad. Sci.*, **150**, 959–975, 1969.

Brady, J. V., Henton, W. W., and Ehle, A.: Some effects of emotional conditioning upon autonomic and electromyographic activity. Paper read at Eastern Psychological Association, Atlantic City, 1970.

Brimer, C. J.: Attention and conditioned suppression. *Psychonomic Sci.*, **22**, 131–132, 1971.

Brimer, C. J., and Dockrill, F. J.: Partial reinforcement and the CER. *Psychonomic Sci.*, **5**, 185–186, 1966.

Brimer, C. J., and Kamin, L. J.: Disinhibition, habituation, sensitization, and the conditioned emotional response. *J. Comp. Physiol. Psychol.*, **56**, 508–516, 1963.

Brimer, C. J., and Wickson, S.: Shock frequency, disinhibition and conditioned suppression. *Learning Motivation*, **2**, 124–137, 1971.

Brodigan, D. L., and Trapold, M. A.: Recovery from conditioned suppression to a partially overlapping compound stimulus. *Anim. Learning Behav.*, **2**, 89–91, 1974.

Brogden, W. J.: Sensory preconditioning. *J. Exp. Psychol.*, **25**, 323–332, 1939.

Brophy, J. C., and Tremblay, A. M.: One-trial CER as a function of shock intensity. *Psychonomic Sci.*, **25**, 13–14, 1971.

Brown, J. S., and Farber, I. E.: Emotions conceptualized as intervening variables—with suggestions toward a theory of frustration. *Psychol. Bull.*, **48**, 465–495, 1951.

Brown, J. S., Kalish, H. I., and Farber, I. E.: Conditioned fear as revealed by the magnitude of startle response to an auditory stimulus. *J. Exp. Psychol.*, **41**, 317–328, 1951.

Brunner, R. L., Roth, T. G., and Rossi, R. R.: Age differences in the development of the conditioned emotional response. *Psychonomic Sci.*, **21**, 135–136, 1970.

Bryant, R. C.: Conditioned suppression of free-operant avoidance. *J. Exp. Anal. Behav.*, **17**, 257–260, 1972.

Buchanan, D. C. Schaefer, G. J., and Caul, W. F.: Effects of infantile handling on heart rate conditioning and response suppression. *Psychonomic Sci.*, **29**, 279–281, 1972.

Bull, J. A., III: An interaction between appetitive Pavlovian CS's and instrumental avoidance responding. *Learning Motivation*, **1**, 18–26, 1970.

Burdick, C. K., and James, J. P.: Spontaneous recovery of conditioned suppression of licking by rats. *J. Comp. Physiol. Psychol.*, **72**, 467–470, 1970.

Burdick, C. K., and James, J. P.: Effects of backward conditioning procedure following acquisition on extinction of conditioned suppression. *Anim. Learning Behav.*, **1**, 137–139, 1973.

Byrum, R. P., and Jackson, D. E.: Response availability and second-order conditioned suppression. *Psychonomic Sci.*, **23**, 106–108, 1971.

Calef, R. S., Kaufman, R. A., Bone, R. N., and Werk, S. A.: Noncontingent nonreinforcement of a response as the aversive event in a CER paradigm. *Psychol. Rep.*, **29**, 1196–1198, 1971.

Cameron, O. G., and Appel, J. B.: Conditioned suppression of bar-pressing behavior by stimuli associated with drugs. *J. Exp. Anal. Behav.*, **17**, 127–137, 1972a.

Cameron, O. G., and Appel, J. B.: Generalization of LSD-induced conditioned suppression. *Psychonomic Sci.*, **27**, 303–304, 1972b.

Campbell, B. A., and Campbell, E. H.: Retention and extinction of learned fear in infant and adult rats. *J. Comp. Physiol. Psychol.*, **55**, 1–8, 1962.

Cannon, W. B.: Recent studies of bodily effects of fear, rage, and pain. *J. Philosophy, Psychol. Sci. Methods,* **11,** 162–165, 1914.

Cannon, W. B.: The James-Lange theory of emotions: a critical examination and alternate theory. *Am. J. Psychol.,* **39,** 106–204, 1927.

Cannon, W. B.: Again the James-Lange theory and the thalamic theories of emotion. *Psychol. Rev.,* **38,** 281–295, 1931.

Cannon, W. B., Lewis, J. T., and Britton, S. W.: The dispensibility of the sympathetic division of the ANS. *Boston Med. Surg. J.,* **197,** 514–515, 1927.

Cappel, H. D., Herring, B., and Webster, C. D.: Discriminated conditioned suppression: further effects of stimulus compounding. *Psychonomic Sci.,* **19,** 147–149, 1970.

Cappel, H. D., Ginsberg, R., and Webster, C. D.: Amphetamine and conditioned "anxiety." *Br. J. Pharmacol.,* **45,** 525–431, 1972.

Carlton, P. L., and Didamo, P.: Some notes on the control of conditioned suppression. *J. Exp. Anal. Behav.,* **3,** 255–258, 1960.

Carlton, P. L., and Vogel, J. R.: Habituation and conditioning. *J. Comp. Physiol. Psychol.,* **63,** 348–351, 1967.

Carman, J. B.: Time-out from a short mean-interval reinforcement schedule. *Psychonomic Sci.,* **15,** 259–260, 1969.

Carman, J. B.: Deprivation levels and conditioned suppression. *Psychol. Rep.,* **27,** 599–602, 1970.

Carr, A. P.: Latent inhibition and overshadowing in conditioned emotional response conditioning with rats. *J. Comp. Physiol. Psychol.,* **86,** 718–723, 1974.

Catania, A. C.: Concurrent operants. In, W. K. Honig (ed.): *Operant behavior: areas of research and application.* New York, Appleton-Century-Crofts, 1966.

Chaddock, T. E.: Visual detection of X ray by the rhesus monkey. *J. Comp. Physiol. Psychol.,* **78,** 190–201, 1972.

Church, R. M.: Response suppression. In, B. A. Campbell and R. M. Church (eds.): *Punishment and aversive behavior.* New York, Appleton-Century-Crofts, 1969.

Church, R. M., Wooten, C. L., and Mathews, T.: Discriminative punishment and the conditioned emotional response. *Learning Motivation,* **1,** 1–17, 1970.

Cicala, G. A., and Hartley, D. L.: Drugs and the learning and performance of fear. *J. Comp. Physiol. Psychol.,* **64,** 173–178, 1967.

Corson, A., and Corson, E. O.: Pavlovian conditioning as a method for studying the mechanism of action of minor tranquilizers. In, H. Brill (ed.): *Proceedings of the Fifth International Conference of Neuropharmacology,* Amsterdam, 1967.

Coughlin, R. C.: The aversive properties of withdrawing positive reinforcement: a review of the recent literature. *Psychol. Record,* **22,** 333–354, 1972.

Coulson, G., and Walsh, M.: Facilitation of avoidance responding in white rats during a stimulus preceding food. *Psychol. Rep.,* **22,** 1277–1284, 1968.

Coulter, X., Collier, A. C., and Campbell, B. A.: Long-term retention of early Pavlovian fear conditioning in infant rats. *J. Exp. Psychol. [Anim. Behav. Processes],* **2,** 48–56, 1976.

Cousins, L. S., Zamble, E., Tait, R. W., and Suboski, M. D.: Sensory preconditioning in curarized rats. *J. Comp. Physiol. Psychol.,* **77,** 152–154, 1971.

Dalton, L. W., Jr.: Conditioned suppression as a technique for determination of auditory sensitivity in pigeons. *J. Auditory Res.,* **7,** 25–29, 1967.

Daly, H. B.: Disruptive effects of scopolamine on fear conditioning and on instrumental escape learning. *J. Comp. Physiol. Psychol.,* **66,** 579–583, 1968.

Dantzer, R., and Baldwin, B. A.: Changes in heart rate during suppression of operant responding in pigs. *Physiol. Behav.,* **12,** 385–391, 1974.

Dantzer, R., and Delacour, J.: Modification of a phenomenon of conditioned suppression by a thalamic lesion. *Physiol. Behav.,* **8,** 997–1003, 1972.

Darwin, C.: *Expression of the Emotions in Man and Animals.* London, Murray, 1872.

Davenport, J. W.: Higher-order conditioning of fear. *Psychonomic Sci.,* **4,** 27–28, 1966.

Davis, H.: Conditioned suppression: a survey of the literature. *Psychonomic Monogr. [Suppl.],* **2,** 283–291, 1968.

Davis, H., and Kreuter, C.: Conditioned suppression of an avoidance response by a stimulus paired with food. *J. Exp. Anal. Behav.,* **17,** 277–285, 1972.

Davis, H., and McIntire, R. W.: Conditioned suppression under positive, negative, and no contingency between conditioned and unconditioned stimuli. *J. Exp. Anal. Behav.,* **12,** 633–640, 1969.

Davis, H., McIntire, R. W., and Cohen, S. I.: Fixed and variable duration warning stimuli and conditioned suppression. *J. Psychol.,* **73,** 19–25, 1969.

Davis, H., Memmott, J., and Hurwitz, H. M. B.: Effects of signals preceding and following shock on baseline responding during a conditioned suppression procedure. *J. Exp. Anal. Behav.,* **25,** 263–277, 1976.

Davis, R. G.: Olfactory psychophysical parameters in man, rat, dog, and pigeon. *J. Comp. Physiol. Psychol.,* **85,** 221–232, 1973.

Davitz, J. P.: Decreased autonomic functioning and extinction of a conditioned emotional response. *J. Comp. Physiol. Psychol.,* **46,** 311–313, 1953.

DeCosta, M. J., and Ayres, J. J. B.: Suppression of operant vs consummatory behavior. *J. Exp. Anal. Behav.,* **16,** 133–142, 1971.

Desiderato, O.: Generalization of conditioned suppression. *J. Comp. Physiol. Psychol.,* **57,** 434–437, 1964.

Desiderato, O.: Generalization of extinction and inhibition in control of avoidance responding by Pavlovian CSs in dogs. *J. Comp. Physiol. Psychol.,* **68,** 611–616, 1969.

Desiderato, O., and Newman, A.: Conditioned suppression produced in rats by tones paired with escapable and inescapable shock. *J. Comp. Physiol. Psychol.,* **77,** 427–431, 1971.

de Toledo, L.: Changes in heart rate during conditioned suppression in rats as a function of US intensity and type of CS. *J. Comp. Physiol. Psychol.,* **77,** 528–538, 1971.

de Toledo, L., and Black, A. H.: Heart rate: changes during conditioned suppression in rats. *Science,* **152,** 1404–1406, 1966.

DeVietti, T. L., and Holliday, J. H.: Retrograde amnesia produced by electroconvulsive shock after reactivation of a consolidated memory trace: a replication. *Psychonomic Sci.,* **29,** 137–138, 1972.

DeVietti, T. L., and Porter, P. B.: Modification of the autonomic component of the conditioned emotional response. *Psychol. Rep.,* **24,** 951–958, 1969.

Dews, P. B.: Psychopharmacology. In, A. J. Bachrach (ed.): *Experimental Foundations of Clinical Psychology.* New York, Basic Books, 1962.

Dexter, W. R., and Merrill, H. K.: Role of contextual discrimination in fear conditioning. *J. Comp. Physiol. Psychol.,* **69,** 677–681, 1969.

Dickinson, A., and Morriss, R. G. M.: Conditioned acceleration and free-operant wheel-turn avoidance following septal lesions in rats. *Physiol. Psychol.,* **3,** 107–112, 1975.

Di Giusto, J. A., Di Giusto, E. L., and King, M. G.: Heart rate and muscle tension correlates of conditioned suppression in humans. *J. Exp. Psychol.,* **103,** 515–521, 1974.

Domjan, M., and Siegal, S.: Conditioned suppression following CS preexposure. *Psychonomic Sci.,* **25,** 11–12, 1971.

Donegan, N. H., Whitlow, J. W., and Wagner, A. R.: Posttrial reinstatement of the CS in Pavlovian conditioning: facilitation or impairment of acquisition as a function of individual differences in responsiveness to the CS. *J. Exp. Psychol.* [*Anim. Behav. Processes*], **3,** 357–376, 1977.

Dubin, W. J., and Levis, D. J.: Influence of similarity of components of a serial conditioned stimulus on conditioned fear in rats. *J. Comp. Physiol. Psychol.,* **85,** 304–312, 1973.

Duffy, E.: The psychological significance of the concept of "arousal" or "activation." *Psychol. Rev.,* **64,** 265–275, 1957.

Egger, M. D., and Miller, N. E.: Secondary reinforcement in rats as a function of information value and reliability of the stimulus. *J. Exp. Psychol.,* **64,** 97–104, 1962.

Estes, W. K.: Discriminative conditioning. I. A discriminative property of conditioned anticipation. *J. Exp. Psychol.,* **32,** 150–155, 1943.

Estes, W. K.: Discriminative conditioning. II. Effects of a Pavlovian conditioned stimulus upon a subsequently established operant response. *J. Exp. Psychol.,* **38,** 173–177, 1948.

Estes, W. K.: The statistical approach to learning theory. In S. Koch (ed.): *Psychology: A Study of Science, vol. 2.* New York, McGraw-Hill, 1959.

Estes, W. K.: Outline of a theory of punishment. In, B. A. Campbell and R. M. Church (eds.): *Punishment and Aversive Behavior*. New York, Appleton-Century-Crofts, 1969.

Estes, W. K., and Skinner, B. F.: Some quantitative properties of anxiety. *J. Exp. Psychol., 29,* 390–400, 1941.

Evans, H. L., and Patton, R. A.: Scopolamine effects on conditioned suppression: influence of diurnal cycle and transitions between normal and drugged states. *Psychopharmacologia. 17,* 1–13, 1970.

Fehr, F. S., and Stern, J. A.: Peripheral physiological variables and emotion: the James–Lange theory revisited. *Psychol. Bull., 74,* 411–424, 1970.

Ferster, C. B., and Skinner, B. F.: *Schedules of Reinforcement*. New York, Appleton-Century-Crofts, 1957.

Field, G., and Boren, J. J.: An adjusting avoidance procedure with multiple auditory and visual warning stimuli. *J. Exp. Anal. Behav., 6,* 537–543, 1963.

Findley, J. D.: An experimental outline for building and exploring multi-operant behavior repertoires. *J. Exp. Anal. Behav. [Suppl.], 5,* 113–166, 1962.

Finnocchio, D.: Changes in temporally space responding as a measure of conditioned emotional behavior. Paper read at Eastern Psychological Association, New York, 1963.

Fleshler, M., and Hoffman, H. S.: Stimulus generalization of conditioned suppression. *Science, 133,* 753–755, 1961.

Fontaine, O., and Richelle, M.: Comparative study of the effects of chlorpromazine and chlordiazepoxide on a series of programs of positive and negative reinforcement of behavior in the rat. *Psychol. Belg., 9,* 17–29, 1969.

Freeman, F. G., Mikulka, P. J., and d'Auteuil, P.: Conditioned suppression of a licking response in rats with hippocampal lesions. *Behav. Biol., 12,* 257–263, 1974.

Frey, A. H.: Modification of the conditioned emotional response by treatment with small negative air ions. *J. Comp. Physiol. Psychol., 63,* 121–125, 1967.

Frey, P., Eng, S., and Gavin, W.: Conditioned suppression in the gerbil. *Behav. Res. Methods Instr. 4,* 245–249, 1972.

Frieman, J. P., Warner, L., and Riccio, D. C.: Age differences in conditioning and generalization of fear in young and adult rats. *Develop. Psychol., 3,* 119–123, 1970.

Frieman, J. P., Frieman, J., Wright, W., and Hegberg, W.: Developmental trends in the acquisition and extinction of conditioned suppression in rats. *Develop. Psychol., 4,* 425–428, 1971.

Geller, I.: The acquisition and extinction of conditioned suppression as a function of the baseline. *J. Exp. Anal. Behav., 3,* 235–240, 1960.

Geller, I.: Conditioned suppression in goldfish as a function of shock-reinforcement schedule. *J. Exp. Anal. Behav., 7,* 345–349, 1964.

Geller, I., Sidman, M., and Brady, J. V.: The effect of electroconvulsive shock on a conditioned emotional response: a control for acquisition recency. *J. Comp. Physiol. Psychol., 48,* 130–131, 1955.

Gleitman, H., and Holmes, P. A.: Retention of incompletely learned CER in rats. *Psychonomic Sci., 7,* 19–20, 1967.

Glick, S. D.: Effects of d-amphetamine and frontal ablations on response suppression in rats. *J. Comp. Physiol. Psychol., 69,* 49–54, 1969.

Goddard, G. V.: Amygdaloid stimulation and learning in the rat. *J. Comp. Physiol. Psychol., 58,* 23–30, 1964.

Goddard, G. V.: Analysis of avoidance conditioning following cholinergic stimulation of amygdala in rats. *J. Comp. Physiol. Psychol. Monogr., 68,* (2, pt 2), 1969.

Goldberg, M. E., Sledge, K., Hefner, M., and Robichaud, R. C.: Learning impairment after three classes of agents which modify cholinergic function. *Arch. Int. Pharmacodyn. Ther., 193,* 226–235, 1971.

Goldberg, M. E., Sledge, K., Robichaud, R. C., and Dubinsky, B.: A comparative study of the behavioral effects of scopolamine and 4-(1-naphthylvinyl) pyridine hydrochloride (NVP), an inhibitor of choline acetyltransferase. *Psychopharmacologia, 23,* 34–47, 1972.

Goldberg, S. R., and Schuster, C. R.: Conditioned suppression by a stimulus associated with nalorphine in morphine-dependent monkeys. *J. Exp. Anal. Behav., 10,* 235–242, 1967.

Goldberg, S. R., and Schuster, C. R.: Conditioned nalorphine-induced abstinence changes: persistance in morphine dependent monkeys. *J. Exp. Anal. Behav.*, **14**, 33–36, 1970.

Goldstein, R.: Effects of non-contingent septal stimulation on the CER in the rat. *J. Comp. Physiol. Psychol.*, **61**, 132–135, 1966.

Gonzalez, S. C., Karinol, I. G., and Carlini, E. A.: Effects of Cannabis sativa extract on conditioned fear. *Behav. Biol.*, **7**, 83–94, 1972.

Goodman, L. S., and Gilman, A. (eds.): *The Pharmacological Basis of Therapeutics*, 4th ed. New York, MacMillan, 1970.

Gottwald, P.: The role of punishment in the development of conditioned suppression. *Physio. Behav.*, **2**, 283–286, 1967.

Gottwald, P.: Adventitious punishment in two conditioned suppression procedures. *Psychol. Rep.*, **25**, 699–703, 1969.

Goy, R. W., and Hunt, H. F.: The resistance of an instrumental response to suppression by conditioned fear. *Am. Psychol.*, **8**, 509, 1953.

Gray, T., and Appignanesi, A. A.: Elimination of the blocking effect. *Learning Motivation*, **4**, 374–380, 1973.

Grossen, N. E., and Bolles, R. C.: Effects of classical conditioned "fear signal" and "safety signal" on nondiscriminated avoidance behavior. *Psychonomic Sci.*, **11**, 321–322, 1968.

Grossen, N. E., Kostansek, D. J., and Bolles, R. C.: Effects of appetitive discriminative stimuli upon avoidance behavior. *J. Exp. Psychol.*, **81**, 340–343, 1969.

Grossman, S. P.: *A Textbook of Physiological Psychology*. New York, Wiley, 1967.

Gustafson, J. W., Lidsky, T. I., and Schwartzbaum, J. S.: Effects of hippocampal stimulation on acquisition, extinction and generalization of conditioned suppression in the rat. *J. Comp. Physiol. Psychol.*, **10**, 1136–1147, 1975.

Hake, D. F., and Powell, J.: Positive reinforcement and suppression from the same occurrence of the unconditioned stimulus in a positive conditioned suppression paradigm. *J. Exp. Anal. Behav.*, **14**, 247–257, 1970.

Hammond, L. J.: Increased responding to CS − in differential CER. *Psychonomic Sci.*, **5**, 337–339, 1966.

Hammond, L. J.: A traditional demonstration of the active properties of Pavlovian inhibition using differential CER. *Psychonomic Sci.*, **9**, 65–66, 1967.

Hammond, L. J., and Maser, J.: Forgetting and conditioned suppression: role of temporal discrimination. *J. Exp. Anal. Behav.*, **13**, 333–338, 1970.

Hancock, R. A., and Ayres, J. J. B.: Within-subject effects of sucrose concentration on conditioned suppression of licking. *Psychol. Record*, **24**, 325–331, 1974.

Hanson H. M.: Effects of discrimination training on stimulus generalization. *J. Exp. Psychol.*, **58**, 321–323, 1959.

Hartmann, G. J., and Geller, I.: P-Chlorophenylalanine effects on a conditioned emotional response in rats. *Life Sci.*, **10**, 927–933, 1971.

Harvey, J. A., Lints, C. E., Jacobson, L. E., and Hunt, H. F.: Effects of lesions in the septal area on conditioned fear and discriminated instrumental punishment in the albino rat. *J. Comp. Physiol. Psychol.*, **59**, 37–48, 1965.

Haworth, J. T.: Conditioned emotional response phenomena and brain stimulation. *Br. J. Psychol.*, **62**, 97–103, 1971.

Hearst, E.: Stress-induced breakdown of an appetitive discrimination. *J. Exp. Anal. Behav.*, **8**, 135–146, 1965.

Hebb, D. O.: *The organization of behavior*. New York, Wiley, 1949.

Heffner, H., and Masterton, B.: Hearing in primitive primates: slow loris (Nycticebus coucang) and potto (Perodicticus potto). *J. Comp. Physiol. Psychol.*, **71**, 175–182, 1970.

Heffner, R., Heffner, H., and Masterton, B.: Behavioral measurement of absolute and frequency-difference thresholds in the guinea pig. *J. Acoust. Soc. Am.*, **49**, 1888–1895, 1971.

Hendersen, R. W.: Conditioned and unconditioned fear inhibition in rats. *J. Comp. Physiol. Psychol.*, **84**, 554–561, 1973.

Hendersen, R. W.: Compounds of conditioned fear stimuli. *Learning Motivation*, **6**, 28–42, 1975.

Hendricks, J.: Flicker thresholds as determinted by a modified conditioned suppression procedure. *J. Exp. Anal. Behav.*, **9**, 501–506, 1966.

Hendry, D. P.: Conditioned inhibition of conditioned suppression. *Psychonomic Sci.*, **9**, 261–262, 1967.

Hendry, D. P., and Van Toller, C.: Alleviation of conditioned suppression. *J. Comp. Physiol. Psychol.*, **59**, 458–460, 1965.

Hendry, D. P., Switalski, R., and Yarczower, M.: Generalization of conditioned suppression after differential training. *J. Exp. Anal. Behav.*, **12**, 799–806, 1969.

Henton, W. W.: Suppression behavior to odorous stimuli in the pigeon. Unpublished Doctoral Dissertation, Florida State University, 1966.

Henton, W. W.: Conditioned suppression to odorous stimuli in pigeons. *J. Exp. Anal. Behav.*, **12**, 175–185, 1969.

Henton, W. W.: The effects of pre-schedule change stimuli upon avoidance responding. *Rep. Neurophysiol. Inst. (Kbh)*, 34–35, 1970.

Henton, W. W. Avoidance response rates during a pre-food stimulus in monkeys. *J. Exp. Anal. Behav.*, **17**, 269–275, 1972.

Henton, W. W., and Brady, J. V.: Operant acceleration during a pre-reward stimulus. *J. Exp. Anal. Behav.*, **13**, 205–209, 1970.

Henton, W. W., and Iversen, I. H.: Concurrent response rates during preevent stimuli. Paper read at the Easter Conference, Cambridge, March 1973.

Henton, W. W., and Jordan, J. J.: Differential conditioned suppression during pre-shock stimuli as a function of shock intensity. *Psychol. Record*, **20**, 9–16, 1970.

Henton, W. W., Smith, J. C., and Tucker, D.: Odor discrimination in pigeons. *Science*, **153**, 1138–1139, 1966.

Henton, W. W., Smith, J. C., and Tucker, D.: Odor discrimination in pigeons following section of the olfactory nerves. *J. Comp. Physiol. Psychol.*, **69**, 317–323, 1969.

Herrnstein, R. J.: On the law of effect. *J. Exp. Anal. Behav.*, **13**, 243–266, 1970.

Herrnstein, R. J., and Morse, W. H.: Some effects of response-independent positive reinforcement on maintained operant behavior. *J. Comp. Physiol. Psychol.*, **50**, 461–467, 1957.

Herrnstein, R. J., and Sidman, M.: Avoidance conditioning as a factor in the effects of unavoidable shocks on food-reinforced behavior. *J. Comp. Physiol. Psychol.*, **51**, 380–385, 1958.

Heth, C. D., and Rescorla, R. A.: Simultaneous and backward fear conditioning in the rat. *J. Comp. Physiol. Psychol.*, **82**, 434–443, 1973.

Hilton, A.: Partial reinforcement of a conditioned emotional response in rats. *J. Comp. Physiol. Psychol.*, **69**, 253–260, 1969.

Hoffman, H. S.: Discrimination processes are relative to aversive controls. In, R. Gilbert (ed.): *Discrimination Learning*. Aberdeen, University of Aberdeen, 1967.

Hoffman, H. S.: Stimulus factors in conditioned suppression. In, B. A. Campbell and R. M. Church (eds.): *Punishment and Aversive Behavior*. New York, Appleton-Century-Crofts, 1969.

Hoffman, H. S., and Barrett, J.: Overt activity during conditioned suppression: a search for punishment artifacts. *J. Exp. Anal. Behav.*, **16**, 343–348, 1971.

Hoffman, H. S., and Fleshler, M.: Stimulus factors in aversive controls: the generalization of conditioned suppression. *J. Exp. Anal. Behav.*, **4**, 371–378, 1961.

Hoffman, H. S., and Fleshler, M. The course of emotionality in the development of avoidance. *J. Exp. Psychol.*, **64**, 288–294, 1962.

Hoffman, H. S., and Fleshler, M.: Stimulus aspects of aversive controls: stimulus generalization of conditioned suppression following discrimination training. *J. Exp. Anal. Behav.*, **7**, 233–239, 1964.

Hoffman, H. S., and Fleshler, M.: Stimulus aspects of aversive controls: the effects of response contingent shock. *J. Exp. Anal. Behav.*, **8**, 89–96, 1965.

Hoffman, H. S., Fleshler, M., and Jensen, P.: Stimulus aspects of aversive controls: the retention of conditioned suppression. *J. Exp. Anal. Behav.*, **6**, 575–583, 1963.

Hoffman, H. S., Selekman, W., and Fleshler, M.: Stimulus aspects of aversive controls: long term effects of suppression procedures. *J. Exp. Anal. Behav.*, **9**, 659–662, 1966a.

Hoffman, H. S., Selekman, W. L., and Fleshler, M.: Stimulus factors in aversive controls: conditioned suppression after equal training to two stimuli. *J. Exp. Anal. Behav.*, **9**, 649–653, 1966b.

Holland, P. C., and Rescorla, R. A.: The effect of two ways of devaluing the unconditioned stimulus after first- and second-order appetitive conditioning. *J. Exp. Psychol.* [*Anim. Behav. Processes*], **1**, 355–363, 1975.

Holmes, P.: Conditioned suppression with extinction as the signalled stimulus. *J. Exp. Anal. Behav.*, **18**, 129–132, 1972.

Holtzman, S. G., and Villarreal, J. E.: The effects of morphine on conditioned suppression in rhesus monkeys. *Psychonomic Sci.*, **17**, 161–162, 1969.

Homzie, M. J., Shucard, D. W., and Trost, R. C.: Effects of percentage of reinforcement in fear conditioning upon the acquisition of an instrumental response. *Psychonomic Sci.*, **17**, 143–145, 1969.

Houser, V. P.: Modulation of avoidance behavior in squirrel monkeys after chronic administration and withdrawl of d-amphetamine or α-methyl-p-tyrosine. *Psychopharmacologia*, **28**, 213–234, 1973.

Houser, V. P. and Houser, F. L.: The effects of agents that modify muscarinic tone upon behavior controlled by an avoidance schedule that employs signalled shock. *Psychopharmacologia*, **32**, 133–150, 1973.

Houser, V. P., Rothfeld, B., and Varady, A., Jr.: Effects of chlordiazepoxide upon fear-motivated behavior in dogs. *Psychol. Rep.*, **36**, 987–998, 1975.

Hughes, R. A.: Retrograde amnesia in rats produced by hippocampal injections of potassium chloride: gradient of effect and recovery. *J. Comp. Physiol. Psychol.*, **68**, 637–644, 1969.

Hunt, H. F.: Some effects of drugs on classical (type S) conditioning. *Ann. N. Y. Acad. Sci.*, **65**, 258–267, 1956.

Hunt, H. F.: Some effects of meprobanate on conditioned fear and emotional behavior. *Ann. N. Y. Acad. Sci.*, **67**, 712–723, 1957.

Hunt, H. F., and Brady, J. V.: Some effects of electro-convulsive shock on a conditioned emotional response ("anxiety"). *J. Comp. Physiol. Psychol.*, **44**, 88–98, 1951a.

Hunt, H. F., and Brady, J. V.: Some quantitative and qualitative differences between "anxiety" and "punishment" conditioning. *Am. Psychol.*, **6**, 276–277, 1951b.

Hunt, H. F., and Brady, J. V.: Some effects of punishment and intercurrent "anxiety" on a simple operant. *J. Comp. Physiol. Psychol.*, **48**, 305–310, 1955.

Hunt, H. F., Jernberg, P., and Brady, J. V.,: The effect of electroconvulsive shock (ECS) on a conditioned emotional response: the effect of post-ECS extinction on the reappearance of the response. *J. Comp. Physiol. Psychol.*, **45**, 589–599, 1952.

Hunt, H. F., Jernberg, P., and Lawlor, W. G.: The effect of electro-convulsive shock on a conditioned emotional response: the effect of electro-convulsive shock under anesthesia. *J. Comp. Physiol. Psychol.*, **46**, 64–68, 1953.

Hurwitz, H. M. B., and Roberts, A. E.: Suppressing an avoidance response by a pre-aversive stimulus. *Psychonomic Sci.*, **17**, 305–306, 1969.

Hurwitz, H. M. B., and Roberts, A. E.: Conditioned suppression of an avoidance response. *J. Exp. Anal. Behav.*, **16**, 275–281, 1971.

Jackson, D. E., and Delprato, D. J.: Aversive CSs suppress lever pressing for food, but not the eating of free food. *Learning Motivation*, **5**, 448–458, 1974.

James, J. P.: Acquisition, extinction and spontaneous recovery of conditioned suppression. *Psychonomic Sci.*, **22**, 156–158, 1971a.

James, J. P.: Latent inhibition and the preconditioning–conditioning interval. *Psychonomic Sci.*, **24**, 97–98, 1971b.

James, J. P., and Mostoway, W. W.: Conditioned suppression of licking as a function of shock intensity. *Psychonomic Sci.*, **13**, 161–162, 1968.

James, W.: What is emotion? *Mind*, **9**, 188–204, 1884.

James, W.: *Principles of Psychology*. New York, Holt, 1890.

Jones, M. C.: A laboratory study of fear: the case of Peter. *J. Genet. Psychol.*, **31**, 308–315, 1924a.

Jones, M. C.: The elimination of children's fears. *J. Exp. Psychol.*, **7**, 382–390, 1924b.

Kamano, D. K.: Effects of an extinquished fear stimulus on avoidance behavior. *Psychonomic Sci.,* **13,** 271–272, 1968.

Kamil, A. C.: The second-order conditioning of fear in rats. *Psychonomic Sci.,* **10,** 99–100, 1968.

Kamil, A. C.: Some parameters on the second-order conditioning of fear in rats. *J. Comp. Physiol. Psychol.,* **67,** 364–369, 1969.

Kamin, L. J.: Trace conditioning of the conditioned emotional response. *J. Comp. Physiol. Psychol.,* **54,** 149–153, 1961.

Kamin, L. J.: Backward conditioning and the conditioned emotional response. *J. Comp. Physiol. Psychol.,* **56,** 517–519, 1963.

Kamin, L. J.: Temporal and intensity characteristics of the conditoned stimulus. In, W. F. Prokasy (ed.): *Classical Conditioning.* New York, Appleton-Century-Crofts, 1965.

Kamin, L. J.: "Attention-like" processes in classical conditioning. In, M. Jones (ed.): *Miami Symposium on the Prediction of Behavior: Aversive Stimulation.* Miami, University of Miami Press, 1968.

Kamin, L. J.: Predictability, surprise, attention and conditoning. In, B. Campbell and R. Church (eds.): *Punishment: a Symposium.* New York, Appleton-Century-Crofts, 1969.

Kamin, L. J., and Brimer, C. J.: The effects of intensity of conditioned and unconditioned stimuli on a conditioned emotional response. *Can. J. Psychol.,* **17,** 194–200, 1963.

Kamin, L. J., and Gaioni, S. J.: Compound conditioned emotional response conditioning with differentially salient elements in rats. *J. Comp. Physiol. Psychol.,* **87,** 591–597, 1974.

Kamin, L. J., and Schaub, R. E.: Effects of conditioned stimulus intensity on the conditioned emotional response. *J. Comp. Physiol. Psychol.,* **56,** 502–507, 1963.

Kamin, L. J., Brimer, C. J., and Black, A. H.: Conditioned suppression as a monitor of fear of the CS in the course of avoidance training. *J. Comp. Physiol. Psychol.,* **56,** 497–501, 1963.

Kaufman, A.: Response suppression in the CER paradigm with extinction as the aversive event. *Psychonomic Sci.,* **15,** 15–16, 1969.

Kelleher, R., Riddle, W., and Cook, L.: Persistent behavior maintained by unavoidable shocks. *J. Exp. Anal. Behav.,* **6,** 507–517, 1963.

Kellicut, M. H., and Schwartzbaum, J. S.: Formation of a conditioned emotional response (CER) following lesions of the amygdaloid complex in rats. *Psychol. Rep.,* **12,** 351–358, 1963.

Kelly, D. D.: Long-term prereward suppression in monkeys unaccompanied by cardiovascular conditionining. *J. Exp. Anal. Behav.,* **20,** 93–104, 1973a.

Kelly, D. D.: Suppression of random-ratio and acceleration of temporally spaced responding by the same prereward stimulus in monkeys. *J. Exp. Anal. Behav.,* **20,** 363–373, 1973b.

Kenshalo, D. R., and Hall, E. C.: Thermal thresholds of the rhesus monkey (Macaca mulatta). *J. Comp. Physiol. Psychol.,* **86,** 902–910, 1974.

Kesner, R. P., Gibson, W. E., and Leclair, M. J.: ECS as a punishing stimulus: dependency on route of administration. *Physiol. Behav.,* **5,** 683–686, 1970.

Kimble, G. A.: *Hilgard and Marquis' Conditioning and Learning.* New York, Appleton-Century-Crofts, 1961.

Kinnard, W. J., Aceto, M. D. G., and Buckley, J. P.: The effects of certain psychotropic agents on the conditioned emotional response behavior pattern of the albino rat. *Psychopharmacologia, ***3,** 227–230, 1962.

King, N. W., Justesen, D. R., and Clarke, R. L.: Behavioral sensitivity to microwave irradiation. *Science,* **172,** 398–401, 1971.

Kling. J. O.: Interstimulus intervals in conditioned suppression. *J. Gen. Psychol.,* **87,** 297–299, 1972.

Kling. J. O., and Kling, K.: Spontaneous recovery of conditioned suppression. *J. Gen. Psychol.,* **88,** 151—152, 1973.

Kling, J. W., and Riggs, L. A.: *Woodworth and Schlosberg's Experimental Psychology.* New York, Holt, Rinehart & Winston, 1971.

Kluver, H., and Bucy, P. C.: "Psychic blindness" and other symptoms following bilateral temporal lobectomy in rhesus monkeys. *Am. J. Physiol.,* **119,** 352–353, 1937.

Kluver, H., and Bucy, P. C.: An analysis of certain effects of bilateral temporal lobectomy in the rhesus monkey with special reference to "psychic blindness." *J. Psychol.,* **5,** 33–54, 1938.

Koch, S. (ed.): *Psychology: a Study of Science,* vol. 2. New York, McGraw-Hill, 1959.

Kohlenberg, R., and Trabasso, T.: Recovery of a conditioned emotional response after one or two electroconvulsive shocks. *J. Comp. Physiol. Psychol.,* **65,** 270–273, 1968.

Konorski, J.: *Integrative Activity of the Brain.* Chicago, University of Chicago Press, 1967.

Konorski, J.: Some ideas concerning physiological mechanisms of so-called internal inhibition. In, R. S. Boakes and M. S. Halliday (eds.): *Inhibition and Learning.* New York, Academic Press, 1972.

Kremer, E. F.: Truly random and traditional control procedures in CER conditioning in the rat. *J. Comp. Physiol. Psychol.,* **76,** 441–448, 1971.

Kremer, E. F.: Properties of a preexposed stimulus. *Psychonomic Sci.,* **27,** 45–47, 1972.

Kremer, E. F.: The truly random control procedure: conditioning to the static cues. *J. Comp. Physiol. Psychol.,* **86,** 700–707, 1974.

Kremer, E. F., and Kamin, L. J.: The truly random control procedure: associative or nonassociative effects in rats. *J. Comp. Physiol. Psychol.,* **74,** 203–210, 1971.

Kruper, D. C.: Effects of a pre-aversive stimulus upon oddity performance in monkeys. *J. Exp. Anal. Behav.,* **11,** 71–75, 1968.

Kruper, D. C., and Haude, R.: Visual exploration in a conditioned emotional response paradigm. *J. Exp. Anal. Behav.,* **7,** 381–382, 1964.

Kumar, R.: Incubation of fear: experiments on the "Kamin effect" in rats. *J. Comp. Physiol. Psychol.,* **70,** 258–263, 1970.

Kumar, R., Stolerman, I. P., and Steinberg, H.: Psychopharmacology. *Annu. Rev. Psychol.,* **21,** 595–628, 1970.

Lange, C. G.: *Om Sindsbevoegesler,* (1885.) Leipzig, Theodor Thomas, 1887.

Lantz, A. E.: Effect of number of trials, interstimulus interval, and dishabituation during CS habituation on subsequent conditioning in a CER paradigm. *Anim. Learning Behav.,* **1,** 273–277, 1973.

Lauener, H.: Conditioned suppression in rats and the effect of pharmacological agents thereon. *Psychopharmacologia,* **4,** 311–325, 1963.

La Vail, M. M., Sidman, M., Rausin, R., and Sidman, R.: Discrimination of light intensity by rats with inherited retinal degeneration: a behavioral and cytological study. *Vision Res.,* **14,** 693–702, 1974.

Leaf, R. C., and Leaf, S. R. P.: Recovery time as a measure of conditioned suppression. *Psychol. Rep.,* **18,** 265–266, 1966.

Leaf, R. C., and Muller, S. A.: Effect of CER on DRL responding. *J. Exp. Anal. Behav.,* **7,** 405–407, 1964.

Leaf, R. C., and Muller, S. A.: Simple method for CER conditioning and measurement. *Psychol. Rep.,* **17,** 211–215, 1965.

Leaf, R. C., Kayser, R. J., Andrews, J. S., Jr., Adkins, J. W., and Leaf, S. R. P.: Block of fear conditioning induced by habituation or extinction. *Psychonomic Sci.,* **10,** 198–199, 1968.

Leitenberg, H.: Conditioned acceleration and conditioned suppression in pigeons. *J. Exp. Anal. Behav.,* **9,** 205–212, 1966.

Leitenberg, H., Bertsch, G. J., and Coughlin, R. C., Jr.: "Time-out from positive reinforcement" as the UCS in a CER paradigm with rats. *Psychonomic Sci.,* **13,** 3–4, 1968.

Lepore, F., Ptito, M., Frieberg, V., and Gullemot, J. P.: Effects of low dose of chlorapromazine on a conditioned emotional response in the rat. *Psychol. Rep.,* **34,** 231–237, 1974.

Levine, M. S., Goldrich, S. G., Pond, F. J., Livesky, P., and Schwartzbaum, J. S.: Retrograde amnestic effects of inferotemporal and amygdaloid seizures upon conditioned suppression of lever-pressing in monkeys. *Neuropsychologia,* **8,** 431–442, 1970.

Lewis, J.: Conditioned suppression of a VI baseline using a two-bar multiple VI shock-avoidance schedule. *Anim. Learning Behav.,* **1,** 247–250, 1973.

Libby, A.: Two variables in the acquisition of depressant properties by a stimulus. *J. Exp. Psychol.,* **42,** 100–107, 1951.

Lidsky, T. I., Levine, M. S., Kreinich, C. J., and Schwartzbaum J. S.: Retrograde effects of amygdaloid stimulation on conditioned suppression (CER) in rats. *J. Comp. Physiol. Psychol.,* **73,** 135–149, 1970.

Linden, D. R.:Attenuation and reestablishment of the CER by discriminated avoidance condition-
ing in rats. *J. Comp. Physiol. Psychol., 69*, 573–578, 1969.
Lindsley, D. B.: Emotions and the electroencephalogram. In, M. L. Reymert (ed.): *Feelings and
Emotions.* New York, McGraw-Hill, 1950.
Lindsley, D. B.: Emotion. In, S. S. Stevens (ed.): *Handbook of Experimental Psychology.* New
York, Wiley, 1951.
Lindsley, D. B.: Psychophysiology and motivation. In, M. R. Jones (ed.): *Nebraska Symposium on
Motivation.* Lincoln, University of Nebraska Press, 1957.
Lo Lordo, V. M.: Similarity of conditioned fear responses based upon different aversive events. *J.
Comp. Physiol. Psychol., 64*, 154–158, 1967.
Lo Lordo, V. M.: Facilitation of food-reinforced responding by a signal for response-independent
food. *J. Exp. Anal. Behav., 15*, 49–55, 1971.
Lo Lordo, V. M., McMillan, J. C., and Riley, A. L.: The effects of food-reinforced pecking and
treadle-pressing of auditory and visual signals for response-independent food. *Learning Motiva-
tion, 5*, 24–41, 1974.
Lubow, R. E.: Latent inhibition. *Psychol. Bull., 79*, 398–407, 1973.
Lubow, R. E., and Siebart, L.: Latent inhibition within the CER paradigm. *J. Comp. Physiol.
Psychol., 68*, 136–138, 1969.
Lyon, D. O.: Frequency of reinforcement as a parameter of conditioned suppression. *J. Exp. Anal.
Behav., 6*, 95–98, 1963.
Lyon, D. O.: Some notes on conditioned suppression and reinforcement schedules. *J. Exp. Anal.
Behav., 7*, 289–291, 1964.
Lyon, D. O.: CER methodology: reply to Blackman. *Psychol. Rep., 20*, 206, 1967.
Lyon, D. O.: Conditioned suppression: operant variables and aversive control. *Psychol. Record,
18*, 317–338, 1968.
Lyon, D. O., and Felton, M.: Conditioned suppression and fixed ratio schedules of reinforcement.
Psychol. Record, 16, 433–440, 1966a.
Lyon, D. O., and Felton, M.: Conditioned suppression and variable-ratio reinforcement. *J. Exp.
Anal. Behav., 9*, 245–250, 1966b.
Lyon, D. O., and Millar, R. D.: Conditioned suppression on a fixed interval schedule of reinforce-
ment. *Psychonomic Sci., 17*, 31–32, 1969.
Mackintosh, N. J.: Blocking of conditioned suppression: role of the first compound trial. *J. Exp.
Psychol. [Anim. Behav. Processes], 1*, 335–345, 1975.
Mackintosh, N. J.: Overshadowing and stimulus intensity. *Anim. Learning Behav., 4*, 186–192,
1976.
MacLean, P. D.: Psychosomatic disease and the "visceral brain:" recent developments bearing on
the Papez theory of emotion. *Psychosom. Med., 11*, 388–353, 1949.
MacLean, P. D.: Some psychiatric implications of physiological studies on frontotemporal portion
of limbic system (visceral brain). *Electroencephal. Clin. Neuropsychiatry, 4*, 407–418, 1952.
Mahoney, W. J., and Ayres, J. J. B.: One-trial simultaneous and backward fear conditioning as
reflected in conditioned suppression of licking in rats. *Anim. Learning Behav., 4*, 357–362,
1976.
Maier, S. F., Rapoport, P., and Wheatley, K.: Conditioned inhibition and the UCS–CS interval.
Anim. Learning Behav., 4, 217–220, 1976.
Malmo, R. B.: Anxiety and behavioral arousal. *Psychol. Rev., 64*, 276–287, 1957.
Malmo, R. B.: Activation. In, A. J. Bachrach (ed.): *Experimental Foundations of Clinical Psychology.* New York, Basic Books, 1962.
Martin, L. K., and Riess, D.: Effects of US intensity during previous discrete delay conditioning on
conditioned acceleration during avoidance extinction. *J. Comp. Physiol. Psychol., 69*, 196–200,
1969.
Maser, J. D., and Hammond, L. J.: Disruption of a temporal discrimination by the minor tranquilizer, oxazepam. *Psychopharmacologia, 25*, 69–76, 1972.
Mason, J. W., and Brady, J. V.: Plasma 17-hydroxycorticosteroid changes related to reserpine effects on emotional behavior. *Science, 124*, 983–984, 1956.
Masserman, J. H.: *Behavior and Neurosis.* Chicago, University of Chicago Press, 1943.

Masterton, B., Heffner, H., and Ravizza, R.: The evolution of human hearing. *J. Acoust. Soc. Am., 45*, 966–985, 1969.

Matthews, T. J., McHugh, T. G., and Carr, L. D.: Pavlovian and instrumental determinants of response suppression in the pigeon. *J. Comp. Physiol. Psychol., 87*, 500–506, 1974.

May, R. B., Tolman, C. W., and Schoenfeldt, M. G.: Effects of pre-training exposure to the CS on conditioned suppression. *Psychonomic Sci., 9*, 61–62, 1967.

McAllister, W. R., and McAllister, D. E.: Behavioral measurement of conditioned fear. In, F. R. Brush (ed.): *Aversive Conditioning and Learning.* New York, Academic Press, 1971.

McIntire, R. W.: Conditioned suppression and self-stimulation. *Psychonomic Sci., 5*, 273–274, 1966.

McIntyre, D. C.: Differential amnestic effect of cortical vs amygdaloid elicited convulsions in rats. *Physiol. Behav., 5*, 747–753, 1970.

McIntyre, D. C., and Molino, A.: Amygdala lesions and CER learning: long term effects of kindling. *Physiol. Behav., 8*, 1055–1058, 1972.

Meltzer, D., and Brahlek, J. A.: Conditioned suppression and conditioned enhancement with the same positive UCS: an effect of CS duration. *J. Exp. Anal. Behav., 13*, 67–73, 1970.

Merrill, H., Lott, W. J., and Bergen, B. J.: Attenuation of a conditioned emotional response via reinforcing intracranial stimulation in rats. *J. Comp. Physiol. Psychol., 71*, 426–434, 1970.

Miczek, K.: Effects of scopolamine, amphetamine, and benzodiazepines on conditioned suppression. *Pharmacol. Biochem. Behav., 1*, 401–411, 1973.

Miczek, K. A., and Grossman, S. P.: Positive conditioned suppression: effects of CS duration. *J. Exp. Anal. Behav., 15*, 243–247, 1971.

Migler, B., and Brady, J. V.: Timing behavior and conditioned fear. *J. Exp. Anal. Behav., 7*, 247–251, 1964.

Miller, G. A., Galanter, E., and Pribram, K.: *Plans and the Structure of Behavior.* New York, Holt, Rinehart & Winston, 1960.

Miller, L.: Compounding of pre-aversive stimuli. *J. Exp. Anal. Behav., 12*, 293–299, 1969.

Miller, N. E.: Studies of fear as an acquirable drive: I. Fear as motivation and fear-reduction as reinforcement in the learning of new responses. *J. Exp. Psychol., 38*, 89–101, 1948.

Miller, N. E.: Learnable drives and rewards. In, S. S. Stevens (ed.): *Handbook of Experimental Psychology.* New York, Wiley, 1951.

Miller, N. E.: Liberalization of basic S–R concepts: extenstion to conflict behavior, motivation and social learning. In, S. Koch (ed.): *Psychology: a Study of Science,* vol. 2. New York, McGraw-Hill, 1959.

Miller, S., and Konorski, J.: Sur une forme particuliere des reflexes conditionnels. *C. R. Soc. Pol. Biol. 99*, 1155–1157, 1928.

Morris, D. D.: Threshold for conditioned suppression using x rays as the pre-aversive stimulus. *J. Exp. Anal. Behav., 9*, 29–34, 1966.

Mowrer, O. H.: A stimulus–response analysis of anxiety and its role as a reinforcing agent. *Psychol. Rev., 46*, 553–565, 1939.

Mowrer, O. H.: Anxiety reduction and learning. *J. Exp. Psychol., 27*, 497–516, 1940.

Mowrer, O. H.: *Learning Theory and Personality Dynamics.* New York, Ronald Press, 1950.

Mowrer, O. H.: *Learning Theory and Behavior.* New York, Wiley, 1960.

Nachman, M., Meinecke, R. O., and Baumbach, H. D.: Temporal gradient of recovery of a conditioned emotional response following a single electroconvulsive shock. *Psychonomic Sci., 17*, 137–138, 1969.

Nadel, L.: Dorsal and ventral hippocampal lesions and behavior. *Physiol. Behav., 3*, 891–900, 1968.

Nageishi, Y., and Imada, H.: Suppression of licking behavior in rats as a function of predictability of shock and probability of conditioned stimulus–shock pairings. *J. Comp. Physiol. Psychol., 87*, 1165–1173, 1974.

Nathan, M. A., and Smith, O. A., Jr.: Differential conditional emotional and caridovascular responses—a training technique for monkeys. *J. Exp. Anal. Behav., 11*, 77–82, 1968.

Nathan, M. A., and Smith, O. A., Jr.: Conditional cardiac and suppression responses after lesions in the dorsomedial thalamus of monkeys. *J. Comp. Physiol. Psychol., 76*, 66–73, 1971.

Olds, J.: Physiological mechanisms of reward. In, M. R. Jones (ed.): *Nebraska Syposium on Motivation.* Lincoln, University of Nebraska Press, 1955.

Olds, J.: A preliminary mapping of electrical reinforcing effects in the rat brain. *J. Comp. Physiol. Psychol.,* **49,** 281–285, 1956.

Oley, N., DeHan, R. S., Tucker, D., Smith, J. C., and Graziadei, P. P. C.: Recovery of structure and function following transection of the primary olfactory nerves in pigeons. *J. Comp. Physiol. Psychol.,* **88,** 477–495, 1975.

Orme-Johnson, D. W., and Yarczower, M.: Conditioned suppression, punishment and aversion. *J. Exp. Anal. Behav.,* **21,** 57–74, 1974.

Overmeir. J. B.: Differential transfer of avoidance responses as a function of UCS duration. *Psychonomic Sci.,* **5,** 25–26, 1966a.

Overmeir, J. B.: Instrumental and cardiac indices of Pavlovian fear conditioning as a function of US duration. *J. Comp. Physiol. Psychol.,* **62,** 15–20, 1966b.

Overmeir, J. B., and Bull, J. A., III: An interaction between appetitive Pavlovian CSs and instrumental avoidance responding. *Learning Motivation, 1,* 18–26, 1970.

Overmeir, J. B., and Leaf, R. C.: Effects of discriminative Pavlovian fear conditioning upon previously or subsequently acquired avoidance responding. *J. Comp. Physiol. Psychol.,* **60,** 213–217, 1965.

Overmeir, J. B., Bull, J. A., III, and Pack, K.: On instrumental response interaction as explaining the influences of Pavlovian CS$^+$s upon avoidance behavior. *Learning Motivation, 2,* 103–112, 1971.

Palfai, T., and Cornell, J. M.: Effect of drugs on consolidation of classically conditioned fear. *J. Comp. Physiol. Psychol.,* **66,** 584–589. 1968.

Papez, J. W.: A proposed mechanism of emotion. *Arch. Neurol. Psychiatry,* **38,** 725–743, 1937.

Pare, W. P.: Interaction of age and shock intensity on acquisition of a discriminated conditioned emotional response. *J. Comp. Physiol. Psychol.,* **68,** 364–369, 1969.

Parker, B., Barker, D. L., and Topping, J.: The differential effects of timeout and shock on DRL responding in the CER paradigm. *Psychonomic Sci.,* **22,** 133–135, 1971.

Parkinson, S. R.: Sensory preconditioning of a conditioned emotional response. *Psychonomic Sci.* **11,** 119, 1968.

Parrish, J.: Classical discrimination conditioning of heart rate and bar press suppression in the rat. *Psychonomic Sci.,* **9,** 267–268, 1967.

Pavlov, I. P.: *Conditioned Reflexes.* New York, Dover, 1927.

Persinger, M. A., and Pear, J. J.: Prenatal exposure to an ELF-rotating magnetic field and subsequent increase in conditioned suppression. *Develop. Psychol.,* **5,** 269–274, 1972.

Pert, A., and Avis, H. H.: Dissociation between scopolamine and mecamylamine during fear conditioning in rats. *Physiol. Psychol.,* **2,** 111–116, 1974.

Pierson, S. C.: Conditioned suppression to odorous stimuli in the rat. *J. Comp. Physiol. Psychol.,* **86,** 708–717, 1974.

Pliskoff, S.: Rate-change effects during a pre-schedule change stimulus. *J. Exp. Anal. Behav.,* **4,** 383–386, 1961.

Pliskoff, S.: Rate-change effects with equal potential reinforcements during the "warning" stimulus. *J. Exp. Anal. Behav.,* **6,** 557–562, 1963.

Pomerleau, O.: The effects of stimuli followed by response-independent shock on shock-avoidance behavior. *J. Exp. Anal. Behav.,* **14,** 11–21, 1970.

Powell, R. W.: The pulse-to-cycle fraction as a determinant of critical flicker fusion in the pigeon. *Psychol. Rec.,* **17,** 151–160, 1967.

Powell, R. W., and Smith, J. C.: Critical-flicker-fusion thresholds as a function of very small pulse-to-cycle fractions. *Psychol. Record,* **18,** 35–40, 1968.

Premack, D.: Reinforcement theory. In, D. Levine (ed.): *Nebraska Syposium on Motivation.* Lincoln, University of Nebraska Press, 1965.

Prewett, E. P.: Number of preconditioning trials in sensory preconditioning using CER training. *J. Comp. Physiol. Psychol.,* **64,** 360–362, 1967.

Price, L. L., Dalton, L. W., Jr., and Smith, J. C.: Frequency DL in the pigeon as determined by conditioned suppression. *J. Auditory Res.,* **7,** 229–239, 1967.

Quinsey, V. L., and Ayres, J. J. B.: Shock induced facilitation of a partially extinquished CER. *Psychonomic Sci.,* **14,** 213–214, 1969a.

Quinsey, V. L., and Ayres, J. J. B.: The effect of CS-induced fear on a partially extinguished CER. *Psychonomic Sci.,* **14,** 242–244, 1969b.

Rand, G. V., Sloane, H. N., and Dobson, W. R.: Some variables affecting conditioned suppression in humans. *Behav. Ther.,* **2,** 554–559, 1971.

Ravizza, R. J., Heffner, H. E., and Masterton, B.: Hearing in primitive mammals: I. Opossum (Didelphis virginianus). *J. Auditory Res.,* **9,** 1–7, 1969.

Ray, O.: Tranquilizer effects on conditioned suppression. *Psychopharmacologia,* **5,** 136–146, 1964.

Ray, O., and Stein, L.: Generalization of conditioned suppression. *J. Exp. Anal. Behav.,* **2,** 357–361, 1959.

Reberg, D.: Compound tests for excitation in early acquisition and after prolonged extinction of conditioned suppression. *Learning Motivation,* **3,** 246–258, 1972.

Reberg, D., and Black, A. H.: Compound testing of individually conditioned stimuli as an index of excitatory and inhibitory properties. *Psychonomic Sci.,* **17,** 30–31, 1969.

Reiss, S., and Wagner, A. R.: CS habituation produces a "latent inhibition effect" but no active "conditioned inhibition." *Learning Motivation,* **3,** 237–245, 1972.

Rescorla, R. A.: Predictability and number of pairings in Pavlovian fear conditioning. *Psychonomic Sci.,* **4,** 383–384, 1966.

Rescorla, R. A.: Inhibition of delay in Pavlovian fear conditioning. *J. Comp. Physiol. Psychol.,* **64,** 114–120, 1967a.

Rescorla, R. A.: Pavlovian conditioning and its proper control procedure. *Psychol. Rev.,* **74,** 71–80, 1967b.

Rescorla, R. A.: Pavlovian conditioned fear in Sidman avoidance learning. *J. Comp. Physiol. Psychol.,* **65,** 55–60, 1968a.

Rescorla, R. A.: Probability of shock in the presence and absence of CS in fear conditioning. *J. Comp. Physiol. Psychol.,* **66,** 1–5, 1968b.

Rescorla, R. A.: Conditioned inhibition of fear. In, W. K. Honig and N. J. Mackintosh (eds.): *Fundamental Issues in Associative Learning.* Halifax, Dalhousie University Press, 1969a.

Rescorla, R. A.: Conditioned inhibition of fear resulting from negative CS–UCS contingencies. *J. Comp. Physiol. Psychol.,* **67,** 504–509, 1969b.

Rescorla, R. A.: Pavlovian conditioned inhibition. *Psychol. Bull.,* **72,** 77–94, 1969c.

Rescorla, R. A.: Reduction in the effectiveness of reinforcement following prior excitatory training. *Learning Motivation,* **1,** 372–381, 1970.

Rescorla, R. A.: Summation and retardation tests of latent inhibition. *J. Comp. Physiol. Psychol.,* **75,** 77–81, 1971a.

Rescorla, R. A.: Variations in the effectiveness of reinforcement and nonreinforcement following prior inhibitory conditioning. *Learning Motivation,* **2,** 113–123, 1971b.

Rescorla, R. A.: Effects of US habituation following conditioning. *J. Comp. Physiol. Psychol.,* **82,** 137–143, 1973.

Rescorla, R. A.: Effect of inflation of the value of the unconditioned stimulus following conditioning. *J. Comp. Physiol. Psychol.,* **86,** 101–106, 1974.

Rescorla, R. A.: Second-order conditioning of Pavlovian conditioned inhibition. *Learning Motivation,* **7,** 161–172, 1976.

Rescorla, R. A., and Furrow, D. R.: Stimulus similarity as a determinant of Pavlovian conditioning. *J. Exp. Psychol.* [*Anim. Behav. Processes*], **3,** 203–215, 1977.

Rescorla, R. A., and Heth, C. D.: Reinstatement of fear to an extinguished conditioned stimulus. *J. Exp. Psychol.* [*Anim. Behav. Processes*], **104,** 88–96, 1975.

Rescorla, R. A., and Lo Lordo, V. M.: Inhibition of avoidance behavior. *J. Comp. Physiol. Psychol.,* **59,** 406–412, 1965.

Rescorla, R. A., and Solomon, R.: Two-process learning theory: relationships between Pavlovian conditioning and instrumental learning. *Psychol. Rev.,* **74,** 151–182, 1967.

Rescorla, R. A., and Wagner, A. R.: A theory of Pavlovian conditioning: variations in the effectiveness of reinforcement and nonreinforcement. In, A. H. Black and W. F. Prokasy (eds.): *Classical Conditioning,* vol. 2. New York, Appleton-Century-Crofts, 1972.

Riess, D.: The buzzer as a primary aversive stimulus: I. Unconditioned acceleration and summation of conditioned and unconditioned acceleration. *Psychonomic Sci., 21*, 167–169, 1970a.

Riess, D.: The buzzer as a primary aversive stimulus: II. Unavoidable buzzer presentation and conditioned acceleration. *Psychonomic Sci., 21*, 302–304, 1970b.

Riess, D.: The buzzer as a primary aversive stimulus: III. Unconditioned and conditioned suppression of barpress avoidance. *Psychonomic Sci., 24*, 212–214, 1971.

Riess, D., and Farrar, C. H.: UCS duration and conditioned suppression: acquisition and extinction between-groups and terminal performance within-subjects. *Learning Motivation, 4*, 366–373, 1973a.

Riess, D., and Farrar, C. H.: Us duration, conditioned acceleration, multiple CR measurement and Pavlovian R-R laws in rats. *J. Comp. Physiol. Psychol., 82*, 144–151, 1973b.

Rioch, D. M.: Certain aspects of the behavior of decorticate cats. *Psychiatry, 1*, 339–345, 1938.

Rizley, R. C., and Rescorla, R. A.: Associations in second-order conditioning and sensory preconditioning. *J. Comp. Physiol. Psychol., 81*, 1–11, 1972.

Roberts, A. E., and Hurwitz, H. M. B.: The effect of a pre-shock signal on a free operant avoidance response. *J. Exp. Anal. behav., 14*, 331–340, 1970.

Roberts, A. E., Copper, K. G., and Richey, T. L.: Rat behaviors during unsignalled avoidance and conditioned suppression training. *Bull. Psychonomic Soc., 9*, 373–376, 1977.

Rogers, J. D.: Stimulus intensity and trace intervals in sensory preconditioning using the CER. *Bull. Psychonomic Soc., 1*, 107–109, 1973.

Rohrbaugh, M., Riccio, D. S., and Arthur, A.: Paradoxical enhancement of conditioned suppression. *Behav. Res. Ther., 10*, 125–130, 1972.

Rosenberger, P. B.: Response-adjusting stimulus intensity. In, W. C. Stebbins (ed.): *Animal Psychophysics: the Design and Conduct of Sensory Experiments*. New York, Appleton-Century-Crofts, 1970.

Rosenberger, P. B., and Ernst, J. T.: Behavioral assessment of absolute visual thresholds in the albino rat. *Vision Res., 11*, 199–207, 1971.

Sachs, D. A., and Keller, T.: Intensity and temporal characteristics of the CER paradigm with humans. *J. Gen. Psychol., 86*, 181–188, 1972.

Sachs, D. A., and May, J. G., Jr.: Conditioned emotional response with humans: the effect of a variable interstimulus interval using a trace conditioning paradigm. *Psychonomic Sci., 9*, 343–344, 1967.

Sachs, D. A., and May, J. G. Jr.: The presence of a temporal discrimination in the conditioned emotional response with humans. *J. Exp. Anal. Behav., 12*, 1003–1007, 1969.

Scheuer, C.: Resistance to extinction of the CER as a function of shock-reinforcement training schedules. *Psychonomic Sci., 17*, 181–182, 1969.

Scheuer, C., and Keeter, W. H.: Temporal vs discriminative factors in the maintenance of conditioned suppression: a test of the information hypothesis. *Psychonomic Sci., 15*, 21–23, 1969.

Schnur, P.: Selective attention: effect of element preexposure on compound conditioning in rats. *J. Comp. Physiol. Psychol., 76*, 123–130, 1971.

Schwartz, B.: Positive and negative conditioned suppression in the pigeon: effects of the locus and modality of the CS. *Learning Motivation, 7*, 86–100, 1976.

Schwartz, B., and Gamzu, E.: Pavlovian control of operant behavior: an analysis of autoshaping and of interactions between multiple schedules of reinforcement. In, W. K. Honig and J. E. R. Staddon (eds.): *Handbook of Operant Behavior*. Englewood Cliffs, N. J., Prentice-Hall, 1977.

Scobie, S. R.: Interaction of an aversive Pavlovian conditioned stimulus with aversively and appetitively motivated operants in rats. *J. Comp. Physiol. Psychol., 79*, 171–188, 1972.

Scobie, S. R.: The response–shock interval and conditioned suppression of avoidance in rats. *Anim. Learning Behav., 1*, 17–20, 1973.

Scobie, S. R., and Garske, G.: Chlordiazepoxide and conditioned suppression. *Psychopharmacologia, 16*, 272–280, 1970.

Sechenov, I. *Selected Works*. Moscow, State Publishing, 1935.

Seger, K. A., and Scheuer, C.: The informational properties of S1, S2, and S1–S2 sequence on conditioned suppression. *Anim. Learning Behav., 5*, 39–41, 1977.

Seligman, M. E.: Chronic fear produced by unpredictable electric shock. *J. Comp. Physiol. Psychol.*, **66**, 402–411, 1968.

Seligman, M. E., Maier, S. F., and Solomon, R. L.: Unsignalled and uncontrollable aversive events. In R. R. Brush (ed.): *Aversive Conditioning and Learning*. New York, Academic Press, 1971.

Shaber, G. S., Ramsey, J. A., III., Dorn, B. C., and Brent, R. L.: Saccharin behavior taste threshold in the rat. *Fed. Proc.*, **26**, 543, 1967.

Sherrington, C. S.: Experiments on the value of vascular and visceral factors for the genisis of emotion. *Proc. R. Soc.*, **366**, 390–433, 1900.

Sherrington, C. S.: *The Integrative Action of the Nervous System*. New Haven, Yale University Press, 1906.

Shimoff, E.: Measurement of behavioral effects of the CER procedure. *Psychol. Rep.*, **30**, 67–71, 1972a.

Shimoff, E.: Avoidance responding as a function of stimulus duration and relation to free shock. *J. Exp. Anal. Behav.*, **17**, 451–461, 1972b.

Shinkman, P. G., and Kaufman, K. P.: Posttrial hippocampal stimulation and CER acquisition in the rat. *J. Comp. Physiol. Psychol.*, **80**, 283–292, 1972a.

Shinkman, P. G., and Kaufman, K. P.: Time course of retroactive effects of hippocampal stimulation on learning. *Exp. Neur.*, **34**, 476–483, 1972b.

Shipley, R.: Extinction of conditioned fear in rats as a function of several parameters of CS exposure. *J. Comp. Physiol. Psychol.*, **87**, 699–707, 1974.

Shumake, S. A., Smith, J. C., and Taylor, H. L.: Critical fusion frequency in rhesus monkeys using the conditioned suppression technique. 6571st Aeromedical Research Laboratory, Alaomgordo, N. Mex., Tech. Rep. ARL-TR-67-22, 1967.

Shumake, S. A., Smith, J. C., and Taylor, H. L.: Critical fusion frequency in rhesus monkeys. *Psychol. Record*, **8**, 537–542, 1968.

Shumake, S. A., Thompson, R. D., and Caudill, C. J.: A technique for visual threshold measurement in vampire bats. *Physiol. Behav.*, **18**, 325–327, 1977.

Sidman, M.: By-products of aversive control. *J. Exp. Anal. Behav.*, **1**, 265–280, 1958.

Sidman, M.: Normal sources of pathological behavior. *Science*, **132**, 61–68. 1960a.

Sidman, M.: *Tactics of scientific research: evaluating experimental data in psychology*. New York, Basic Books, 1960b.

Sidman, M., Herrnstein, R. J., and Conrad, D. G.: Maintenance of avoidance behavior by unavoidable shock. *J. Comp. Physiol. Psychol.*, **50**, 553–557, 1957.

Sidman, M., Ray, B. A., Sidman, R. L., and Klinger, J. M.: Hearing and vision in neurological mutant mice: a method for their evaluation. *Exp. Neurol.*, **16**, 377–402, 1966.

Siegal, S., and Domjan, M.: Backward conditioning as an inhibitory procedure. *Learning Motivation*, **2**, 1–11, 1971.

Siegal, S., and Domjan, M.: The inhibitory effect of backward conditioning as a function of the number of backward pairings. *Bull. Psychonomic Soc.*, **4**, 122–124, 1974.

Singh, S. D.: Conditioned emotional response in the rat. I. Constitutional and situational determinants. *J. Comp. Physiol. Psychol.*, **52**, 574–578, 1959.

Skinner, B. F.: *The Behavior of Organisms*. New York, Appleton-Century-Crofts, 1938.

Skinner, B. F.: Are theories of learning necessary? *Psychol. Rev.*, **57**, 193–216, 1950.

Skinner, B. F.: *Science and Human Behavior*. New York, MacMillan, 1953.

Skinner, N. P.: Comment on Sachs and May's paper on the conditioned emotional response with humans. *Psychol. Rep.*, **34**, 1069–1070, 1974.

Smith, J. B.: Effects of response rate, reinforcement frequency, and the duration of a stimulus preceding response-independent food. *J. Exp. Anal. Behav.*, **21**, 215–221, 1974.

Smith, J. C.: Conditioned suppression as an animal psychophysical technique. In W. C. Stebbins (ed.): *Animal Psychophysics: the Design and Conduct of Sensory Experiments*. New York, Appleton-Century-Crofts, 1970.

Smith, J. C., and Tucker, D.: Olfactory mediation of immediate x-ray detection. In, C. Pfaffmann (ed.): *Olfaction and Taste III*. New York, Rockfeller University Press, 1969.

Smith, O. A., Jr., and Nathan, M. A.: The development of cardiac and blood flow conditional responses during the acquisition of a differentiated "conditioned emotional response" in monkeys. *Conditional Reflex, 2,* 155–156, 1967.

Snedden, D. S., Spevack, A. A., and Thompson, W. R.: Conditioned and unconditioned suppression as a function of age in rats. *Can. J. Psychol., 25,* 313–322, 1971.

Solomon, R. L., and Wynne, L. C.: Traumatic avoidance learning: acquisition in normal dogs. *Psychol. Monogr., 67,* 1–19, 1953.

Solomon, R. L., and Wynne, L. C.: Traumatic avoidance learning: the principle of anxiety conservation and partial irreversibility. *Psychol. Rev., 61,* 353–385, 1954.

Solyom, L., and Miller, S.: The effect of age differences on the acquisition of operant and classical conditioned responses in rats. *J. Gerontol., 20,* 311–314, 1965.

Spiegal, E. A., and Wycis, H. T.: Physiological and psychological results of thalamontomy. *Proc. R. Soc. Med. [Suppl.], 42,* 1–9, 1949.

St. Claire-Smith, R., and Mackintosh, N. J.: Complete suppression to a compound CS does not block further conditioning to each element. *Can. J. Psychol., 28,* 92–101, 1974.

Stebbins, W. C., and Smith, O. A., Jr.: Cardiovascular concomitants of the conditioned emotional response in the monkey. *Science, 144,* 881–883, 1964.

Stein, L., and Berger, B. D.: Paradoxical fear-increasing effects of tranquilizers: evidence of repression of memory in the rat. *Science, 166,* 253–256, 1969.

Stein, L., Sidman, M., and Brady, J. V.: Some effect of two temporal variables on conditioned suppression. *J. Exp. Anal. Behav., 1,* 153–162, 1958.

Stein, N., Hoffman, H. S., and Stitt, C.: Collateral behavior of the pigeon during conditioned suppresslon of key pecking. *J. Exp. Anal. Behav., 15,* 83–93, 1971.

Stolurow, L. M.: Conditioning. In, B. B. Wolman (ed.): *Handbook of General Psychology.* Englewood Cliffs, N.J., Prentice-Hall, 1973.

Strouthes, A.: Effect of CS-onset, UCS-termination delay, UCS duration, CS-onset interval and number of CS–UCS pairings on conditioned fear response. *J. Exp. Psychol., 69,* 287–291, 1965.

Suboski, M. D., Marquis, H. A., Black, M., and Platenius, P.: Adrenal and amygdala function in the incubation of aversively conditioned responses. *Physiol. Behav., 5,* 283–289, 1970.

Tait, R. W., and Suboski, M. D.: Stimulus intensity in sensory preconditioning of rats. *Can. J. Psychol., 26,* 374–381, 1972.

Tait, R. W., Marquis, H. A., Williams, R., Weinstein, L., and Suboski, M. D.: Extinction of sensory preconditioning using CER training. *J. Comp. Physiol. Psychol., 69,* 170–172, 1969.

Tait, R. W., Simon, E., and Suboski, M. D.: "Partial reinforcement" in sensory preconditioning with rats. *Can. J. Psychol., 25,* 427–435, 1971.

Tait, R. W., Black, M., Katz, M., and Suboski, M. D.: Discriminative sensory preconditioning. *Can. J. Psychol., 26,* 201–205, 1972.

Tarpy, R. M.: Incubation of anxiety as measured by response suppression. *Psychonomic Sci., 4,* 189–190, 1966.

Tenen, S.: Recovery time as a measure of CER strength: effect of benzodiazepines, amobarbital, chloropromazine, and amphetamine. *Psychopharmacologia, 12,* 1–17, 1967.

Testa, T. J.: Effects of similarity of location and temporal intensity pattern of conditioned and unconditioned stimuli on the acquisition of conditioned suppression in rats. *J. Exp. Psychol. [Anim. Behav. Processes], 104,* 114–121, 1975.

Thompson, J. B., and Schwartzbaum, J. S.: Discrimination behavior and conditioned suppression (CER) following localized lesions in the amygdala and putamen. *Psychol. Rep., 15,* 587–606, 1964.

Torres, A. A.: Anxiety vs escape conditioning and tranquilizing agents. *J. Comp. Physiol. Psychol., 54,* 349–353, 1961.

Trafton, C. L.: Effects of lesions in the septal area and cingulate cortical areas on conditioned suppression of activity and avoidance behavior in rats. *J. Comp. Physiol. Psychol., 63,* 191–197, 1967.

Valenstein, E. S.: The effects of reserpine on the conditioned emotional response of the guinea pig. *J. Exp. Anal. Behav., 2,* 219–225, 1959.

Van Dyne, G.: Conditioned suppression with a positive US in the rat. *J. Comp. Physiol. Psychol., 77,* 131–135, 1971.

Van Houten, R., O'Leary, K. D., and Weiss, S. J.: Summation of conditioned suppression. *J. Exp. Anal. Behav.,* **13,** 75–81, 1970.

Vogel, J. R., and Spear, N. E.: Interaction of reward magnitude and conditioned fear on the consumatory response. *Psychonomic Sci.,* **5,** 263–264, 1966.

Vogel, J. R., Hughes, R. A., and Carlton, P. L.: Scopolamine, atropine, and conditioned fear. *Psychopharmacologia,* **10,** 409–416, 1967.

Wagner, A. R.: Stimulus validity and stimulus selection. In, W. K. Honig and N. J. Mackintosh (eds.): *Fundamental Issues in Associative Learning.* Halifax, Dalhousie University Press, 1969.

Wagner, A. R., and Rescorla, R. A.: Inhibition in Pavlovian conditioning: application of a theory. In, R. S. Boakes and M. S. Halliday (eds.): *Inhibition and Learning.* New York, Academic Press, 1972.

Wagner, A. R., Siegal, L. S., and Fein, G. G.: Extinction of conditioned fear as a function of percentage of reinforcement. *J. Comp. Physiol. Psychol.,* **63,** 160–164, 1967.

Waller, M. B., and Waller, D. F.: The effects of unavoidable shocks on a multiple schedule having an avoidance component. *J. Exp. Anal. Behav.,* **6,** 29–37, 1963.

Watson, J. B., and Morgan, J. J. B.: Emotional reactions and psychological experimentation. *Am. J. Psychol.,* **28,** 163–174, 1917.

Watson, J. B., and Raynor, R.: Conditioned emotional reactions. *J. Exp. Psychol.,* **3,** 1–14, 1920.

Weiss, K. M.: Some effects of the conditioned suppression paradigm on operant discrimination performance. *J. Exp. Anal. Behav.,* **11,** 767–775, 1968.

Weiskrantz, L.: Emotion. In, L. Weiskrantz (ed.): *Analysis of Behavioral Change.* New York, Harper & Row, 1968.

Weiskrantz. L., and Wilson, W. A., Jr.: The effects of reserpine on emotional behavior of normal and brain-operated monkeys. *Ann. N. Y. Acad. Sci.,* **61,** 36–55, 1955.

Weisman, R. G., and Litner, J. S.: The course of Pavlovian extinction and inhibition of fear in rats. *J. Comp. Physiol. Psychol.,* **69,** 667–672, 1969.

Weiss, S. J.: Stimulus compounding in free-operant and classical conditioning: a review and analysis. *Psychol. Bull.,* **78,** 189–208, 1972.

Weiss, S. J., and Emurian, H. H.: Stimulus control during the summation of conditioned suppression. *J. Exp. Psychol.,* **85,** 204–209, 1970.

Wenger, M. A.: Emotion as visceral action: an extension of Lange's theory. In, M. L. Reymert (ed.): *Feelings and Emotions.* New York, McGraw-Hill, 1950.

Whitney, G. D., and Trost, J. D.: Response disruption following amphetamine self- and programmed-administration. In, R. T. Harris, W. M. McIsaac, and C. R. Shuster (eds.): *Drug Dependence.* Austin, University of Texas Press, 1970.

Willi, F. J.: The effect of electroconvulsive shock on a conditioned emotional response in the rhesus monkey. *Br. J. Psychol.,* **60,** 509–521, 1969.

Willis, R. D.: The partial reinforcement of conditioned suppression. *J. Comp. Physiol. Psychol.,* **68,** 289–295, 1969.

Willis, R. D., and Lundin, R. W.: Conditioned suppression in the rat as a function of shock reinforcement schedule. *Psychonomic Sci.,* **6,** 107–108, 1966.

Wilson, G. T., and Davison, G. C.: Processes of fear reduction in systematic desensitization: animal studies. *Psychol. Bull.,* **76,** 1–14, 1971.

Wilson, L. M., and Riccio, D. C.: CS facilitation and conditioned suppression in weanling and adult albino rats. *Bull. Psychonomic Soc.,* **1,** 184–186, 1973.

Wilson, W. L., Darcy, J. M., and Haralson, J. V.: Reserpine and conditioned suppression in the fish *Tilapia H* Marcrocephala. *Psychonomic Sci.,* **20,** 47–48, 1970.

Winocur, G., and Mills, J. A.: Aversive consequences of electroconvulsive shock. *Physiol. Behav.,* **5,** 631–634, 1970.

Winograd, E.: Maintained generalization testing of conditioned suppression. *J. Exp. Anal. Behav.,* **8,** 47–51, 1965.

Wise, C. D., Berger, B. D., and Stein, L.: Serotonin: a possible mediator of behavioral suppression induced by anxiety. *Dis. Nerv. Syst.,* **31,** 34–37, 1970.

Witcher, E. S., and Ayres, J. J. B.: Effect of removing background white noise during CS presentation on conditioning in the truly random control procedure. *Bull. Psychonomic Soc.,* **6,** 25–27, 1975.

Wolpe, J.: The formation of negative habits: a neurological view. *Psychol. Rev., 59*, 290–299, 1952.

Wolpe, J.: *Psychotherapy by reciprocal inhibition.* Stanford, Calif., Stanford University Press, 1958.

Wolpe, J.: The experimental foundations of some new psychotherapeutic methods. In, A. J. Bachrach (ed.): *Experimental Foundations of Clinical Psychology.* New York, Basic Books, 1962.

Woodworth, R. S., and Sherrington, C. S.: A pseudoaffective reflex and its spinal path. *J. Physiol., 31*, 234–243, 1904.

Yamahiro, H. S., Bell, E. C., and Hill, H. E.: The effects of reserpine on a strongly conditioned emotional response. *Psychopharmacologia, 2*, 197–202, 1961.

Yeo, A. G.: The acquisition of conditioned suppression as a function of interstimulus interval duration. *Q. J. Exp. Psychol., 26*, 405–416, 1974.

Yeo, A.: The acquisition of conditioned emotional response as a function of intertrial interval. *Q. J. Exp. Psychol., 28*, 449–458, 1976.

Young, P. T.: *Emotion in Man and Animal.* New York, Wiley, 1943.

Young, P. T.: Motivation and emotion. In, B. B. Wolman (ed.): *Handbook of General Psychology.* Englewood Cliffs, N.J.: Prentice-Hall, 1973.

Zeiner, A. R., Nathan, M. A., and Smith, O. A., Jr.: Conditioned emotional responding (CER) mediated by interference. *Physiol. Behav., 4*, 645–648, 1969.

Zelhard, P. F.: Conditioned reinforcement based on shock termination. *J. Gen. Psychol., 86*, 131–139, 1972.

Zielinski, K.: The direction of change versus the absolute level of noise intensity as a cue in the CER situation. *Acta Biol. Exp., 25*, 337–357, 1965.

Chapter 2

Empirical Analysis of Concurrent Classical–Operant Schedules

Wendon W. Henton

The following series of experiments is loosely based upon the competing response interpretation of conditioned suppression by Brady and Hunt (1955). This type of analysis also seems to account for the effects of conditioned stimuli paired with food as well as shock, and the interpretation has been slightly extended to a more general analysis of concurrent schedules controlling concurrent responses (Henton and Brady, 1970). The present studies were conducted between 1970 and 1973 as a developing experimental analysis of the response patterns within all classical–operant schedule combinations. The experiments were consequently designed to purposely manipulate and directly record the response interactions generated by the various possible classical–operant combinations.

Interactions Between Sidman Avoidance and Appetitive Classically Conditioned Responses (Experiment I)*

Our behavioral analysis was actually initiated at the Walter Reed laboratories in 1968 with a study on the effects of CS–food pairings upon shock avoidance behavior (described by Brady, 1971). The results simply suggested that avoidance rates of monkeys were highly dependent upon response contingencies buried within the superimposed appetitive conditioning procedure. The lever-pressing response was accelerated by a visual CS, in spite of an explicit contingency preventing UCS delivery within 5 sec of a previous operant avoidance

---

* Experiments conducted at the University of Copenhagen, from September, 1970 to February 1971, with portions previously reported by W. Henton (1972).

response. Suspiciously, lever pressing also increased when the classical conditioning was presented alone, without any shock avoidance contingency. Additional manipulations demonstrated that the acceleration was primarily maintained by spurious reinforcement of lever pressing *during* rather than preceding the 3-sec UCS pellet delivery cycle. Another contributing factor was a substantial decrease in shock avoidance rates during the intertrial interval, with bursts of responses alternating with 3- to 15-sec periods of pawing at the unilluminated CS or orienting toward and licking the UCS dispenser.

The observed behavioral interactions were then rather similar to the adventitious chaining of two responses described by Sidman (1958) when defensive classical conditioning was superimposed upon a similar shock avoidance baseline. Following Sidman's lead, schedule manipulations and a physical separation of the responses eliminated the response alternation during the intertrial interval, and also produced a suppression of avoidance rates and acceleration of orienting and approach responses during the CS. Figure 2.1 shows the typical performance of two monkeys with the latter procedures.

At that time, however, the effects of positive classical conditioning procedures upon negatively reinforced operants had received only limited experimental attention and were not entirely understood. The latency of a shuttle box avoidance response was reported to increase during stimuli formerly paired with either response-independent or response-contingent food (Grossen et al., 1969). Using a transfer of training design, Bull and Overmeir (1969) also found a decreased operant rate when a stimulus associated with shock avoidance was combined with a second stimulus formerly paired with food. Yet, our preliminary data seemed to indicate that maintained shock avoidance rates would be

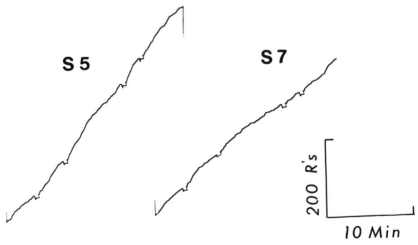

Figure 2.1. Cumulative records demonstrating the suppression of avoidance responses by superimposed stimulus–food pairings for two monkeys. Each presentation of the 30-sec CS is indicated by downward displacement of recording pen. UCS was delivery of five response-independent food pellets. Avoidance responding maintained by response–shock = shock–shock = 50 sec schedule.

either accelerated or suppressed by a prefood stimulus, dependent upon specific experimental arrangements.

The next experiment was simply a replication of our previous preliminary study and sought to further examine the control of avoidance rates by manipulating the characteristics of the superimposed CS–UCS pairing procedure. Within each procedural phase, a stimulus terminated by two food pellets was superimposed upon a free operant shock avoidance baseline. In Phase A, the pellets remained indefinitely available in a food cup until retrieved by a simple movement of the subject's right hand. In Phase B, the UCS retrieval sequence was extended to a slightly longer response chain by locating the CS and UCS immediately behind the subject's head. Furthermore, the pellets were only available during a limited interval, comparable to the duration of UCSs such as electric shock, grain reinforcement, intracranial stimulation, etc. In Phase C, the UCS pellets were again available during a limited interval, and the chain of pellet retrieval responses was further extended by delivering the pellets at a distance from the shock avoidance lever.

Experiment I

Figure 2.2 presents the general features of the apparatus used in each phase of the experiment. In initial acquisition, the subjects were placed in a standard primate restraint chair, and UCS food pellets were delivered into a cup mounted on the right-hand side of the restraint chair. A 3-W red light, which would later be used as the CS, was mounted on a response panel in front of the subject's head, and a Plexiglas response lever was centered in front of the subject's waist. A 7.0-ma, 1500-V, 0.5-sec shock was delivered through wire electrodes attached around the waist and to a brass footplate.

All subjects had a previous shock avoidance history, and were retrained on a response–shock = shock–shock = 30 sec schedule for 35 additional sessions; that is, shocks occurred every 30 sec in the absence of responses, and a lever

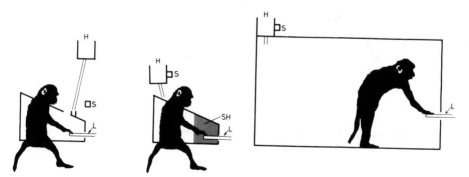

Figure 2.2. Apparatus used to study the effects of CS and UCS location upon lever-press avoidance responding by monkeys. H, UCS food hopper; S, blinking red light CS; L, lever for operant avoidance responses; SH, shield to prevent lever pressing with left hand (reacquisition I only). Left, acquisition; middle, reacquisition 1; right, reacquisition 2.

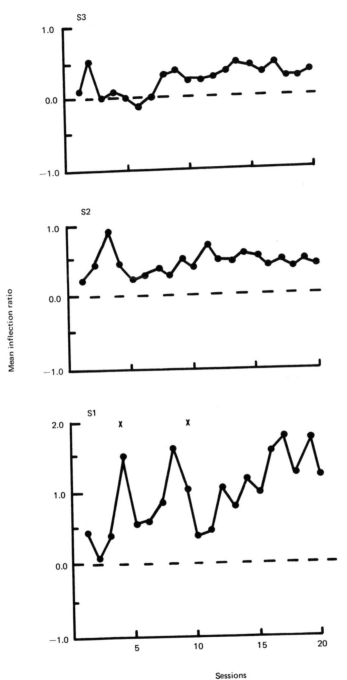

Figure 2.3.   Mean inflection ratio for avoidance responses during stimulus–food pairings for each acquisition session and subject. Each data point is the mean of five trials. The frequency of delivered shock is shown by the X's above each session. Adapted from Henton: *J. Exp. Anal. Behav.*, **17**, 269–275, 1972.

press postponed shock for 30 sec. After the avoidance rates had stabilized, each subject was habituated to a 15-sec blinking red light that was presented 5 times per session for 10 sessions (stimulus adaptation). Finally, the red light was terminated by delivery of two food pellets, with the food hopper activated 13 sec after CS onset and actual pellet delivery occuring 1.5 and 2.3 sec later. (A delay procedure prevented activation of the food hopper until 0.5 sec had elapsed since the previous avoidance response.)

Figure 2.3 presents the mean inflection ratio for avoidance rates in each of the 20 sessions with superimposed classical conditioning. Positive values indicate accelerated avoidance rates during the CS, and negative values indicate suppressed avoidance rates. The inflection ratio for each subject increased to a maximum during the first two to four sessions, followed by an approximate stabilization at a somewhat lower value over the final acquisition sessions. During the CS, each subject continued to emit shock avoidance responses and only initiated the pellet-retrieval sequence following actual pellet delivery into the food cup. One crucial consequence was that one or more avoidance responses were frequently emitted during the 2.3-sec pellet delivery cycle and were therefore immediately contiguous with the actual pellet delivery. The lower baseline avoidance rate of subject 1 was relatively more accelerated, and the higher baseline rate of subject 3 was less accelerated by these stimulus–food pairings.

Of some interest, the variability in the computed inflection ratio was equally determined by the variability in responding during the intertrial interval as well as during the CS (Table 2.1). In addition, the local rate and pattern during the intertrial interval was relatively disrupted when compared to previous avoidance sessions, especially for subject 1 with the lowest baseline avoidance rate. Monitored on a closed-circuit television system, each subject alternated bursts of avoidance responses with various idiosyncratic behaviors, such as head and hand movements toward the unilluminated CS during the intertrial interval. Although such collateral responses are difficult to anticipate and record electronically, unprogrammed lever-holding responses were fortuitously recorded throughout the acquisition sessions for subject 2.

Figure 2.4 presents a sample strain gauge recording of the form and amplitude of lever pressing by subject 2 compared to previous avoidance baselines. The normal avoidance pattern was a regular and cyclical stream of responses with relatively fixed amplitude. The superimposed conditioning procedure disrupted this cyclical responding and generated holding of the response lever at maximum depression, which required 450 g of pressure and a 3-inch displacement of the lever. This lever-holding behavior was occasionally correlated with and perhaps maintained by activation of the food hopper, as in Figure 2.4. Second, the amplitude rather than the frequency of responding was most disrupted, with irregular response amplitude during both the intertrial interval and the CS. In Figure 2.4, only 11 of the 20 lever presses in the prestimulus control period and 15 of the 22 lever presses during the CS were sufficient to cross both the upper and lower force requirements of the response microswitch. The irregular disruption of lever-pressing amplitude was associated with collateral responses, such as observing and pawing responses toward the

Table 2.1   Avoidance response frequencies during control and stimulus periods

Session and trial	Subject 1	Subject 2	Subject 3
1			
1	10/12	18/17	27/30
2	8/9	18/22	21/21
3	17/19	16/19	21/24
4	10/18	13/17	17/19
5	9/20	13/19	16/18
5			
1	7/11	15/17	20/21
2	7/11	18/21	23/18
3	5/9	15/19	24/22
4	5/13	13/19	25/26
5	12/12	15/19	16/21
10			
1	7/11	17/22	27/21
2	7/10	19/26	22/33
3	8/15	19/24	26/29
4	12/14	20/26	25/38
5	12/10	14/20	26/37
20			
1	6/21	11/14	27/28
2	7/20	9/19	22/29
3	12/16	16/16	19/30
4	8/20	16/23	24/30
5	7/13	13/17	19/24

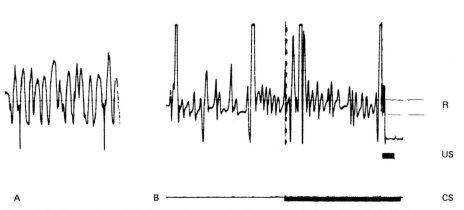

Figure 2.4.   Comparison of the form and amplitude of lever pressing by subject 2. **A.** During avoidance baselines. **B.** During control and stimulus intervals of acquisition. R, upper and lower microswitch response requirements; US, delivery of UCS food pellets; CS, 15-sec blinking red light.

red light. Similar head and hand movements were clearly apparent in subject 1, but occurred only infrequently in subject 3, who had the least disrupted avoidance rate.

The second phase of the study began with classical conditioning extinction, in which the red light was merely presented without pellet delivery for 20 sessions. The inflection ratio for avoidance responses decreased and stabilized at approximately 0.00 across the first three to five extinction sessions. The apparatus was then modified after the 10th session, with the food hopper and red light mounted immediately behind the subject's head (Figure 2.2). This modification would then require the subject to rotate its head approximately 180 degrees to orient toward the red light and food hopper. A sheet metal shield was placed 2 inches to the left of the avoidance lever and prevented lever pressing with the left hand. [The shield was added in an unsuccessful attempt to examine physical incompatibility between lever-pressing and pellet-retrieval resonses. If the subject retrieved the food pellets by clockwise rotation of the head and shoulders, then pellet retrieval would be incompatible with lever pressing with the right hand, and the shield would prevent lever pressing with the left hand. Conversely, if the subject retrieved the food pellets by counterclockwise rotation of the head and shoulders, then pellet retrieval would be compatible with lever pressing with the right hand. All subjects, however, retrieved the pellets by clockwise rotation of the body, and pellet retrieval was therefore incompatible with avoidance responses for each subject].

Given stable shock avoidance baselines, the red light was again terminated by response-independent pellet delivery in each of the next 20 sessions (classical conditioning reacquisition). As before, the food hopper was activated 13 sec after CS onset, but the food pellets now did not remain constantly available. Instead, the pellets fell from the delivery tube 0.8 and 1.5 sec later, and those pellets not retrieved during the pellet delivery cycle fell onto the floor and were "lost."

Figure 2.5 presents the inflection ratio for each subject during the 20 reacquisition sessions of Phase B. The inflection ratio initially increased and then stabilized at a positive value (acceleration) for subjects 1 and 2, but at a negative value (suppression) for subject 3. Changing the location and temporal characteristics of the CS and UCS thus resulted in relatively lower inflection ratios compared to the previous Phase A for all subjects. The inflection ratio was again higher for the subject with the lowest baseline avoidance rate (subject 1) and relatively lower, and suppressed, for the subject with the highest baseline rate (subject 3). However, the overall suppression for subject 3 resulted from a progressive diminution in the amplitude rather than the frequency of avoidance responses throughout the CS–UCS interval.

Similar to the initial acquisition phase, each subject again alternated bursts of avoidance responses with various unprogrammed behaviors during the intertrial interval. Figure 2.6 presents strain gauge recordings of lever holding by subject 2, which again occurred during Phase B. Although the frequency of lever pressing was approximately equal during the control and CS intervals, the response amplitude was nevertheless relatively more disrupted during the con-

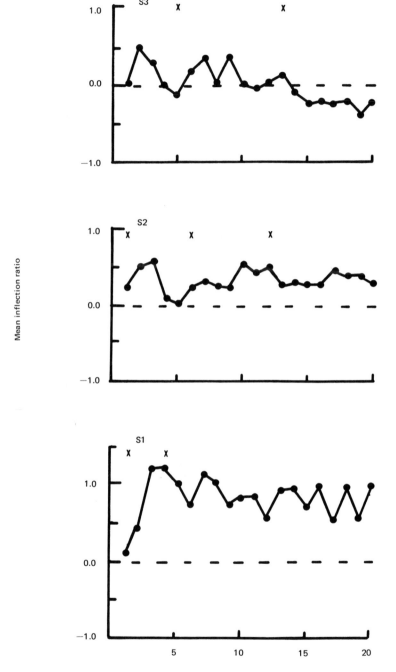

Figure 2.5.   Mean inflection ratio for avoidance responses during stimulus–food pairings of reacquisition 1. Each data point is the mean of five trials. Shock frequency is shown by the X's above each session. Adapted from Henton: *J. Exp. Anal. Behav.*, **17**, 269–275, 1972.

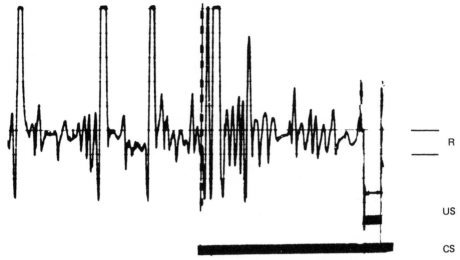

Figure 2.6. Strain gauge recording of lever holding by subject 2 during control and stimulus intervals of reacquisition 1. R, upper and lower microswitch response requirement; US, delivery of UCS food pellets; CS, 15-sec blinking red light.

trol period. This differential response amplitude thus resulted in more responses being counted during the CS. For all subjects, the local rate of avoidance responses during the intertrial interval appeared to be associated with head and hand movements toward the unilluminated CS. As in Phase A, the variability in the inflection ratio was therefore equally determined by the avoidance patterning during the control and CS–UCS intervals. One variable which determined this local avoidance rate was the recent history of shock. Shock delivered on the operant schedule immediately increased avoidance rates and decreased the frequency of unprogrammed behaviors during both the control and CS intervals throughout the remainder of the session.

In the final Phase C, avoidance rates were first reestablished by extinguishing the classical conditioning component. The red light was merely presented but not terminated by UCS food pellets in each of 20 extinction sessions. The extinction procedure was interrupted after the 10 session, and each subject was retrained in a 79 × 60 × 51 cm metal and Plexiglas cage (Figure 2.2). The avoidance lever was positioned in the front left corner, 26 cm above the floor, and the red light and food hopper were mounted on top of the cage in the back right corner. The subjects were trained only on the Sidman avoidance schedule for 5 sessions, and then the classical conditioning extinction procedure was resumed for 10 additional sessions.

In this apparatus, stimulus-orienting and pellet-retrieval responses would physically direct the subject away from the shock avoidance lever. Therefore, one of two possibilities existed. Either orienting and retrieval responses would occur during the stimulus, with a concomitant suppression of the spatially distant operant responses, or, conversely, avoidance responses would be emitted with a resulting suppression of orienting and retrieval responses.

The results of stimulus–food pairings in this apparatus are shown in Figure 2.7. Again, the food pellets were presented for a short duration (approximately 1.3 sec), and pellets not retrieved during the delivery cycle were lost to the subject. In contrast to Phases A and B, the superimposed classical conditioning produced a suppression of avoidance rates for all subjects. The inflection ratio progressively changed across sessions and followed a slightly different pattern for each subject. Avoidance rates were moderately decreased (subjects 2 and 3) or relatively unchanged (subject 1) during sessions 1 to 9. This initial phase was followed by a more marked suppression over the final reacquisition sessions. The sequential changes in the inflection ratio were associated with the temporal pattern of pellet retrieval responses adopted by each subject. Initially, the changeover from avoidance to retrieval responses occurred only following actual pellet delivery. However, since the duration of the changeover response sequence was longer than the availability of the food pellets, this response pattern resulted in retrieval of approximately 30% of the delivered pellets. Over the latter sessions, the changeover to pellet retrieval responses was initiated at CS onset rather than UCS onset, and avoidance responses were consequently suppressed through the prefood stimulus.

During the intertrial interval, bursts of avoidance responses again alternated with idiosyncratic responses, including jumping or climbing responses (subject 1), rocking back and forth with the lever in the right foot (subject 2), and brief orienting and postural responses (subject 3). The range in local avoidance rates was approximately equal to the variability observed in Phases A and B (Table 2.1) and was similarly dependent upon the local history of delivered shock, as noted in Phase B.

Discussion

The results then demonstrate that avoidance rates during the prefood stimuli may be controlled by selecting the appropriate apparatus and schedule characteristics. Throughout the study, avoidance responses were decreased when concurrent pellet-retrieval responses were increased, either after pellet delivery (Phase A), during pellet delivery (Phase B), or during the stimulus preceding pellet delivery (Phase C). In the initial acquisition, pellet-retrieval responses were at low rates during the prefood stimulus and only increased after actual pellet delivery into the food cup. Concomitantly, avoidance responses emitted throughout the stimulus were temporally contiguous with the subsequent delivery of the UCS food pellets. This unscheduled relationship would favor adventitious operant reinforcement and maintenance of avoidance responses by the response-independent food (Skinner, 1948). (The brief 0.5-sec delay contingency between avoidance responses and pellet delivery used in Phase A would preserve the response-independent delivery of the UCS, but it was less than the avoidance interresponse times of each subject and would not therefore be expected to prevent the adventitious effect.) This ever-present relationship between behavior and response-independent events has been previously described in other classical–operant combinations (Herrnstein and Morse, 1957; Sidman et al., 1957; Gottwald, 1967).

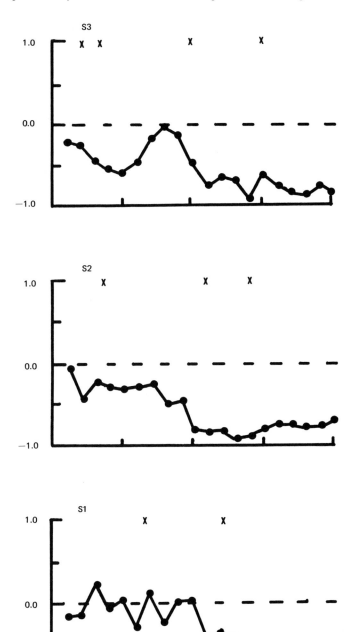

Figure 2.7. Mean inflection ratio for avoidance responses during stimulus–food pairings in reacquisition 2. Each data point is the mean of five trials, and shock frequency is given by the X's above each session. Adapted from Henton: *J. Exp. Anal. Behav.,* **17,** 269–275, 1972.

The response patterning was altered, however, by changing the characteristics of pellet delivery over subsequent experimental phases. In the last phase, for example, avoidance responses contiguous with the more distant pellet delivery would result in a loss of pellets. Avoidance rates were therefore suppressed by the changeover to pellet retrieval responses during the CS rather than during the UCS. The location of pellet retrieval responses within the classical conditioning component might then be determined by the temporal characteristics of the UCS relative to the duration of the UCS retrieval responses. As a consequence, the pattern of operant responses and retrieval responses should be dependent upon the temporal probabilities of response-contingent and response-independent events, as reported for operant rates in other classical–operant combinations (Stein et al., 1958; Meltzer and Brahlek, 1970; Pomerleau, 1970). More importantly, additional studies have now reported qualitative observations of concurrent response patterns in these classical–operant schedules.

Konorski (1967), for example, reported that operant suppression during pre-food stimuli was associated with approach responses to the UCS food tray (also see Stein et al., 1971). In contrast, Azrin and Hake (1969) replicated the Konorski experiment but added that the suppression could not be explained by "appealing" to competing responses. Hake and Powell (1970), however, seemed to reverse the claim of Azrin and Hake, and also seemed to support the response interaction interpretation (see also Van Dyne, 1971). [Azrin and Hake (1969) had superimposed stimuli paired with intracranial stimulation, food, or water upon positively reinforced operant responses and concluded that the operant suppression could not be explained by competing responses. The Azrin and Hake interpretation is somewhat complicated by the inclusion of freely available water and food within the conditioning chamber for different subgroups. The authors believed that food-deprived rats would respond very little for food reinforcers unless water was freely available, or that water-deprived rats would respond very poorly for water reinforcers unless food was also available (Azrin and Hake, 1969, p. 168; see also Hake and Powell, 1970). The remarkable absence of approach and orienting responses to the CS, food trays, and freely available water is not wholly consistent with previous data on schedule-induced drinking (Falk, 1961) or stimulation-induced orienting and consummatory responses (e.g., Pliskoff et al., 1964; Mogenson and Stevenson, 1966; Glickman and Schiff, 1967; Valenstein and Cox, 1970; Huston and Brozek, 1972).]

The current data thus suggest that overt responses may be directly if adventitiously affected by the UCS if all other responses are at a zero rate during the superimposed CS. Conversely, conditioned suppression may be dependent upon the schedule parameters generating an increased rate of concurrent responses during the CS–UCS interval. Operant rates during superimposed classical conditioning may thus be determined by the many parameters that control the frequency and temporal patterning of each concurrent response as well as the changeover between responses.

As a related issue, the analysis of classical–operant combinations has been primarily influenced by theoretical interpretations that emphasize operant rates only within the CS–UCS interval. Recent data would suggest, however, that superimposed conditioning procedures may have more extensive effects, and under some conditions may also influence response rates during the intertrial interval. Smith (1970) noted that intertrial response rates are often disrupted by CS–shock pairings, and that the frequency of such pausing may be controlled by the CS and UCS parameters. The pausing and bursts of avoidance responses in the present study would further suggest that stimulus–food pairings similarly disrupt baseline avoidance rates. The additional observations of competing responses then at least tentatively indicate that response disruption during both the intertrial interval and the CS are equally associated with increased frequencies of other behaviors.

These behavioral patterns are particularly congruent with the incompatible respondent analysis (Brady and Hunt, 1955) and the incompatible operant analysis (Weiskrantz, 1968) of negative classical conditioning superimposed upon positive operant baselines. Both concurrent response analyses may be extended to account for the effects of positive or negative classical conditioning combined with positive or negative operant reinforcement schedules. However, the distinctions between classical and operant processes are theoretical rather than empirical (Anohkin, 1958; Kimmel, 1965; Rescorla and Solomon, 1967). A more atheoretical position would suggest that classical–operant combinations may be viewed as concurrent schedules in which two components are operative during the CS (Henton and Brady, 1970).

Formally, classical conditioning procedures superimposed upon operant schedules are temporally concurrent schedules of response-independent and response-dependent events (Ferster and Skinner, 1957). Moreover, similar mutual interactions have been described in concurrent classical–operant schedules and concurrent operant—operant schedules. Disruption of response rates in both forms of concurrent schedules are (1) observed when the responses are conditioned in each component prior to schedule combination, (2) similarly affected by unprogrammed or adventitious reinforcement, and (3) dependent upon similar parameters (e.g., Catania, 1966; Davis, 1968; Lyon, 1968). Classical and operant combinations may therefore have many of the functional as well as formal characteristics of concurrent schedules controlling concurrent responses.

Such concurrent classical–operant schedules are most commonly interpreted in terms of interactions between underlying processes and states. Recent data, however, demonstrate that the conditioned suppression of operant responses is not clearly correlated with presumed covert or autonomic indicators of underlying associative states, such as heart rate, blood pressure, or EMG activity (e.g., Brady et al., 1969; Brady et al., 1970). A similar independence between operant responding and conditioned salivation was previously reported by Knitisch and White (1962). The experimental evidence thus supports Skinner's suggestion that overt responses are not an index or measure of physiological responses, not to mention presumed emotional constructs or states (Skinner, 1950). We might then conclude that classical and operant conditioning procedures may be more amenable to an empirical analysis of concurrently scheduled events, at least until the assumed mental states are directly measurable. In contrast to previous accounts that emphasize inferred and interposed constructs, a concurrent schedules analysis might advantageously emphasize observed events.

Concurrent Response Rates During Positive
Classical–Positive Operant Conditioning
(Experiments II and III)*

The original behavioral analysis of Brady and Hunt (1955) suggested that response interactions must occur when defensive classical conditioning is superimposed upon appetitive operant baselines. We have reason to believe that stimuli terminated by food, intracranial stimulation, and other positive reinforcers also control overt responses (Pavlov, 1927; Pliskoff et al., 1964; Konorski, 1967; Brown and Jenkins, 1968; Huston and Brozek, 1972), which in turn inductively suggests that respondents and operants also interact when appetitive classical conditioning procedures are combined with operant baselines. Davis and Kreuter (1972), for example, reported changes in shock avoidance rates during prefood stimuli may be associated with food cup approach responses—a finding confirmed by our Experiment I. A concurrent response–concurrent schedules analysis has also been applied to the changes in positively reinforced operants during stimuli paired with food (Henton and Brady, 1970) and intracranial stimulation (Van Dyne, 1971). The present experiments were therefore designed to examine various aspects of a more general concurrent responses interpretation.

The primary purpose was to record the response patterns maintained by a positive classical–positive operant conditioning procedure. To investigate the relationship between concurrent responses, the parameters in Experiments II and III were selected to generate high and low operant rates, respectively, during the prefood stimulus, with the suspicion that concurrent conditioned responses would be at reciprocally low and high rates.

Second, the previous competing response analyses have emphasized that physically incompatible responses are competing responses, by definition. The reverse assertion—that competing responses are necessarily physically incompatible—would be misleading. Interactions between compatible responses have been previously reported during classical conditioning (Pavlov, 1927) and operant conditioning (Sidman, 1958). Unless classical–operant schedules are assumed to have unique properties, physical incompatibility may also be sufficient but not necessary for response interactions during positive classical–positive operant conditioning. The apparatus in the following studies was purposely arranged such that retrieval of the UCS food pellet was physically compatible

---

* Experiments conducted at the University of Copenhagen, from June to September 1971, by W. Henton and I. Iversen.

with lever pressing. Monkeys of the same size and species have been trained with response chaining contingencies in our laboratory to simultaneously contact and hold one manipulandum while repeatedly lever pressing with the other hand. Based on this information, the distance between the operant response lever and the UCS food cup was selected to be well within the known limits of simultaneous responding. Thus, the concurrent responses were behaviorally compatible as well as physically compatible.

Third, operant suppression during classical–operant procedures has been proposed to be dependent upon qualitative or quantitative differences between the response-independent and response-dependent reinforcers (Azrin and Hake, 1969). To examine the reinforcer value interpretation, the operant and Pavlovian reinforcers were quantitatively and qualitatively equivalent in the present experiments.

Three experimentally naive African green monkeys were trained in the metal and Plexiglas cage described in Experiment I and Figure 2.2. The operant response lever was mounted in the right corner (10 cm from the right wall and 26 cm from the floor), and response-contingent reinforcers were delivered into a food cup 11.1 cm to the left of the response lever. The UCS food pellets were delivered into a second food cup mounted on the right wall. With the subject seated directly in front of the response lever, the UCS pellets were delivered approximately 19 cm to the right of the subject's head and within easy reach of the right arm (approximately 27 cm). Both the response-independent and response-contingent reinforcers were 1-g banana-flavored food pellets. Contact with the UCS food cup was recorded with a voltage comparator and measured in 200 millisec units. A 5-W flashing light (on/off phases of 100 millisec) was used as the CS and was placed 12.7 cm directly above the UCS delivery tube.

Experiment II

The specific purpose of Experiment II was to analyze the concurrent response patterns when the parameters were purposely selected to yield relatively high and unchanged operant rates during the prefood stimulus. Specifically, lever pressing was reinforced after an average of 100 responses by pellet delivery into food cup 1 (VR 100 schedule). Initially, the subjects were trained on this operant schedule for 30 sessions. A 30-sec flashing red light was then presented five times per session and terminated by one food pellet delivered into food cup 2. The UCS food pellet remained indefinitely available until retrieved by the subject. Retrieval of the UCS was recorded in all sessions and was physically compatible with lever pressing.

Figure 2.8 presents the results of this classical–operant schedule for each subject and acquisition session compared to the effects of stimulus only presentation during two adaptations sessions. Lever-pressing rates were relatively high and unchanged during the prefood stimulus for all subjects. The duration of retrieval responses was simultaneously zero (sessions 1 to 6) or low (less than 5 millisec/sec, sessions 7 to 15) for each subject. One informative exception, however, was that the lever-pressing rate of subject 2 in session 13 de-

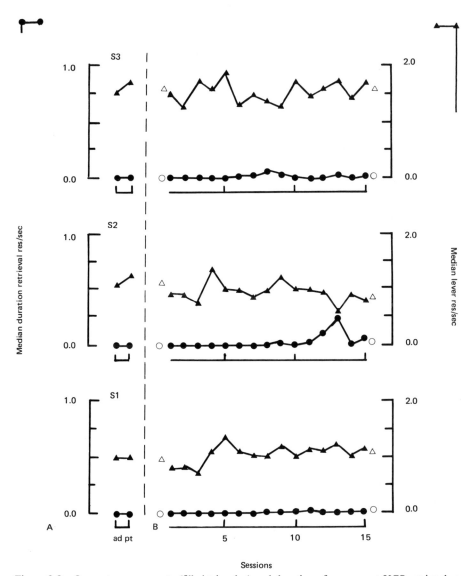

Figure 2.8. Operant response rate (filled triangles) and duration of concurrent UCS retrieval responses (filled circles) **A.** During stimulus adaptation. **B.** During sumperimposed stimulus–food pairings. For comparison, the open triangles and open circles show the operant rate and retrieval response duration, respectively, during control periods of sessions 1 and 15. Each data point is the mean of five trials.

creased approximately 34% when concurrent pellet retrieval responses increased to approximately 200 millisec/sec during the prefood stimuli.

Five control trials were also presented each session in which lever pressing and pellet retrieval responses were merely recorded during two consecutive 30-sec periods. Lever pressing was at a high rate and retrieval responses occurred less than 5 millisec/sec for each subject during these control trials.

   Strip chart records for individual conditioning trials are presented in Figure
2.9. Operant responses were emitted at high rates when the retrieval response
duration was zero during both the intertrial interval and the prefood stimulus.
However, lever pressing was consistently suppressed by pellet retrieval responses during the 1 to 3 sec following UCS delivery on each trial. The local
lever-pressing rate was also transiently suppressed when retrieval responses
briefly occurred during the intertrial interval or during the stimulus (Figure 2.9,
subject 1, trial 75; subject 2, trials 25 and 50). For each subject, a high rate of
one recorded response was therefore associated with a low rate of a second
recorded response. The data further indicate that reciprocal interactions occur
when the responses maintained by the classical and operant schedules are physically compatible. Moreover, the reciprocal interactions were not limited to
the two specific responses of lever pressing and retrieval of the response-independent pellets, but also included the effects of other physically compatible responses, such as retrieval of the operant reinforcers. Lever pressing and retrieval responses were both at zero rates, for example, following delivery and
retrieval of the operant reinforcers on the VR 100 schedule.
   The temporal patterning of positively reinforced operant responses might
therefore be related to alterations in the rate of other concurrently available responses. The results in fact imply that conditioned stimuli that do not control
competing responses have little if any disruptive effect upon baseline operant
responses. Similarly, other stimuli, such as UCS pellet delivery, were disruptive only to the degree and duration that concurrent responses were increased.
The results are then consistent with the suggestion that the superimposed ef-

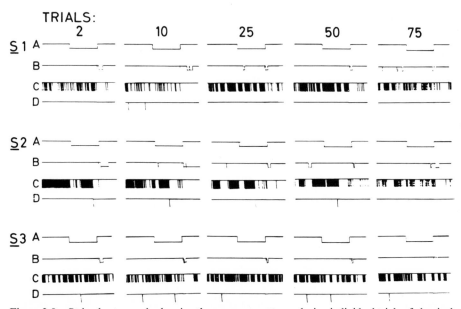

Figure 2.9.   Strip chart records showing the response patterns during individual trials of classical–
operant conditioning for each subject. A, CS duration; B, UCS retrieval responses; C, operant
lever pressing; D, delivery of operant reinforcer.

fects of Pavlovian conditioning are limited to those temporal intervals in which concurrent responses increase and interact with the reference operant response. This possibility was further investigated in the next experiment.

Experiment III

The basic purpose of Experiment III was to determine the response patterns generated by schedules selected to suppress operant rates during the prefood stimulus. The schedule manipulations were based on previous reports that operant suppression is an inverse function of relative CS duration (Stein et al., 1958; Meltzer and Brahlek, 1970). However, acceleration of operant responding during even relatively brief stimuli (Azrin and Hake, 1969; Henton, 1972) clearly indicated that manipulation of CS duration alone would not precisely control operant rates during the CS. Alternatively, the experimental literature suggests that manipulation of both CS and UCS parameters might be sufficient to specify and maintain a low operant response rate during the superimposed stimulus. A concurrent response analysis suggests that any such parametric manipulations will also increase the rate of competing responses during the prefood stimulus. To eliminate lever pressing during the CS, the duration of the red light was reduced to 15 sec and the response-independent pellets were available only during the 200-millisec pellet delivery cycle.

Second, if the concurrent response analysis is correct, then the sporadic occurrence of retrieval responses during the intertrial interval should also be controllable by manipulating the competing rate of lever pressing. We could, for example, increase retrieval responses during the intertrial interval by decreasing the rate of concurrent lever pressing. However, a low lever-pressing rate during the intertrial interval would counter the primary purpose of demonstrating a conditioned suppression of lever pressing during the CS. Therefore, the parameters were also manipulated to completely eliminate retrieval responses from the intertrial interval by increasing concurrent lever pressing to a slightly higher and more uniform rate. To this end, the operant schedule was changed from the previous VR 100 to a VR 80 reinforcement schedule.

Each subject from Experiment II was consequently trained in two 50-min sessions on each of the next 5 days. Session A and session B were separated by 3 hr. During session A, lever pressing was reinforced on a VR 80 schedule, and the prefood stimulus was not presented. During session B, the operant response lever and associated food cup were removed, and the subjects were trained to retrieve the UCS pellets directly from a delivery tube. The flashing red light was presented for 15 sec and terminated by the response-independent delivery of one food pellet from feeder 2. The pellets fell directly from the delivery tube approximately 200 millisec after feeder operation, and those pellets not retrieved were lost to the subject. Five stimulus trials and five control trials were given each session in an irregular sequence.

The operant conditioning from session A and the classical conditioning from session B were then combined in each of the next 15 sessions. Figure 2.10 presents the overall response patterns with this schedule combination for each

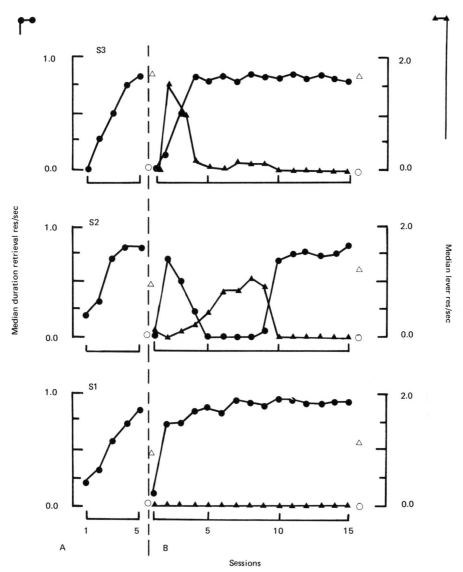

Figure 2.10. Operant response rate (filled triangles) and retrieval response duration (filled circles) **A.** During simple classical conditioning. **B.** During concurrent classical–operant conditioning. Open triangles and open circles give the operant response rate and retrieval response duration, respectively, during control periods of session 1 and session 15. Each data point is the mean of five trials.

subject and session. Strip chart records of lever pressing and retrieval responses for individual trials are presented in Figure 2.11. During the preliminary training with stimulus–food pairings in separate off-the-baseline sessions, retrieval response durations progressively increased to 700 or 800 millisec/sec for all subjects (Figure 2.10A). Each subject oriented the head and body toward

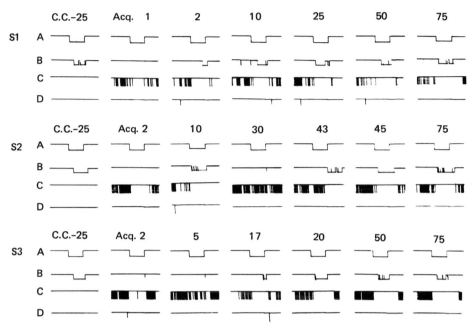

Figure 2.11. Strip chart records of individual trials of simple classical conditioning (C.C.-25) and concurrent classical–operant conditioning (Acq. 1, 2, etc.). A, CS duration; B, UCS retrieval responses; C, operant lever pressing; D, delivery of operant reinforcer.

the stimulus during the first 1 to 3 sec of each trial, followed by a changeover to retrieval responses throughout the remaining 10 to 12 sec of the stimulus (Figure 2.11). Following UCS delivery, the pellets were transferred to the mouth, either by a simple movement of the right hand or by covering the end of the delivery tube with the mouth. Subsequent combination of the operant and classical conditioning procedures produced a transient suppression of both lever pressing and recorded retrieval responses during the first one to three trials. All subjects, monitored with the television system, oriented the head and eyes toward the red light and feeder 2 throughout the stimulus but did not physically contact the pellet delivery tube during these initial trials. Over subsequent trials, the pattern of lever pressing and retrieval responses was slightly different for each subject.

Subject 1 made a retrieval response during the last 3 sec of the second acquisition trial (Figure 2.11), and retrieval responses increased to approximately 700 millisec/sec by the 10th trial (Figure 2.10). Lever pressing was therefore suppressed throughout the remaining acquisition trials.

For subject 2, retrieval responses similarly increased across the first 10 to 15 trials, then decreased to zero until trial 43 (Figure 2.11), followed by an immediate increase to a high and stable rate after trial 45. Reciprocally, the lever-pressing rate of subject 2 was initially low, progressively increased to baseline rates until trial 43, and then decreased to near zero over subsequent trials.

For subject 3, retrieval responses were suppressed until trial 17, then systematically increased to approximately 800 millisec/sec across trials 17 to 20, and remained high over subsequent trials. Lever pressing concurrently increased to baseline rates until trial 17, then decreased to near zero during the remaining trials of the experiment.

During the intertrial interval and control trials, retrieval response duration was zero and lever-pressing rates remained high and unchanged for all subjects. However, Figure 2.11 shows that lever pressing and UCS retrieval responses were both locally suppressed during and immediately following delivery of the operant reinforcers. Again, observation indicated that each subject oriented toward food cup 1 and physically retrieved the food pellets following the VR 80 reinforcement.

The recorded behavioral patterns then indicate that suppressed operant rates may be associated with a high rate of concurrent responses during a prefood stimulus. The response transitions of subjects 2 and 3 especially demonstrate that even phasic changes in lever-pressing rates are associated with reciprocal alterations in concurrent retrieval responses. The alterations in operant responding in the present study were not dependent upon any qualitative or quantitative difference between the response-independent and response-dependent reinforcers; rather, the reciprocal rate patterns may be dependent upon quantitative and qualitative differences between concurrent responses, not concurrent reinforcers. The operant suppression may thus be dependent upon an increase in the rate of topographically different responses rather than a strict behavioral or physical incompatibility.

In contrast to Experiment II, the selected parameters in the present study suppressed the intermittent pellet retrieval rate to zero during the intertrial interval. In consequence, the results suggest that response patterns during the intertrial interval also may be controlled by competing response manipulations.

Discussion

Experiments II and III therefore suggest that the rate of positively reinforced operants may be controlled by specifying the temporal location of competing responses during superimposed appetitive classical conditioning. Increased pellet retrieval responses produced a decrease in concurrent lever pressing following UCS pellet delivery in Experiment II, but during the prefood stimulus in Experiment III. In both experiments, the changeover from exclusive lever pressing to exclusive retrieval responses could not be attributed to reinforcer differences or response incompatibility, nor were the reciprocal interactions restricted to a simple correlation between the two specifically manipulated and recorded responses. The findings thus suggest that any parameter that alters the local rate of one response may very well have more elaborate effects, and may also modify the concurrent rates of a variety of topographically different responses.

Sidman (1960) has previously suggested that typically unrecorded behaviors may effectively alter the frequency and temporal patterning of the experimenter-selected response. The present data would also argue that recording only one response may not provide a sufficient description of classical–operant interactions. One typically unrecorded interaction, for example, is the effect of the operant schedule upon the classical conditioning procedure. Most contemporary theories assume the operant responses passively measure but do not actively determine the superimposed Pavlovian processes. Classical–operant analyses therefore usually emphasize only the modulation of operant rates by classical conditioning procedures. The present results instead suggest that the modulation effects are reciprocal: responses maintained by the classical conditioning procedure may be altered and disrupted by the operant conditioning schedule. The initial disruption of UCS retrieval responses of all subjects in Experiment III, and the subsequent response transitions of subjects 2 and 3, demonstrate that responses controlled by the classical conditioning component may be neither constant nor unaffected by classical–operant combination. Similar modulation effects occur in concurrent classical–classical conditioning (reviewed in Part III) and in concurrent operant–operant conditioning (see Part II). The combined literature suggests that mutual modulation effects occur in each of the four general types of concurrent schedules involving an operant or Pavlovian procedure combined with a second operant or Pavlovian procedure. Interdependent response patterns therefore seem to be ordered and empirical characteristics of concurrent schedules in general, rather than a haphazard collection of passive or unobstrusive devices of inferrential measurement.

Concurrent Response Rates During Preevent Stimuli (Experiments IV, V, VI, and VII)*

Classical–operant schedules have attracted numerous theoretical perspectives and treatments since their inception some 30 years ago (Estes and Skinner, 1941). The observed effects can and have been attributed to general emotional states (Azrin and Hake, 1969), emotional–motivational interactions (Rescorla and Solomon, 1967), reinforcer value (Hake and Powell, 1970), motivational states (Estes, 1969), incompatible responses (Brady and Hunt, 1955), multiple schedule effects (Hake and Powell, 1970), and concurrent schedule effects (Henton and Brady, 1970), among others. The multiple schedule and the concurrent schedules analyses similarly identify observable events as the variables that directly control behaviors during classical–operant combinations, and therefore both interpretations are amenable to direct examination.

The multiple schedule interpretation, a derivative of the general emotional state account, suggests that a superimposed UCS may be equivalent to a change in the ongoing operant reinforcement rate. Superimposed CS–UCS pairings might then have some of the same effects as a stimulus signaling a change in the rate of operant reinforcement (Hake and Powell, 1970). The concurrent schedules analysis, a derivative of the incompatible response interpre-

---

* Experiments conducted at the University of Copenhagen, from February to December 1971, by W. Henton.

tation, proposes that a superimposed CS–UCS procedure is a concurrent schedule that controls different responses and would therefore be more analogous to a discriminative stimulus controlling a competing operant response. If the multiple schedule or concurrent schedules analogies are correct, then classical–operant effects should be duplicated either by stimuli paired with sequential transitions in the baseline operant schedule, or stimuli paired with changes in a second, concurrent operant schedule. Given the context of previous reports on relative CS duration in the classical–operant literature (Stein et al., 1958; Meltzer and Brahlek, 1970; Pomerleau, 1970), we might then expect that manipulating stimulus duration would yield similar behavioral functions with stimuli paired with multiple or concurrent schedule changes. The purpose of the following experiments was simply to compare operant response rates during different duration stimuli paried with various response-independent events. The parameters of the response-independent changes were systematically altered across experiments to progressively approximate the characteristics of superimposed stimuli paired with food or shock.

Experiment IV

Experiment IV began with the multiple schedule interpretation, and the suggestion that the value of the operant reinforcer will increase or decrease, respectively, during stimuli signaling a subsequent decrease or increase in the probability of operant reinforcement. This account further suggests that operant response rates will correspondingly increase or decrease during the stimulus to match the calculated value of the reinforcer (Azrin and Hake, 1959; Hake and Powell, 1970). Increased operant rates during stimuli terminated by time out (Leitenberg, 1966) and decreased rates during stimuli terminated by a more dense reinforcement schedule (Pliskoff, 1961, 1963) support the multiple schedule interpretation. The purpose of Experiment IV was to determine the function relating response rate to the duration of stimuli terminated by time out from positive reinforcement.

   Initially, three experimentally naive monkeys (*Cercopithicus aethiops*) were trained in the previously described metal and Plexiglas cage. For this study, two transparent Plexiglas levers were mounted on the front wall 26 cm apart, and a panel containing a food cup and red, green, and white lights was centered between lever 1 and lever 2. Each lever could be transilluminated by an internally mounted white light, and responses on the illuminated lever 1 (right lever) were reinforced with food pellets on a VR 80 schedule (range 1 to 371). Lever 2 was used in the succeeding experiments but had no programmed consequences in this experiment. When lever 1 response rates had stabilized (30 sessions), the light within the lever was turned off for 3-min periods at irregular intervals throughout each session. The VR 80 schedule was then in effect for a total of 36 min, and the 3-min time out (TO) periods were scheduled six times per session (i.e., *mult* VR 80 TO). Training with this multiple schedule continued until responses occurred at a high and uniform rate during the VR 80 component, and at a stable virtually zero rate during the TO component (sessions 31 to 76).

After five stimulus habituation sessions (sessions 77 to 81), the TO component was preceded by either a 15-sec white light, a 50-sec red light, or a 100-sec green light in each of the next 25 sessions (sessions 82 to 106). The stimuli were each presented twice per session in an irregular order, with response rates during each stimulus compared to a control interval of comparable duration preceding stimulus onset. This procedure would thus yield a function relating

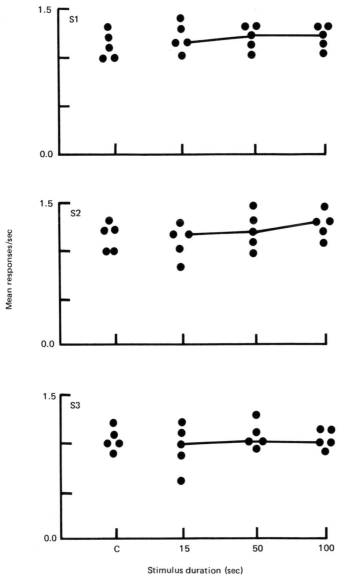

Figure 2.12. Relationship between operant response rate and the duration of pre-TO stimuli. For comparison, the data plotted at C are the response rates during the control periods preceding the 15-sec stimulus. Each data point is the mean of two trials for each of the final five sessions.

operant response rates to the duration of the pre-TO stimuli within each session.

Figure 2.12 presents the operant rates during each stimulus for each subject. The VR 80 response rates were unchanged during the pre-TO stimuli relative to baseline rates throughout the acquisition sessions. Strip chart records of individual trials at each stimulus duration are presented in Figure 2.13; they similarly provide little indication of altered response patterns during the pre-TO stimuli. The negligible effects of stimulus duration are then in sharp contrast to the behavioral effects of CS duration in classical–operant schedules. This finding would suggest that a sequential alteration in the proportional value of reinforcers may not be sufficient to change response rates during pre-schedule change stimuli. Previous results have also been unclear, with indications that operant rates may be unchanged, increased, or decreased during stimuli terminated by time out from positive reinforcement (Pliskoff, 1963; Leitenberg, 1966; Leitenberg et al., 1968; Kaufman, 1969). Similarly, the identical alteration of avoidance rates during stimuli terminated by opposing schedule changes suggests that the effects of pre-schedule change stimuli are dependent upon variables other than reinforcer value (Henton, 1970).

Moreover, Brownstein and Hughes (1970) and Brownstein and Newsom (1970) noted that response rate changes in multiple schedules (''contrast'' effects) may be partially dependent upon changes in response rate rather than reinforcer rates during the successive schedule components. In a somewhat related analysis, Dunham (1971) and Iversen (1974) proposed that multiple schedule effects may be dependent upon the concurrent rate of unrecorded responses within a schedule component, and therefore only indirectly related to the recorded operant rate during the subsequent schedule component (see Chapter 4

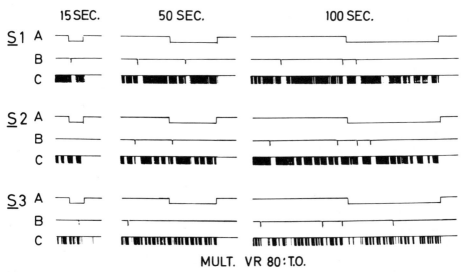

MULT. VR 80 : T.O.

Figure 2.13.   Strip chart records of individual trials using the 15-, 50-, and 100-sec pre-TO stimuli. A, stimulus duration; B, delivery of the operant reinforcer; C, operant responses on lever 1.

for a more detailed review and analysis). The variety of rate alterations associated with multiple schedule changes could thus result from the absence of contingencies specifically controlling the rates of concurrent responses.

An extended competing or concurrent response analysis would in fact suggest that the changeover from baseline responses to concurrently reinforced responses may be a fundamental parameter in classical–operant schedules. Such changeover responses are a distinguishing characteristic of concurrent performances, but not multiple schedules (Catania, 1969). The concurrent response interpretation thus suggests that classical–operant combinations may be more analogous to pre-schedule change stimuli superimposed upon concurrent schedules than to multiple schedules. [The distinction between multiple and concurrent schedules, however, is sometimes confused in current terminology. For example, a two-component procedure in which reinforcement for one response sequentially alternates between positive reinforcement and time-out, while the schedule for a second response simultaneously alternates between time-out and positive reinforcement could be described as a multiple schedule; e.g., *mult* VI VI. This description, however, ignores the TO component and the concurrently available response. Since TO specifies the relationship between stimuli, responses, and reinforcers, and therefore defines a reinforcement schedule, the above procedure would be more accurately described as a concurrent schedule simultaneously controlling two responses; e.g., *conc* (*mult* VI TO) (*mult* TO VI).]

Experiment V

The procedures of Experiment IV were therefore modified to more closely approximate concurrent classical–operant schedules by specifying a changeover from the baseline response to a second response at the offset of each pre-schedule change stimulus. The purpose of Experiment V was to record the rate of each concurrent response as a function of the duration of the pre-schedule change stimuli. Specifically, Experiment IV was repeated, with the addition that responses on a second lever were reinforced during the 3-min TO for lever 1 responses.

As preliminary training, lever 2 was illuminated, and responses on lever 2 were reinforced on the VR 80 schedule in each of the next five sessions (sessions 107 to 111). In these sessions, lever 2 rates increased and equalled the previous lever 1 rates by the third session.

In sessions 112 to 136, lever 1 responses were again reinforced on the *mult* VR 80 TO schedule, and the TO component was again preceded by the 15-sec white light, the 50-sec red light, or the 100-sec green light. However, lever 2 was now illuminated during the 3-min TO for lever 1, and responses on lever 2 were reinforced on the VR 80 schedule. Each stimulus was thus followed by changes in concurrent schedules, from VR 80 to TO for lever 1, and from TO to VR 80 for lever 2 [*conc* (*mult* VR 80 TO) (*mult* TO VR 80)]. Responses on the two levers were physically compatible, and also were compatible with retrieval of the VR 80 reinforcers delivered into the food cup between the levers.

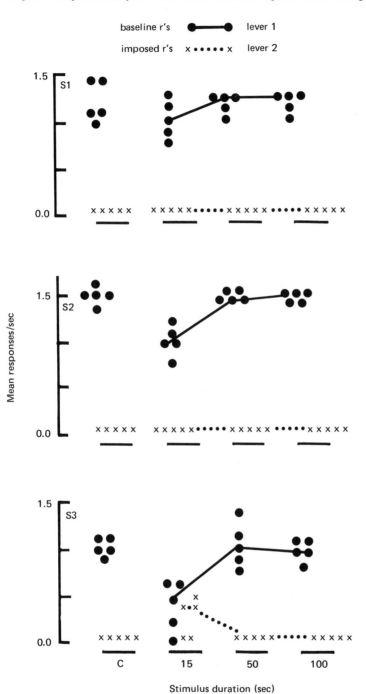

Figure 2.14.   Baseline response rates on lever 1 and concurrent rates on lever 2 as a function of the duration of stimuli terminated by changes in two concurrent schedules. For comparison, the data plotted at C give the response rates during the control period preceding the 15-sec stimulus. Each data point is the mean of two trials in each of the final five acquisition sessions.

With this schedule, lever 1 response rates were decreased during the 15-sec stimulus and remained unchanged during the 50- and 100-sec stimuli throughout the 25 acquisition sessions. The concurrent response rates during stimulus trials are given in Figure 2.14 for each of the final five sessions. Responses on lever 2 increased slightly during the 15-sec stimulus for subject 3, but not for subjects 1 and 2. Lever 2 responses during the 50- and 100-sec stimuli remained unchanged at virtually zero rates for subjects 1 and 2 and at low, irregular rates for subject 3.

Strip chart records of individual trials are given in Figure 2.15. The temporal pattern of lever 1 responses changed during the 15-sec stimulus, but not during the 50- and 100-sec stimuli, for all subjects. Observed on the television monitor, each subject either oriented toward the visual stimulus or made postural adjustments toward lever 2 during the 15-sec trials. Subjects 1 and 2, however, did not physically contact and depress lever 2 during any pre-schedule change stimulus. For subject 3, lever 2 responses increased during the 15-sec stimulus, and also occurred at lower intermittent rates during the intertrial interval and the 50- and 100-sec stimuli. For all subjects, responses on either lever 1 or lever 2 were associated with a zero local rate on the other available lever before, during, and after the pre-schedule change stimuli. Similarly, responses on both

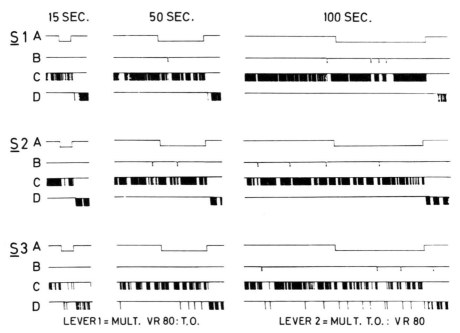

Figure 2.15. Strip chart records of concurrent response patterns during stimuli terminated by simultaneous changes in concurrent operant schedules. A, stimulus duration; B, delivery of operant reinforcer; C, lever 1 responses reinforced on *mult* VR 80 TO; D, lever 2 responses reinforced on *mult* TO VR 80.

levers were suppressed when concurrent pellet retrieval responses were emitted during the delivery of VR reinforcers (Figure 2.15).

In summary, the results of Experiment V demonstrate that operant rates may be decreased during relatively brief stimuli terminated by simultaneous changes in concurrent schedules. Further, the suppressive effects of the 15-sec stimulus appeared to be associated with an increase in other recorded and unrecorded behaviors. The baseline responses on lever 1 were then decreased independent of whether the emitted concurrent response was pressing lever 2, orienting to the pre-schedule change stimuli, or retrieving the operant reinforcer.

The stimulus-bound changes in lever 1 rates would not seem to be wholly dependent upon reinforcer value per se, since reinforcers were delivered on the same VR 80 schedule before, during, and after stimulus presentation. Indeed, lever 1 rates were locally suppressed during the 15-sec stimulus, independent of whether the burst of concurrent responses was associated with explicit operant reinforcement, but were unchanged during the 50- and 100-sec stimuli in spite of the subsequent shift in reinforcer value to a different response. These findings support the contention that operant rates do not necessarily match the sequential value of reinforcers (Brownstein and Hughes, 1970; Brownstein and Newsom, 1970) and that the same distribution of reinforcers may control a diversity of response patterns even in simple operant schedules (Ferster and Skinner, 1957). The local response interactions are, however, at least qualitatively similar to the concurrent response patterns recorded in positive classical–positive operant conditioning (Experiments II and III). The possibility then remains that an increase in the rate of concurrently available responses may be sufficient to alter baseline operant rates during pre-schedule change stimuli, as well as during superimposed prefood or preshock stimuli.

The response-independent presentation of an operant schedule component, however, is fundamentally different from the delivery of food or shock in a typical classical conditioning procedure. One difference is that the baseline operant schedule is usually unchanged during a superimposed classical conditioning procedure but is frequently altered following the offset of pre-schedule change stimuli. More importantly, in the classical conditioning procedure the stimulus is terminated by the immediate delivery of reinforcers, but in the pre-schedule change procedure it is terminated by the intermittent delivery of reinforcers throughout several minutes. The pre-schedule change stimuli in Experiment V, for example, were typically terminated by three pellets scattered throughout a 3-min VR 80 component, rather than the undelayed delivery of Pavlovian reinforcers within milliseconds. These temporal characteristics of the response-independent event are rather powerful controlling variables in classical–operant schedules (e.g., Kamin, 1965), as evidenced by the differential effects of superimposed delay and trace classical conditioning. If pre-schedule change stimuli superimposed upon concurrent operant schedules are in fact analogous to classical–operant combinations, then the response patterns may also be expected to depend upon the parameters of the response-independent event.

Experiment VI

The procedures of the previous experiment were therefore modified to duplicate the temporal characteristics of prefood stimuli superimposed upon an ongoing operant reinforcement schedule. In Experiment VI, the pre-schedule change stimuli were terminated only by a brief change in the contingencies controlling a second operant response. More specifically, responses on lever 2 were maintained on the VR 80 schedule throughout each session. Each of the three pre-schedule change stimuli was terminated by a 3-sec interval in which a concurrent response on lever 1 was immediately reinforced with three food pellets. (The reader may note that the baseline VR 80 was assigned to lever 2 in the present study, but lever 1 in Experiments IV and V. The change was necessitated by the intention of exchanging one of the levers for an additional pellet feeder in the following experiment, and the physical characteristics of the supporting system required that the added feeder replace the right-hand lever 1, leaving lever 2 as the comparable baseline response for both Experiments VI and VII.)

Beginning with the first session (session 137), a fading procedure (Terrace, 1963) was used to establish the changeover from lever 2 to lever 1 during a limited period following stimulus offset. In the first four sessions, each stimulus was terminated by a 10-sec period in which (1) the light in lever 2 was turned off and lever 2 responses had no programmed effect, and (2) lever 1 was illuminated and the first response was followed by three food pellets. The schedules and associated stimuli changed back to VR 80 (lever 2) and TO (lever 1) following the first lever 1 response, or after 10 sec. In all subsequent sessions the VR 80 for lever 2 remained in effect throughout the session and was not changed following stimulus offset. The limited hold for lever 1 reinforcement was reduced to 7.5 sec (three sessions) and 5.0 sec (three sessions). Each subject consistently changed over from lever 2 to lever 1 during this limited hold, with the latency of the changeover approximately 2.0 to 2.5 sec.

In the next 25 sessions (sessions 147 to 171), the 15-sec white light, the 50-sec red light, and the 100-sec green light were paired with a 3.0-sec interval in which the first lever 1 response was reinforced with three food pellets. The behavioral procedure thus consisted of a simple VR 80 for lever 2 and a *mult* TO CRF (limited hold 3 sec) for lever 1. With this concurrent schedules procedure, lever 2 and lever 1 rates were both dependent upon the duration of the pre-schedule change stimuli. The mean response rates on each lever during stimulus periods are given in Figure 2.16 for each subject. For subjects 1 and 3, the baseline rates on lever 2 were suppressed during the 15- and 50-sec stimuli, but remained relatively high and unchanged during the 100-sec stimulus. At the same time, lever 1 rates increased during the 15- and 50-sec stimuli, but were relatively low and unchanged during the 100-sec stimulus. For subject 2, lever 2 rates were decreased, and lever 1 rates irregularly increased during the 15-sec stimulus, and both responses were at unchanged rates during the 50- and 100-sec stimuli.

Interactions in the frequency and patterning of responses during individual

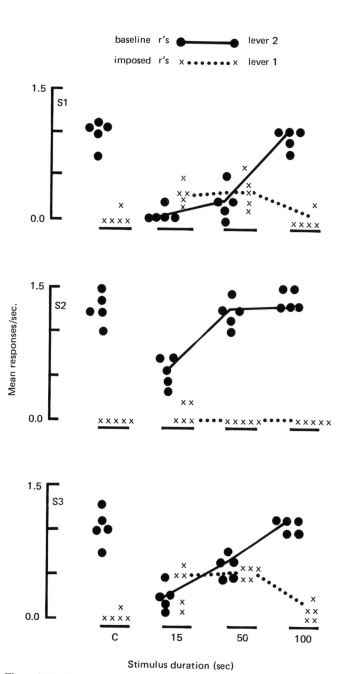

Figure 2.16. Baseline rates on lever 2 and concurrent rates on lever 1 as a function of the duration of stimuli terminated by reinforcement of lever 1 responses. For comparison, the data plotted at C give the concurrent response rates during the control period preceding the 15-sec stimulus. Each data point is the mean of two trials in each of the final five sessions.

trials are given in Figure 2.17. Subject 1 consistently emitted lever 1 responses throughout the 15-sec stimulus, alternated bursts of responses on lever 2 and lever 1 throughout the 50-sec stimulus, and emitted only baseline lever 2 responses during the 100-sec stimulus. Subject 2 alternated responses on lever 2 with orienting responses and occasional lever 1 responses during the 15-sec stimulus, but changed over to lever 1 only following the offset of the 50- and 100-sec stimuli. Subject 3 alternated responses on lever 2 and lever 1 throughout all pre-schedule change stimuli, with the frequency of each response per changeover dependent upon stimulus duration. Bursts of responses on either lever 2 or lever 1 were associated with a zero local rate on the other available lever before, during, and after the pre-schedule change stimuli. Similarly, response rates on both levers were decreased when pellet retrieval responses occurred during delivery of the three food pellets following stimulus offset or during delivery of the baseline VR 80 reinforcers (Figure 2.17). All subjects also emitted other unrecorded behaviors, such as approach and contact with the visual stimuli.

The rate of a positively reinforced operant was therefore altered by increasing the rate of other responses during the pre-schedule change stimuli. The data suggest that the local rates and patterns of the competing responses were dependent upon the duration of the signal for concurrent reinforcement. For each subject, baseline response rates on lever 2 decreased and approximated a direct function of stimulus duration. The concurrent lever 1 rate was increased and approximated an inverse function of stimulus duration. This functional rela-

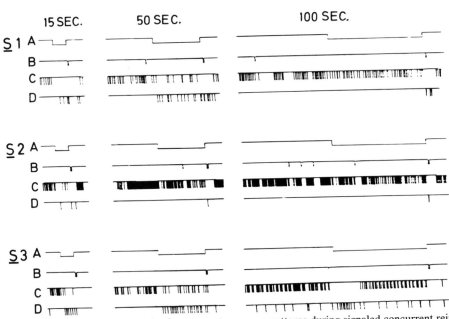

Figure 2.17.   Strip chart records of concurrent response patterns during signaled concurrent reinforcement. A, stimulus duration; B, delivery of operant reinforcers; C, baseline lever 2 responses maintained on VR 80; D, lever 1 responses maintained by signaled reinforcement.

tionship, moreover, is quantitatively comparable to the effects of CS duration in classical—operant schedules (e.g., Stein et al., 1958). Stimulus duration may then be a common parameter controlling concurrent response rates during stimuli paired with concurrent response-contingent or response-independent reinforcers.

One troubling aspect of these observations, however, is that previous authors have reported that baseline rate changes during signaled concurrent reinforcement cannot be attributed to response interactions, but instead match the proportional value of reinforcers (Catania, 1963; Rachlin and Baum, 1969). In contrast, the baseline response rates in the present experiment did not match the proportional rate of obtained reinforcers for any subject. Furthermore, the rate of competing responses maintained by the pre-schedule change stimuli did not match the relative value of the signaled reinforcers. In comparison, both Catania (1963) and Rachlin and Baum (1969) reported low, near zero rates of competing preparatory and observing responses, which therefore also did not match the relatively high rate of signaled reinforcers. The absence of concurrent or competing responses in the previous signaled reinforcement studies is rather puzzling and seemingly inconsistent with response—reinforcer value matching as well as the concurrent response interpretation. The present data are consistent, however, with the suggestion that response rates do not match reinforcer rates except within specific values of changeover delays and other experimental constraints (Catania, 1966), or when all controlling variables are carefully balanced across all responses (Rachlin, 1971). Balancing procedures were not used in the present study and are not used in classical—operant combinations. The response rates would therefore not be expected to conform to the matching theory. Indeed, the constrained matching of concurrent response rates to reinforcer rates may be a specific example of response interactions (Part II).

Experiment VII

We then suspect that the response interdependencies in Experiment VI are closely similar to the behavioral patterns generated by analogous classical—operant schedules. If operant rates are a direct function of the duration of the superimposed CS, then we would expect that the rates of other, competing responses must be inversely related to stimulus duration. Such an inductive speculation is consistent with previous data demonstrating overt orienting responses toward the conditioned stimulus, as well as conditioned consummatory responses, during Pavlovian conditioning (Pavlov, 1927; Razran, 1961; Konorski, 1967; Patton and Rudy, 1967; Brown and Jenkins, 1968). The results then imply that a *variety* of response interactions must occur when conditioned orienting and consummatory responses are scheduled with operant responses in classical—operant conditioning. Although the sequence of orienting and consummatory responses may involve numerous postural changes and head and hand movements, the terminal response of physical contact with the CS and the UCS may be directly recorded. In Experiment VII, contact with the conditioned stimuli was recorded with a voltage comparator connected to uninsulated wire embedded in the stimulus display panel; physical contact with the UCS pellet delivery tube was recorded with a second voltage comparator.

The purpose of the experiment was then to determine the interactions between stimulus-orienting responses, preparatory UCS retrieval responses, and operant lever pressing when prefood stimuli are superimposed upon a positive operant reinforcement schedule. Lever 1 was replaced with a pellet delivery tube and the procedures of Experiment VI were repeated, with the exception that the three food pellets following stimulus offset were delivered independent of the subject's behavior.

To convert the pre-schedule change stimuli to classical conditioning stimuli, an extinction procedure was first used in which each stimulus was presented but not terminated by a schedule change in each of the next 15 sessions (sessions 172 to 186). Baseline responses on lever 2 were reinforced on the VR 80 schedule throughout each session. Lever 2 rates during the stimuli increased to normal baseline rates, and lever 1 responses decreased to a zero rate by the 10th extinction session. The apparatus was then modified and lever 2 was removed and replaced with a UCS pellet delivery tube.

Each subject was trained to retrieve UCS pellets during off-the-baseline sessions following each of the last five extinction sessions. In these additional sessions, lever 2 and the stimulus display panel were removed from the training cage. To match the temporal characteristics of the operant limited-hold procedure of Experiment VI, a white light mounted above the pellet delivery tube was turned on for 3.0 sec, and the UCS pellet feeder was operated 2.0 sec after light onset. The three pellets were delivered approximately 300 millisec after feeder operation, which corresponds to the changeover latency to lever 1 in the previous procedure. Pellets not retrieved fell through the grid floor and were not available to the subject.

The two types of sessions were subsequently combined, with lever 2 responses reinforced on the VR 80, and the 15-, 50-, and 100-sec stimuli were paired with the UCS pellet delivery cycle (sessions 187 to 211). The compatibility of lever 2 responses and UCS retrieval responses was matched to the previous compatibility of lever 2 and lever 1 responses by positioning the pellet delivery tube 26 cm from lever 2. The results of this classical–operant schedule are presented in Figure 2.18. Baseline response rates on lever 2 were dependent upon the duration of the prefood stimulus for all subjects. For subjects 1 and 3, lever 2 rates were suppressed during the 15- and 50-sec stimuli and slightly decreased during the 100-sec stimulus. Concomitantly, the rate of recorded stimulus-orienting responses was most increased during the 15- and 50-sec stimuli and least increased during the 100-sec stimulus. For subject 2, lever 2 rates were suppressed during the 15-sec stimulus, marginally decreased during the 50-sec stimulus, and remained unchanged during the 100-sec stimulus. Stimulus-orienting responses concurrently increased during the 15-sec stimulus, marginally increased during the 50-sec stimulus, and remained relatively unchanged during the 100-sec stimulus. For all subjects, recorded UCS retrieval responses were at a zero rate during the stimulus and only increased during the UCS pellet delivery cycle.

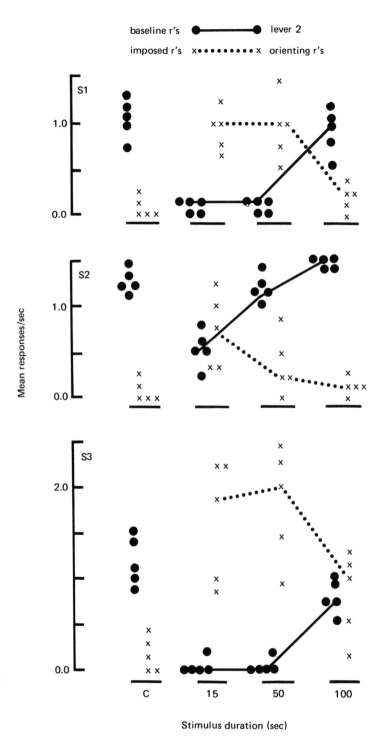

Figure 2.18. Baseline rate on lever 2 and concurrent rate of conditioned orienting responses as a function of the duration of an appetitive Pavlovian CS. For comparison, the data plotted at C give the response rates during the control period preceding the 15-sec stimulus. The rate of orienting responses is the frequency of contact with the CS measured in 200-millisec units divided by CS duration. Each data point is the mean of two trials in each of the final five sessions.

The interactions between lever 2 responses, stimulus-orienting responses, and UCS retrieval responses are presented in Figure 2.19 for individual trials at each stimulus duration. A changeover from lever-pressing to stimulus-orienting responses occurred at the onset of the 15-sec stimulus, followed by a second changeover from orienting responses to UCS retrieval responses after stimulus offset, which in turn was followed by a third changeover from UCS retrieval responses back to lever pressing. Subjects 1 and 3 emitted stimulus-orienting responses throughout the 50-sec stimulus, while subject 2 irregularly alternated between lever pressing and brief orienting responses. During the 100-sec stimulus, each subject only intermittently changed over to stimulus-orienting responses. A high local rate of either lever-pressing, stimulus-orienting, or UCS retrieval responses was associated with a low local rate of the other two available responses. Lever-pressing and UCS retrieval responses were simultaneously decreased during retrieval of the operant reinforcers from food cup 1 mounted on the stimulus display panel (Figure 2.19, traces D and E).

These findings are consistent with the notion that prefood stimuli superimposed upon operant procedures simultaneously control the rates of concurrent responses. The alteration in the rate of each response seems to be intimately related to the duration of the prefood stimulus. For all subjects, the operant rate was decreased and approximated a direct function of stimulus duration, while stimulus-orienting responses concomitantly increased and approximated

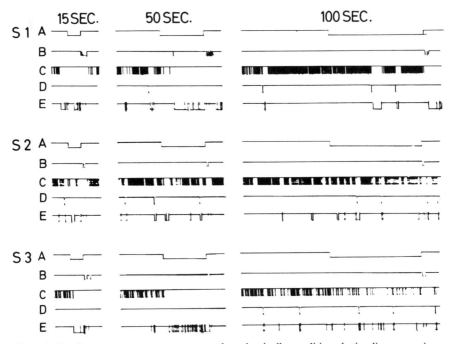

Figure 2.19. Concurrent response patterns when classically conditioned stimuli are superimposed upon operant baselines. A, CS duration; B, contact with UCS food cup; C, baseline lever 2 responses reinforced on VR 80; D, delivery of operant reinforcers; E, contact with CS display panel.

an inverse function of stimulus duration. Similar to the results of Experiment VI, the local rate of one recorded response was inversely related to the local rate of concurrently available responses. Furthermore, the results again indicate that physical incompatibility is not necessary for reciprocal interactions between concurrent responses. The present results, in agreement with previous data (Davis and Kreuter, 1972; Henton, 1972), then amplify the suggestion that prefood stimuli combined with operant schedules may have more extensive effects than the simple alteration of a single response.

The multiple response interactions and changeovers during the prefood stimuli are quite similar to the response interactions during the comparable pre-schedule change stimuli in Experiment VI: in both experiments, baseline operant rates were decreased when the rate of a second response was increased; the rates of both recorded responses were simultaneously decreased when the rate of a third response was increased; and the interactions between responses did not match reinforcer value and were not dependent upon response incompatibility. In combination, the data suggest that the competing response analysis might be successfully applied to a variety of concurrent reinforcement procedures.

Discussion

A common thread binding this series of experiments together is the fact that alterations in the patterning of one response seem to be sufficient to change the rate characteristics of other concurrently available responses. In hindsight, the rate interactions are not limited to a few isolated occurrences, but are found before, during, and after presentation of a stimulus terminated by a response-independent event. The evidence suggests that the pattern of concurrent responses during such preevent stimuli is related to both stimulus duration and the parameters of the response-independent event. The mutual response interactions recorded in Experiments V, VI, and VII are particularly consistent with the competing response analyses of Brady and Hunt, Weiskrantz, and others. The competing response interpretation is also quite similar to analyses that suggest that conditioned reinforcers, such as stimuli paired with food or shock, may function as discriminative stimuli that control specific responses (review by Kelleher and Gollub, 1962). More recent results, for example, demonstrate that stimuli paired with intracranial stimulation, which do not "require" responses, nevertheless control the rate of preparatory and orienting behaviors (e.g., Pliskoff et al., 1964; Huston and Brozek, 1972).

A general form of the competing response interpretation has suggested that concurrent classical–operant schedules may be analyzed as procedures that superimpose one set of responses upon a second, divergent set of responses (Henton and Brady, 1970; Henton, 1972). The local rate of individual elements in each response set may be intimately dependent upon the local rate of other behaviors in the subject's repertoire. Additive response interactions ("summation of excitation") as well as competing response interactions ("inhibition") may then be at least partially dependent upon the qualitative and quantitative topographical characteristics of each response element.

Unfortunately, this type of analysis clashes with contemporary emotional, motivational, and inhibition theories, which argue that classical–operant interactions are independent of peripheral response patterns. Nevertheless, the data are consistent with suggestions that subjects are in fact responding during behavioral "pauses" and inhibition procedures, and that the patterns of unrecorded responses are determined by observable events (Sidman, 1960). The interactions between stimulus-orienting responses and operant responses observed in Experiments V and VI and recorded in Experiment VII also indicate that relevant behaviors may be omitted by recording only a single response. The results of Experiment VII, for example, demonstrate that appetitive classical–appetitive operant conditioning may have multiple behavioral effects and may not be a simple interaction between Pavlovian and operant processes. This rich variety and complexity of local response interactions is simply not effectively described by one or two explanatory states. Perhaps the diversity of observed rates and patterns of responding could be assumed to match a corresponding molecular diversity of emotions, motivations, or other underlying processes. In the latter assumption, however, the hypothesized state variable would be redundant and little more than the specific response pattern from which it is inferred; rather, the interactions between lever-pressing responses, orienting responses, retrieval responses, changeover responses, etc., may be more directly related to empirical parameters. This interpretation, of course, is simply the reiteration of previous functional analyses in which response rates are directly related to real variables and experimental procedures (Sidman, 1960).

Interactions Between Programmed and Superstitious Operants (Experiment VIII)*

Experiment VIII

Our next concern was the application of the response pattern analysis to the third schedule combination of negative classical–positive operant conditioning. Hoffman and Barrett (1971) and Stein et al. (1971) had just reported that suppression of operant responses may be associated with freezing during preshock stimuli. A concurrent response interpretation would then anticipate that the interactions between freezing and operant responses must be keyed to schedule parameters such as UCS intensity and CS duration. The initial purpose of this study was to record the concurrent rates of operant and classical conditioned responses as a function of UCS shock intensity. However, a flaw in the shock delivery system resulted in an unprogrammed or adventitious operant avoidance contingency—all behaviors with the common property of moving the shock electrodes would disrupt electrical continuity in the shock circuit and

---

* Experiment conducted at the University of Oxford, from October to December 1972, by W. Henton.

modify the 30-millisec shock. The equipment artifact effectively altered the negative classical conditioning into a discrete trial operant avoidance schedule. The resultant behaviors, although clearly artifactual, are directly relevant to several conflicting interpretations. Weiskrantz (1968) suggested that suppression during a preshock stimulus may be due to unprogrammed competing responses that operantly modify the unconditioned stimulus. Second, negative classical conditioning and discrete trial operant avoidance conditioning might have common properties when superimposed upon reference baselines (e.g., Henton and Iversen, 1973). Alternatively, Maier et al. (1969) argued that adventitious reinforcement has received limited experimental examination and may not be sufficient to generate superstitious behaviors in procedures using response-independent shock. The present experiment was therefore continued in order to examine the theoretical and empirical implications of superstitious behaviors generated by preshock stimuli. The serendipitous purpose was to record the mutual interactions between unprogrammed shock avoidance responses and positively reinforced operant responses as a function of shock intensity.

The subjects were two white Careneaux pigeons trained in a standard Camden Instrument pigeon box. Pecking responses on the center key were reinforced with 3.0-sec access to grain on a random interval 64-sec schedule. Click rates of 5, 15, and 50/sec were used as the preshock stimuli and were diffusely presented throughout the experimental room containing the conditioning chamber (to prevent specific orienting responses elicited by a localized CS). Each auditory stimulus was presented for three 30-sec trials in each of five adaptation sessions and then terminated by a 30-millisec shock of 0.1, 1.3, and 2.6 ma, respectively. The subject's activity was observed via a closed-circuit television system and was recorded with an ultrasonic activity recorder. Key pecking and overt activity were recorded during each stimulus and during the immediately preceding 30-sec interval.

Key-pecking rates during the three preshock stimuli are given in Figure 2.20 for each subject and session. The acquisition of differential key-pecking rates during the stimuli followed a similar biphasic pattern for both subjects. Initially, key-pecking rates were approximately equal during all stimuli and independent of the shock intensity terminating each trial. Over subsequent sessions, key pecking stabilized at baseline rates during the 0.1-ma stimulus but was progressively and differentially suppressed during the 1.3- and 2.6-ma stimuli.

Observed daily on the closed-circuit television system, each subject progressively developed idiosyncratic, stereotyped behaviors during the stimuli. Onset of either the 1.3- or 2.6-ma stimulus produced a changeover from key pecking to pecking the shock electrodes and vigorous jumping (subject 1), or to wing flapping and clockwise turning movements (subject 2). Both subjects continued to key peck during the 0.1-ma stimulus. The stereotyped behaviors prompted a reexamination of the shock system following the 12th session, and we found that the shock circuit was closed only when the shock commutator was stationary. Virtually any rotation or vibration of the commutator resulted in a disruption of the electrical continuity within the circuit. Secondly, shock was deliv-

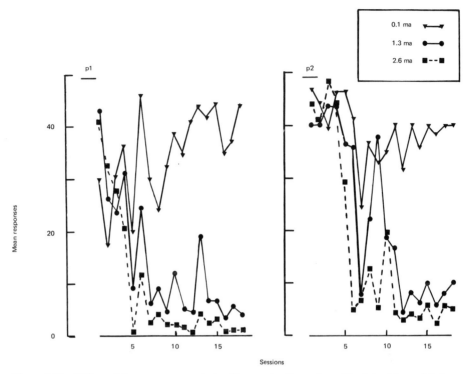

Figure 2.20. Differential response rates during 30-sec stimuli terminated by 0.1-, 1.3-, and 2.6-ma shocks. Each data point is the mean of three trials per session.

ered through beaded-chain wing-band electrodes, which also have poor electrical continuity when in motion. The flaws in the shock circuit thus combined to define an unprogrammed class of behaviors that would attenuate the response-independent shock. The experiment was nevertheless continued, and the interactions between key pecking and stereotyped avoidance behaviors were recorded during the preshock stimuli.

Figure 2.21 presents the relationship between key pecking and activity as a function of shock intensity. Key pecking decreased and molar activity concurrently increased as monotonic functions of the shock intensity paired with each stimulus. Relative to control periods, the wing flapping and electrode pecking during the preshock stimuli generated more gross activity than key pecking at the moderately high rate of approximately 1.3 responses/sec. As a supplement to the gross activity data, the avoidance behaviors observed throughout the experiment were manually recorded during sessions 17 and 18 (one observer). The mean frequency of pecking the shock electrodes by subject 1 was 0.0, 12.0, and 19.5, and the mean frequency of wing flapping by subject 2 was 0.0, 8.5, and 14.0 during the stimuli terminated by 0.1, 1.3, and 2.6 ma, respectively. At all shock intensities for both subjects, key pecking was at a zero rate when the unprogrammed behaviors increased, and conversely, key pecking was at locally high rates when wing flapping or electrode pecking was at a zero rate.

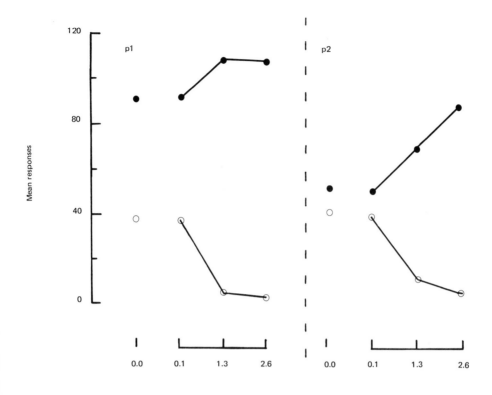

Shock ma

Figure 2.21. Key pecking and activity during 30-sec preshock stimuli as a function of shock intensity. For comparison, the data plotted at 0.0 are the response rates during the 30-sec control period preceding the 0.1-ma stimulus. Each data point is the mean of the final 10 trials. Black circles, activity; white circles, key peck.

Discussion

The results suggest that key pecking by pigeons may be suppressed during discrete stimuli that maintain a high rate of unprogrammed shock avoidance response. The results also demonstrate that adventitious reinforcement by the response-independent delivery of shock is not only sufficient to generate superstitious behaviors, but that the effects are differential and dependent upon shock intensity. The graded suppression is quite similar to the differential effects of shock intensity in negative classical–positive operant conditioning (Annau and Kamin, 1961; Henton and Jordan, 1970). This behavioral comparison suggests that operant responses may be suppressed by unprogrammed shock avoidance responses as well as classical conditioned freezing responses during discrete trial procedures.

One distinction between the competing respondent and competing operant analyses of conditioned suppression (Brady and Hunt, 1955; Weiskrantz, 1968) is this possibility of adventitious operant reinforcement by the response-independent UCS. The competing operant and competing respondent accounts, however, are frequently placed in theoretical opposition as mutually contradictory systems. Alternatively, the effects of classical–operant and operant–operant combinations may be quite similar and equally dependent upon mutual interactions between the local rates of concurrent resonses (Henton, 1972; Henton and Iversen, 1973; Iversen, 1974, 1975a, 1975c). The competing operant and competing respondent interpretations may then be both accurate and similar concurrent schedules analyses rather than mutually conflicting interpretations.

Suppression of Classically Conditioned Responses by Superimposed Operant Responses (Experiment IX)*

The influence of emotional theories upon conditioned suppression research has resulted in a singular emphasis upon the alteration of operant rates during the superimposed classical conditioning procedures. The strength and perhaps weakness of such emotional interpretations is the proposition that underlying classical conditioning processes are measured not by classically conditioned responses, but by the concurrent operant response (Rescorla and Soloman, 1967). Nevertheless, we have reason to believe that the behavioral effects may be more extensive than the stimulus-bound disruption of operant responses. As one instance, the responses controlled by the classical conditioning procedures may be reciprocally disrupted by the superimposed operant responses (Experiment III). Behaviors maintained by the classical conditioning contingencies may then be suppressed by concurrent operant responses, in the same fashion that baseline operant responses are altered by concurrent classical conditioning. In this perspective, operant rates would substantially alter rather than measure classical conditioning processes.

The current literature, unfortunately, does not provide a direct comparison of conditioned responses in the presence and absence of concurrent operant procedures. However, previous data indicate that activity by pigeons is *increased* during simple negative classical conditioning (Longo et al., 1962), but *decreased* when the negative classical conditioning is combined with operant conditioning (Hoffman and Barrett, 1971; Stein et al., 1971). Together, the two sets of data imply that the operant procedure must suppress the behaviors elicited by superimposed classical conditioning.

Experiment IX

The purpose of the present study was to further examine the suppressive effects of operantly reinforced key pecking upon classically conditioned freezing responses. In Phase A, three different auditory stimuli were randomly presented and terminated by different shock intensities. In Phase B, key pecking

---

* Experiment conducted at the University of Oxford, from January to April 1973, by W. Henton.

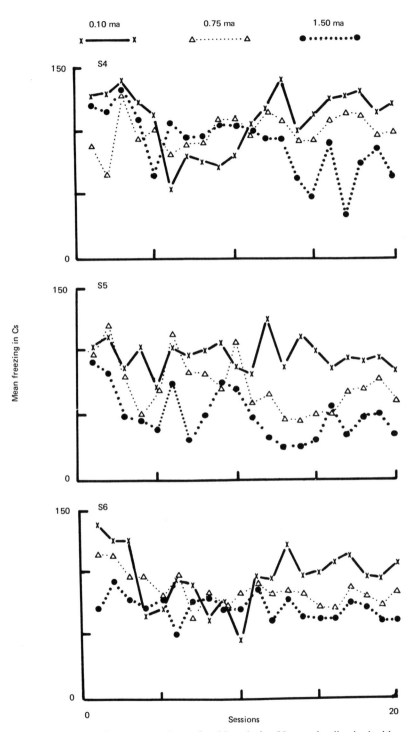

Figure 2.22. Freezing responses by each subject during 30-sec stimuli paired with response-independent shock of 0.10, 0.75, and 1.50 ma. Each data point is the mean of three trials per session.

reinforced on an operant schedule was superimposed upon the classical conditioning baseline of Phase A. The previous reports (Longo et al., 1962; Hoffman and Barrett, 1971) suggest that freezing responses would be an inverse function of shock intensity in Phase A, but a direct function of shock intensity in Phase B. Further, a response interaction analysis suggests that the local rate of concurrent key pecking would be inversely related to the freezing response rate across all shock intensities.

The apparatus described in Experiment VIII was repaired and used in the present study. Three experimentally naive pigeons were first habituated to the experimental chamber (3 sessions) and then given 20 sessions of classical conditioning acquisition. The 5, 15, and 50 clicks/sec stimuli were presented in a randomized order within each session and terminated by a 30-millisec shock of 0.10, 0.75, and 1.50 ma, respectively. Stimulus duration was 30 sec on all trials, and each stimulus was presented three times per session. A freezing response was defined as a zero frequency of activity recorded by the ultrasonic monitor during a 200-millisec interval.

The results of this simple classical conditioning procedure are given in Figure 2.22. Freezing during each stimulus was rather variable across the first 5 to 10 sessions for each subject. A differential pattern during the conditioned stimuli was apparent over the final 10 sessions, with freezing at low rates during the 1.50-ma stimulus, and at progressively higher rates during the 0.75- and 0.10-ma stimuli. Freezing was an inverse function of shock intensity for all subjects over the final sessions. Freezing was relatively unchanged during additional blank control trials, and was approximately comparable to the freezing recorded during the 0.10-ma stimulus.

The seemingly inconsistent pattern of freezing across subjects during early acquisition (Figure 2.22) was partially determined by a sequential dependence of freezing upon the preceding UCS, and therefore at least partially determined by the randomized sequence of CS–UCS trials. Figure 2.23 presents the frequency of freezing during each CS as a function of the shock intensity on the preceding trial ($N - 1$) during the initial and final sessions. In the first five sessions, freezing during each CS was related to the UCS intensity on the immediately preceding trial, with the amount of freezing during any stimulus a direct function of the preceding UCS intensity. The single exception is that freezing by subject 6 during the 0.75-ma stimulus was independent of the preceding trial. In comparison, over the final five sessions, freezing during one trial was relatively independent of the UCS on the preceding trial.

For a more detailed analysis, freezing was also recorded in successive 6-sec intervals within the prestimulus, stimulus, and poststimulus periods of each trial. Figure 2.24 presents the within-trial analysis for trials 1, 15, and 60 with each CS. Each column compares the pattern of freezing across successive trials with each CS, and each row compares freezing across the three different stimuli within the same trial. The trial-by-trial data for subjects 5 and 6 were qualitatively comparable to the data for subject 4. In the prestimulus period, freezing had no systematic pattern either within or across successive trials. Within each CS, the freezing pattern was initially dependent upon the previous UCS (trial

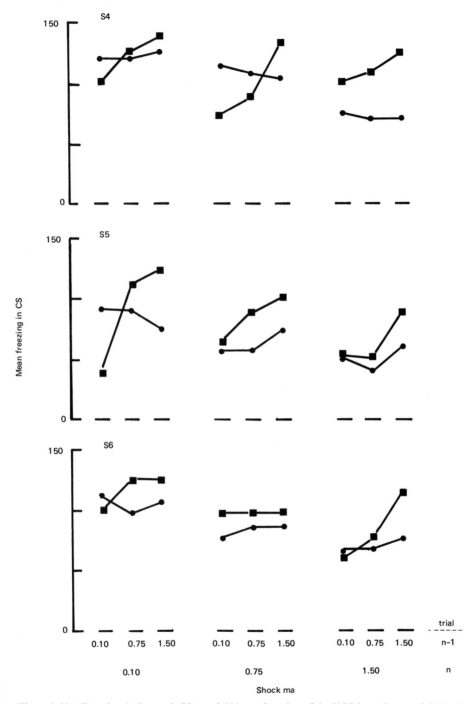

Figure 2.23. Freezing during each CS on trial N as a function of the UCS intensity on trial $N - 1$. Data for the first five sessions (squares) and the last five sessions (circles) are presented for each subject.

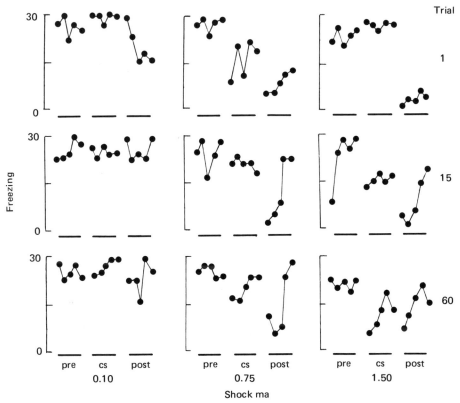

Figure 2.24. Distribution of freezing in the 30-sec pre-CS, CS, and post-CS intervals of individual trials by subject 4. Each data point represents the absolute frequency of freezing in successive 6-sec intervals within trials 1, 15, and 60 of each CS.

1), but only dependent upon the paired shock intensity during trial 60. In these final trials, freezing decreased at CS onset, followed by an increase to higher rates across succeeding 6-sec periods within the CS–UCS interval. Both the initial decrease and final rate of freezing was an inverse function of UCS intensity. During the postshock period of each trial, freezing was generally an inverse function of UCS intensity in the early acquisition sessions. However, the freezing elicited by the 1.50-ma UCS gradually increased over sessions and eventually equalled the pattern of freezing elicited by the lower 0.75-ma UCS in the final acquisition sessions. Postshock freezing had no systematic pattern following the 0.10-ma UCS either within trials or across subjects.

In Phase B, stimulus and control trials were not presented during the next 20 sessions, and each subject was operantly trained to peck the center response key. The reinforcement schedule was gradually changed from continuous reinforcement to random interval (RI) 64 sec across the first 12 sessions, with keypecking rates stabilizing over the next 8 sessions with the RI 64 sec schedule. The operant reinforcement procedure was then superimposed upon the previously established defensive classical conditioning baseline for 20 additional sessions.

As shown in Figure 2.25, the superimposed operant schedule disrupted the pattern of freezing during each CS for all subjects. Freezing was most disrupted, and suppressed, during the 0.10-ma CS, and least disrupted during the 1.50-ma CS throughout the 20 classical–operant sessions. For subjects 4 and 6, freezing decreased to zero during the 0.10-ma CS, when the rate of key pecking was relatively high. Conversely, key pecking was reduced to zero by concurrent freezing during the 0.75- and 1.50-ma stimuli. For subject 5, key pecking suppressed freezing during the 0.10-ma CS, freezing suppressed key pecking during the 1.50-ma CS, and there was intermediate rates of both responses during the 0.75-ma CS.

Patterns of key pecking and freezing during successive 6-sec intervals within individual trials are described in Figure 2.26 for subject 4. Again, the behavior of subjects 5 and 6 was qualitatively comparable to the response patterns of subject 4. During trial 1, a changeover from key pecking to freezing occurred at the onset of each of the three different CSs. A differential response pattern gradually developed over sessions, with key pecking at relatively high and un-changed rates during the 0.10-ma CS but suppressed during the CSs paired with the 0.75- and 1.50-ma shock. On the other hand, freezing was at a zero rate throughout the 0.10-ma CS, but progressively increased to higher rates during

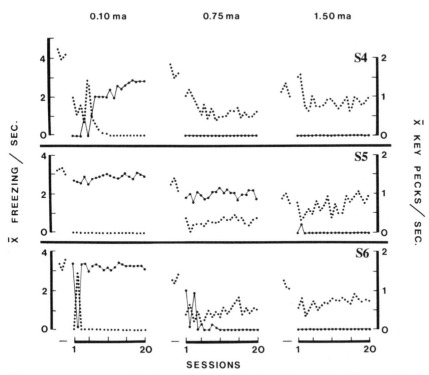

Figure 2.25. Mean rate of freezing (unconnected dots) and key pecking (connected dots) during superimposed 30-sec stimuli paired with 0.10-, 0.75-, and 1.50-ma shock (columns) for each of three subjects (rows). For comparison, freezing during the preceding simple classical conditioning is given in the left portion of each panel. All data points are the means of three trials per session.

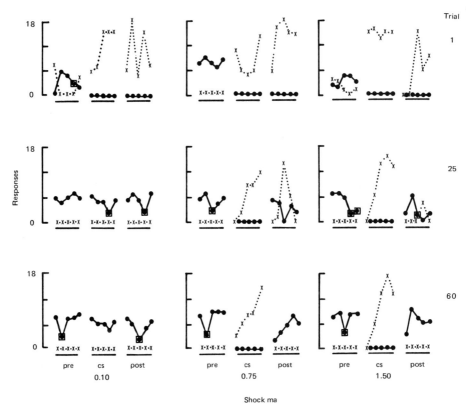

Figure 2.26. Distribution of freezing (x) and key pecking (circles) within the 30-sec pre-CS, CS, and post-CS intervals of individual trials for subject 4. Each data point is the absolute frequency of each response in successive 6-sec intervals within trials 1, 25, and 60 for each CS. Squares represent the delivery of grain reinforcement contingent upon key pecking.

the 0.75- and 1.50-ma CSs. Within the post-UCS interval, freezing occurred at high rates during the initial trials and then systematically decreased with increasing key-pecking rates over trials with each CS. The local rate of key pecking was also suppressed during the 3-sec presentation of the response-contingent operant reinforcer (for example, during the prestimulus periods of trial 60 with each CS). Thus, a high rate of either key pecking or freezing would predict a low rate of the alternative response. However, a low rate of one recorded response would not invariably predict a high rate of the second response rather than the third response of consuming the operant reinforcer.

Discussion

The present data clearly demonstrate that the pattern of classically conditioned freezing was markedly altered by the superimposed operant reinforcement schedule; that is, freezing was an inverse function of shock intensity with the simple classical conditioning procedure (Phase A), but a direct function of shock intensity with the concurrent classical–operant procedure (Phase B). The disruptive effects of a concurrent operant schedule were therefore quite substantial, and in fact reversed the functional relationship between conditioned freezing and UCS intensity. The CS effects then replicate the seemingly paradoxical reports of decreased freezing during defensive classical conditioning (Longo et al., 1962) but increased freezing when the classical conditioning is superimposed upon operant baselines (Stein et al., 1971).

The paradoxical effects of classical and concurrent classical–operant conditioning might be resolved, however, by an analysis of the reciprocal relationship between key pecking and freezing. Because of this relationship, freezing was not only differentially affected during each CS, but was also disrupted during the intertrial interval. As a result, freezing during the CS is compared to different control levels in the two procedures, with opposite response patterns of high freezing–low key-pecking rates during the intertrial interval of the classical conditioning (Phase A), but low freezing–high key-pecking rates during the same intertrial interval with the classical–operant procedure (Phase B). As one example, the CS paired with 1.50-ma shock elicited approximately equal freezing during the classical conditioning and the concurrent classical–operant conditioning. However, the same rate of freezing was decreased relative to the high control rates in Phase A, but increased relative to the low control rates in Phase B. Similar effects are apparent in a comparison of the freezing pattern across the different CSs, with the inverse relationship between freezing and UCS intensity changed to a direct function by the reciprocal interactions with key pecking. The seemingly contradictory effects of classical conditioning in the presence and absence of a concurrent operant schedule may thus be due to systematic response interactions, which in turn provides some strong evidence for reciprocal response patterning in classical–operant schedules.

The interdependent nature of classical and operant responses would also address the frequent attribution of invariant and unconditional properties to the Pavlovian UCS. Previous investigators such as Kimmel (1965) have observed that the responses elicited by a UCS may be neither constant nor unconstrained. Kimble (1961), for example, reported changes in the magnitude of unconditioned responses elicited by the UCS in classical eyelid conditioning, and concluded that the unconditioned responses may be inhibited by the sequential pairing of CS and UCS. Similarly, the progressive changes in postshock freezing in Phase A also argue that the effects of a UCS are not constant over successive acquisition trials. The point that we wish to make here, however, is that freezing elicited by each UCS was also markedly altered by superimposing a concurrent operant reinforcement schedule in Phase B. The unconditioned behavioral effects of a UCS, like the conditioned effects of a CS, might therefore be equally conditional upon concurrent as well as sequential experimental events.

Such conditional rather than unconditional UCS effects would then be intimately involved in concurrent classical–operant schedules. Although post-UCS effects are not frequently discussed, occasional papers have reported transient changes in baseline operant rates following UCS delivery (Smith,

1970). Key pecking rates in the present study were similarly disrupted follow-ing UCS delivery in the early sessions of Phase B (i.e., trial 1, Figure 2.26). The transiently decreased operant rates were generated by an equally transient high rate of freezing responses following the UCS and extending into the subsequent intertrial interval. As noted above, however, this pattern quickly reversed after a few trials or sessions, with operant key pecking returning to baseline rates immediately postshock with a concomitant suppression of the unconditioned freezing elicited by the UCS. We therefore have some reason to believe that extensive response interactions occur throughout classical–operant schedules, including interactions with unconditioned as well as conditioned Pavlovian re-sponses.

As a final note, reciprocal interactions of this type do not seem to be re-stricted to the concurrent responses separately maintained by each condition-ing component. The within-trial analysis also shows similar behavioral interac-tions occurring within the operant schedule. For all subjects, key pecking was locally inhibited by the retrieval and consumption of the grain reinforcers deliv-ered on the operant schedule. Identical local interactions were observed be-tween operant lever pressing and consummatory responses in Experiments II to VII, and also between operant and schedule-induced collateral responses (Iversen, 1975b, 1976). Apparently, reciprocal interactions occur between the responses generated within each conditioning component and are not limited to concurrent responses generated by different conditioning components.

The primary and secondary response interactions in the present study might therefore extend the generality of a competing or concurrent response analysis. The alteration and indeed reversal of classical conditioning functions, however, is not wholly consistent with the traditional conception of baseline response rates as measures of potential processes underlying a superimposed schedule. Thus, operant rates may not measure superimposed classical conditioning processes, or, in the present study, classical conditioned responses may not measure superimposed operant processes. Rather, the "measuring" response may fundamentally alter the "measured" process. In a similar fashion, the pat-tern of one response may be a determinant, not a measure, of other responses and processes in simple and complex operant schedules (Part II). Behavioral conditioning procedures therefore seem to be more accurately characterized by response interdependence rather than response independence.

Summary

The present set of experiments consistently shows that the local rate of one recorded response will be effected by changes in the local rate of other concur-rently available responses. The interdependent relationship seems to be true across a variety of parameters and classical–operant schedules, ranging from CS duration to UCS intensity across positive or negative classical conditioning procedures scheduled with positive or negative operant conditioning proce-dures. Our current working generality is summarized in Figure 2.27. Four gen-eral types of concurrent schedules may be generated by superimposing a classi-

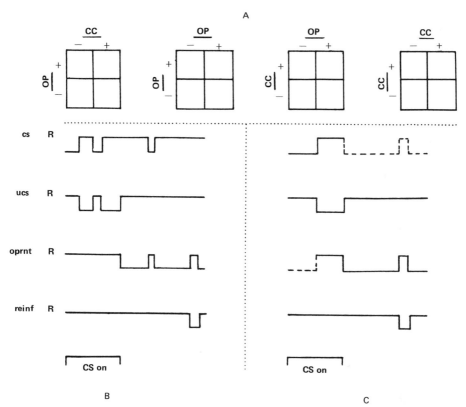

Figure 2.27. **A.** Graph of the possible combinations of positive and negative classical or operant conditioning superimposed upon positive or negative classical or operant baselines. **B.** Mutual interactions between physically incompatible responses when classical conditioning is superimposed upon operant conditioning. Event pens deflect downward for the duration of each response. **C.** Interactions between classical and operant conditioned responses when two responses are physically identical. CS R, orienting responses to the CS; UCS R, responses elicited by UCS; oprnt R, operant or reinforced response; reinf R, responses generated by contingent reinforcer.

cal or operant conditioning schedule upon another classical or operant schedule. Within each of the general combinations, a positive or negative conditioning procedure may be superimposed upon another positive or negative conditioning procedure, yielding four specific procedures within each general combination. The first general concurrent schedule is the more common classical conditioning superimposed upon operant baselines (Experiments I, II, and VII). Second, a discrete-trial operant procedure could be combined with a more continuous operant conditioning baseline (Experiments V and VI; see also Part II). Third, operant procedures may be superimposed upon preestablished classical conditioning baselines (Experiments III and IXB). Finally, positive or negative classical conditioning could be superimposed upon another positive or negative classical conditioning procedure (Part III).

Each of the four general combinations, or 16 specific procedures, may control the rate of at least four responses in the subject's repertoire. Classical–operant schedules, for example, may control (1) orienting or "autoshaping" responses toward or away from a CS paired with food or shock, (2) retrieval of the UCS food pellet or responses elicited by shock, (3) baseline operant responses, and (4) the reinforcing or contingent response. If the responses are topographically dissimilar (Figure 2.27B), then an increase in the local rate of one response may be sufficient to suppress the local rate of the other three responses. For instance, any procedure that increases stimulus-orienting responses during the CS would simultaneously decrease the rate of preparatory UCS responses. Conversely, procedures that increase UCS responses may decrease CS-orienting responses. This is, if you will, a competing response analysis within the classical conditioning component itself. Similar relationships have also been described within the operant conditioning schedule (e.g., Dunham, 1972; review in Part II, this volume). This interpretation has some obvious similarities with Premack's suggestion that response–response relationships may be critical factors within conditioning schedules. However, the Premackian analysis is primarily concerned with the reinforcing and punishing effects of sequential responses (Schaeffer and Premack, 1961; Premack, 1965, 1971; Schaeffer, 1965), whereas the present formulation is an analysis of the incremental and decremental effects of concurrent responses.

If two of the responses controlled by the classical and operant schedules are identical, as the operant and CS-orienting responses in Figure 2.27C, then an increase in the rate of one response would obviously increase the "alternate" identical response. Lo Lordo (1971) has previously suggested that key pecking by pigeons will be increased by the addition of autoshaped responses to the same key during a prefood stimulus. If this type of analysis is accurate, then we should be able to increase as well as decrease operant rates during superimposed classical conditioning procedures by (1) separately controlling low or moderate rates of the same physical response with each schedule component, and (2) maintaining a low or zero rate of other concurrent responses.

The incremental effect has been confirmed in unpublished student projects in the Oxford laboratories, in which CS location was manipulated relative to the operant manipulandum. Key pecking by pigeons was relatively higher during a prefood stimulus when the auditory CS was placed immediately below the operant manipulandum, but suppressed when the CS was presented on the other side of the chamber. Observation indicated that orienting responses toward the location of the CS directed the subject to the operant pecking key in the former case, but led the subject away from the pecking key in the latter case. Of some interest, a reverse interaction occurs during preshock stimuli, with the subject moving away from rather than approaching the CS. In this case, we have found that operant key pecking is more suppressed when the negative CS is located immediately beneath the pecking key rather than at some distance. The relative location of the CS also seems to play a role in the relative location of rats during superimposed stimuli formerly paired with shock or food. Although tentative, these results are consistent with Lo Lordo's suggestion and would be supportive of a concurrent responses–concurrent schedules analysis. We suspect, however, that space, like time, may be a rather empty variable, with the more important aspect being the pattern of responses elicited by the different spatial and temporal characteristics of the CS. The CS location per se may be as ineffectual and irrelevant as any experimentally neutral stimulus, and may only effectively alter classical–operant rates when the different CS proximities control different overt response patterns (see also Lo Lordo et al., 1974).

Changes in operant responding during a superimposed CS, however, are only relative descriptions comparing response rates in two different time samples, the intertrial interval versus the CS–UCS interval. Previous investigators have importantly noted that operant acceleration may be only relative to a disrupted intertrial interval response rate, not to previous operant baselines (e.g., Meltzer and Brahlek, 1970). Conversely, operant responding during a negative classical conditioning procedure may be suppressed relative to previous operant baselines, but unchanged relative to the equally suppressed intertrial interval response rate (Brady, 1953). The relative characterization of CS response rates in classical–operant schedules can then be substantially dependent upon changes in responding during the intertrial interval. In the present Experiment I, for example, baseline avoidance rates gradually decreased across classical–operant sessions as well as gradually increasing during the CS. As a result, the recorded CS avoidance rate was slightly accelerated if compared to previous avoidance baselines, but markedly accelerated when compared to the disrupted avoidance pattern during the intertrial interval. An increased CS rate is then not necessarily an excitation of operant responding by superimposed classical conditioning, but may also involve a partial disruption of response patterns during the intertrial interval control period.

A similar alternation of classically conditioned freezing was found before and after superimposing a positive operant procedure in Experiments IXA and B. The freezing responses were maximally decreased during the intertrial interval and differentially suppressed during the CS as a function of UCS intensity. The description of increased freezing during the CS is then only relative to the low rates during the intertrial interval, and not an absolute facilitation of freezing by superimposed operant responses. The present results as well as previous data suggest that relatively increased CS response rates should not be categorically attributed to a generalized summation or facilitation of classical and operant processes; rather, relative and absolute acceleration could involve divergent operations of disrupting intertrial interval rates or accelerating CS response rates, respectively.

The above analysis is admittedly an oversimplification of the behaviors controlled by concurrent schedules. Given the four basic responses within classical–operant schedules, there must be sequences of changeover responses—a changeover from lever pressing to CS orienting responses, for example. Figure 2.28 presents a more detailed representation of the sequence of primary and changeover responses controlled by classical–operant conditioning. We believe that the changeover responses are both important and basically similar to the four primary responses. The changeover from operant responses to concur-

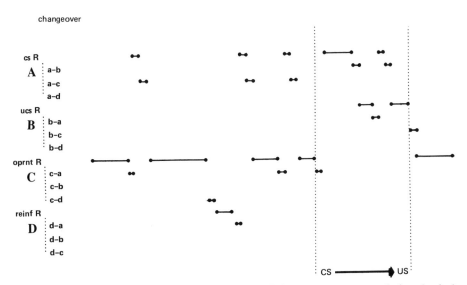

Figure 2.28. Interactions between basic responses and changeover responses during classical–operant conditioning. Time scale from left to right.

rent UCS responses, for example, may be partially controlled by the spatial and temporal characteristics of the response-independent event during CS–food pairings (Experiments I, II, and III) or preschedule change stimuli (Experiments V and VI). The changeover characteristics may be especially involved in determining the relative rates and patterning of physically incompatible responses—incompatible responses generally having longer sequences and durations of changeover responses than compatible responses. As shown in Experiment I, the changeover from lever pressing to UCS retrieval responses may be dependent upon the duration of the changeover sequence relative to the latency and duration of the UCS; that is, the changeover to UCS pellet retrieval occurred during the UCS when the changeover response was brief relative to the indefinitely available food pellets, but occurred during the CS when the changeover sequence was relatively longer than the limited availability of the UCS. Quite simply, any effective response must precede the delivery of a brief UCS. The schedule control of unrecorded changeover responses may therefore specify the temporal location of operant suppression either during the CS or during the UCS. Indeed, the continuum of changeover response duration may be at least one of the defining dimensions of physical compatibility–incompatibility. All this again emphasizes that the unrecorded changeover responses sum to an important fraction of the subject's behavior and may be an interesting set of variables in the analysis of classical–operant schedules. Unfortunately, we have at best been recording only one-fourth of the data during classical–operant combinations; at worst, one-sixteenth. This is not a very good record for any empirical science.

As shown in Figure 2.27, the present analysis holds that the effects of superimposed classical conditioning procedures may be duplicated by superimposed discrete-trial operant procedures. Previous data would suggest, for example, that discrete-trial avoidance procedures and CS shock pairings may have analogous effects upon baseline operant response rates. This interpretation is derived from the previous data of Desiderato and Newman (1971), the adventitious discrete-trial avoidance procedure of Experiment VIII, and previous comparisons of superimposed discriminative punishment and negative classical conditioning procedures (Brady and Hunt, 1955; Church, 1969; Orme-Johnson and Yarczower, 1974). In general, the previous studies indicate an approximately similar suppression of baseline responding, with perhaps slightly different parametric relationships, within discriminative punishment and negative classical conditioning procedures. More basically, the striking difference between signaled response-contingent and response-independent shock seems to be the changes in concurrent responses during the two procedures. Brady and Hunt (1955) reported that the response-contingent shock procedure engendered only a passive avoidance of the baseline response, with bursts of various other behaviors emitted throughout the discriminative stimulus. The response-independent shock procedure, however, had an opposite effect, with a high rate of one specific concurrent response (freezing) and a low rate of all other responses throughout the conditioned stimulus. The divergent response patterns suggest fundamentally different mechanisms underlying the admittedly similar operant suppression during superimposed discriminative punishment and negative classical conditioning procedures. In the former case, the punishment contingency only *eliminates* one response from the subject's repertoire, with no explicit control over other concurrent responses. In the latter case, the negative classical conditioning schedule actively *increases* the rate of one concurrent response, with a concomitant local suppression of all other responses (including the recorded baseline response). To speak loosely, the baseline suppression is a "cause" in the discriminative punishment procedure, but an "effect" in the negative classical conditioning procedure, of increased concurrent response rates.

The previous results could then suggest that conditioned suppression may be more analogous to a superimposed discrete-trial avoidance procedure, specifically controlling an increased rate of one response, than to a passive avoidance or discriminative punishment procedure, which specifically decreases the rate of one response. [Dinsmoor (1954) and Sidman (1960) have previously discussed the opposing functional contingencies in punishment and avoidance schedules.] The more recent work of Desiderato and Newman (1971) does suggest that a superimposed discrete-trial active avoidance procedure will generate concurrent response patterns similar to the conditioned suppression paradigm. Related experiments by Hoffman and Fleshler (1962) also demonstrate a suppression of operant baselines during a superimposed avoidance discriminative stimulus. Furthermore, the results of Experiment VIII suggest that discrete-trial shock avoidance responses and conditioned suppression of baseline responses are symmetrically related to UCS intensity. Thus, the preliminary data consistently demonstrate analogous response patterning when active avoidance or negative classical conditioning is superimposed upon operant baselines.

The discriminative punishment analogy, however, would seem to be especially appropriate during the acquisition of conditioned suppression in the on-the-baseline procedure. Initially, baseline response rates are suppressed during the CS without accompanying freezing responses; rather, the subjects move away from the operant manipulandum with abortive approach and tentative operant responses throughout the CS. The initial behavioral pattern is typical of the passive avoidance responses noted in discriminative punishment procedures. A consistent pattern of increased freezing throughout the CS only develops after elimination of the serial responses within the operant response chain. Our current interpretation is that conditioned suppression is a two-stage acquisition process in the on-the-baseline procedure, with passive avoidance effects in early trials followed by the classically conditioned acquisition of specific response patterns over subsequent trials.

Additional data suggest a similar equivalence of concurrent response patterns during superimposed stimuli paired with response-independent and response-contingent food. A comparison across the matched parameters and procedures of Experiments VI and VII, for example, would demonstrate a qualitative and quantitative similarity of interdependent behaviors when discriminative or conditioned stimuli are superimposed upon operant baselines. A concurrent response analysis would therefore be commensurate with the behavioral effects of discrete operant and classical conditioning procedures scheduled with continuous, ongoing operant baselines.

The concurrent response analysis is, of course, neither new nor currently unique. The examination of behavioral patterns in negative classical–positive operant schedules has been a signal feature of the competing response analysis of Brady and co-workers (reviews by Brady, 1971, 1975). The present analysis is at the same time somewhat more extensive yet more restricted than the original competing response interpretation. Given the expanded data base, the current interpretation is an extension of the formulation to include additional concurrent schedules (Henton and Brady, 1970; Henton, 1972). The approach is more restricted, however, in the analysis of only overt response interactions and does not include overt–covert response patterns. In addition, the interdependent relationship between responses during superimposed positive classical conditioning was previously discussed by Konorski (1967), and further concurrent response interpretations have more recently been reported by other investigators (Lo Lordo, 1971; Van Dyne, 1971; Miczek, 1973; Lo Lordo et al., 1974). Moreover, response interactions within operant conditioning were previously emphasized by Sidman (1960). Finally, some of the recording techniques and procedures described in the present experiments were rapidly replicated by Divas and Wikmark, in our laboratory, and subsequently by their associate E. Hearst in another laboratory.

And yet, in spite of substantial amounts of data, many theorists routinely "disprove" the existence of concurrent responses in classical–operant schedules. Indeed, the logical derivation of virtually all mediating hypothetical states within the conditioned suppression paradigm rests on the denial of behavioral interactions. One logic proposes that conditioned suppression must be due to fear, not competing behaviors, when the classical and operant procedures are separately conditioned prior to test combinations of the two components. The particular argument usually emphasizes the absence of any response requirement and the stimulus–stimulus contiguous nature of classical conditioning. Since classical conditioning does not "require" any particular response, no responses are available to interact with baseline operants during the classical–operant test sessions. The argument, however, would require a rather sweeping denial of some 50 years of data describing orienting, approach, and consummatory responses during classical conditioning procedures (Pavlov, 1927; Zener, 1937; Razran, 1961; Konorski, 1967). Most laboratory psychologists are more than reluctant to accept such an extreme and negative theoretical position. A related argument proposes that classical conditioning under curare somehow eliminates behavioral interactions in subsequent classical–operant sessions. However, curare administration hours or days before testing does not in any way eliminate behavior in the subsequent noncurarized state. Experiments using response prevention techniques during conditioning have clearly reported the presence, not the absence, of responses following the removal of the physical restraints (Pavlov, 1927; Zener, 1937; also see Solomon and Turner, 1962). The fundamental issue of conditioning under curare is not whether behavior is or is not required for classical conditioning, but whether classical conditioning is sufficient to generate behavior. The implication that procedural necessity is equivalent to behavioral sufficiency would seem to be inaccurate but is obviously amenable to empirical rather than logical demonstration.

A more common argument disproves response interactions by describing the responses that are *not* elicited during classical–operant schedules. The conspicuous element is a reluctance to describe the responses that *are* occurring. One paper "proved" that conditioned suppression could not be due to concurrent responses since CS-orienting behaviors occurred at a very low rate during the CS–UCS interval. Only later, in criticizing a different formulation, did the authors mention that the subjects spent most of the CS with the head in the food hopper. The absence of CS-orienting responses in this example is at best a rather elliptical description of the presence of competing food cup responses. The multitude of responses that are not occurring simply provides little or no information about the actual behaviors that are occurring. A zero rate of one response displayed on electronic counters does not exhaust the subject's response repertoire, not demonstrate a "behavioral inhibition" or a "behavioral pause," only a "recording pause". The empirical difficulty is that behavior is continuous and always occurring. Total inhibition may well be more descriptive of the observing behavior of the experimenter than the conditioned behavior of the subject.

A related issue is the absence of perfect negative correlations between the frequencies of any two responses in classical–operant conditioning. Imperfect correlational pairs are occasionally offered as a statistical demonstration of the independence of concurrent responses. However, as shown in Figures 2.9, 2.11, 2.13, 2.15, 2.17, and 2.19, operant responses may be locally suppressed by a number of different concurrent behaviors, ranging from CS-orienting responses, preparatory UCS approach responses, adventitious UCS avoidance responses, retrieval of the operant reinforcer, changeover responses, etc. A perfect correlation between the absence of one response and the presence of a second response would require a subject with but two responses in the behavioral repertoire. The expectation of a perfect "match" between one arbitrary pair of responses would be as improbable as expecting a response to "match" only one variable selected from the host of known controlling variables. An analogous error would be the negative proof that shock avoidance occurs in the absence of food reinforcement contingencies, with the proposition that positive reinforcement therefore cannot control operant responses. The fact that behavior can be controlled by a variety of different contingencies does not refute the fact that a specific contingency is sufficient, although not necessary, to control response rates. In a similar manner, a negative logic that the absence of response A does not specify concurrent behaviors is fundamentally irrelevant. The suppression of one response A neither requires nor specifies the specific presence of response B rather than response C, or D, or N. The argument is misleading and surely does not deny that the occurrence of response A is sufficient to decrease response B, as well as C, D, and N—sufficient but not necessary, since many other competing responses will also decrease the rate of response B. A partial independence of "not responding" should not be accepted as an independence "of responding." Such partial correlations summed over responses and time may accurately describe the complex interdependence of behaviors, but not response independence.

Our previous papers prepared over the last few years have uniformly accepted the theory based device of relabeling positive and negative classical conditioning as *prefood* or *preshock* stimuli. We have become progressively concerned with both the neutrality and accuracy of the relabeled terms. Traditionally, *prefood* and *preshock* stimuli are used as noncommital terms to prevent even the appearance of implying two-process dichotomies between operant and classical conditioning. The traditional theory testing of operant–respondant distinctions, such as the skeletal–autonomic or overt–covert dichotomies (Kimble, 1961), has resulted in the dismissal of "suspect" responses that do not neatly fit into the theoretical requirements. Overt motor responses are frequently ignored or denied in classical conditioning as irrelevant to the proper analysis of stimulus–stimulus association processes. The recent rediscovery of overt responses in classical conditioning (Pavlov, 1927, Zenor, 1937; Patton and Rudy, 1967) has now promoted the relabeling of positive classical conditioning as *autoshaping*. If overt motor responses are recorded during stimuli paired with food, then the procedure is autoshaping. However, if salivation is recorded, then the procedure is true classical conditioning. This segregation of overt responses from classical conditioning maintains the view that Pavlovian conditioning is the autonomic, covert, contiguity conditioning of associative states, uncontaminated by offending overt autoshaping responses.

The role of stimulus-reinforcer and response-reinforcer effects in autoshaping (Brown and Jenkins, 1968; Boakes et al., 1975; Schwartz and Gamzu, 1977) currently parallels previous discussions of associative states versus overt responses in "conditioned anxiety." Rather oddly, the autoshaping argument uniformly concedes whereas the "anxiety" argument most frequently denies that classical conditioning controls overt behaviors. The growing concern is that the description of overt responses during prefood and preshock stimuli are all too easily dismissed as mere examples of autoshaping rather than proper classical conditioning and may actually circumvent the accurate analysis of classical conditioning effects. If so, the cost of theory maintenance would be a subservient and segregated data analysis in place of the accepted view of inductive and deductive theory subservient to data. Hopefully, the time has at least recently past when theoretical explanations could profitably gainsay behavioral patterns in favor of more convenient "behavioral pauses" during superimposed Pavlovian conditioning.

In conclusion, the present data seem to be fundamentally inconsistent with the current use of a few molar state variables to explain classical and operant schedule effects. If response rates were in fact a measure of explanatory constructs, then the broad expanse of response patterns and interactions would seem to require an equal number of explanatory emotions, general emotional states, incentives, expectancies, inhibitions, etc. The varied effects of manipulating CS location, for example, could be attributed to a corresponding number of underlying motivations. Alternatively, the changes in operant baselines might be more directly attributed to the altered environmental space, or perhaps still more directly to the elicited behaviors maintained by the altered environment. The purpose of the present experiments, however, was not to create problems for other interpretations but to analyze the concurrent response patterns within a variety of different procedures and parameters. Ultimately, our argument is not so much that emotional–motivational theory cannot specify the patterns and distributions of concurrent responses, but that they should. Eventually, all interpretations, including the concurrent response analysis, will have to describe and explain the total pattern of responses within classical–operant conditioning.

Note:

This review of our work between 1970 and 1973 is taken from a prepared speech first presented at the Easter Conference, Cambridge, England, in March 1973. To emphasize that the analysis is neither new nor unique, related experiments and similar interpretations have now been reported by Hearst and Jenkins (1974), Karpicke et al. (1977), Roberts et al. (1977), and Schwartz and Gamzu (1977).

References

Annau, Z., and Kamin, L. J.: The conditioned emotional response as a function of the intensity of the US. *J. Comp. Physiol. Psychol., 54,* 428–432, 1961.
Anohkin, P. K.: The role of the orienting–exploratory reflex in the formation of the conditioned

reflex. In, L. G. Voronin, A. N. Leontiev, A. R. Luria, E. N. Sokolov, and O. S. Vinogradova (eds.): *Orienting Reflex and Exploratory Behavior.* Moscow, Academy of Pedagogical Science, 1958.

Azrin, N. H., and Hake, D. F.: Positive conditioned suppression: conditioned suppression using positive reinforcers as the unconditioned stimuli. *J. Exp. Anal. Behav.,* **12,** 167–173, 1969.

Boakes, R. A., Halliday, M. S., and Poli, M.: Response additivity: effects of superimposed free reinforcement on a variable-interval baseline. *J. Exp. Anal. Behav.,* **23,** 177–191, 1975.

Brady, J. V.: Does tetraethylammonium reduce fear. *J. Comp. Physiol. Psychol.,* **46,** 307–310, 1953.

Brady, J. V.: Emotion revisited. *J. Psychiatr. Res.,* **8,** 363–384, 1971.

Brady, J. V.: Toward a behavioral biology of emotion. In, L. Levi (ed.): *Emotions—Their Parameters and Measurement.* New York, Raven Press, 1975.

Brady, J. V., and Hunt, H. F.: An experimental approach to the analysis of emotional behavior. *J. Psychol.,* **40,** 313–325, 1955.

Brady, J. V., Kelly, D. D., and Plumlee, L.: Autonomic and behavioral responses of the rhesus monkey to emotional conditioning. *Annu. N. Y. Acad. Sci.,* **159,** 959–971, 1969.

Brady, J. V., Henton, W. W., and Ehle, A.: Some effects of emotional conditioning upon autonomic and electromyographic activity. Paper read at the Eastern Psychological Association, 1970. (Also described in Brady, 1971.)

Brown, P. L., and Jenkins, H. M.: Auto-shaping of the pigeon's key-peck. *J. Exp. Anal. Behav.,* **11,** 1–8, 1968.

Brownstein, A. J., and Hughes, R. G.: The role of response suppression in behavioral contrast: signalled reinforcement. *Psychonomic Sci.,* **18,** 50–52, 1970.

Brownstein, A. J., and Newsom, C.: Behavioral contrast in multiple schedules with equal reinforcement rates. *Psychonomic Sci.,* **18,** 25–26, 1970.

Bull, J. A., and Overmeir, J. B.: Incompatibility of appetitive and aversive conditioned motivation. *Proceedings of the 77th Annual Convention of the American Psychological Association,* vol. 4 (part 1), 1969, pp. 97–98.

Catania, A. C.: Concurrent performances: reinforcement interaction and response independence. *J. Exp. Anal. Behav.,* **6,** 253–263, 1963.

Catania, A. C.: Concurrent operants. In, W. K. Honig (ed.): *Operant Behavior: Areas of Research and Application.* New York, Appleton-Century-Crofts, 1966.

Catania, A. C.: Concurrent performances: inhibition of one response by reinforcement of another. *J. Exp. Anal. Behav.,* **12,** 731–734, 1969.

Church, R. M.: Response suppression. In, B. A. Campbell and R. M. Church (eds.): *Punishment and Aversive Behavior.* New York, Appleton-Century-Crofts, 1969.

Davis, H.: Conditioned suppression. a survey of the literature. *Psychonomic Monogr. [Suppl.],* **2,** 1968.

Davis, H., and Kreuter, C.: Conditioned suppression of an avoidance response by a stimulus paired with food. *J. Exp. Anal. Behav.,* **17,** 277–285, 1972.

Desiderato, O., and Newman, A.: Conditioned suppression produced in rats by tones paired with escapable or inescapable shock. *J. Comp. Physiol. Psychol.,* **77,** 427–431, 1971.

Dinsmoor, J. A.: Punishment: I. The avoidance hypothesis. *Psychol. Rev.,* **61,** 34–46, 1954.

Dunham, P. J.: Punishment: method and theory. *Psychol. Rev.,* **78,** 58–70, 1971.

Dunham, P. J.: Some effects of punishment upon unpunished responding. *J. Exp. Anal. Behav.,* **17,** 443–450, 1972.

Estes, W. K.: Outline of a theory of punishment. In, B. A. Campbell and R. M. Church (eds.): *Punishment and Aversive Behavior.* New York, Appleton-Century-Crofts, 1969.

Estes, W. K., and Skinner, B. F.: Some quantatative properties of anxiety. *J. Exp. Psychol.,* **29,** 390–400, 1941.

Falk, J. L.: Production of polydipsia in normal rats by an intermittent food schedule. *Science,* **133,** 195–196, 1961.

Ferster, C. B., and Skinner, B. F.: *Schedules of Reinforcement,* New York, Appleton-Century-Crofts, 1957.

Glickman, S. E., and Schiff, B. B.: A biological theory of reinforcement. *Psychol. Rev.,* **74,** 81–109, 1967.

Gottwald, P.: The role of punishment in the development of conditioned suppression. *Physiol. Behav.*, **2**, 283–286, 1967.

Grossen, N. E., Kostansek, D. J., and Bolles, R. C.: Effects of appetitive discriminative stimuli on avoidance behavior. *J. Exp. Psychol.*, **81**, 340–343, 1969.

Hake, D. F., and Powell, J.: Positive reinforcement and suppression from the same occurrence of the unconditioned stimulus in a positive conditioned suppression procedure. *J. Exp. Anal. Behav.*, **14**, 247–257, 1970.

Hearst, E., and Jenkins, H. M.: *Sign Tracking: The Stimulus–Reinforcer Relation and Directed Action.* Monograph of the Psychonomic Society, Austin, Texas, 1974.

Henton, W. W.: The effects of pre-schedule change stimuli upon avoidance behavior. *Rep. Neurophysiol. Inst.* (Kbh.) 34–35, 1970.

Henton, W. W.: Avoidance response rates during a pre-food stimulus in monkeys. *J. Exp. Anal. Behav.*, **17**, 269–275, 1972.

Henton, W. W., and Brady, J. V.: Operant acceleration during a pre-reward stimulus. *J. Exp. Anal. Behav.*, **13**, 205–211, 1970.

Henton, W. W., and Iversen, I. H.: Concurrent response rates during pre-event stimuli. Paper presented at the Easter Conference, Cambridge, March 1973, Abstract pp. 2–3.

Henton, W. W., and Jordan, J. J.: Differential conditioned suppression during pre-shock stimuli as a function of shock intensity. *Psychol. Record,* **20**, 9–16, 1970.

Herrnstein, R. J., and Morse, W. H.: Some effects of response independent positive reinforcement on maintained operant behavior. *J. Comp. Physiol. Psychol.*, **50**, 461–467, 1957.

Hoffman, H. S., and Barrett, J.: Overt activity during conditioned suppression: a search for punishment artifacts. *J. Exp. Anal. Behav.*, **16**, 343–348, 1971.

Hoffman, H. S., and Fleshler, M.: The course of emotionality in the development of avoidance. *J. Exp. Psychol.*, **64**, 288–294, 1962.

Huston, J. P., and Brozek, G.: Attempt to classically condition eating and drinking elicited by hypothalamic stimulation in rats. *Physiol. Behav.*, **8**, 973–977, 1972.

Iversen, I. H.: Behavioral interactions in concurrent reinforcement schedules. Paper presented at the English Experimental Analysis of Behavior Group, Bangor, 1974.

Iversen, I. H.: Concurrent responses during multiple schedules in rats. *Scand. J. Psychol.*, **16**, 49–54, 1975a.

Iversen, I. H.: Interactions between lever pressing and collateral drinking during VI with limited hold. *Psychol. Record,* **25**, 47–50, 1975b.

Iversen, I. H.: Reciprocal response interactions in concurrent variable-interval and discrete-trial fixed-ratio schedules. *Scand. J. Psychol.*, **16**, 280–284, 1975c.

Iversen, I. H.: Interactions between reinforced responses and collateral responses. *Psychol. Record,* **26**, 399–413, 1976.

Kamin, L. J.: Temporal and intensity characteristics of the conditioned stimulus. In, W. F. Prokasy (ed.): *Classical Conditioning.* New York, Appleton-Century-Crofts, 1965.

Karpicke, J., Christoph, G., Petersen, G., and Hearst, E.: Signal location and positive vs negative conditioned suppression in the rat. *J. Exp. Psychol. [Anim. Behav. Processes]*, **3**, 105–118, 1977.

Kaufman, A.: Response suppression in the CER paradigm with extinction as the aversive event. *Psychonomic Sci.,* **15**, 15–17, 1969.

Kelleher, R. T., and Gollub, L. R.: A review of positive conditioned reinforcers. *J. Exp. Anal. Behav.*, **5**, 543–595, 1962.

Kimble, G. A.: *Hilgard and Marquis' Conditioning and Learning.* New York, Appleton-Century-Crofts, 1961.

Kimmel, H. D.: Instrumental inhibitory factors in classical conditioning. In, W. F. Prokasy (ed.): *Classical Conditioning: A Symposium.* New York, Appleton-Century-Crofts, 1965.

Knitisch, W., and White, R. S.: Concurrent conditioning of bar press and salivation responses. *J. Comp. Physiol. Psychol.*, **55**, 863–968, 1962.

Konorski, J.: *Integrative Activity of the Brain.* Chicago, University of Chicago Press, 1967.

Leitenberg, H.: Conditioned acceleration and conditioned suppression in pigeons. *J. Exp. Anal. Behav.*, **9**, 205–212, 1966.

Leitenberg, H., Bertsch, G. J., and Coughlin, R. C.: "Timeout from positive reinforcement" as the UCS in a CER paradigm with rats. *Psychonomic Sci.,* **13**, 3–4, 1968.

Lo Lordo, V. M.: Facilitation of food-reinforced responding by a signal for response-independent food. *J. Exp. Anal. Behav.,* **15,** 49–55, 1971.

Lo Lordo, V. M., McMillan, J. C., and Riley, A. L.: The effects of food-reinforced pecking and treadle-pressing of auditory and visual signals for response-independent food. *Learning Motivation,* **5,** 24–41, 1974.

Longo, N., Milstein, S., and Bitterman, M.: Classical conditioning in the pigeon: effects of partial reinforcement. *J. Comp. Physiol. Psychol.,* **55,** 983–986, 1962.

Lyon, D. O.: Conditioned suppression: operant variables and aversive control. *Psychol. Record,* **18,** 317–338, 1968.

Maier, S. F., Seligman, M. E. P., and Solomon, R. I.: Pavlovian fear conditioning and learned helplessness: effects on escape and avoidance behavior of (a) the CS-US contingency and (b) the independence of the US and voluntary responding. In, B. A. Campbell and R. M. Church (eds.): *Punishment and Aversive Behavior.* New York, Appleton-Century-Crofts, 1969.

Meltzer, D., and Brahlek, J. A.: Conditioned suppression and conditioned enhancement with the same positive UCS: an effect of CS duration. *J. Exp. Anal. Behav.,* **13,** 67–75, 1970.

Miczek, K.: Effects of scopolamine, amphetamine, and benzodiazepines on conditioned suppression. *Pharmac., Biochem., Behav.,* **1,** 401–411, 1973.

Mogenson, G. J., and Stevenson, J. A. F.: Drinking and self-stimulation with electrical stimulation of the lateral hypothalamus. *Physiol. Behav.,* **1,** 251–254, 1966.

Orme-Johnson, D. W., and Yarczower, M.: Conditioned suppression, punishment, and aversion. *J. Exp. Anal. Behav.,* **21,** 57–74, 1974.

Patton, R. L., and Rudy, J. W.: Orienting during classical conditioning: acquired vs. unconditioned responding. *Psychonomic Sci.,* **7,** 27–28, 1967.

Pavlov, I. P.: *Conditioned Reflexes.* London, Oxford Press, 1927.

Pliskoff, S.: Rate change effects during a pre-schedule change stimulus. *J. Exp. Anal. Behav.,* **4,** 383–386, 1961.

Pliskoff, S.: Rate-change effects with equal potential reinforcements during the "warning" stimulus. *J. Exp. Anal. Behav.,* **6,** 557–562, 1963.

Pliskoff, S. S., Hawkins, T. D., and Wright, J. E.: Some observations on the discriminative stimulus hypothesis and rewarding electrical stimulation of the brain. *Psychol. Record,* **14,** 179–184, 1964.

Pomerleau, O. F.: The effects of stimuli followed by response-independent shock on shock-avoidance behavior. *J. Exp. Anal. Behav.,* **14,** 11–21, 1970.

Premack, D.: Reinforcement theory. In, D. Levine (ed.): *Nebraska Symposium on Motivation.* Lincoln, University of Nebraska Press, 1965.

Premack, D.: Catching up on common sense, or two sides of a generalization: reinforcement and punishment. In, R. Glazer (ed.): *On the Nature of Reinforcement.* New York, Academic Press, 1971.

Rachlin, H.: On the tautology of the matching law. *J. Exp. Anal. Behav.,* **15,** 249–251, 1971.

Rachlin, H., and Baum, W. M.: Response rate as a function of the amount of reinforcement for a signalled concurrent response. *J. Exp. Anal. Behav.,* **12,** 11–16, 1969.

Razran, G.: The observable unconscious and the inferable conscious in current Soviet psychophysiology: Interoceptive conditioning, semantic conditioning, and the orienting reflex. *Psychol. Rev.,* **68,** 81–147, 1961.

Rescorla, R. A., and Solomon, R. L.: Two-process learning theory: relationships between Pavlovian conditioning and and instrumental learning. *Psychol. Rev.,* **74,** 151–184, 1967.

Roberts, A. E., Cooper, K. G., and Richey, T. L.: Rat behaviors during unsignalled avoidance and conditioned suppression training. *Bull. Psychonomic Soc.,* **9,** 373–376, 1977.

Schaeffer, R. W.: The reinforcement relation as a function of instrumental response base rate. *J. Exp. Psychol.,* **69,** 419–425, 1965.

Schaeffer, R. W., and Premack, D.: Licking rates in infant albino rats. *Science,* **134,** 1980–1981, 1961.

Schwartz, B., and Gamzu, E.: Pavlovian control of operant behavior. In, W. K. Honig and J. E. R. Staddon (eds.): *Handbook of Operant Behavior.* Englewood Cliffs, N. J., Prentice-Hall, 1977.

Sidman, M.: By-products of aversive control. *J. Exp. Anal. Behav.,* **1,** 265–280, 1958.

Sidman, M.: *Tactics of Scientific Research: Evaluating Experimental Data in Psychology*. New York, Basic Books, 1960.

Sidman, M., Herrnstein, R. J., and Conrad, D. G.: Maintenance of avoidance behavior by unavoidable shock. *J. Comp. Physiol. Psychol.*, **50**, 553–557, 1957.

Skinner, B. F.: "Superstition" in the pigeon. *J. Exp. Psychol.*, **38**, 168–172, 1948.

Skinner, B. F.: Are theories of learning necessary. *Psychol. Rev.*, **57**, 193–216, 1950.

Smith, J. C.: Conditioned suppression as an animal psychophysical technique. In W. Stebbins (ed.): *Animal Psychophysics*. New York, Appleton-Century-Crofts, 1970.

Solomon, R. L., and Turner, L. H.: Discriminative classical conditioning in dogs paralyzed by curare can later control discriminative avoidance responses in the normal state. *Psychol. Rev.*, **69**, 202–219, 1962.

Stein, L., Sidman, M., and Brady, J. V.: Some effects of two temporal variables on conditioned suppression. *J. Exp. Anal. Behav.*, **1**, 153–162, 1958.

Stein, N., Hoffman, H. S., and Stitt, C.: Collateral behavior of the pigeon during conditioned suppression of key pecking. *J. Exp. Anal. Behav.*, **15**, 83–93, 1971.

Terrace, H.: Discrimination learning with and without "errors." *J. Exp. Anal. Behav.*, **6**, 1–27, 1963.

Valenstein, E. S., and Cox, V. C.: Influence of hunger, thirst, and previous experience in the test chamber on stimulus bound eating and drinking. *J. Comp. Physiol. Psychol.*, **70**, 189–199, 1970.

Van Dyne, G.: Conditioned suppression with a positive US in the rat. *J. Comp. Physiol. Psychol.*, **77**, 131–135, 1971.

Weiskrantz, L.: Emotion. In, L. Weiskrantz (ed.): *Analysis of Behavioral Change*. New York, Harper & Row, 1968.

Zener, K.: The significance of behavior accompanying conditioned salivary secretion for theories of the conditioned response. *Am. J. Psychol.*, **50**, 384–403, 1937.

SECTION II

OPERANT CONDITIONING PROCEDURES

Chapter 3

Concurrent Schedules: Response versus Reinforcement Interaction

Iver H. Iversen

The Issue of Response Versus Reinforcement Interaction

The fact is now well established that presentation of reinforcers contingent upon a specific response will usually increase the rate of that response, and subsequent removal of reinforcers will decrease the response rate (Skinner, 1938). Skinner once briefly introduced and quickly withdrew a principle stating that the rate (strength) of one response (R) might be directly proportional to the *absolute* reinforcement rate (r) for that response; expressed mathematically,

$$R = Kr. \tag{1}$$

This simplistic relationship between an independent variable (reinforcement rate, r) and a dependent variable (response rate, R) was abandoned because experimental findings did not accord well with the assumption of a direct proportionality between response and reinforcement rates. Rather, Skinner (1938, 1950, 1953, 1969) clearly argued that the rate of one response may realistically be dependent upon more than just one variable.

More recently, a principle reminiscent of equation 1 has been put forward as applicable to a wide range of behavioral settings. Thus, Herrnstein (1970) suggested that the rate of one response might be directly proportional to the *relative* rate of reinforcement for that response; expressed mathematically,

$$R = K \frac{r}{r + r_0}. \tag{2}$$

Herrnstein argued that the reinforcement rate assigned to one response should be considered within the context of (or relative to) the total operating reinforcement rate for all responses. The symbol r_0 thus refers to the aggregate reinforcement rate from all responses concurrent with the reference response.

The assumptions encompassed by equation 2 explicitly express, first, an independence between the absolute rate of one response and the absolute rates of concurrently occurring responses. The right-hand side of equation 2 simply does not contain a parameter representing the rates of concurrent responses (Catania, 1963, 1969; Pliskoff et al., 1968; Rachlin and Baum, 1969; Nevin, 1973). Second, the absolute rate of one response is considered to be inversely related to the absolute reinforcement rates of concurrent responses (increases in r_0 enlarge the denominator and thereby decrease the size of R). The first assumption has been referred to as *response independence* or *constancy* (Catania, 1966) and the second as *reinforcement interaction* or *contrast,* or as an *inhibitory effect of concurrent reinforcement* (Catania, 1969, 1973; Herrnstein, 1970). Significantly, equation 2 proposes that the rate of one response is fully described by the reinforcement rate for that response and the reinforcement rate for concurrent responses.

These assumptions of response independence and reinforcement interaction —referred to as the *reinforcement model*—have mainly been supported by experiments with combinations of positive operant conditioning procedures, better known as *concurrent reinforcement schedules.*

In a previous review, Catania summarized the theoretical position of reinforcement interaction:

> Concurrent performances, therefore may be described as the product of reinforcement interaction, in that the rate of each operant is determined not only by its own rate of reinforcement but also by the concurrent rates of reinforcement of other operants, and response independence, in that the rate of each operant is not determined by the concurrent rates of other operants. (Catania, 1966, p. 248)

Response independence and reinforcement interaction would appear, however, to be somewhat different from, if not directly opposed to, the principle of response interaction that applies for other conditioning procedures. Thus, response interactions are said to describe well the findings from combinations of operant and classical conditioning procedures (Chapter 2), classical conditioning procedures (Chapter 6), positive operant and avoidance conditioning procedures (Sidman, 1962), and some avoidance conditioning procedures (Verhave, 1961). Nevertheless, response interaction has been vigorously dismissed as a possible characterization of concurrent performances in combinations of positive operant reinforcement procedures. Response interactions have therefore not been generalized to an extent warranting any serious limitation of the response independence principle in concurrent operant schedules. Instead, negatively, we must conclude that one and the same behavioral principle apparently cannot encompass the different conditioning procedures.

The purpose of this chapter is to examine the opposing models of concurrent performances as they apply to combinations of positive operant conditioning procedures.

Response Independence and Reinforcement Interaction

In the early literature on concurrent reinforcement schedules the emphasis was on establishing generality of schedule control obtained with single-response schedules. A significant question was whether the rate and pattern of a response continuously maintained on one schedule (an ongoing response) was the same whether or not a second concurrently available response was simultaneously maintained on a separate schedule.* Ferster and Skinner (1957), for example, reported that each of two responses separately maintained on VI schedules occurred at a uniform rate characteristic of VI. Ferster (1957) also reported that concurrent responses maintained by different schedules such as FR and VI showed patterns characteristic of the same schedules in isolation: a "break and run" pattern of FR responding and a more uniform rate of VI responding. These early results led to the more general definition that concurrent operants are "capable of being executed with little mutual interference" (Ferster and Skinner, 1957, p. 724). Ferster suggested that concurrent schedules could then be used to study "bilateral independence" and that "the performance on one key could be used as a baseline for the emotional side effects of a change in the schedule of reinforcement on a second key" (Ferster, 1957, p. 1091).

The study of changes of an ongoing response after schedule changes for a second response has in fact been a major concern of subsequent research on concurrent schedules. A more general finding, if not the prime feature of concurrent performances, has been that increased reinforcement for a concurrent response not only increases the rate of that response, but also simultaneously decreases the rate of an ongoing response (Catania, 1963, 1966, 1969, 1973; Herrnstein, 1961, 1970, 1974; Baum, 1973, 1974; Rachlin, 1973). In this sense, the rate of an ongoing response may certainly be affected by the schedule per se for a second concurrent response.

The terminology employed in concurrent performances is now slightly more descriptive, and the term *emotional effect* has been abandoned. However, the fundamental assumption of response independence proved to be far more influential. Since both the response and the reinforcement rate vary in the same direction under the manipulated schedule, a significant question has been whether the rate change of the ongoing response should be attributed to the response or the reinforcement rate change on the manipulated schedule.

With response interaction, the increased time allocated to concurrent responding after an increase in concurrent reinforcement rate must decrease the time available to, and thereby the rate of the ongoing response. With reinforcement interaction, on the other hand, the decreased rate of the ongoing response is said to be independent of the increased time allocated to concurrent responding.

While an abundant number of experiments have been done with concurrent schedules, relatively few have investigated the issue of response versus reinforcement interaction. The experimental approach has been to separate or pre-

---

* In the following, an *ongoing response* refers to a response continuously maintained by a schedule. *Concurrent responses* refers to other responses available within the same session as the ongoing response. *Concurrent performances,* on the other hand, is used in describing the overall situation of two or more responses maintained on separate but concurrently operating schedules. *Reinforcements* refer to reinforcers delivered contingent on an ongoing response, delivered contingent upon a concurrent response, or delivered independent of any response.

vent concomitant changes in concurrent response and reinforcement rates. Catania (1963) reported that the rate of an ongoing response was inversely related to the rate of concurrent reinforcement on a signaled VI schedule (i.e., a signal was presented when a concurrent reinforcer was eligible, and the first concurrent response during the signal produced signaled reinforcement). This finding was replicated in subsequent experiments with roughly similar procedures (Catania, 1969; Rachlin and Baum, 1969; Catania and Dobson, 1972; Catania et al., 1974). Rachlin and Baum (1972) further reported that the rate of an ongoing response was inversely related to the rate of concurrent reinforcement on a response-independent schedule (i.e., no responses were required for concurrent reinforcements). Since both procedures maintained a low or zero recorded concurrent response rate, the change of the ongoing response was said to be dependent upon concurrent reinforcement rates and to be independent of concurrent response rates.

Simply, the demonstrations of apparent response independence within these procedures were considered to provide substantial confirmation of the assumption of reinforcement interaction (Herrnstein, 1970; Catania, 1973; Rachlin, 1973). Herrnstein, for example, in a review of signaled reinforcement, concludes that ''contrast depends upon the reinforcement for the other alternative, not on the responding there'' (1970, p. 257). Importantly, the implication is that the rate of an ongoing response decreases not because of the simultaneously increased rate of the concurrent response, but only because of the increased reinforcement rate for the concurrent response.

The data obtained with the signaled and response-independent procedures appear to constitute the empirical support for the claim of reinforcement interaction in the absence of response interaction (Catania, 1969; Herrnstein, 1970, 1974; Rachlin and Baum, 1972; Nevin, 1973; Rachlin, 1973). Note that the particular logic of reinforcement interaction requires not only that the procedures yield an unchanged (low or zero) rate of the second response, but also that they do not otherwise generate concurrent responses that compete for time with the ongoing response. Some emphasis was therefore placed in arguing against the possibility that concurrent responses other than those recorded might have affected the rate of the ongoing response. The generation and eventual influence of observing responses toward the signal in the signaled reinforcement procedure, and of superstitious responses in the response-independent procedure, were clearly dismissed by various arguments (Catania, 1969; Rachlin and Baum, 1969, 1972; Catania and Dobson, 1972). (The details of the arguments are given in full in Experiments VI, VII, VIII, and IX in this chapter).

The characterization of concurrent performances in terms of response independence and reinforcement interaction appears to have received tremendous support during the past decade. A relatively large number of experimental and theoretical papers have been devoted to an application of the reinforcement theory to concurrent schedules in general, and the obtained reciprocal response rate relations were treated as an example of reinforcement interaction. This hegemony of the reinforcement model would suggest an apparent settlement of the issue of response versus reinforcement interaction.

In general, the results from concurrent schedules are treated as a relationship between relative response and reinforcement rates. When the response ratio equals the reinforcement ratio, the response distribution is said to match the reinforcement distribution (Herrnstein, 1970, 1974). Expressed mathematically, this matching law is

$$\frac{R}{R + R_0} = \frac{r}{r + r_0}.$$ (3)

We will not go into detail as to whether or not relative response rates invariably match relative reinforcement rates. Several experiments have in fact demonstrated deviations from matching. Suffice to mention here that systematic deviations from matching tend to be obtained when parameters other than reinforcement are scheduled asymmetrically on concurrent schedules with equal reinforcement rates, or are symmetrically arranged on schedules with unequal reinforcement rates (Chung, 1965; Shull and Pliskoff, 1967; Thomas, 1968; Todorov, 1971; Deluty, 1976a). Shull and Pliskoff (1967), for example, reported that the difference between the relative response and reinforcement rates on VI schedules with unequal reinforcement rates was a decreasing function of the duration of a changeover delay (COD) scheduled in both components (see also Brownstein and Pliskoff, 1968; Schroeder, 1975). Similarly, relative response and reinforcement rates did not match when response-contingent punishment was presented with different rates in equal RI schedules (Deluty, 1976a; see also Carlson and Aroksaar, 1970; Katz, 1973).

Direct or Indirect Reinforcement Interaction

Before turning to the experimental analysis of response versus reinforcement interaction, we may briefly consider the theoretical consequences of an eventual change in emphasis from response independence to response interaction in the characterization of concurrent performances. Certainly, the rate of an ongoing response (as the dependent variable) has been shown to be inversely related to the rate of concurrent reinforcement (as the independent variable) in several experiments. If this well-established functional relationship is not mediated by changes in concurrent response rates, a relevant question is how the relationship then comes about. This issue has long been explained by saying that an ongoing response is affected *directly* by concurrent reinforcements (Catania, 1966, 1973). However, the interpretative emphasis on a direct connection between concurrent reinforcement and ongoing response may not necessarily imply a final settlement of the empirical analysis of concurrent performances. The relationship between concurrent reinforcement and an ongoing response might be further investigated, and perhaps the theoretical issues have not yet been sufficiently debated to warrant a complete rejection of alternative interpretations.

In the literature of concurrent schedules, the alternative interpretation of response interactions has occasionally questioned response independence and reinforcement interaction. While response interaction has been dismissed several times, the possible characterization of concurrent performances in terms of observed response interactions was in fact recognized at least to have the advantage of not appealing to unobserved inhibitory processes that are implicit in the reinforcement model (Catania, 1969).

Let us accept for the sake of argument the alternative interpretation of response interaction. The inverse relationship between the rate of an ongoing response and concurrent reinforcement rates would still hold as a functional relationship, but now the relation would be indirect rather than direct. If the rate of concurrent reinforcement is increased, for example, and the rate of concurrent responses thereby increases simultaneously, then a decreased rate of the ongoing response would be attributed directly to the increased concurrent response rate, and only indirectly to the increased concurrent reinforcement rate. With response interaction, concurrent reinforcements simply act upon concurrent responses, which in turn directly influence the ongoing response.

The following experiments will argue in favor of a change in the causal vocabulary from a *direct* to *indirect* dependent relationship between an ongoing response and concurrent reinforcement rates. This vocabulary change may appear small and insignificant in itself. The assumptions of response independence and exclusive reinforcement interaction would, however, be abandoned if concurrent performances could be sufficiently described as interactions between responses.

Response Pattern Reciprocity in Concurrent FR VI Schedules (Experiments I and II)*

While overall changes in an ongoing response are generally considered to be independent of a second concurrent response, more local changes were not thought to be entirely independent of concurrent responses in the early literature. Ferster (1957, 1959) noted, for example, that VI responding was temporally interrupted during high local rates of a concurrent FR response. More gross local inversions were also described between the rates of responses maintained on schedules such as concurrent (*conc*) FR FI (Ferster and Skinner, 1957), *conc* VI FR (Catania, 1966), and *conc* VI FI (Nevin, 1971). In the Nevin study, for example, the FI response occurred in the typical scallop, with a gradually increasing rate between reinforcements. The concurrent VI response was disrupted, however, with a gradually decreasing rate between the FI reinforcements. Thus the pattern of an ongoing response may, at least under some conditions, show a partial dependence on the simultaneous pattern of a concurrent response.

Since response interactions already have been admitted at the level of local response rates, a good starting point for a concurrent response analysis would be a further investigation of the relationships between local response patterns in concurrent schedules. In the following two experiments, the pattern of FR responding was simply compared to the pattern of concurrent VI responding.

---

* Experiments were conducted at the University of Copenhagen, from January to October 1971, and reported by I. Iversen (1974).

Experiment I

The beginning experiment examined changes in FR and VI response patterns established by successively presented schedules when the schedules were made simultaneously available. More specifically, two male pigeons were maintained at 80% of their free-feeding body weights. The pigeons had served in previous experiments with single and *conc* VI FR schedules. When the center key of a three-key pigeon chamber (Iversen, 1975a) was red, pecks on this key were reinforced on VI 2 min. The interreinforcement intervals were distributed according to the formula of Fleshler and Hoffman (1962). A reinforcer set up on this schedule was only accessible for a 3-sec period. The first peck in this period produced the reinforcer, but reinforcer delivery was canceled if no pecks occurred [limited hold (LH) procedure]. When the left key was lit green, pecks on this key were reinforced on FR 50. The FR counter was only reset after reinforcer delivery for FR responding. The right key was never lit and pecks on this key had no effect. In the first experimental phase (30 sessions), the schedules were presented successively. A session of 3200 sec was divided into eight 400-sec periods. During each period, only one key was lit, and reinforcers were only scheduled for pecks on that key. Pecks on the other, nonilluminated key had no effect. The schedules were always presented in strict alternation.

In the second phase (18 sessions), both keys were lit simultaneously and the associated schedules operated concurrently throughout a session. The schedules were independently programmed so that pecks on one key did not affect the response–reinforcement contingency on the second key. Reinforcer delivery was 3 sec of access to mixed grain.

With the *conc* VI FR in the second phase, the terminal performance was invariably a substantially reduced rate on one key and an approximately unchanged rate on the second key (Table 3.1). The pauses in FR responding increased for both pigeons and VI responding occurred in bursts after FR reinforcement. For pigeon A5, the FR pauses were short with few interspersed VI responses, whereas for pigeon A6, the pauses were long with a high number of VI responses (Table 3.1).

Table 3.1   Response and reinforcement rates (responses/min, reinforcements/min) for FR and VI responding, pause durations and run times (sec) in FR responding, and the number of VI responses emitted during FR pauses and runs

Pigeon no.	Schedules	Response rates		Reinforce- ment rates		FR pause[a]	FR run time	Number of VI responses	
		FR	VI	FR	VI			FR pause[a]	FR run
A5	in isolation	89.8	61.2	1.79	0.44	6.8	26.6	0.0	0.0
	simultaneously	83.4	8.6	1.66	0.15	9.4	27.0	4.1	1.1
A6	in isolation	119.6	63.6	2.38	0.43	6.3	18.8	0.0	0.0
	simultaneously	10.2	66.0	0.20	0.44	89.5	205.6	103.5	221.5

[a] FR pauses were measured to the first FR response after FR reinforcement. Values are means of the last six sessions of each phase.

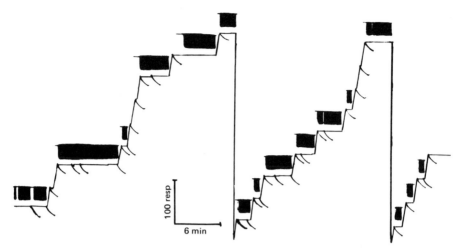

Figure 3.1. Sample cumulative record showing reciprocity between FR responding and VI responding. VI responding is shown on the event pen with segments displaced to the appropriate pause for easy comparison. Reinforcements for both responses are indicated as hatchmarks on the stepping pen.

The cumulative record of FR responding and the event traces of VI responding in Figure 3.1 clearly show the response pattern reciprocity. The burst of VI responding and the concomitant pause in FR responding were closely covariant, and the FR pause was apparently independent of whether or not the burst of VI responding was reinforced.

We should note that the recorded responses were physically incompatible, which by necessity assures some degree of response interdependence. Thus, pauses in one response clearly cannot be shorter than bursts of a concurrent incompatible response. However, the pause in one response can be indefinitely longer than (and therefore patrially independent of) the burst of a second response. Since the FR pause approached the burst duration of VI responding in this study, FR pausing was then not totally independent of the concurrent VI response. The results would then seem to suggest some form of interdependence between concurrently reinforced responses.

Experiment II

To further analyze the interrelationships between concurrent FR and VI responding, the next experiment directly manipulated the duration of access to VI responding. The experiment also sought to determine whether physical incompatibility is necessary for inverse response rate relations. Therefore, monkeys were trained in a cage with two response levers that could easily be depressed simultaneously. The experimentally naive monkeys were *Cercopithecus aethiops* (African green monkeys) and were deprived of food for approximately 21 hr prior to each daily session. The levers were 9.0 cm long and 2.0 cm in diameter: they operated a switch when depressed 2.0 cm with a

force of 150 g. The distance between the levers was 26.0 cm. The 1-g food pellets were delivered from a food cup centered between the two levers. During
sessions, presses on the left lever were followed by response feedback of a 0.1-
sec darkening of a white light in the lever and a 0.1-sec 4000-Hz tone. When a
red stimulus light was lit above the right lever, presses on the right lever were
followed by a 0.1-sec illumination of a white light in the lever and a 0.1-sec 400-
Hz tone.

After pretraining, the terminal schedules in effect throughout a session were
either an FR 100 (monkey 1) or FR 80 (monkey 2) on the left lever. The right
lever was programmed with a discrete-trial VI 40 sec with a limited hold of 5
sec. In the first phase, the discrete VI trials and intertrials (EXT) occurred in
strictly alternating 150-sec periods. In the second phase, trial durations of 10,
20, 40, 60, 120, 240, or 300 sec occurred in mixed order separated by variable
intertrial intervals of 40 to 360 sec. In both phases, shifts between trial and intertrial intervals were independent of responses on any lever. A session was
terminated after delivery of 50 pellets.

This paradigm of presenting and retracting the discriminative stimulus for
right lever responding could formally be described either as a discrete-trial procedure or a multiple schedule. In the following, *trials* therefore refers to the VI
component of the *mult* VI (LH) EXT schedule for the right lever, and *intertrial
intervals* refers to the EXT component.

Presenting the VI discriminative stimulus resulted not only in large rate increases in VI responding, but also in decreases in FR responding (Table 3.2).
The manipulated trial durations, furthermore, produced different burst durations of VI responding, which in turn affected the ongoing pattern of FR responding.

Figure 3.2 presents sample cumulative records for the fixed and variable trial
durations. The interruption in FR responding was complete and closely followed the trial duration for monkey 2 since trial onset controlled an immediate
changeover to VI responding (a) and trial offset controlled an immediate
changeover back to FR responding (d and m). For monkey 1, FR responding

Table 3.2   Mean response and reinforcement rates calculated for the last five
sessions of each phase

| Monkey no. | Trial duration | Response rates (responses/min) | | | | Reinforcement rates (reinforcements/min) | | | |
| | | Left lever | | Right lever | | Left lever | | Right lever | |
		VI[a]	EXT[a]	VI[a]	EXT[a]	VI[a]	EXT[a]	VI[a]	EXT[a]
1	fixed	38.1	153.1	70.4	2.4	0.38	1.53	1.36	0.0
	variable	38.3	190.0	61.5	1.8	0.38	1.90	1.40	0.0
2	fixed	0.3	66.5	75.2	0.3	0.0	0.83	1.43	0.0
	variable	0.3	61.4	70.2	0.2	0.0	0.77	1.39	0.0

[a] Schedule for right lever.

MONKEY 1   **MONKEY 2**

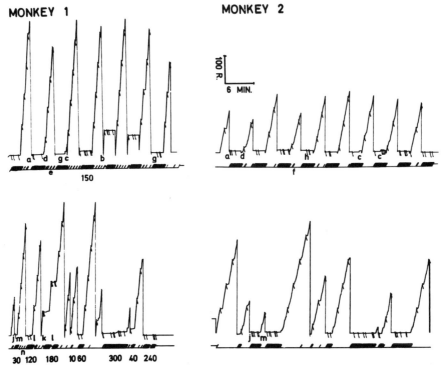

Figure 3.2. Sample cumulative records illustrating the effects of discrete VI trials upon ongoing FR responding. VI responding is shown on the event pen as downward deflections during trials and upward deflections during intertrial intervals. Pellet deliveries for both responses are shown as hatchmarks on the stepping pen. Upper records are from the first phase, with fixed trial duration; lower records are from the second phase, with variable trial duration. Numbers refer to the trial duration, and letters refer to details discussed in the text.

continued occasionally after trial onset, with the changeover to VI responding then occurring immediately after FR pellet delivery (b and k). Moreover, changeovers from VI responding to brief bursts (c) or complete runs (l) of FR responding occurred during some trials for monkey 1. Therefore, FR responding was suppressed during trials to the extent that trial presentation controlled emission of VI responses. For both monkeys, trials presented immediately after FR reinforcement produced a postreinforcement pause approximating the duration of the concurrent VI trial. In a similar fashion, trials presented during the FR run increased the run time by an amount approximating the trial duration (h and j). During intertrial intervals, VI responding was at zero rate with the major exception of brief bursts after FR pellet deliveries for monkey 1 (e and n), and occasionally for Monkey 2.

Overall, the interruptions in FR responding more closely approximated the actual duration of VI responding than the programmed trial duration. Furthermore, the responses were physically compatible rather than incompatible, hence one response did not prevent the occurrence of the second response. Reciprocal interactions in concurrent schedules may therefore not necessarily result from or be reduced to response incompatibility.

Discussion

Demonstrations of response pattern interdependence in concurrent schedules may involve two levels of comparison. At the level of averaged response and reinforcement rates, the reinforcement model specifically states that inhibition of an ongoing response does not result from an increased rate of a concurrent response but only from an increased concurrent reinforcement rate. The present data would not disagree qualitatively with this model for averaged, overall response and reinforcement rates (Tables 3.1 and 3.2); that is, the decreased FR response rate was associated with increases in both concurrent response and reinforcement rates. At the molecular level of response changes during individual trials, however, the reinforcement model only uneasily explains the response rate changes. The burst duration of concurrent VI responding ranged widely in Experiment I and was purposely manipulated between 10 and 300 sec in Experiment II. Therefore, the local VI reinforcement rate was highly variable from one VI trial to the next, with an absence of VI reinforcement during many of the trials. If the reinforcement model can be applied to the consistent response rate changes during trials, the inhibition from VI reinforcement upon FR responding *must* exactly match the duration of VI responding, not the variable rate of obtained VI reinforcement.

In the present experiments, alterations of the ongoing FR response pattern were far more closely associated with the concurrent pattern of VI responding than with the actually delivered VI reinforcers. Similarly, FR pauses may be directly affected by bursts of collateral responding that does not require delivery of reinforcers (Iversen, 1976). Alterations of FR responding are thus more closely accounted for by interacting response patterns than by interacting reinforcement patterns.

The reinforcement model would seem to require essentially that inhibition by concurrent reinforcement must somehow be tightly associated with the emission of a concurrent response. This analysis does not appear to be peculiar to the specific procedures of the present experiments. As mentioned before, Nevin (1971) employed continuously operating concurrent VI and FI schedules and found a gradually decreasing VI response rate between FI reinforcements. Again, the effect of the FI schedule on the VI response pattern must somehow be connected with the generation of a scallop of FI responding.

Response changes at a more local level go beyond the premises of the reinforcement model, and are therefore usually excluded from analysis. Thus Baum, for example, asserted that "orderly relations between behavior and environment should emerge at the level of aggregate flow in time, rather than momentary events" (1973, p. 137). A critical question then is the degree of data averaging. Whether reinforcement interaction can account for local response rate changes remains unclear. In contrast, response interaction may easily account for both overall and local changes in responding.

Changeover Responses Under Discriminative Control with Discrete-Trial Procedures (Experiments III, IV, and V)*

A changeover from an ongoing response to a concurrent response may involve not only concurrent changes but also sequential alternation between responses. The sequential changes were not explicitly controlled in Experiment I, with the changeover from FR to VI responding consistently only after FR reinforcement. The more explicit experimental control of burst durations in Experiment II established changeovers controlled by the onset of the VI discriminative stimulus. The results would suggest that changeover responses might profitably be investigated by various paradigms of discriminative stimulus control. The explicit investigation of the discriminative control of changeover responses, however, has been undertaken in only a few experiments.

Sidman (1956) studied the changes in DRL responding during a discriminative stimulus controlling a concurrent response. With this design, the probability of the second response was a decreasing function of the time of stimulus onset within the DRL requirement. Boren (1961) similarly studied the effects upon an FR response of an added stimulus during which a concurrent response was reinforced on a CRF schedule for only one reinforcement. The superimposed discriminative stimulus was presented at different positions within the FR run. The probability of a changeover to the concurrent response was a decreasing function of the number of FR responses emitted prior to presentation of the discriminative stimulus. (In the experiments by Sidman and Boren, the response contingencies were not exactly independent. The DRL in Sidman's experiment and the FR in Boren's experiment were both "reset" by the second response.) The procedure of signaling reinforcement for a second response has subsequently been used in a series of experiments with VI schedules (Catania, 1963, 1969; Rachlin and Baum, 1969; Pliskoff and Green, 1972).

The changeover response has also been investigated when the second response changed over to merely alters the schedule for the first response changed over from (Findley, 1958; Sherman and Thomas, 1968). More recently, discriminative control of changeovers has been studied with concurrent operant and classical conditioning procedures (Henton and Iversen, 1973; Chapter 2, this volume). In these schedules, a changeover from the operant to the classically conditioned response immediately occurred at onset of conditioned stimuli controlling a high rate of the classically conditioned response.

The following three experiments were an attempt to investigate further the variables that control changeover responses within concurrent schedules. A central question is: To what extent is the interruption of an ongoing response related to concurrent responses controlled by a discriminative stimulus?" All three experiments maintained one response on a continuously accessible schedule and a second response on a discrete-trial procedure. The advantage of the trial procedure, in addition to the elaborate discriminative control of

---

* Experiments conducted at the University of Copenhagen, from January 1971 to January 1974, and reported by I. Iversen (1974, 1975a).

changeovers, is the explicit within-session manipulation and dissociation of concurrent response and reinforcement parameters.

Experiment III

This experiment was designed to study the rate and pattern of VI responding during the acquisition, extinction, and reacquisition of discriminative control of concurrent FR responding (Iversen, 1975a). Pigeons were maintained on 80% of their free-feeding body weights and pecking one red key was reinforced on a VI 2 min, with an LH of 3.6 sec. The concurrent discrete trial was illumination of a second key by green light. In the first phase (acquisition), responding on the green key was reinforced on FR 40. After 40 pecks, a reinforcer was presented and the green light was turned off. To assess the effects of FR extinction, pecks on the green key were no longer reinforced and the trial duration was 40 sec in the second phase (EXT). Finally, pecking the green key was again reinforced on FR 40 in the third phase (reacquisition). In all phases, 12 trials occurred with variable intertrial intervals and were independent of pecks on any key. Each phase consisted of fifteen 70-min sessions and the reinforcer was access to mixed grain for 4 sec.

The intermittent trial presentation during acquisition controlled an immediate changeover from VI to FR responding. VI responding was completely suppressed during all trials (Figure 3.3). Removal of the concurrent FR reinforcer

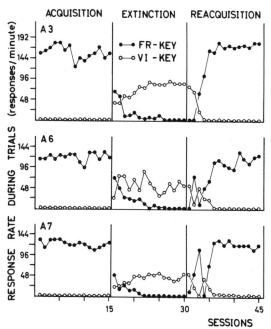

Figure 3.3. Relationships between FR and VI response rates during the acquisition, extinction and reacquisition of discrete-trial FR responding. Data are means of 12 trials presented during each session. From Iversen: *Scand. J. Physiol.,* **16,** 280–284, 1975.

(EXT) resulted in a gradual increase in the VI response rate along with the decrease in the FR response rate. Reacquisition of FR responding reversed the response pattern changes, with a gradually decreased rate of VI responding along with the increased rate of FR responding.

According to the reinforcement model, removal of reinforcers for a concurrent response increases an ongoing response rate because of an increased relative reinforcement rate. The model would thus seem to predict an abrupt increase in VI response rates to match the immediate increase in relative VI reinforcement rate during the FR EXT. Therefore, the reinforcement model may apparently not account for the *gradually* increasing VI response rate during extinction of FR responding, unless an additional inhibitory effect of previous FR reinforcers is assumed to decay gradually. Such an inferred inhibitory after-effect of previous concurrent reinforcement must at least closely follow if not exactly mimic the extinction curve for the concurrent response. However, the VI response rate was precisely decreased only during those EXT trials in which FR responding still occurred, not during trials in which FR responses were absent. Similarly, during reacquisition, the VI response rate decreased only when FR responses occurred during trials. Examples of the minute interrelationships between the responses are shown in sample event records in Figure 3.4.

The influence of FR reinforcement must then closely follow changes in the FR response if an inhibitory effect is to cogently explain changes in the VI response rate. More importantly, perhaps, changes in the VI response rate would then seem to be as well described by reference to the FR response rate changes in and of themselves, as by reinforcement inhibition inferred from changes in VI responding.

Although the reinforcement model does not address local or molecular response changes (Catania, 1966; Baum, 1973), the very close negative correlations between local rates of an ongoing response and a concurrent response nevertheless remain to be explained. Molecular response changes have in fact been left in limbo for quite sometime. Perhaps the argument against local or

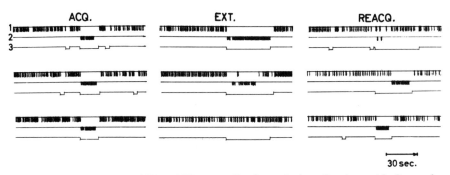

Figure 3.4. Event records of VI and FR responding for each phase for pigeon A3. On pen 3, extended deflections refer to trial presentations and brief deflections refer to reinforcer delivery. 1, VI-Key; 2, FR-Key; 3, FR-trials or reinforcement. Adapted from Iversen: *Scand. J. Physiol.,* **16,** 280–284, 1975.

transitional interactions could be reversed, so that any general description of concurrent performances might attempt to account for all performance aspects rather than only overall response rates.

Experiment IV

In Experiment III both the response rate and the reinforcement rate were relatively higher for the concurrent response than for the ongoing response. This finding raises the question of whether the relatively higher rate of the concurrent response is necessary for the complete suppression of the ongoing response. The first purpose of Experiment IV was to examine this question; it's second purpose was to determine the immediacy of the discriminative control of the changeover as a function of the concurrent reinforcement rate.

Three male pigeons were maintained at 80% of their free-feeding body weights. The pigeons had served in a previous experiment with simple VI schedules, and one pigeon (A1) had served in a preliminary experiment. Pecking of a red key (key 1), centered on the chamber wall with the food hopper, was reinforced on a VI 120 sec with an LH of 3.6 sec throughout sessions. Pecking of a second key (key 2), centered on the adjoining left-hand wall, was reinforced on a discrete-trial procedure.

One-minute trials of white or green illumination of key 2 each occurred six times per session, intermixed with intertrial intervals (key 2 dark) of 90 to 360 sec. During white trials, key 2 pecking was reinforced on VI 60 sec (Phase A), VI 40 sec (Phase B), VI 120 sec (Phase C), and VI 40 sec again (Phase D). During green trials, key 2 pecking was always reinforced on VI 180 sec. To prevent variability in the key 2 reinforcement rate over sessions (because of the relatively brief exposure time to the discrete trials), the programmer was arranged so that each schedule would assign a fixed number of reinforcer deliveries during a session. The number of sessions in Phases A, B, C, and D was 18, 18, 30, and 10, respectively, for pigeon A1; for pigeon A2 it was 41, 30, 43, and 40, respectively; and for pigeon A4 it was 30, 30, 50, and 32, respectively.

Figure 3.5 presents the results of this *conc* VI (*mult* VI VI EXT) schedule. During trials, the concurrent key 2 response rate was an increasing function, and the ongoing key 1 response rate was a decreasing function of the key 2 reinforcement rate. Note that the key 1 response rate decreased to zero with the highest key 2 reinforcement rates. For pigeons A2 and A4, the decrease in key 1 response rate exceeded the increase in key 2 response rate from intertrial to trial intervals. The complete suppression of key 1 responding thus did not require a changeover to a relatively higher key 2 response rate; that is, the key 1 baseline rate was higher than the key 2 trial rate. In other words, the key 1 decrease did not necessarily balance the key 2 increase in responses/min. Hence, the interruption or total suppression of an ongoing response would not seem to require changeover to a relatively higher concurrent response rate.

At the level of averaged data, the change in the ongoing response was related to both an increased rate of concurrent responding as well as an increased rate of concurrent reinforcement. However, analyzed during individual trials, the

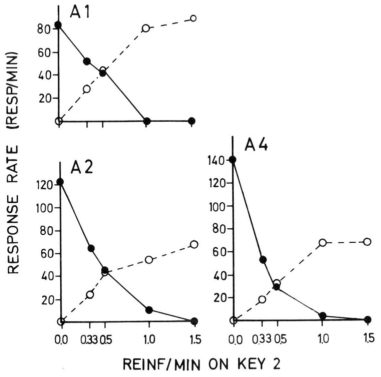

Figure 3.5.   Mean key 2 (white circles) and key 1 (black circles) response rates as a function of the key 2 reinforcement rate. The response rates were averaged for all trials with equal key 2 schedules, and for intertrial intervals (zero key 2 reinforcement rate). Data are presented as means for the last 10 sessions of each phase.

ongoing key 1 rate appeared to be related only to the concurrent response rate on key 2. Figure 3.6 shows the suppression of key 1 responding during trials and the key 2 reinforcement rate (Figure 3.6A,B) compared with the key 2 response rate (Figure 3.6C,D) for overall and local response measures. For comparison of means (Figure 3.6A,C), the percent suppression of key 1 responding is an increasing function of the key 2 reinforcement rate as well as the key 2 response rate. For individual trials (Figure 3.6B,D), the percent suppression of key 1 responding is unrelated to the key 2 reinforcement rate but remains an increasing function of the key 2 response rate. In spite of the scatter in data points (each dot represents the rates for only one 1-min period), the key 1 rate is minimally suppressed *only* when the key 2 response rate is low, but is maximally suppressed *only* when the key 2 response rate is high. The formally confounded effects of key 2 response rate and reinforcement rate upon the key 1 suppression is clearly apparent only at the level of mean comparisons. An inverse relationship between concurrent responses was obtained, however, for overall as well as local data analysis. These data therefore support a model based on response interaction, rather than response independence, of concurrent performances.

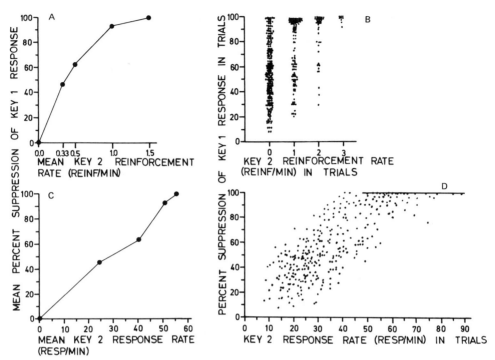

Figure 3.6.   Percent suppression of ongoing key 1 responding. **A** and **B**: As a function of the concurrent key 2 reinforcement rate. **C** and **D**: As a function of key 2 response rate. Average data (panels A and C) and raw data from individual trials (panels B and D) are presented. Data are from the last 10 sessions of Phases A, B, and C for pigeon A2. To avoid crowding of data, the horizontal line in panel D represents the absolute range of key 2 response rates during trials with 100% suppression of key 1 responding.

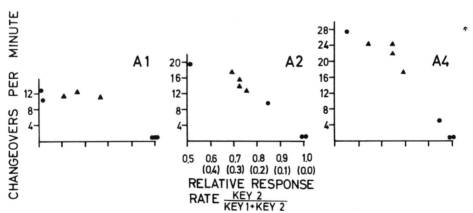

Figure 3.7.   Relationship between the mean rate of changeovers and the mean relative key 2 response rate. Means are based upon the last 10 sessions of each phase. Eight data points are presented for each pigeon, corresponding to VI 60, 40, 120, and 40 sec scheduled during white trials plus four replications of VI 180 sec during green trials. Relative response rates are plotted as symmetrical values around 0.5. A relative response rate of 0.2, for example, is plotted at 0.8. Triangles, <0.5; circles, ≥0.5.

As a further analysis, the mean changeover rates are shown in Figure 3.7 as a function of the relative key 2 response rate. The changeover rate was highest when the relative response rate was approximately 0.5 and then decreased as the relative response rate approached the extremes of 1.0 or 0.0. An example of the symmetry between changeover rate and relative key 2 response rate for individual trials is presented in Figure 3.8.

Previous reports suggest similar relationships between the changeover rate and relative response rate for continuously operating concurrent reinforcement schedules (LaBounty and Reynolds, 1973; Schneider, 1973).

The discriminative control of changeover responses and the interresponse relationships are perhaps best illustrated by sample event recorder segments (Figure 3.9). During intertrial intervals, key 1 responding occurred at a uniform rate, only interrupted by feeder operation (a). With key 2 reinforcement rate of 1.5/min, an immediate changeover from key 1 to key 2 occurred at trial onset (b). Key 2 responding then occurred at a high uniform rate, again only interrupted by feeder operation (c), and key 1 responding was simultaneously suppressed throughout trials (d). With a different key 2 reinforcement rate of 1.0/min. a changeover to key 2 responding also occurred immediately at trial presentation, and key 1 responding was suppressed during trials for pigeon A1 (e). For pigeons A2 and A4, the changeover to key 2 also typically occurred at trial presentation (f), but with intermittent changeovers back to brief bursts of

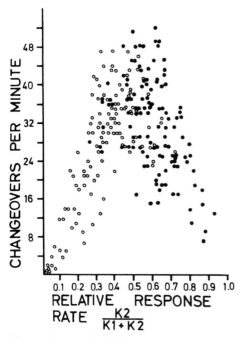

Figure 3.8. Relationship between changeover rate and relative key 2 response rate during individual trials with 0.5/min (black circles) and 0.33/min (white circles) key 2 reinforcement rates for pigeon A4.

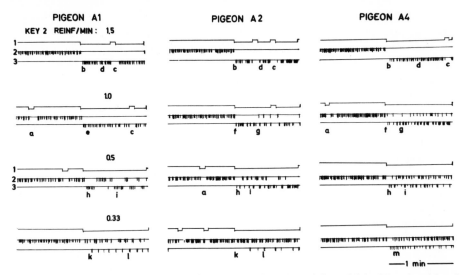

Figure 3.9. Sample event records for pigeons A1, A2, and A4 (left to right) of key 1 and key 2 responding during trials and intertrial intervals for each key 2 reinforcement rate and pigeon. Pen 1 was deflected during trials and reinforcer delivery. 1, trials or reinforcements; 2, key 1; 3, key 2.

key 1 responding (g). The third key 2 reinforcement rate of 0.5/min produced far more frequent changeovers back and forth between the keys (h). With the lowest key 2 reinforcement rate of 0.33/min, changeovers to key 2 were somewhat delayed, and usually occurred within the first 0 to 10 sec after trial onset (k). The key 1 rate was only moderately decreased during these trials, with several key 1 response bursts typically interspersed between a single or a few key 2 responses (l).

In a recent review of concurrent schedules, deVilliers (1977) suggested that relative response rates can be used to quantify the underlying reward value of different reinforcement conditions. Opposed to this view is a previous suggestion by Skinner (1950) that preference or choice merely lies in changing over between responses. With the relationship between changeover rates and relative response rates obtained in the present experiment, an intermediate relative response rate is associated with frequent changeovers or choices, whereas a high or low relative response rate occurs with few choices. Therefore, the relative response rate may be simply related to frequency of choice (e.g., changeovers) rather than unequivocally measuring "value" of choice outcome.

Experiment V

If a response model of concurrent performances is accurate, then one response should be affected by alterations in concurrent response–reinforcement relations only to the extent that such alterations change concurrent responding. The purpose of Experiment V was simply to investigate the changes in an ongo-

ing response after alterations in concurrent response–reinforcement relationships. In principle, the previous results (e.g., Experiment III) suggest that an
ongoing response may be interrupted during a stimulus only if that stimulus
controls the emission of a concurrent response. This relationship was further
investigated in the present experiment by occasionally presenting either one of
two discrete stimuli during sessions of FR reinforcement. During one stimulus,
concurrent reinforcement was contingent on a concurrent VI response. During
the second stimulus, however, concurrent reinforcement was contingent on *not*
emitting the concurrent response. The rates of delivered concurrent reinforcers
were exactly equal during the two stimuli, which nonetheless differentially controlled high and low concurrent response rates. According to the reinforcement
model, the ongoing response should be equally interrupted during the two stimuli because the concurrent reinforcement rates are equal. According to the response model, the ongoing response should in contrast be interrupted only during a stimulus controlling changeovers to a concurrent response.

The experiment used two male and one female African green monkeys maintained at 21 hr of food deprivation prior to each daily session. The monkeys
were trained to respond on two levers that could be depressed simultaneously
using the same equipment as in Experiment II. After pretraining, left lever responding was maintained on FR 80 throughout sessions. Each lever press was
followed by response feedback of a 0.1 sec darkening of the lever and a high-
pitch tone. Phase A analyzed the discriminative control of changeovers from
left to right lever responding. Therefore, right lever responding was maintained
on a two-ply discrete-trial procedure (or multiple schedule).

For most of the session, the red and green stimulus lights above the right
lever were off and right lever responding was not reinforced (EXT). Occasionally, the red light was turned on for 100 sec and right lever responding was reinforced on VI 1 min. Occasionally the green light was turned on for 100 sec and
right lever responding was then reinforced on a variable-time schedule with a
differential reinforcement of other behavior contingency (VT_{DRO}) for 1 min.
During green trials, food pellets were merely delivered on the VT schedule provided right lever responding was at low or zero rate. The DRO contingency was
fixed at 5 sec and was introduced to force right lever responding to a low or
zero rate during green while maintaining the rate of pellet delivery similar to
that during red. Two red and green trials occurred in each session and were
always separated by a variable intertrial interval (no stimuli) associated with
extinction of right lever responding.

A complementary procedure was used in Phase B, with discriminative control of the reverse changeover, from right to left lever responding. The schedule
for the right lever was consequently altered so that VI (red stimulus) was in
effect for most of the session with occasional 100-sec trials of either EXT (the
red light turned off) or VT_{DRO} (the red light turned off and the green light turned
on). Essentially, VI and EXT (and their associated stimuli) were reversed from
the previous phase. Each phase lasted 15 sessions, and each session terminated
after delivery of fifty 1-g food pellets. The schedules were procedurally independent so that responding on one lever did not affect the response–reinforcement contingency on the second lever.

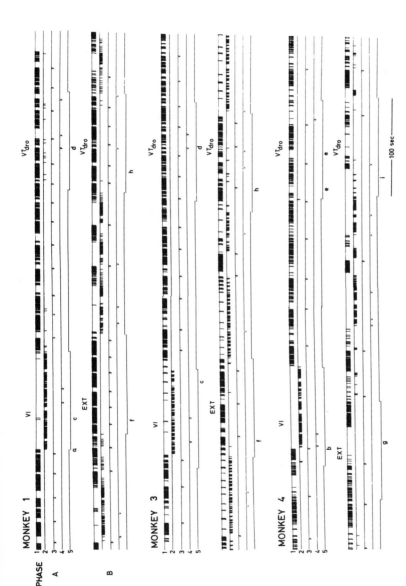

Figure 3.10. Event records showing the interactions between FR responding on the left lever and VI responding on the right lever. For each monkey, the upper record is from Phase A with VI and VT_DRO trials, and the lower record is from Phase B with EXT and VT_DRO trials. The schedule for right lever responding is indicated for each trial. 1, Left lever; 2, right lever; 3, pellet for left lever; 4, pellet for right lever; 5, trial.

183

Figure 3.10 presents sample event records under the two procedural conditions. In Phase A, onset of VI trials controlled a changeover from the left to the right lever immediately (a) or shortly after completion of the ongoing ratio run (b). The response rate on the right lever was typically high during the discrete VI trials, with only occasional changeovers back to bursts of left lever responding (c). Presentation of the red light then led to a radical suppression of left lever responding along with the almost exclusive emission of right lever responding. During VT_{DRO} trials, on the other hand, right lever responses were infrequent and the pattern of left lever responding was unchanged relative to intertrial intervals, except for brief interruptions after concurrent VT_{DRO} reinforcement (d). However, for monkey 4, left lever responding was intermittently interrupted during VT_{DRO} trials (e).

With the reversed discriminative control of changeovers in Phase B, right lever responding decreased at the onset of EXT or VT_{DRO} trials, with a simultaneously marked increase of left lever responding for monkeys 1 and 3 (f amd h). For monkey 4, right lever responding also decreased during trials, but left lever responding did not simultaneously increase. Instead, changeovers occurred to idiosyncratic responses such as exaggeratedly turning the head upward or left lever responding at insufficient force to activate the recording system (g). These behaviors were rarely seen during intertrial intervals. Consequently, recorded left lever responding did not typically increase during trials relative to intertrials for this monkey (i).

The overall schedule effects of Phases A and B are summarized in Figure 3.11. A stimulus signaling increased concurrent reinforcement rates may interrupt an ongoing response only when that stimulus also controls a changeover to a concurrent response. Furthermore, a stimulus effecting a changeover away from a concurrent response *may* control a simultaneous changeover to and hence increased rate of a specific ongoing response, in spite of maintained concurrent reinforcement rates. The latter relationship is deliberately expressed with some caution, as a changeover from one response would not necessarily result in a changeover to only one particular response. For monkey 4, for example, the stimuli controlling a decreased rate of right lever responding in Phase B simultaneously controlled changeovers to observed but unrecorded concurrent responses in addition to the ongoing left lever response. The overall data seem to establish that an ongoing response rate will be decreased by concurrent reinforcements that generate increased rates of concurrent responses.

Discussion

The present series of experiments systematically examined the concurrent response analysis previously developed for the study of behavioral interactions generated within combinations of operant and classical conditioning procedures (Chapter 2). The application of the discrete-trial analysis to concurrent operant schedules significantly established that the interruption of an ongoing response was related to the changeover to a concurrent response, rather than to a changed concurrent reinforcement rate.

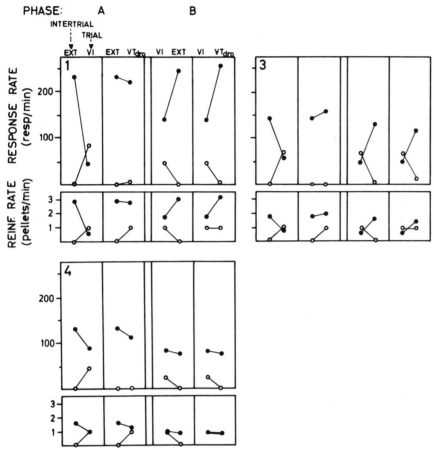

Figure 3.11. Relationship between the mean response and reinforcement rates for each phase. For each monkey, the two left-hand columns are from Phase A, and the two right-hand columns are from Phase B. Response rates during intertrial intervals and during trials are given as the left and right data points within each column. The first column for each monkey, for example, compares the rates during intertrial intervals (EXT) to the rates during VI trials; the next column compares the rates during intertrial intervals to the rates during VT_{DRO} trials. Black circles, left lever; white circles, right lever.

The results seem to be consistent with previous research using continuously operating concurrent schedules. With a variety of parametric manipulations, the rate of an ongoing response may thus be inversely related to the rate of a concurrent reinforced response without a simultaneous "match" to reinforcement rates (Chung, 1965; Chung and Herrnstein, 1967; Shull and Pliskoff, 1967; Brownstein and Pliskoff, 1968; Carlson and Aroksaar, 1970; Herbert, 1970; Moffit and Shimp, 1971; Todorov, 1971; Katz, 1973; Schroeder, 1975; Deluty, 1976a).

The response model would in fact emphasize that suppression of an ongoing response is importantly dependent upon a changeover to concurrent responses.

Likewise, enhancement of an ongoing response may be dependent upon a changeover away from a concurrent response to the ongoing response. However, the response model certainly does not deny a relationship between the rate of one response and concurrent reinforcement rates; rather, this relationship is considered to be indirect rather than direct. The ongoing response rate may then more broadly be affected by changes in concurrent reinforcement rates *by virtue* of simultaneous changes in concurrent response rates. At the level of local performances, we clearly saw that the inhibitory influence of concurrent reinforcement closely coincides with emission of concurrent responses. The pattern of one response was then typically in close inversion to the pattern of a concurrent response—from the minute interruption associated with a brief burst of a concurrent response to the more radical suppression associated with the steady emission of a concurrent response. Indeed, a response may be "inhibited" by concurrent reinforcements only during periods of emission of concurrent responses.

Observing Responses with Signaled Reinforcement
(Experiments VI, VII, and VIII)*

Given the response model, the interest centers on the special procedures hitherto employed to demonstrate reinforcement interaction in the absence of response interaction. In particular, the procedure of signaling concurrent reinforcement has been used to examine response competition in concurrent schedules. The data from the signaled reinforcement procedure have been cited as critical evidence in support for a reinforcement interaction as opposed to a response interaction interpretation of concurrent performances (Catania, 1966; Herrnstein, 1970; Rachlin, 1973).

In the typical concurrent VI VI experiment, the effects of manipulating concurrent reinforcement parameters are usually confounded with the simultaneous changes in the rate of the concurrent response. Thus, as the reinforcement rate is increased for a concurrent response, the rate of that response also increases. Any change in the ongoing response could be attributed to either the increased rate of concurrent responses or concurrent reinforcers. To prevent the concomitant variation of response and reinforcement rates, Catania (1963) designed an experiment in which concurrent reinforcement could be manipulated while maintaining a very low concurrent response rate. Employing a changeover-key procedure (Findley, 1958), Catania changed one of two concurrent VI schedules to a signaled VI; that is, one VI was continuously in effect, and occasionally a second, signal key was lit. A response on this key during the signal switched the main key from VI to continuous reinforcement for only one reinforcer delivery. The experiment showed that the response rate on the main key was inversely related to the rate of signaled reinforcement. As the

---

* Experiments VI and VII were conducted at the University of Copenhagen, from January to November 1974, and reported by I. Iversen (1975b); Experiment VII was conducted at the University of Copenhagen, from September to December 1977.

procedure required only a single response for each signaled reinforcement, the results were said to show that the response rate decrease on the main key was determined directly by the signaled reinforcers and not by response interference.

Subsequently, Rachlin and Baum (1969) argued that the suppressive effect of signaled reinforcement might have come about by changes in the rate of unmeasured responses, such as observing and orienting toward the stimulus signaling availability of the concurrent reinforcer. Rachlin and Baum then hypothesized that competing observing responses toward the signal source could be measured by latencies between signal onset and the response to the signal. Rachlin and Baum repeated the experiment by Catania (1963), with a somewhat simplified procedure and with a manipulation of duration rather than rate of signaled reinforcement. A VI was continuously assigned to one key. A second key was lit on a VT schedule, and the first response on the second key during the signal produced a signaled reinforcer. The results showed that the VI response rate was inversely related to the reinforcer duration on the signal key. Rachlin and Baum also suggested that the decreased VI response rate was not a result of increased observing responses toward the stimulus source since the response latencies to the signal key were uncorrelated with the VI response rate. However, whether observing responses actually occurred toward the signal key was not reported. The data thus confirmed the previous position that the ongoing response is directly influenced by concurrent reinforcement rather than by concurrent responses.

Catania (1969) then replicated the procedure by Rachlin and Baum, with the exception that the VI key was darkened whenever the concurrent signal key was lit. This procedural change would make observing responses redundant, and thus reduce the likelihood of observing responses toward the signal key as a competing response. (In Catania's experiment, however, the VI key was also darkened during reinforcer deliveries. The dark VI key therefore did not reliably indicate signal key illumination.) The results again confirmed the findings of the previous experiments. Catania did not report, however, whether the experimental procedures actually prevented the development of observing responses toward the signal key. The relationship between an ongoing response and concurrent reinforcement was then generalized to propose that the rate of an ongoing response is directly inhibited by reinforcement of a concurrent response.

Using similar procedures, Catania and Dobson (1972) suggested that responding might have been interrupted frequently by observing responses but reported that visual inspection did not reveal any consistent head movements specific to the schedule component with signaled reinforcement. Catania et al. similarly argued that "the effects of signaled reinforcement might be attributed to observing responses . . . , but it is not plausible that such looking would consume as much time as the movement between the two keys when concurrent reinforcement is unsignalled" (1974, p. 106).

In contrast, a recent experiment found that changeovers between concurrently reinforced responses appeared to be associated with high rates of observing responses toward the discriminative stimulus (Iversen, 1975a). The sheer observation of any signal-observing response with a signaled reinforcement procedure suggests that the previous experiments might profitably be replicated with the additional recording and manipulation of observing responses. The issue of response versus reinforcement interaction might be considerably clarified by a direct and quantitative analysis of response interactions within the signaled reinforcement procedure.

Experiment VI

This experiment simply investigated the extent to which an ongoing VI response and concurrent signaled reinforcement might be associated with changes in observing responses toward the signal source. More specifically, two male homing pigeons were trained with VI on one key and a signaled reinforcement procedure on a second key. The pigeons had a previous history of key pecking reinforced on *conc* VI FR. The experimental chamber had a floor area of 30 × 30 cm and a height of 36 cm. Three 2.5-cm diameter keys with a center to center distance of 5.0 cm were positioned 20.0 cm above the floor. Pecks on the left key were reinforced on a VI 3 min with arithmetically distributed interreinforcement intervals. The left key was transilluminated by orange light during sessions except during grain delivery for pecks on this key.

The experiment was conducted in three phases. In Phase A, only the VI for left key responding was in effect. Signaled reinforcement was introduced in Phases B and C. Consequently, the right key (10 cm from the left key) was occasionally lit green. A single peck on this lit key produced grain delivery and turned off the green light. The trials on the right key were distributed arithmetically on a VT schedule with a mean intertrial interval of 2 min in Phase B and 1 min in Phase C. The rates of signaled reinforcement on the right key were thus 0.0, 0.5, and 1.0/min during Phases A, B, and C, respectively. A session was terminated after 50 min for Phases A and B but after 40 min for Phase C due to the higher rates of grain delivery. Reinforcer delivery was 3 sec of access to mixed grain. Phases A, B, and C lasted 18, 10, and 15 sessions, respectively.

To record observing responses toward the right key, a 0.4-cm diameter photocell was positioned 3.0 cm below the center of the key. The chamber was illuminated by one white light in the ceiling, 8.5 cm from the left cage wall and 4.0 cm from the back wall of the chamber. The houselight was thus behind and above the head of the pigeon when pecking the left VI key. Movements of the head and upper neck to the right of the chamber midline toward the area around the right key occluded the photocell and defined observing responses.

The times allocated to responses in concurrent schedules are typically measured as the cumulative time elapsing from a changeover to one response and the subsequent changeover to a concurrent response. The indirect measure of time allocation therefore includes long interresponse times (IRT) presumeably devoted to unrecorded, not explicitly reinforced responses. Inclusion of such unmeasured response durations as time allocated to a recorded response would be avoided by the direct recording of response durations (Dunham, 1972). A second advantage of actual response durations is the applicability of units of measure across behaviors of different topography, such as pecking one key and observing toward a second key (Premack, 1965). The time spent pecking the left key was defined as the number of 0.5-sec periods in which pecking occurred on the left key. Only one time unit was counted if more than one key peck occurred within the 0.5-sec period. The time spent observing was defined as the number of 0.5-sec periods with the photocell occluded. For each session, the probabilities (or relative durations) of key pecking and observing were calculated by dividing the number of 0.5-sec units entered for each response by the total session duration minus the duration of reinforcer delivery (Dunham, 1972).

The experimental procedures established that observing responses may not only occur toward the signal source, but may also increase in probability with increases in the signaled reinforcement rate (Figure 3.12). The increased proba-

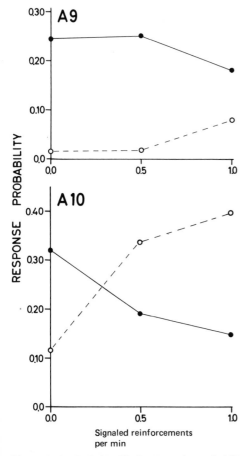

Figure 3.12. Relationship between the probability of pecking the VI key (black circles) and the probability of observing the signal key (white circles) as a function of the signaled reinforcement rate. Data points are means calculated from the last five sessions of each phase.

bility of observing responses as a function of the signaled reinforcement rate would suggest that observing responses may be systematically affected by manipulations of signaled reinforcement parameters. The simultaneously decreased probability of the ongoing response was at least correlated with an increased probability of observing responses. Note that the VI response and the observing probabilities remained unchanged for pigeon A9 when the signaled reinforcement rate was increased from 0.0 to 0.5 reinforcements/min. Overall, the probability of VI responding was then in fact more closely correlated with the probability of observing than with the rate of signaled reinforcement.

The present data tentatively suggest an alternative interpretation of the signaled reinforcement procedure. The decreased probability of the VI response may simply have come about by the increased probability of observing responses toward the signal source.

Experiment VII

The purpose of this experiment was to investigate directly the influence of observing responses upon VI responding. The probability and pattern of observing the signal key was manipulated by inserting an opaque shield between the signal key and the VI key, without simultaneously changing the reinforcement parameters.

A second purpose was to measure the time allocation between schedule components. However, the traditional measure as elapsed time between changeover responses cannot be applied to the signaled reinforcement procedure. Because of the low number of changeovers to the signal key response (only one for each signal presentation) and the brief duration of the signaled component (from signal onset to the first response on the signal key), virtually all of the session time is spent in the VI component. Hence, the time allocated to VI remains relatively invariant across the range of reinforcement parameters on the signaled VI. A similar argument applies to the relative response rate measure. Thus, neither time allocation nor relative response rate in VI can equal the relative reinforcement rate with the procedure of signaled reinforcement.

Time allocation between schedule components has also been measured as the time elapsed in either half of experimental chambers associated with each response and schedule component (Rachlin and Baum, 1969; Bacotti, 1977). Such a measure was used in the present experiment. Therefore, the experimental chamber, which was the same as in Experiment VI, had the following modifications: a 2.5-mm diameter metal bar was fixed under the midline of the grid floor, and the floor would tilt lightly whenever the pigeon moved from one side of the chamber to the other.

To manipulate the probability of observing responses an opaque shield was inserted between the response keys in Phases C and D. The 0.01-cm metal shield protruded 4.0 cm into the cage at a right angle to the wall with the keys. The shield was 12.5 cm long and was positioned with the lower edge 15.0 cm from the floor. The shield thus extended 7.5 cm above and 5.0 cm below the keys. Observations made during a preliminary experiment with one pigeon indicated that the insertion of a shield between the keys resulted in observing responses more directly in front of the signal key. A second houselight was therefore added to record observing responses with the altered topography. Houselight 2 was positioned in the ceiling, 4.0 cm from the right cage wall and 4.0 cm from the back wall of the chamber. With the addition of the second houselight, the photocell under the signal key would also be occluded by the pigeon standing closely in front of the signal key. The two types of observing responses are shown in Figure 3.13. In Figure 3.13A, pigeon A12 is standing in front of the signal key; in Figure 3.13B, pigeon A13 is shown with an excursion of the head away from the VI key and toward the signal key.

Experimentally naive homing pigeons were initially trained to peck on the left key with reinforcement on VI 150 sec (arithmetically distributed interreinforcement intervals). Only the VI for left key pecking was in effect in Phase A, and this established the baseline of photocell activation in the absence of signaled reinforcement. The nonzero observing probability with no signaled reinforcement in Phase A resulted from the relative positions of the pigeon during VI key pecking and collateral behaviors such as turning and bending motions.

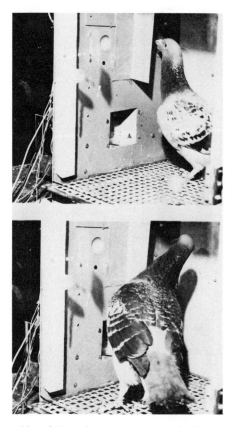

Figure 3.13. Two topographies of observing responses recorded by the photocell under the right key (signal key) following insertion of the opaque shield. Top, pigeon A12; Bottom, pigeon A13.

For example, during bursts of VI key pecking pigeon A11 stood along the floor diagonal. The pulling back of the head and upper neck between individual pecks on the VI key would then briefly occlude the photocell under the signal key. A high rate of very brief photocell occlusions was therefore the baseline of observing responses for this pigeon in Phase A.

In direct replication of Experiment VI, a signaled VI 150 sec was introduced on the right key in Phase B. The probability of observing responses was then experimentally increased by inserting the shield between the keys in Phase C. Finally, the change in ongoing VI responding following extinction of observing responses was studied in Phase D by preventing reinforcement after the signal. Pecks on the right key then merely terminated the signal. Sessions were 40 min,

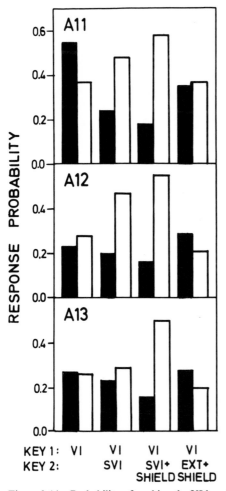

Figure 3.14. Probability of pecking the VI key (black bars) and probability of observing the signal key (white bars) for each experimental phase. SVI: signaled VI on key 2. Data are means from the last five sessions of each phase.

and grain delivery was 3 sec throughout the experiment. Phases A, B, C, and D lasted 24, 30, 12, and 12 sessions, respectively.

The probability measures generally provided both direct and systematic replication of the data from previous experiments (Figure 3.14). First, the VI response decreased and the observing response increased after the introduction of signaled reinforcement. Second, the VI response further decreased when the observing response was increased by inserting the sheild between the keys. Finally, the VI response increased again when the observing response decreased with extinction of the signal key response. The data then clearly show an inverse relationship between VI responding and concurrent observing responses.

The time allocation measures showed that the proportion of time allocated to the signal side did not equal the proportion of reinforcer delivery for any pigeon (Table 3.3). Furthermore, the marked change in the time allocated to the signal side from Phase B to Phase C (when the shield was inserted) was not associated with any alterations of the rates of reinforcer delivery. The rate of shifting chamber side roughly covaried with the proportion of the time spent on the signal side. The proportion of time allocation then appears not to be an unequivocal "measure" of the reinforcement value of the associated schedule components.

The minute interactions between VI responding, observing, and standing on the signal side are probably best described with reference to sample event records (Figure 3.15). For all pigeons, the VI response pattern changed concomitantly with the development of observing responses toward the signal key in Phase B. The number of long IRT on the VI key increased for each pigeon, with virtually all of the long IRT associated with an instance of observing. Standing on the signal side frequently occurred in synchrony with observing. The pattern

Table 3.3   Proportion of time on signal side, rate of shifting side (shifts/min), and proportion of signaled reinforcement for each phase

Pigeon no.	Phase	Proportion of time on signal side	Rate of shifting side	Proportion of signaled reinforcement
A11	A	0.09	8.1	0.0
	B	0.39	28.7	0.5
	C	0.54	32.7	0.5
	D	0.35	22.5	0.0
A12	A	0.60	36.3	0.0
	B	0.74	40.2	0.5
	C	0.64	36.6	0.5
	D	0.28	28.9	0.0
A13	A	0.18	10.5	0.0
	B	0.25	14.3	0.5
	C	0.40	23.9	0.5
	D	0.17	14.0	0.0

Data are means of the last five sessions of each phase.

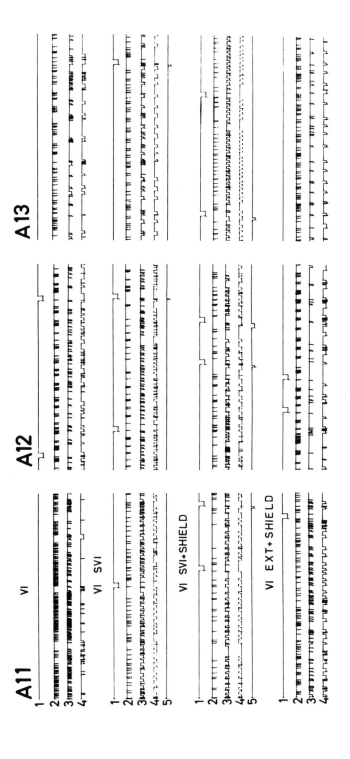

Figure 3.15. Segments of event records showing interactions between ongoing VI responding, observing, and standing on the signal side for each experimental phase. 1, reinforcement; 2, key pecking; 3, observing; 4, signal side; 5, signal.

30 SEC

194

of VI responding and observing further changed when the shield was inserted between the keys (Phase C). The duration of each observing response instance then increased, and the duration of the concomitant IRT in VI responding increased accordingly for pigeons A11 and A12. For pigeon A13, observing response episodes decreased somewhat in duration but markedly increased in number. At the same time the number of intermediate IRTs and VI responding increased for pigeon A13. When pecking the signal key was no longer reinforced in Phase D, the observing response disappeared for all pigeons, resulting in a return of photocell activation to baseline. The patterns of VI responding simultaneously increased to approach those obtained in Phase A.

To provide an analysis of the reliability of the automatic recording of observing responses, the observing behavior was recorded by two human observers in Phase C. An observing response was recorded by pressing a button as long as "the pigeon looked or moved directly toward the right key behind the shield." *As an accuracy check, the pigeons were observed from the left, and the observer could not see the exact moment of photocell occlusion* (Figure 3.13). The observers also recorded turning behavior whenever "the pigeon made a turn in whichever direction."

Figure 3.16 presents sample event records of the automatically recorded behaviors and the behaviors recorded by the human observers. Recordings of observing responses from both observers precisely covaried with the photocell occlusions for pigeons A11 and A13, whereas observing responses were occasionally recorded by both observers without a simultaneous occlusion of the photocell for pigeon A12. For all pigeons, photocell occlusions rarely occurred without a simultaneous recording of observing responses from the observers. Photocell occlusions and instances of observing responses recorded by the observers were thus closely covariant. The duration of individual photocell occlusions was also closely covariant with the simultaneous observing durations recorded by the observers. Observing responses were frequently observed simultaneously with the behavior of turning in circles. For each pigeon, one or more instances of observing the signal key typically occurred during the turning behavior.

Experiment VIII

To further establish the species generality of interacting responses with concurrent schedules, Experiment VIII examined the development of signal-observing responses in rats. Our previous emphasis was on affecting the ongoing VI response by manipulating concurrent observing responses. This experiment examined the interdependency between the responses by instead manipulating the VI response to change the concurrent observing response. First, observing responses were developed with a signaled VI. Then a VI for lever pressing was introduced to suppress the probability of observing. Third, to further suppress the observing probability without changing the rate of VI reinforcement, the probability of VI responding was increased experimentally by adding a differential reinforcement of high rate (DRH) contingency.

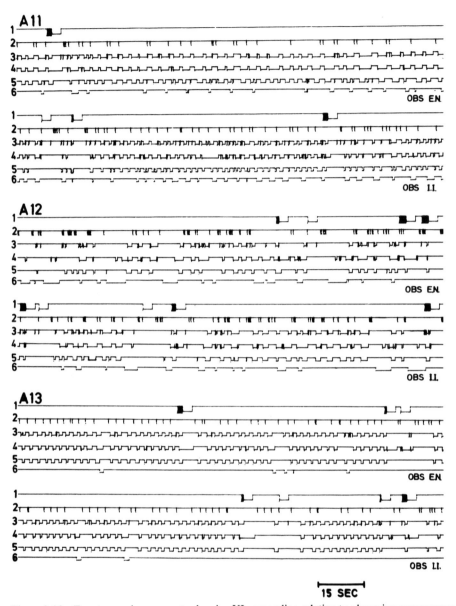

Figure 3.16. Event recorder segments showing VI responding relative to observing responses recorded automatically (A) and observing responses recorded by observers (B). Observers also recorded turning motions. Note that the recording speed is higher than for the records in Figure 3.15. 1, signal or reinforcement; 2, key pecking; 3, observing A; 4, signal side; 5, observing B; 6, turning.

Observing responses directed toward the source of signaled reinforcement were analyzed in a modified Campden Instruments rodent test chamber. An aluminum plate (0.2 × 8.0 × 8.0 cm) was centered on a Plexiglas wall opposite to the lever and the food tray. This left a floor area of 21.0 × 21.0 cm. The signal was a blinking white light, with on–off phases of 0.15 sec, which appeared behind a 1.6-cm diameter hole centered on the aluminum plate, 9.0 cm above the floor. In previous experiments, signaled reinforcement was contingent upon emission of one peck on the key with the signal, the signal response. In this experiment, nose poking to the signal source served as the signal response and was recorded as a 3.0-mm forward push of the 4.0-mm arm of a microswitch recessed 4.0 mm behind the hole.

The observing responses were automatically recorded by a body-capacitance sensitivity system adjusted to detect any activity within 1.0 cm of the aluminum plate. Direct contact with the plate also activated the sensing system. This response served as an equivalent to the observing response recorded as photocell occlusion in the previous experiments.

The additional response of entry into the food tray was recorded by an electrical contact attached to the covering flap. Lever pressing, observing, signal responses, and food tray entry were recorded in 0.3-sec bins.

The three male Wistar albino rats were maintained at 80% of their free-feeding body weights and had a previous history of response-independent reinforcement on a VT 1 min for 60 sessions. The reinforcer was a 45-mg food pellet and sessions lasted 30 min.

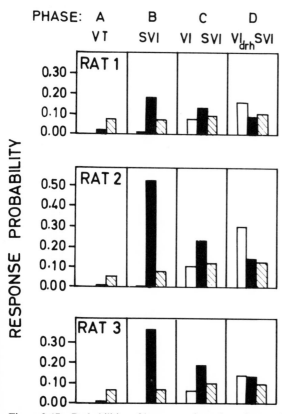

Figure 3.17. Probabilities of lever pressing, observing, and food tray entry for each experimental phase. Data are means from the last three sessions of each phase. White bars, lever; black bars, observing; shaded bars, tray.

Baseline probabilities of lever pressing, observing, signal responses, and food-tray entry were first established with food pellets merely delivered response independently on a VT 1 min for 10 sessions (Phase A). Observing responses were then introduced by changing the schedule to a signaled VI 1 min. The signal was turned on by the VT schedule and the first signal response produced a food pellet and turned off the signal (Phase B, 10 sessions).

This change to signaled VI dramatically increased the probability of observing for all rats (Figure 3.17). The topography of the observing responses included sniffing the signal source without emission of the signal response, fixating the nose about 0.5 cm from the signal, or touching the plate with a forepaw during sniffing at the signal. The signal response (activation of the nose contact in the hole) rarely occurred in the absence of the signal and was clearly dissociated from the observing response in the absence of the signal (Figure 3.18 and Table 3.4). The observing response necessarily occurred in conjunction with the signal response during the signal. These results lend considerable support to the conclusion that signaled reinforcement gives rise to observing responses directed toward the source of the signal.

The probability and pattern of the developed observing response was then affected by increasing the concurrent probability of lever pressing in Phase C (10 sessions). Lever pressing was first shaped with 10 extra food pellets in the first 5 min of the first session, and thereafter reinforced on a VI 1 min. The probability of lever pressing of course increased, but the observing probability simultaneously decreased for all rats (Figure 3.17). The pattern of observing also appreciably changed with the increased lever-pressing probability. Now bursts of observing were shorter and more frequent, and they commonly occurred in rapid alternation with a single or a few lever presses (Figure 3.18). The probability and pattern of observing responses developed on signalled VI are then clearly modifiable by concurrent lever pressing on a VI. However, the increase in lever pressing with VI is formally confounded with the increase in reinforcement rate of lever pressing (from zero to 1.0/min).

Table 3.4 Average signal response latency (seconds) and rate of the signal response (response/min) for each phase

Rat no.		Phase					
		A	B	C	D	E	F
1	signal latency	—	3.0	3.4	4.1	2.9	1.6
	signal response	1.2	5.4	2.8	2.3	4.4	21.2
2	signal latency	—	2.1	2.8	3.1	2.4	1.9
	signal response	1.0	2.1	1.1	1.5	1.6	6.0
3	signal latency	—	5.4	5.4	5.2	4.4	1.4
	signal response	1.0	15.8	10.3	10.6	7.6	17.8

Data are calculated from the last five sessions of each phase, except for Phase F, for which the data are calculated from the last 10 min of the session.

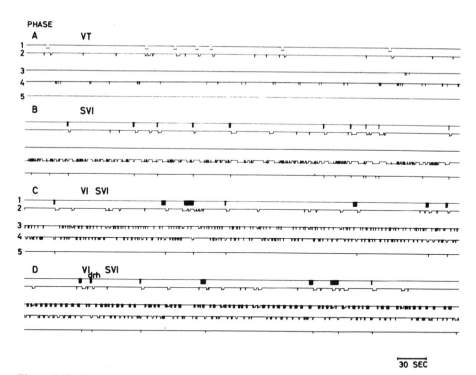

Figure 3.18.   Event recorder segments for rat 2 showing the interactions between the recorded responses for each experimental phase. 1, signal; 2, food tray entry; 3, lever/pellet; 4, observing; 5, signal response.

The probability of lever pressing was therefore further increased without any changes in reinforcement parameters by adding a DRH contingency to lever pressing (Phase D, 12 sessions). The DRH was introduced gradually, with a VI reinforcer contingent upon emission of two lever presses within 0.75 sec (first session), three lever presses within 2.0 sec (second and third sessions), and then four lever presses within 2.0 sec (remaining sessions).

The added DRH contingency increased the probability of lever pressing and concomitantly decreased the probability of observing (Figure 3.17). Lever pressing now occurred in brief bursts, which is typical of VI schedules incorporating a DRH contingency (Ferster and Skinner, 1957). The pattern of observing also changed from frequent short bursts to less frequent bursts of a slightly longer duration relative to Phase C (Figure 3.18).

The results clearly extend the previous experiments in showing a direct modification of both the probability and pattern of observing responses by manipulating the concurrent probability and pattern of lever pressing. In a complimentary fashion, increasing observing responses decreased the probability of VI responding (Experiment VII), and an increase in VI responding decreased the probability of observing (this experiment) without any corresponding changes in reinforcement parameters.

In previous signaled reinforcement experiments, interest focused on the signal response latency as a possible measure of the extent of observing responses (Rachlin and Baum, 1969). In the present experiment, the signal response latency and the observing probability were not clearly related (Table 3.4 and Figure 3.17). Therefore, an increase in observing is apparently not unequivocally associated with a decrease in signal response latency and vice versa.

However, the signal response latency may still be determined by the response context. A more molecular analysis reveals that one can indeed predict the signal latency from the particular response occurring at signal onset. The event records presented in Figure 3.18 show long signal latencies when the rat was in the food tray at signal onset, whereas the latency was quite brief when the signal occurred during observing responses.

Table 3.5 gives the matrix of signal response latencies associated with specific responses at signal onset. The initial response (either lever pressing, food tray entry, or observing) was noted at each signal presentation along with the corresponding latency of the signal response. Short, intermediate, and long latencies occurred with observing, lever pressing, and food tray entry as the emitted response at signal onset, respectively. These results indicate that a subsequent signal response latency may be predicted simply on the basis of the response occurring at signal onset. For this reason, the extent of observing or any other particular response cannot be predicted by the average latency of the signal response. This analysis is particularly consistent with the predictions of VI IRT from the initiating collateral response (Experiment VI in Chapter 5).

In sum, the results leave little doubt that observing responses do occur under schedules that signal reinforcement. Perhaps more importantly for a concurrent response analysis, the observing responses modify concurrent responses and are themselves modified by alterations in concurrent responses.

Table 3.5 Signal response latency (seconds) with respect to the response occurring at signal onset

Rat no.	Occurring response	Phase		
		A	B	C
1	lever pressing	3.7	4.1	4.1
	food tray entry	14.5	8.7	8.4
	observing	1.4	2.2	1.1
2	lever pressing	3.4	4.4	3.1
	food tray entry	7.7	8.0	5.9
	observing	1.8	1.1	1.6
3	lever pressing	5.9	5.9	3.6
	food tray entry	11.2	13.0	12.0
	observing	1.7	1.8	1.3

Data are calculated from event records from the last three sessions of each phase.

Discussion

The results extend the response model to the theoretically important signaled reinforcement procedure by showing that the probability of an ongoing response may be inversely related to the probability of observing responses controlled by a concurrent schedule of signaled reinforcement.

The signaled reinforcement procedure is important historically because of the apparent demonstration that an ongoing response is directly dependent upon concurrent reinforcement rates. The argument is predicated on the fact that the signaling procedure controls a very low response probability on the signal key, and the inhibitory effect upon the ongoing VI response therefore does not result from "some kind of competition between the two responses for available time" (Catania, 1973, p. 518). However, can the absence of responses on the signal key support the broader generalization that response competition is absent in the signaled reinforcement procedure? More clearly, is responding on the signal key really representative of *all* responses concurrent to the VI response? This problem was in fact recognized in previous theoretical discussions of the signaled reinforcement experiments, which clearly dismissed observing as a possible interfering response.

One argument raised against response competition was that observing responses would presumeably not consume as much time as the required movement between the response keys in regular *conc* VI VI. Therefore, the similar effect of concurrent signaled and unsignaled reinforcement upon an ongoing VI response could not depend upon response competition (Catania et al., 1974). Whatever the relationship may be between the movement between response keys and observing responses with different procedures, the present experiments do demonstrate competition between VI responding on one key and concurrent observing toward a second signal key. In fact, the rate of moving from side to side in the experimental chamber (Experiment VII) did increase with introduction of signaled reinforcement, indicating considerable "movement between the keys."

A second argument against response competition is based upon the assumption that the key peck latency "measures" the extent of observing responses toward the signal key (Rachlin and Baum, 1969). Rachlin and Baum found no consistent relationship between the signal latency and the VI response rate, and concluded that changes in the VI response did not result from interference from observing responses toward the signal key. A similar inconsistent relationship was obtained in the present experiments, with the response latency to the signal and the observing probability negatively correlated in Experiment VI, positively correlated in Experiment VII (Figure 3.19), but not clearly correlated in Experiment VIII. Nevertheless, the present results cannot support the additional assumption that observing responses therefore do not occur or cannot interfere with VI responding. The results instead clearly demonstrate that observing responses are in fact generated by signaled concurrent reinforcement. The observing responses were furthermore systematically related to the rate of signaled reinforcement and apparatus manipulations, and they were

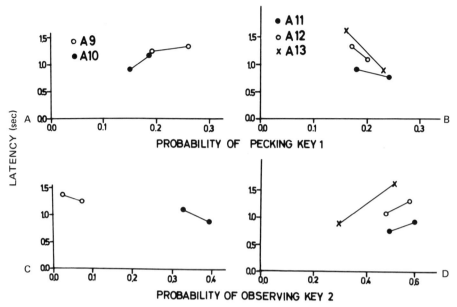

Figure 3.19. Relationships between the latency of pecking the signal key 2 and: **A,B.** Probability of pecking the VI key or **C,D.** Probability of observing key 2. Data from Experiments VI (panels A and C) and VII (panels B and D) are shown.

directly recorded and observed rather than indirectly derived through other "measures" such as the signal response latency.

Observing responses toward the source of a discriminative stimulus may perhaps be a *necessary* outcome of the functional control of discriminative stimuli. A changeover to the reinforced response controlled by the discriminative stimulus would seem to require a prior orientation of the relevant exteroceptor toward the source of the stimulus (Iversen, 1975a). The emphasis on the necessity of observing responses is by no means unique or new. Spence, for example, argued as follows:

> The animal learns many other responses in addition to the final, selective approaching reaction. Prominent and important among these are what have been termed, for want of a better name, "preparatory" responses. These latter consist of the responses which lead to the reception of the appropriate aspects of the total environmental complex on the animals' sensorium, eg., the orientation and fixation of the head and eyes toward the critical stimuli. That is, an animal learns to "look at" one aspect of the situation rather than another because of the fact that this response has always been followed within a short temporal interval by the final goal response. (Spence, 1937, p. 432)

More recently, Browne and Dinsmoor similarly argued that "in order to respond differentially to stimuli in their environment, animals must learn to observe those stimuli, i.e., to establish contact between the stimulus energy and the sensory receptors" (1972, p. 745).

Clearly, the present data do not support the assumptions of response independence and reinforcement interaction within the signaled reinforcement procedure. On the contrary, the probability of an ongoing response appears to be inversely related to the concurrent signaled reinforcement rate precisely because the procedures generate specific observing responses that interfere with the VI response. The present results therefore suggest a change in the emphasis from a direct to an indirect relationship between the probability of an ongoing response and concurrent reinforcement rates. Importantly, the prior claims of reinforcement interaction and simultaneous response independence are thus inconsistent with the present data. On the other hand, the single claim of response interaction would appear to be consistent not only with the present data but also with the previous effect described by the data giving rise to the reinforcement model.

Superstitious Responding with Response–Independent Reinforcement (Experiment IX)*

The preceding experiments showed that a decrement in an ongoing response after introduction of signaled concurrent reinforcement cannot be considered an unequivocal demonstration of reinforcement interaction. A second procedure of presenting concurrent reinforcers independently of responding has also been used as an apparent demonstration of reinforcement interaction. Thus, Rachlin and Baum (1972) reported that the rate of ongoing VI responding was inversely related to the rate of concurrent reinforcers presented independently of any response on a VT schedule. FR, FI, or RI responding may also be decreased by response-independent concurrent reinforcement on fixed-time (FT) or VT schedules (Edwards et al., 1970; Deluty, 1976b; Lattal and Bryan, 1976; Zeiler, 1976).

Within the controversy of response versus reinforcement interaction, the rationale behind response-independent reinforcement is that responses are not required for concurrent reinforcer delivery; therefore changes in the rate of the ongoing response are said *not* to depend upon concurrent response rate changes (Rachlin and Baum, 1972; Catania, 1973). The procedure of response-independent reinforcement is thus logically equivalent to that of signaled reinforcement; both manipulate concurrent reinforcement rates with an assumed absence of any changes in concurrent response rates. As with signaled reinforcement, this assumption can only be upheld provided response-independent reinforcement does not alter or generate concurrent competing responses.

Clearly, response independence does not seem to hold for the signaled reinforcement procedures of Experiments VI, VII, and VIII. What about the response-independent procedure? One suggestive feature of response-independent reinforcement is that responses of various topographies may increase in rate in spite of the absence of any requirement between responses and reinforcer delivery; this is, of course, the well-known finding of superstitious re-

---

* Experiment was conducted at the University of Copenhagen, from February to April 1976.

sponding (Skinner, 1948). Almost a century of research has similarly showed alterations in responses of various topographies with classical conditioning procedures, genuinely characterized by an absence of response requirements (Pavlov, 1927; Zener, 1937; Kimble, 1967).

Applied to the procedure employed by Rachlin and Baum (1972), response-independent concurrent reinforcement might then decrease the rate of an ongoing response because of an increased rate of concurrent superstitious responses. Rachlin and Baum specifically argued, however, that superstitious responses could not explain the decrement of the ongoing response. Similar to observing responses in the signaled reinforcement procedure, "other" responses were in fact admitted a possible existence but certainly no importance in the response-independent reinforcement procedure. Rachlin and Baum thus argued that "other" responses might be changed but would not affect the rate of the ongoing response. Instead, response-independent reinforcement was claimed to make the subjects "distractable," "that is, the procedures somehow enhance the value . . . of sources of reinforcement (grooming, exercise, exploration, etc.) other than reinforcement -A and -B" (Rachlin and Baum, 1972, p. 240). (The terms reinforcement -A and -B were used for the response-dependent and response-independent reinforcements, respectively.) In essence, "other" responses were defined as "other" sources of reinforcement and were not affected by temporal contiguity with the response-independent reinforcers.

An opposite conclusion supporting the development of superstitious responding was reached in related research on response-independent reinforcement effects in simple schedules. Zeiler, for example, concluded that changing a simple schedule from response-dependent to response-independent reinforcement "acts to make this particular competing behavior predominate, thereby resulting in the rapid decrease in the frequency of emission of the original response" (1971, p. 404). Similar conclusions were reached by Schoenfeld and Farmer (1970), Lachter (1971), Lattal (1972), Davis et al. (1973), Alleman and Zeiler (1974), and Buel (1975).

A considerable complication for the eventual resolution of the theoretical opposition is that "other" responses have not been recorded with either procedure. Since the relationship between "other" responses and response-independent reinforcement is so essential, observation and recording of "other" responses would seem to be a natural prerequisite for the eventual solution of the issue of response versus reinforcement interaction.

Experiment IX

One purpose of this experiment was simply to repeat the procedure of Rachlin and Baum with the additional recording of such "other" responses concurrent to an ongoing response. Second, a variety of experiments suggest that a critical determinant of response rates is the frequency with which response-independent reinforcement is actually in close temporal contiguity with a particular response (Davis and Bitterman, 1971; Lachter, 1971; Henton, 1972; Lattal, 1973, 1974). Applied to concurrent schedules, the effect of concurrent reinforcers might then depend upon how many of such reinforcers occur in close temporal contiguity with "other" responses. A second purpose of the experiment was then to assess more precisely multiresponse changes following manipulations of the temporal contiguity between "other" responses and response-independent reinforcement.

Two albino rats maintained at 80% of their free-feeding body weights were used as subjects. They had a previous history of reinforcement of lever pressing on *conc* VI VI. The experiment was done in a two-lever Campden Instruments rodent test chamber with the right lever removed and the hole covered with a metal plate.

The rats were routinely observed through a one-way window in the sound-attenuating chamber, and behaviors other than lever pressing and food tray entry (movement of the flap covering the food tray) were recorded by the experimenter during the last two sessions of each phase. Exploration was recorded when a rat walked around and sniffed corners, walls, or the floors. Standing (rearing) was recorded when the rat was in an upright position sniffing the ceiling of the chamber. Finally, grooming was recorded during scratching and licking of the body. A fourth response, being immobile, was only observed and recorded in Phase G. For each response, the investigator pressed a button for as long as the response occurred. Each response was recorded in 0.3-sec units.

To establish an ongoing response, lever pressing was maintained on VI 1 min in Phases A to E. Reinforcer delivery was always one 45-mg food pellet. The effects of concurrent response-independent reinforcement were analyzed in Phase B, in which a VT 1-min was simply presented concurrently with the ongoing VI response. For ease of description and consistency with the Rachlin and Baum terminology, pellets delivered on VI were termed *A* pellets, whereas pellets delivered on VT or the subsequent modifications of the VT schedule were termed *B* pellets. The programmers for *A* and *B* pellets ran independently in all phases. Each phase lasted eight sessions and each session was 40 min long.

The introduction of concurrent response-independent pellets in Phase B decreased the probability of lever pressing for both rats and simultaneously increased the probability of some of the "other" responses (Figure 3.20). This finding is in agreement with the previously reported effects of response-independent reinforcement in concurrent schedules (Rachlin and Baum, 1972). However, the previous argument (that the changes in VI responding were exclusively determined by concurrent reinforcement per se and not by changes in "other" responses) was based upon a logical interpretation of procedures other than truly response-independent reinforcement. Rachlin and Baum added a second procedure, in which the response contingencies were manipulated to increase the possibility of temporal contiguity between "other" responses and concurrent reinforcement. Their manipulation was to never deliver concurrent reinforcers within 2 sec of emission of the ongoing VI response. The VI response rate was reported to be equally changed whether the concurrent reinforcers were response independent or delayed, in spite of the possibility of dif-

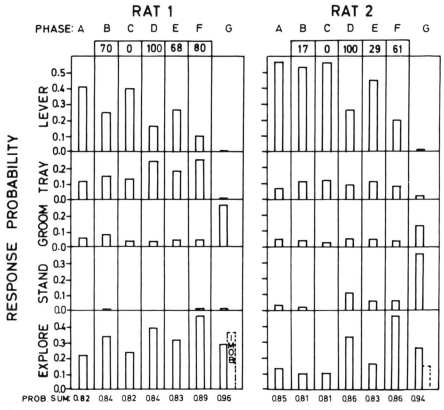

Figure 3.20. Probabilities of lever pressing, food tray entry, grooming, standing, and exploration for each rat and experimental phase. Percentages of the delivered *B* pellets preceded by a 1.0-sec pause in lever pressing are shown at the top of the columns for Phases B to F. Summed response probabilities are shown at the bottom of each column. A new response, imobility, is added in Phase G and is shown in the row for exploration. Data are means of the last two sessions of each phase.

ferential rates of "other" competing responses. Rachlin and Baum then argued that the similar effects on the ongoing VI response must be directly related to the similar rates of concurrent reinforcement rather than differential rates of concurrent responses. The Rachlin and Baum manipulations were repeated in the present experiment, but with somewhat different results.

Although *B* pellets were delivered response independently in Phase B, they were in fact in close temporal contiguity with emitted responses. Thus some of the *B* pellets happened to be temporally close to a lever press, with the rest of the *B* pellets close to the "other" responses. The number of such contiguities between "other" responses and a *B* pellet was defined as the number of instances in which a *B* pellet was delivered in the absence of a lever press for 1 sec. An operate–reset timer remained on as long as lever pressing occurred with IRT less than 1 sec. A *B* pellet delivered while this "response timer" was *off* thus counted as a *B* pellet contiguous with "other" responses.

The first step in the manipulation of temporal contiguity between B pellets and "other" responses involved the simple prevention of delivery of B pellets in contiguity with "other" responses (Phase C). The procedure was modified so that B pellets were now conjointly contingent upon the VT schedule and the *occurrence* of a lever press within 1 sec preceding B pellet delivery. Simply, B pellets were now only delivered when the response timer was on; that is, between zero and 1 sec of the emission of a lever press.

As a result, the fraction of B pellets closely contiguous with "other" responses was experimentally decreased to zero. The effect of this manipulation was that the lever-pressing probability became the same as in the absence of B pellets in Phase A (Figure 3.20). Introduction of concurrent reinforcement thus reduces an ongoing response only when at least some of the concurrent reinforcers occur in close temporal contiguity with "other" responses.

To further pursue this relationship the possibility of close contiguity between "other" responses and B pellet delivery was increased to maximal in Phase D. The B pellets were conjointly contingent upon the VT schedule and the *absence* of a lever press within 1 sec preceding B pellet delivery. Thus, B pellets could only be delivered when the response timer was off; that is, B pellets were never delivered between zero and 1 sec of the emission of a lever press.

With this optimal condition for the development of superstitious responding, the probability of some of the "other" responses increased, and simultaneously the probability of lever pressing decreased relative to the truly response-independent procedure in Phase B (Figure 3.20). The reliability of the findings were then assessed by again changing the procedure back to truly response-independent B pellet delivery (Phase E). The probability of lever pressing then increased to approximately the same level as in Phase B.

In the two final procedures, the influence of B pellets upon lever pressing was further analyzed by first changing the operant schedule to extinction (no A pellets were delivered, Phase F) and then totally preventing pellet delivery (neither A nor B pellets were delivered, Phase G). Lever pressing decreased, but not to zero, by removing the explicitly contingent A pellets in Phase F. At the same time, some of the "other" responses showed marked increases. The entire organization of recorded responses changed with the total elimination of all pellet deliveries in Phase G, with increases in immobility and grooming, and decreases in lever pressing, food tray entry, and exploration.

Discussion

Overall, the probability of lever pressing was rather precisely related to the sum of the probabilities of the "other" responses. Note that the probability of *all* recorded responses did not sum to unity. The sums ranged between 0.81 and 0.96, and were highest in Phase G. Although an attempt was made to record all responses exhaustively, some fraction of the session time was not represented in the measured response durations. Related analysis shows that differences in the sum of recorded response durations may be directly related to changes in the additional set of changeover responses controlled by the different schedules (Chapters 4 and 6).

One essential finding was that equal B pellet rates did not generate equal VI response probabilities across experimental phases (B, C, D, and E). B pellets simply had no decremental effect upon the ongoing VI response when none of them were contiguous with "other" responses. Given the premise of reinforcement interaction, equal rates of concurrent reinforcement should produce equal decrements in an ongoing response regardless of how the concurrent reinforcers are delivered. A previous very crucial argument was that concurrent reinforcement can be explicitly contingent upon concurrent responses, independent of any response, either signaled or delayed with respect to a specific ongoing response; the "source" of concurrent reinforcement should *not* matter for the decremental effect upon an ongoing response (Rachlin and Baum, 1972; Catania, 1973; Rachlin, 1973). The results of the present experiment clearly indicate, however, that the probability of an ongoing response may in fact be differently affected by equal rates of delivered concurrent reinforcers.

Recent reports provide substantial support for the present findings. Zeiler (1976, 1977) found that the rate of ongoing FI, VI, or VR responding was relatively higher when concurrent reinforcements were truly response independent than when explicitly contiguous with pauses in the ongoing response (i.e., delivered on a DRO schedule). Similarly, for a previously reinforced response undergoing extinction, the response rate may be higher when concurrent reinforcers are response independent then when contingent upon pausing in the extinguishing response (Davis and Bitterman, 1971; Lowry and Lachter, 1977).

Therefore, the effects of concurrent reinforcements upon either an ongoing response or a response undergoing extinction are not sufficiently described by the mere overall rates of delivered concurrent reinforcers. The probabilities of lever pressing and the summed probabilities of all "other" recorded responses were instead clear functions of the percentage of all pellet deliveries contiguous with the "other" responses (Figure 3.21). (Note that the abscissa does not give the relative rates of obtained reinforcement, which were 0.5 in Phases B, C, D, and E.) For both rats, the summed probabilities of the "other" responses and the lever-pressing probabilities were simply increasing and decreasing functions, respectively, of the percentages of all pellets contiguous with "other" responses. Thus, across all phases, the higher the percent of pellets contiguous with the "other" responses, the higher the probability of the "other" responses, and the lower the probability of lever pressing. The present data therefore rather specifically indicate that the decremental or "inhibitory" effect of a given rate of concurrent reinforcement upon an ongoing response may depend upon the fraction of the concurrent reinforcements being contiguous with "other" responses.

The previous argument that an ongoing response is inhibited by concurrent reinforcements independently of source (Rachlin and Baum, 1972; Catania, 1973; Rachlin, 1973) might, however, be formally preserved by arguing that only those concurrent reinforcements that are contingent on or contiguous with "other" responses can be classified as coming from another source. If that is

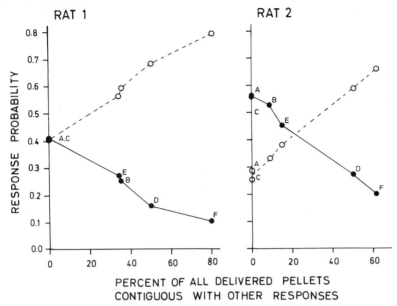

Figure 3.21. Lever-pressing probability (black circles) and the summed probabilities of "other" responses (white circles) for each rat as a function of the percent of all pellet deliveries contiguous with "other" responses. Letter for each data point indicates experimental phase.

the case, then concurrent reinforcements that are contiguous with the ongoing response might be added to the reinforcements that are directly contingent on that response. In essence, the inhibitory effect of concurrent reinforcement would be smaller if some fraction of the concurrent reinforcements were contiguous with the ongoing response. Applied to the present experiment, an ongoing response would not be inhibited by the concurrent response-independent reinforcements that "happened" to be contiguous with the ongoing response. [The absence of an incremental effect by the addition of reinforcements in close temporal contiguity with the VI response may not be empirically exceptional. The function relating rate of VI responding to rate of reinforcement may be roughly asymptotic at the reinforcement rates used in the present study (Catania and Reynolds, 1968). Therefore, the addition of reinforcements may not necessarily increase the overall response probability].

Therefore, the functional effect attributed to concurrent reinforcement depends upon the precise definition given to concurrent or "other" reinforcement. If only reinforcements contiguous with "other" responses qualify as concurrent reinforcement, then concurrent reinforcement is always inhibitory. Conversely, if response-independent reinforcements contiguous with an ongoing response qualify as concurrent reinforcement, then concurrent reinforcement is not always inhibitory. However, with either definition, the present experiment suggests that concurrent reinforcements decrease an ongoing response to the extent that they are contiguous to and increase the probability of concurrent responses.

1   T L T W_1 L C_1 L W_1 L W_1 L W_1 C_1 L W_1 S L W_1 S L C_1 L C_1 L C_1 W_2 L W_2 L W_2 L W_2 L W_2 L–

    W_2 L W_2 L C_1 S L F L C_4 S C_3 S C_2 L T W_1 L C_1 L C_1 L C_1 L C_1 L C_1 L C_4–

    $W_1 C_2$ L W_1 L W_1 L T L P

2   T L W_1 L W_1 L T W_1 L W_1 (T) P

3   (T) L P

4   T L (T) L W_1 L (T) L W (T) L $W_1 C_1$ L C (T) W_1 L P

5   T L W_1 L W_1 L T L W_1 L C_1 L W_1 L T L W_1 L T P

6   T L P

7   T W_1 L T W_1 L W_1 L W_1 L T L F T L W_1 L C_1 L W_1 C_4 L W_1 L W_1 L W_1 L W_1 L W_1 S T W_1 L W_1–

    L W_1 L W_1 L W_1 C_4 L W_1 L (C_4) P

8   T (C_4) L T W_1 L (C_4) L (C_4) T L (C_4) T L W_1 L T W_1 (C_4) L (C_4) L (C_4) L (C_4) T L (C_4) L P

9   T L T [W_1 1] P

10 T L T [W_1 1] [W_1 1] C_1 L W_1 L W_1 L W_1 L W_1 T L W_1 L C_1 C_4 L W_1 L W_1 L C_1 L C_3 G P

11 T L T L C_1 L C_1 W_2 L W_2 C_3 F L F W_4 P

12 T L T L T W_1 L W_4 L T W_1 L C_4 S F L C_1 L T L W_1 L T (W_4) P

13 T L C_4 L T L C_3 (W_4) S C_3 (W_4) C_4 S F (W_4) L P

14 T L T L C_4 L F L C_4 (W_4) C_4 L (W_4) S (W_4) C_4 (W_4) C_4 C_2 W_2 L (W_4) G F L (W_4) C_3 (W_4) F W_2 L T (W_4) C_3–

    S (W_4) F L C_1 C_2 C_3 (W_4) F G L P

15 T L C_1 T L C_1 L C_1 L C_1 L C_1 [W_1 1] P

16 T L [W_1 1] T L W_1 T L [W_1 1] [W_1 1] W_1 S C_4 L [W_1 1] C_4 L T [W_1 1] C_1 L C_1 L C_1 T [W_1 1] [W_1 1] C_1–

    L T L T L C_1 L W_1 L C_1 L C_1 L W_1 L W_1 L T L C_1 L W_1 L C_1 T W_1 L C_1 L C_1–

    L W_1 L W_1 L W_1 L P

17 T L T L P

18 T L T L C_1 L T L W_1 L C_4 L W_1 L W_1 L W_1 L C_1 L W_1 L W_1 L W_1 L C_1 L W_1 S F C_1 L P

19 (T) P

20 (T) P

21 T F L (T) [W_1 L (T)] P

22 T F (T) [W_1 L (T)] W_1 L [W_1 L (T)] L [W_1 L (T)] [W_1 L (T)] W_1 L [W_1 L (T)] L (T) L P

23 T L P

24 T L [W_1 L T] [W_1 L (T)] P

25 T [W_1 L (T)] W_1 L [W_1 L (T)] L [W_1 L (T)] L W_1 (T) W_1 L W_1 L W_1 (T) [W_1 L (T)] W_1 L C_1 W_1 L W_1 L W_1 C_1 P

26 T (session stop)

Figure 3.22. Successive response sequences for rat 1 from the last session of Phase E. Each letter represents one burst of a given response class (see text). Each sequence starts from the left with T (food tray entry after pellet delivery) and ends in P (pellet delivery). A bar at the end of a row indicates that the sequence is continued in the next row.

The above analysis was concerned with the overall or molar relationship between ongoing response and contingency of concurrent reinforcement. What would be convincing evidence that concurrent reinforcements provide a source for the development of "other" superstitious responses, and thereby alter the probability of the ongoing response? Perhaps a mere increase in the overall probability of some "other" response is not sufficient to label these responses superstitious. Therefore, the present experiment provided a more molecular analysis of sequential alterations in bursts of individual responses.

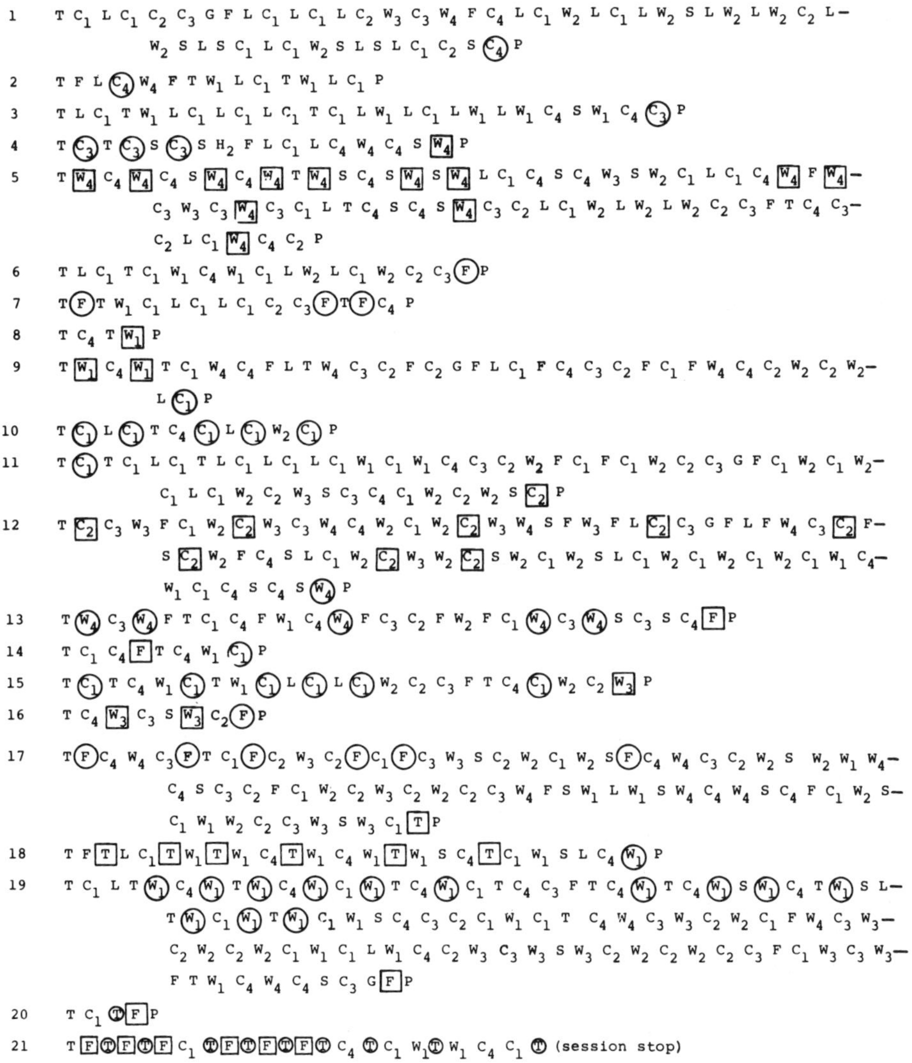

1   T C₁ L C₁ C₂ C₃ G F L C₁ L C₁ L C₂ W₃ C₃ W₄ F C₄ L C₁ W₂ L C₁ L W₂ S L W₂ L W₂ C₂ L—
    W₂ S L S C₁ L C₁ W₂ S L S L C₁ C₂ S (C₄) P

2   T F L (C₄) W₄ F T W₁ L C₁ T W₁ L C₁ P

3   T L C₁ T W₁ L C₁ L C₁ L C₁ T C₁ L W₁ L C₁ L W₁ L W₁ C₄ S W₁ C₄ (C₃) P

4   T (C₃) T (C₃) S (C₃) S H₂ F L C₁ L C₄ W₄ C₄ S [W₄] P

5   T [W₄] C₄ [W₄] C₄ S [W₄] C₄ [W₄] T [W₄] S C₄ S [W₄] S [W₄] L C₁ C₄ S C₄ W₃ S W₂ C₁ L C₁ C₄ [W₄] F [W₄]—
    C₃ W₃ C₃ [W₄] C₃ C₁ L T C₄ S C₄ S [W₄] C₃ C₂ L C₁ W₂ L W₂ L W₂ C₂ C₃ F T C₄ C₃—
    C₂ L C₁ [W₄] C₄ C₂ P

6   T L C₁ T C₁ W₁ C₄ W₁ C₁ L W₂ L C₁ W₂ C₂ C₃ (F) P

7   T (F) T W₁ C₁ L C₁ L C₁ C₂ C₃ (F) T (F) C₄ P

8   T C₄ T [W₁] P

9   T [W₁] C₄ [W₁] T C₁ W₄ C₄ F L T W₄ C₃ C₂ F C₂ G F L C₁ F C₄ C₃ C₂ F C₁ F W₄ C₄ C₂ W₂ C₂ W₂—
    L (C₃) P

10 T (C₃) L (C₁) T C₄ (C₁) L (C₁) W₂ (C₃) P

11 T (C₁) T C₁ L C₁ T L C₁ L C₁ L C₁ W₁ C₁ W₁ C₄ C₃ C₂ W₂ F C₁ F C₁ W₂ C₂ C₃ G F C₁ W₂ C₁ W₂—
    C₁ L C₁ W₂ C₂ W₃ S C₃ C₄ C₁ W₂ C₂ W₂ S (C₂) P

12 T [C₂] C₃ W₃ F C₁ W₂ [C₂] W₃ C₃ W₄ C₄ W₂ C₁ W₂ [C₂] W₃ W₄ S F W₃ F L [C₂] C₃ G F L F W₄ C₃ [C₂] F—
    S [C₂] W₂ F C₄ S L C₁ W₂ [C₂] W₃ W₂ [C₂] S W₂ C₁ W₂ S L C₁ W₂ C₁ W₂ C₁ W₂ C₁ W₁ C₄—
    W₁ C₁ C₄ S C₄ S [W₄] P

13 T (W₄) C₃ (W₄) F T C₁ C₄ F W₁ C₄ (W₄) F C₃ C₂ F W₂ F C₁ (W₄) C₃ (W₄) S C₃ S C₄ [F] P

14 T C₁ C₄ [F] T C₄ W₁ (C₃) P

15 T (C₁) T C₄ W₁ (C₁) T W₁ (C₁) L (C₁) L (C₁) W₂ C₂ C₃ F T C₄ (C₁) W₂ C₂ [W₃] P

16 T C₄ [W₃] C₃ S [W₃] C₂ (F) P

17 T (F) C₄ W₄ C₃ (F) T C₁ (F) C₂ W₃ C₂ (F) C₁ (F) C₃ W₃ S C₂ W₂ C₁ W₂ S (F) C₄ W₄ C₃ C₂ W₂ S W₂ W₁ W₄—
    C₄ S C₃ C₂ F C₁ W₂ C₂ W₃ C₂ W₂ C₂ C₃ W₄ F S W₁ L W₁ S W₄ C₄ W₄ S C₄ F C₁ W₂ S—
    C₁ W₁ W₂ C₂ C₃ W₃ S W₃ C₁ [T] P

18 T F [T] L C₁ [T] W₁ [T] W₁ C₄ [T] W₁ C₄ W₁ [T] W₁ S C₄ [T] C₁ W₁ S L C₄ (W₁) P

19 T C₁ L T (W₁) C₄ (W₁) T (W₁) C₄ (W₁) C₁ (W₁) T C₄ (W₁) C₁ T C₄ C₃ F T C₄ (W₁) T C₄ (W₁) S (W₁) C₄ T (W₁) S L—
    T (W₁) C₁ (W₁) T (W₁) C₁ W₁ S C₄ C₃ C₂ C₁ W₁ C₁ T C₄ W₄ C₃ W₃ C₂ W₂ C₁ F W₄ C₃ W₃—
    C₂ W₂ C₂ W₂ C₁ W₁ C₁ L W₁ C₄ C₂ W₃ C₃ W₃ S W₃ C₂ W₂ C₂ W₂ C₂ C₃ F C₁ W₃ C₃ W₃—
    F T W₁ C₄ W₄ C₄ S C₃ G [F] P

20 T C₁ (T) [F] P

21 T [F] (T) [F] (T) [F] (T) C₁ (T) [F] (T) [F] (T) [F] (T) C₄ (T) C₁ W₁(T) W₁ C₄ C₁ (T) (session stop)

Figure 3.23.   Successive response sequences for rat 1 from the last session of Phase F. See Figure 3.22 legend and text for definitions.

Figures 3.22 and 3.23 present representative samples of successive interpellet response sequences from the last sessions of Phases E and F for rat 1. Similar data were obtained for rat 2. Each response sequence is identified by number (left-hand column) and shows all responses occurring between pellet deliveries. The specific sequence of all emitted responses was recorded throughout the session, and each possible response was identified by location within the chamber. The recorded responses included: exploring or sniffing each corner of the chamber (C_1, C_2, C_3, and C_4), each wall (W_1, W_2, W_3, and W_4) or the grid floor (F), as well as lever pressing (L), food tray entry (T), grooming (G), and standing (S). [Corner one, C_1, was between the wall with the lever and food tray (wall one, W_1) and the left-hand wall (wall two, W_2); corner two, C_2, was between the left-hand wall and the back wall, etc.] This method recorded the number of bursts but not the relative duration of individual responses.

The last 25 sequences in the last session of Phase E are shown in Figure 3.22. The first sequence (*seq* 1) consisted mainly of alterations between L and W_1, L and W_2, and L and C_1. T preceded pellet delivery in *seq* 2, and in the brief *seq* 3, and then became more frequent in *seq* 4. (Examples of significant changes in structural composition from one sequence to the next are indicated by circles or squares around the last response in one sequence and the same response in the next sequence.) The long *seq* 7 terminated in C_4 preceding pellet delivery, and C_4 was immediately apparent as a dominant response throughout *seq* 8. (C_4 was typically a very rare response.) In *seq* 9, W_1L preceded pellet delivery as a response pair and then dominated *seq* 10. *Seqs* 11 and 12 both terminated in W_4, and W_4 was a most frequent response in the relatively long *seq* 14. Then in *seq* 15, the response pair W_1L again preceded pellet delivery and appeared frequently in *seq* 16. T terminated the very brief *seqs* 19, 20, and 21 and was then a very frequent response in *seq* 22 compared to many of the preceding sequences. T again terminated *seq* 24 and appeared frequently in *seq* 25. Note that the minisequence W_1LT that preceded pellet delivery in *seq* 21 was repeated in *seqs* 22, 24, and 25.

Similar response sequence changes were clearly apparent in Phase F. The last 21 sequences of the last session are shown in Figure 3.23. C_4 terminated *seq* 1 and then appeared in *seq* 2. In *seq* 2, the response pair LC_1 preceded pellet delivery and dominated *seq* 3. In virtually all of the following sequences, the last response preceding pellet delivery in one sequence not only occurred frequently in the next sequence, but also was immediately emitted after pellet retrieval (after T); see *seqs* 4, 5, 7 through 13, 17, and 21. In the last three sequencies, F terminated *seq* 19 and the response pair TF terminated the brief *seq* 20. Both F and T entirely dominated the last *seq* 21. L was typically not as dominant as in Phase E and was either entirely absent or emitted at low frequency (see for example, *seqs* 13, 17, and 19 in Figure 3.23).

These examples clearly show that the particular response preceding pellet delivery was often emitted again soon after pellet retrieval. Typically, the effect was relatively transient but became more persistent, perhaps dominating one or more successive sequences, if that response was followed relatively quickly by a second pellet delivery. This clear incremental effect upon exactly the response that preceded reinforcer delivery beyond doubt extends the principle of superstitious responding to include response-independent reinforcement in concurrent schedules. Skinner (1938), Fenner (1969), and Neuringer (1970) previously found that a very few pairings, even only one, between a given response and reinforcement was similarly sufficient for a marked increase in the frequency of that specific response.

In the present experiment, the relatively increased frequency of a given response after temporal contiguity with reinforcer delivery appeared to supplant the previously dominating responses. In many response sequences, the probability of a previously infrequent response was locally increased after contiguity with reinforcer delivery. In fact, a particular composition of response frequencies could be radically altered by only a few contiguities between reinforcer delivery and a "new" response. The recorded "other" responses then did not merely constitute a class of homogeneous responses passively filling the pauses of the operant response. On the contrary, they participated in the formation of the pattern of the operant response.

In summary, the present data do not provide much support for recent arguments that question the development of superstitious responding with response-independent reinforcement (Rachlin and Baum, 1972, Staddon, 1975). More critically, the present results extend the response interaction model to the hitherto theoretically important procedure of response-independent concurrent reinforcement. The results are specifically congruent with the results from Experiment V and with Henton (1972). These results also combine with the results from the signaled reinforcement procedures of Experiments VI, VII, and VIII and suggest that contiguities between concurrent responses and concurrent reinforcements are basic to concurrent schedule effects. In general, the inhibitory effect of concurrent reinforcements may literally depend upon the extent to which they control concurrent responses that compete with the ongoing response.

Concluding Comments

The behavioral effects of the various concurrent schedules have proven to be well described in terms of interactions between response. Briefly, an ongoing response was characteristically interrupted during emission of a concurrent response. The features of response interaction within combinations of operant and classical conditioning procedures were easily replicated in the present experiments. An ongoing response was interrupted only when stimulus presentation controlled a changeover to a concurrent response (i.e., when the stimulus was a discriminative stimulus for a different response). Furthermore, the procedure of withdrawing rather than presenting a discriminative stimulus suggested at least some conditions in which the elimination of a concurrent response may be followed by a changeover back to and enhancement of the ongoing response. Finally, the ongoing response was not suppressed when the discriminative stimulus did not control a changeover to concurrent responses.

In previous investigations specific concurrent responses were physically prevented in an attempt to assess whether response interactions are important for concurrent schedules, either classical–operant or concurrent operant–operant schedules. As in recent analyses of classical–operant combinations, the present analysis also encountered the "discovery" of concurrent responses and response interactions within the operant procedures hitherto throught to disprove response interactions. The extensive response interdependencies suggest that the central assumption of response independence cannot be upheld as a universal description of concurrent performances. Consequently, the empirical basis for a strict reinforcement model is rather weakened, and the model may not provide a satisfactory description of concurrent performances.

The present results therefore confront the assumptions and predictions based upon previous criticisms of the role of response competition for concurrent performances. Some of the more critical arguments are elaborated below.

Traditionally, changes in an ongoing response associated with the emission of a concurrent response are, first of all, confounded with the reinforcements for the concurrent response. This confounding is usually separated by a logical resolution that only concurrent reinforcements and not concurrent responses are responsible for the altered probability of an ongoing response. In the present experiments, however, the probability changes of the ongoing response were more clearly related to the probability of concurrent responses than to the rates of delivered concurrent reinforcers. For example, in Experiment II, the pauses in FR responding covaried with the manipulated burst durations of concurrent VI responding. This effect was perhaps even more clear in Experiment III, in which an ongoing VI response was interrupted precisely during those trials in which the extinguishing concurrent response still occurred, not during trials without the concurrent response. Furthermore, in Experiment IV, an ongoing response was maximally suppressed during trials only when the concurrent response rate was high, and minimally suppressed only when the concurrent response rate was low, irrespective of the associated rate of concurrent reinforcers delivered during trials.

The point raised by these examples is, of course, that response interactions and reinforcement interactions are experimentally separated at the level of local response changes. Moreover, in the case of interactions involving a concurrent response undergoing extinction, any confounding of concurrent responses and concurrent reinforcements is obviously eliminated. Only an inferred "inhibitory aftereffect" of previously delivered concurrent reinforcers might provide a reinforcement explanation in the absence of actually delivered reinforcers—and even then, only when the assumed decaying aftereffects of previous reinforcers precisely follow the local pattern of the extinguishing response. In all cases, the local rate and pattern of an ongoing response were more closely related to the concurrent response rate than to the concurrent reinforcement rate.

The claim of reinforcement interaction was previously supported with demonstrations of inhibition in the apparent absence of concurrent responses within the procedures of signaled and response-independent concurrent reinforcement. These procedures were repeated in four of the present experiments. Clearly, the concurrent reinforcements did in fact control concurrent responses, and the effects may come about by virtue of changes in concurrent responses. Furthermore, the proportional rate of delivered reinforcers was not sufficient to describe the probability of the ongoing response. In Experiment VII, for example, the probability of the ongoing VI response decreased when the probability of concurrent observing responses was increased, without any changes in reinforcement rates. Similarly, in Experiments V and XI, equal rates of delivered concurrent reinforcers yielded different probabilities of an ongoing response, and different rates of concurrent reinforcers generated equal response probabilities. Therefore, reinforcement factors are not sufficiently precise to provide a satisfactory description of response changes.

The primary question is whether concurrent reinforcements can have an inhibitory effect *without reference to concurrent response changes.* The very close response–response correlations in the present experiments, even within quite minute response patterns, simply suggest that the inhibitory influence of concurrent reinforcements must somehow be related to the simultaneous occurrence of concurrent responses. Ultimately, the response model states that an ongoing response is "inhibited" by concurrent reinforcements exactly and only during the emission of concurrent responses.

Catania (1969) has argued in a historical perspective that the concept of inhibition has been ambiguously applied because of failures to specify clearly the inhibited and the inhibiting events. Catania suggested that the property of inhibition should encompass not only a reduction of an ongoing response but also the agent responsible for the reduction. In the case of concurrent operant schedules, the inhibitory agent was said to be concurrent reinforcements. This now standard and often cited definition, that "concurrent reinforcements are inhibitory" (Catania, 1969), would seem to be imprecise, since the introduction of concurrent reinforcements does not always lead to a reduction of an ongoing response (Experiment V). When concurrent reinforcements do lead to a reduction, that effect stems from an increase in concurrent responses (e.g., Experiments VI, VII, VIII, and IX). Response reductions may also be produced by increases in concurrent responses experimentally dissociated from increases in concurrent reinforcement rates (Experiment VII). In summary, the term *inhibition* is misleading if the inhibiting event refers to concurrent reinforcement, and superfluous if the inhibiting event refers to a concurrent response. Assigning inhibitory properties to concurrent responses simply does not add to the observed fact that an ongoing response decreases after increases in concurrent responses.

The reinforcement model essentially states that interactions in concurrent schedules are sufficiently accounted for by *one* functional relationship between concurrent reinforcement rate and ongoing response probability. Hence, an ongoing response is said to be acted upon *directly* by concurrent reinforcements.

The present experiments suggest that the action of concurrent reinforcement on the ongoing response may be further analyzed as *two* rather than just one functional relationship. Concurrent reinforcements seem to control concurrent responses directly (one functional relationship), with concurrent responses then directly affecting the ongoing response (a second functional relationship). Apparently, concurrent reinforcements affect an ongoing response only indirectly, via alterations in concurrent responses.

The identification of concurrent responses as independent variables therefore argues that response probabilities are dependent upon more than just the rates of contingent and concurrent reinforcement. This conclusion does not appear to be peculiar to the present analysis as previous experiments have shown that response probabilities do not "match" reinforcement rates in a range of procedures involving additional parameters. At best, each additional parameter influencing a given response could be represented as a quantifier in a general mathematical formulation predicting the probability of responding. Of course, the task of quantifying all behavioral variables into one large formula may be a thankless attempt to outrun infinity. The problem here is that one particular formula might fit the data from one procedure but might not equally apply to a different procedure in which previous conditions "held constant" were now changed.

Attempts have been made to extend the generality of reinforcement interaction to other than reinforcement parameters by introducing the terms *spontaneous* or *hidden* reinforcement (Herrnstein, 1970). The spontaneous reinforcement is not an empirical parameter but rather is a quantity extracted from obtained data. Of late, spontaneous reinforcement has been considered to be intimately related to or imbedded in unspecified concurrent responses (Herrnstein, 1974; deVilliers, 1977). This assignment of reinforcement value to unknown or at best potential concurrent responses apparently preserves the theoretical claim that response probability is only determined by reinforcement context (Herrnstein, 1970). We believe, however, that as long as spontaneous reinforcement value is only indirectly derived, such that it exactly covaries with the probability of a response, then a change in reinforcement value is a circular explanation of behavioral changes (Powers and Osborne, 1976).

Important to note, nevertheless, is that both the reinforcement and the response models apparently concur that the probability of an ongoing response and of concurrent responses may change in opposite directions. Reinforcement interaction might positively propose that a change of one response is indirectly *associated* with a change of concurrent responses. The response model would push the critical step further and propose that a change of one response is directly *dependent* upon changes of concurrent responses in and of themselves. As Herrnstein has noted, "choice is nothing but behavior set into the context of other behavior" (1970, p. 255). Within the reinforcement model, however, the "other" behaviors are represented not in terms of their rate or probability, but in terms of their contingent and inferred (inherent) reinforcement value. This is precisely where the analyses separate. The reinforcement model specifies that an ongoing response is at least partially dependent upon derived and inferred entities. In contrast, the concurrent response analysis highlights that an ongoing response is only dependent upon empirical parameters.

Response interaction, of course, emphasizes foremost concurrent responses as determinants of an ongoing response. However, concurrent reinforcements are also potent parameters. The present experiments suggest that concurrent reinforcements and concurrent response parameters combine, so that the probability of an ongoing response may be decreased by concurrent reinforcements to the extent that they increase the probability of concurrent responses. Concurrent performances may then be described as the precise relationship between concurrent reinforcements and concurrent responses, on the one hand, and the equally precise relationship between the concurrent responses and the ongoing response on the other hand.

This analysis of concurrent schedules most satisfactorily meets the analysis of operant–classical conditioning combinations. The effect of various arrangements of concurrent operant and classical conditioning procedures could thus be accounted for by the direct relationship between concurrent reinforcements and concurrent responses. An ongoing baseline response is suppressed when concurrent responses precede concurrent reinforcements but is unchanged or facilitated when the baseline response precedes concurrent reinforcement (Henton, 1972). A further consistency is that the probability of an ongoing response appears to be inversely related to the probability of concurrent responses across a wealth of parametric manipulations in concurrent schedules.

In conclusion, the considerable mutual reinforcement provided by these related analyses suggests that the functional characteristics of concurrent operant–classical-conditioning schedules and concurrent operant schedules may be encompassed by the same basic behavioral principles. Additionally, the response–response emphasis has been extended to complex sequential conditioning procedures (multiple schedules; Chapter 4), to simple operant conditioning procedures (Chapter 5), and to combinations of classical conditioning procedures (Chapter 6).

This analysis of concurrent performances furthermore ties in well with both previous (Skinner, 1950; Sidman, 1960) and more recent arguments (Dunham, 1971, 1972; Staddon, 1977) emphasizing the importance of interacting responses in conditioning procedures. A particular tribute is paid to the long held insistence by Kantor that a behavior occurs in a field of other behaviors, never in isolation (Kantor and Smith, 1975).

The growing generality of interresponse patterns strengthens the argument that response factors are essential elements in concurrent performances. Such repeated observations of interbehavioral relationships across many different procedures suggest that response interactions are real and relevant and merit systematic investigation.

References

Alleman, H. D., and Zeiler, M. D.: Patterning with fixed-time schedules of response-independent reinforcement. *J. Exp. Anal. Behav.*, **22**, 135–141, 1974.

Bacotti, A. V.: Matching under concurrent fixed-ratio variable-interval schedules of food presentation. *J. Exp. Anal. Behav.*, **27**, 171–182, 1977.

Baum, W. M.: The correlation-based law of effect. *J. Exp. Anal. Behav.*, **20**, 137–153, 1973.

Baum, W. M.: On two types of deviation from the matching law: bias and undermatching. *J. Exp. Anal. Behav.*, **22**, 231–242, 1974.

Boren, J. J.: Stimulus probes of the fixed ratio run. Paper delivered at Eastern Psychological Association, Philadelphia, 1961.

Browne, M. P., and Dinsmoor, J. A.: Selective observing of discriminative stimuli. *Proceedings of the 80th Annual Convention of the American Psychological Association,* 1972, pp. 745–746.

Brownstein, A. J., and Pliskoff, S. S.: Some effects of relative reinforcement rate and changeover delay in response-independent concurrent schedules of reinforcement. *J. Exp. Anal. Behav.*, **11**, 683–688, 1968.

Buel, C. L.: Investigation of the temporal parameters in omission training with humans in a two-key situation. *Psychol. Record*, **25**, 99–109, 1975.

Carlson, J. G., and Aroksaar, R. E.: Effects of time-out upon concurrent operant responding. *Psychol. Record,* **20,** 365–371, 1970.

Catania, A. C.: Concurrent performances: reinforcement interaction and response independence. *J. Exp. Anal. Behav.,* **6,** 253–263, 1963.

Catania, A. C.: Concurrent operants. In, W. K. Honig (ed.): *Operant Behavior: Areas of Research and Application.* New York, Appleton-Century-Crofts, 1966.

Catania, A. C.: Concurrent performances: inhibition of one response by reinforcement of another. *J. Exp. Anal. Behav.,* **12,** 731–744, 1969.

Catania, A. C.: Self-inhibiting effects of reinforcement. *J. Exp. Anal. Behav.,* **19,** 517–526, 1973.

Catania, A. C., and Dobson, R.: Concurrent performances: rate and accuracy of free-operant oddity responding. *J. Exp. Anal. Behav.,* **17,** 25–35, 1972.

Catania, A. C., and Reynolds, G. S.: A quantitative analysis of the responding maintained by interval schedules of reinforcement. *J. Exp. Anal. Behav.,* **11,** 327–383, 1968.

Catania, A. C., Silverman, P. J., and Stubbs, D. A.: Concurrent performances: stimulus-control gradients during schedules of signaled and unsignaled concurrent reinforcement. *J. Exp. Anal. Behav.,* **21,** 99–107, 1974.

Chung, S. H.: Effects of delayed reinforcement in a concurrent situation. *J. Exp. Anal. Behav.,* **8,** 439–444, 1965.

Chung, S. H., and Herrnstein, R. J.: Choice and delay of reinforcement. *J. Exp. Anal. Behav.,* **10,** 67–74, 1967.

Davis, H., Iriye, C., and Hubbard, J.: Response independent food as an extinction procedure for responding on DRL schedules. *Psychol. Record,* **23,** 33–38, 1973.

Davis, J., and Bitterman, M. E.: Differential reinforcement of other behavior (DRO): a yoked-control comparison. *J. Exp. Anal. Behav.,* **15,** 237–241, 1971.

Deluty, M. Z.: Choice and the rate of punishment in concurrent schedules. *J. Exp. Anal. Behav.,* **25,** 75–80, 1976a.

Deluty, M. Z.: Excitatory and inhibitory effects of free reinforcers. *Anim. Learning Behav.,* **4,** 436–440, 1976b.

deVilliers, P.: Choice in concurrent schedules and a quantitative formulation of the law of effect. In, W. K. Honig and J. E. R. Staddon (eds.): *Handbook of Operant Behavior.* Englewood Cliffs, N.J., Prentice-Hall, 1977.

Dunham, P. J.: Punishment: method and theory. *Psychol. Rev.,* **78,** 58–70, 1971.

Dunham, P. J.: Some effects of punishment upon unpunished responding. *J. Exp. Anal. Behav.,* **17,** 443–450, 1972.

Edwards, D. D., Peek, V., and Wolfe, F.: Independently delivered food decelerates fixed ratio rates. *J. Exp. Anal. Behav.,* **14,** 301–307, 1970.

Fenner, D. H.: Key pecking in pigeons maintained by short-interval adventitious schedules of reinforcement. *Proceedings of the 77th Annual Convention of the American Psychological Association,* 1969, pp. 831–832.

Ferster, C. B.: Concurrent schedules of reinforcement in the chimpanzee. *Science,* **125,** 1090–1091, 1957.

Ferster, C. B.: A complex concurrent schedule of reinforcement. *J. Exp. Anal. Behav.,* **2,** 65–80, 1959.

Ferster, C. B., and Skinner, B. F.: *Schedules of Reinforcement.* New York, Appleton-Century-Crofts, 1957.

Findley, J. D.: Preference and switching under concurrent scheduling. *J. Exp. Anal. Behav.,* **1,** 123–144, 1958.

Fleshler, M., and Hoffman, H. S.: A progression for generating variable-interval schedules. *J. Exp. Anal. Behav.,* **5,** 529–530, 1962.

Henton, W. W.: Avoidance response rates during a pre-food stimulus in monkeys. *J. Exp. Anal. Behav.,* **17,** 269–275, 1972.

Henton, W. W., and Iversen, I. H.: Concurrent response rates during pre-event stimuli. Paper presented at the Easter Conference: English Experimental Analysis of Behavior Group, Cambridge, March 1973.

Herbert, E. W.: Two-key concurrent responding: response-reinforcement dependencies and blackout. *J. Exp. Anal. Behav.,* **14,** 61–70, 1970.

Herrnstein, R. J.: Relative and absolute strength of response as a function of frequency of reinforcement. *J. Exp. Anal. Behav.*, **4**, 267–272, 1961.

Herrnstein, R. J.: On the law of effect. *J. Exp. Anal. Behav.*, **13**, 243–266, 1970.

Herrnstein, R. J.: Formal properties of the matching law. *J. Exp. Anal. Behav.*, **21**, 159–164, 1974.

Iversen, I. H.: Behavioral interactions in concurrent reinforcement schedules. Paper presented at
Easter Conference of the English Experimental Analysis of Behavior Group, Bangor, April
1974.

Iversen, I. H.: Reciprocal response interactions in concurrent variable-interval and discrete-trial
fixed-ratio schedules. *Scand. J. Psychol.*, **16**, 280–284, 1975a.

Iversen, I. H.: Response versus reinforcement interaction in concurrent reinforcement schedules.
Paper presented at Easter Conference of the English Experimental Analysis of Behavior Group.
Exeter, March 1975b.

Iversen, I. H.: Interactions between reinforced responses and collateral responses. *Psychol. Record*, **26**, 399–413, 1976.

Kantor, J. R., and Smith, N. W.: *The Science of Psychology: An Interbehavioral Survey*. Chicago,
Ill., Principia Press, 1975.

Katz, R. C.: Effects of punishment in an alternative response context as a function of relative reinforcement rate. *Psychol. Record*. **23**, 65–74, 1973.

Kimble, G. A.: *Foundations of Conditioning and Learning*. New York, Appleton-Century-Crofts,
1967.

LaBounty, C. E., and Reynolds, G. S.: An analysis of response and time matching to reinforcement in concurrent ratio-interval schedules. *J. Exp. Anal. Behav.*, **19**, 155–166, 1973.

Lachter, G. D.: Some temporal parameters of non-contingent reinforcement. *J. Exp. Anal. Behav.*,
16, 207–217, 1971.

Lattal, K. A.: Response–reinforcer independence and conventional extinction after fixed-interval
and variable-interval schedules. *J. Exp. Anal. Behav.*, **18**, 133–140, 1972.

Lattal, K. A.: Response–reinforcer dependence and independence in multiple and mixed schedules. *J. Exp. Anal. Behav.*, **20**, 265–271, 1973.

Lattal, K. A.: Combinations of response–reinforcer dependence and independence. *J. Exp. Anal.
Behav.*, **22**, 357–362, 1974.

Lattal, K. A., and Bryan, A. J.: Effects of concurrent response-independent reinforcement on
fixed-interval schedule performance. *J. Exp. Anal. Behav.*, **26**, 495–504, 1976.

Lowry, M. A., and Lachter, G. D.: Response elimination: a comparison of four procedures. *Learning Motivation*, **8**, 69–76, 1977.

Moffit, M., and Shimp, C. P.: Two-key concurrent paced variable-interval paced variable-interval
schedules of reinforcement. *J. Exp. Anal. Behav.*, **16**, 39–49, 1971.

Neuringer, A. J.: Superstitious key pecking after three peck-produced reinforcements. *J. Exp.
Anal. Behav.*, **13**, 127–134, 1970.

Nevin, J. A.: Rates and patterns of responding with concurrent fixed-interval and variable-interval
reinforcement. *J. Exp. Anal. Behav.*, **16**, 241–247, 1971.

Nevin, J. A.: The maintenance of behavior. In, J. A. Nevin and G. S. Reynolds (eds.): *The Study of
Behavior*. Glenview, Ill., Scott, Foresman, 1973.

Pavlov, I. P.: *Conditioned Reflexes* (Translated by G. V. Anrep). London, Oxford, 1927 (reprinted,
New York, Dover, 1960).

Pliskoff, S. S., and Green, D.: Effects on concurrent performances of stimulus correlated with reinforcer availability. *J. Exp. Anal. Behav.*, **17**, 221–227, 1972.

Pliskoff, S. S., Shull, R. L., and Gollub, L. R.: The relation between response rates and reinforcement rates in a multiple schedule. *J. Exp. Anal. Behav.*, **11**, 271–284, 1968.

Powers, R. B., and Osborne, J. G.: *Fundamentals of Behavior*. San Francisco, West, 1976.

Premack, D.: Reinforcement theory. In, D. Levine (ed.): *Nebraska Symposium on Motivation*.
Lincoln, University of Nebraska Press, 1965.

Rachlin, H.: Contrast and matching. *Psychol. Rev.*, **80**, 217–234, 1973.

Rachlin, H., and Baum, W. M.: Response rate as a function of amount of reinforcement for a signalled concurrent response. *J. Exp. Anal. Behav.*, **12**, 11–16, 1969.

Rachlin, H., and Baum, W. M.: Effects of alternate reinforcement: Does the source matter? *J. Exp.
Anal. Behav.*, **18**, 231–241, 1972.

Schneider, J. W.: Reinforcer effectiveness as a function of reinforcer rate and magnitude: a comparison of concurrent performances. *J. Exp. Anal. Behav.,* **20,** 461–471, 1973.

Schoenfeld, W. N., and Farmer, J.: Reinforcement schedules and the "behavior stream." In, W. N. Schoenfeld (ed.): *The Theory of Reinforcement Schedules.* New York, Appleton-Century-Crofts, 1970.

Schroeder, S. R.: Perseveration in concurrent performances by the developmentally retarded. *Psychol. Record,* **25,** 51–64, 1975.

Sherman, J. A., and Thomas, J. R.: Some factors controlling preference between fixed-ratio and variable-ratio schedules of reinforcement. *J. Exp. Anal. Behav.,* **11,** 689–702, 1968.

Shull, R. L., and Pliskoff, S. S.: Changeover delay and concurrent schedules: some effects on relative performance measures. *J. Exp. Anal. Behav.,* **10,** 517–527, 1967.

Sidman, M.: Time discrimination and behavioral interaction in a free operant situation. *J. Comp. Physiol. Psychol.,* **49,** 469–473, 1956.

Sidman, M.: *Tactics of Scientific Research: Evaluating Experimental Data in Psychology.* New York, Basic Books, 1960.

Sidman, M.: Time out from avoidance as a reinforcer: a study of response interactions. *J. Exp. Anal. Behav.,* **5,** 423–434, 1962.

Skinner, B. F.: *The Behavior of Organisms.* New York, Appleton-Century-Crofts, 1938.

Skinner, B. F.: Superstition in the pigeon. *J. Exp. Psychol.,* **38,** 168–172, 1948.

Skinner, B. F.: Are theories of learning necessary? *Psychol. Rev.,* **57,** 193–216, 1950.

Skinner, B. F.: *Science and Human Behavior.* New York, Macmillan, 1953.

Skinner, B. F.: *Contingencies of Reinforcement.* New York, Appleton-Century-Crofts, 1969.

Spence, K. W.: The differential response in animals to stimuli varying within a single dimension. *Psychol. Rev.,* **44,** 430–444, 1937.

Staddon, J. E. R.: Learning as adaptation. In, W. K. Estes (ed.): *Handbook of Learning and Cognitive Processes,* vol. 2. Hillsdale, N. J., Lawrence Erlbaum, 1975.

Staddon, J. E. R.: Schedule-induced behavior. In, W. K. Honig and J. E. R. Staddon (eds.): *Handbook of Operant Behavior.* Englewood Cliffs, N. J., Prentice-Hall, 1977.

Thomas, J. R.: Fixed-ratio punishment by timeout of concurrent variable-interval behavior. *J. Exp. Anal. Behav.,* **11,** 609–616, 1968.

Todorov, J. C.: Concurrent performances: effect of punishment contingent on the switching response. *J. Exp. Anal. Behav.,* **16,** 51–62, 1971.

Verhave, T.: Some observations concerning prepotency and probability of postponing shock with a two-lever avoidance procedure. *J. Exp. Anal. Behav.,* **4,** 187–192, 1961.

Zeiler, M. D.: Eliminating behavior with reinforcement. *J. Exp. Anal. Behav.* **16,** 401–405, 1971

Zeiler, M. D.: Positive reinforcement and the elimination of reinforced responses. *J. Exp. Anal. Behav.* **26,** 37–44, 1976.

Zeiler, M. D.: Elimination of reinforced behavior: intermittent schedules of not-responding. *J. Exp. Anal. Behav.* **27,** 23–32, 1977.

Zener, K.: The significance of behavior accompanying conditioned salivary secretion for theories of the conditioned response. *Am. J. Psychol.,* **50,** 384–403, 1937.

Chapter 4

Concurrent Responses with Multiple Schedules

Iver H. Iversen

Explanations of Behavioral Contrast

The response rate in the presence of one stimulus and its associated schedule depends also upon the schedules associated with temporally adjacent stimuli. Alternations between schedule components associated with different stimuli are traditionally referred to as *multiple schedules* (Ferster and Skinner, 1957). Reynolds (1961b) suggested that interactions in multiple schedules might be described as *contrast* or *induction,* depending upon whether the changes in response rate diverge or converge across schedule components. Furthermore, contrast and induction may be either positive or negative, depending upon direction of change in response rate. *Positive contrast,* for example, refers to an increase in response rate in one schedule component simultaneously with a decreased rate in an adjacent component.

Several interpretations have been offered to account for or explain interactions in multiple schedules. However, since most interpretations primarily deal with positive contrast the following brief overview only deals with this phenomenon.

Perhaps the most well-known explanation is an extension of reinforcement interaction outlined in Chapter 3. Based on experiments that assessed response rate in one schedule component when the reinforcement rate was manipulated in an adjacent component (Reynolds, 1961a, 1961b, 1961c; Bloomfield, 1967; Nevin, 1968), the reinforcement model specifically suggests that the response rate in one component depends upon the relative reinforcement rate (Herrnstein, 1970; Catania, 1973). However, the reinforcement model of multiple schedules does not easily account for response changes occurring in one component when the response rate but not the reinforcement rate changes in the adjacent component (Brownstein and Hughes, 1970; Brownstein and Newsom,

1970; Hughes, 1971; Lander, 1971; Wilkie, 1973). Conversely, positive contrast may not occur after a decrease in reinforcement in an adjacent component with particular errorless discrimination procedures (Terrace, 1963; compare to Rilling, 1977) or in conjunction with certain brain lesions (Henke et al., 1972) or drugs (Bloomfield, 1972). Apparently, a change in relative reinforcement rate may be neither necessary nor sufficient for positive contrast.

Frustration and emotions have also been evoked in the explanation of positive contrast. One theory holds that positive contrast is a manifestation of emotional responses, generated by the aversiveness of not receiving reinforcement for previously reinforced responses under an adjacent component (Terrace, 1966). However, as mentioned above, reinforcement rate changes are neither necessary nor sufficient for positive contrast, therefore positive contrast may be produced in situations that do not involve emission of nonreinforced responses. Moreover, several experiments have shown positive contrast without nonreinforced responses in an adjacent component (Reynolds, 1961b; Freidman and Guttman, 1965; Vieth and Rilling, 1972; Sadowsky, 1973: Halliday and Boakes, 1974) and, conversely, an absence of positive contrast with nonreinforced responses in an adjacent component (Halliday and Boakes, 1971; Mackintosh et al., 1972). The occurrence of nonreinforced responses is then neither necessary nor sufficient for positive contrast.

Changes in preference among schedule components have also been offered as an explanation of positive contrast. Specifically, positive contrast has been suggested to result when the adjacent component is relatively less preferred (Bloomfield, 1969; Premack, 1969). However, relative preference for one schedule component, as assessed with concurrent schedules, may not be a reliable predictor of positive contrast with the same schedule components arranged as a multiple schedule. Wilkie (1973), for example, reported that positive contrast was obtained with signaled reinforcement in an adjacent component, whether or not preference for signaled reinforcement had been obtained in the same subjects when the schedules were arranged concurrently. Also, Halliday and Boakes (1972) found preference for response-dependent reinforcement over response-independent reinforcement but not positive contrast when the same schedules were arranged as a multiple schedule. Therefore, relative preference for schedule components also appears to be neither necessary nor sufficient for positive contrast.

According to a more recent formulation, interactions between classical and operant conditioning may produce positive contrast (the response additivity theory; Gamzu and Schwartz, 1973; Hemmes, 1973; Redford and Perkins, 1974; Schwartz and Gamzu, 1977). The response additivity theory suggests that responses directed toward a stimulus associated with a relatively higher reinforcement rate (stimulus–reinforcer relation) may add to the operant response producing the reinforcer (response–reinforcer relation). Positive contrast then results when the component stimuli are located on the operant manipulandum, with stimulus-directed responses and operant responses thereby activating the same manipulandum. Experiments accordingly demonstrated that positive contrast may not occur when the component stimuli are not on the operant manipulandum (Keller, 1974; Schwartz, 1975; Schwartz et al., 1975; Spealman, 1976). However, other experiments have shown that positive contrast may easily be obtained when the component stimuli are not located on the manipulandum for the operant response (Beecroft, 1969; Bloomfield, 1972; Boakes, 1972; Chitwood and Griffin, 1972; Coates, 1972; Henke et al., 1972; Gaffan, 1973; Hemmes, 1973; Bradshaw, 1975; Farthing, 1975; Gutman et al., 1975; Gutman and Minor, 1976; Henke, 1976; Bradshaw et al., 1978; Gutman, 1977). On the other hand, contrast is not invariably obtained when the component stimuli are in fact located on the operant manipulandum (Terrace, 1963). Placement of the component stimuli on the operant manipulandum therefore seem to be neither necessary nor sufficient for positive contrast.

A relatively novel account suggests that positive contrast results from the stimulus of the adjacent component signaling a decrease in local reinforcement rate (Marcucella, 1976; B. A. Williams, 1976; Wilkie, 1977). For example, with a maintained overall reinforcement rate, positive contrast appears to depend upon the temporal characteristics of reinforcement in the adjacent component (B. A. Williams, 1976). Positive contrast thus occurred when reinforcement was available late but not early in the adjacent component. This model has not yet been extended further and any determination of whether the critical variable is either necessary or sufficient for contrast is perhaps premature. However, the available evidence that positive contrast may not occur with some forms of errorless training (Terrace, 1963) or in subjects with certain central nervous system lesions (Henke et al., 1972) suggests that a change in local reinforcement rate in an adjacent component is perhaps not sufficient for positive contrast.

Each of the above theoretical positions suggests that positive contrast results from one common effect. The theories differ according to what sort of "change" best describes the common effect. Changes in reinforcement rate, response rate, stimulus-directed responses, frustration, aversiveness, preference, or local reinforcement rate have each been proposed to account for positive contrast. None of the explanations, however, seems to be able to account for all the various experimental findings with multiple schedules. Some of the theoretical positions make reference to intervening variables, such as frustration or aversiveness, and generally suggest that a number of experimental manipulations affect the intervening variable, which in turn affects the response rates. Measurement of intervening emotions by responses such as wing-flapping and attack has been attempted, but a comparison of reports indicates that the "measures" are inconsistently related to both the independent and dependent variables of interest (Terrace, 1971; Coughlin, 1973; Rilling and Caplan, 1973, 1975; Rilling et al., 1973).

A significant feature of multiple schedules is that interactions occur across components and are therefore separated temporally. Interactions in multiple schedules are thereby critically different from interactions obtained with concurrent reinforcement schedules. Response rate changes, however, are often very similar in concurrent and multiple schedules. For example, changing *mult* VI VI to *mult* VI EXT, or changing *conc* VI VI to *conc* VI EXT, will equally decrease the response rate under EXT and increase the response rate under VI (Herrnstein, 1970). In concurrent schedules, the time allocated to one response detracts from the time available to a second concurrent response. In multiple schedules, however, the time allocated to responding in one component cannot (directly) affect the time available for responding in temporally adjacent components. Response interactions *across* components in multiple schedules would therefore seem to be formally different from response interactions *between* components of concurrent schedules.

Recently, investigations have attempted to assess how or by what means response interactions across multiple schedule components may be related to concurrent response rate changes in each component.

The stimulus-directed responses generated by differential reinforcement rates across multiple schedule components suggest one possible route to an understanding of positive contrast under at least some procedural arrangements. Note that the stimulus-directed responses are generated *concurrently* with the operant rate changes described as positive contrast effects. Furthermore, procedures that prevent positive contrast do so by selectively adding more concurrent responses to the component with the relatively higher reinforcement rate (Keller, 1974; Redford and Perkins, 1974; Schwartz, 1975). Concurrent responses dissociated across multiple schedule components may therefore critically participate in the formation of positive contrast.

The purpose of the following three experiments was to offer an analysis of multiple schedules in terms of interactions among concurrently occurring responses. These experiments represent an attempt to interrelate changes in the rate and pattern of operant responses and collateral responses under the components of multiple schedules. In two experiments, the operant response and the collateral responses were explicitly manipulated to cast some light upon possible mechanisms whereby responses in one component may be acted upon by events in a second, temporally adjacent component.

Component Duration and Collateral Responses (Experiment I)*

In the first study, interactions between reinforced and collateral responses were merely illustrated, with an experimental manipulation of component durations of a multiple schedule.

Experiment I

Three male naive Wistar albino rats were trained on a *mult* FR 20 FR 40 schedule. The rats responded for a 20% sucrose solution in a two-lever chamber (described by Iversen, 1975b) and were maintained at 80% of their free-feeding body weights. Lever pressing was reinforced according to a two-ply multiple schedule. In one component (A), responses on the left lever (*A*) were rein-

* Experiment was conducted at the University of Copenhagen, from January to August 1972.

forced on FR 20 and responses on the right lever (*B*) had no scheduled consequences. In the other component (B), responses on lever *B* were reinforced on FR 40 and responses on lever *A* had no effect. Responses on the appropriate lever were followed by a relay click in each schedule component. A 900-Hz tone sounded from the ceiling of the chamber when component B (FR 40) was scheduled. Licking on the sucrose delivery tube was recorded by a drinkometer circuit.

Initially the duration of each component was 240 sec (for 45 sessions) and was then changed to 400 sec (15 sessions), 120 sec (15 sessions), and 600 sec (15 sessions). A session was terminated after 40 min. Component changes were independent of responses on any lever, and the FR counters were not reset at component changes. The components occurred in strict alternation with the first component in a session selected at random.

The results of this parametric manipulation are presented in Table 4.1. For

Table 4.1   Means of the last five sessions of each component duration

Rat no.	Schedule	Component duration	Response rate for reinforced lever (resp/min)	Licking duration (sec/min)	Response rate for other lever (resp/min)
S1	FR 20	120	104.4	7.8	0.7
		240	93.7	7.9	0.6
		400	97.7	9.6	0.2
		600	82.1	21.9	0.2
	FR 40	120	28.8	13.4	7.7
		240	37.2	13.1	8.0
		400	35.4	17.3	6.1
		600	28.8	19.9	6.0
S2	FR 20	120	88.6	13.2	0.6
		240	103.0	9.4	0.8
		400	85.7	13.6	0.1
		600	53.5	30.1	0.1
	FR 40	120	19.8	14.4	7.0
		240	23.4	12.5	7.8
		400	19.8	12.4	6.4
		600	16.8	30.8	5.7
S3	FR 20	120	64.6	6.0	0.7
		240	73.8	3.0	0.5
		400	66.6	6.3	0.2
		600	61.1	16.9	0.1
	FR 40	120	26.4	5.3	5.0
		240	21.6	4.8	5.9
		400	25.8	6.0	5.0
		600	22.8	11.6	4.7

all rats, the overall rate of reinforced lever pressing was higher under FR 20 than under FR 40. The only systematic effect of the component duration was a tendency for a decreased rate under FR 20 for the longest component duration.

Although the overall response measures remained relatively invariant, the postreinforcement pause and the run rate measures depended upon the manipulated component duration (Figure 4.1). Under FR 40, both the postreinforcement pause and the run rate were increasing functions of the component duration. These effects approximately balanced, resulting in an almost constant overall response rate. Under FR 20, the postreinforcement pause increased for the longest component duration, whereas the run rate remained approximately the same for all component durations. The overall rate under FR 20 was therefore decreased during the longest component duration because of an increased postreinforcement pause.

Hence, invariant overall response rates do not necessarily signify invariant response patterns. In particular, opposing changes may balance one another and leave the overall response rate unchanged. However, more molecular changes may be systematically related to experimental manipulations.

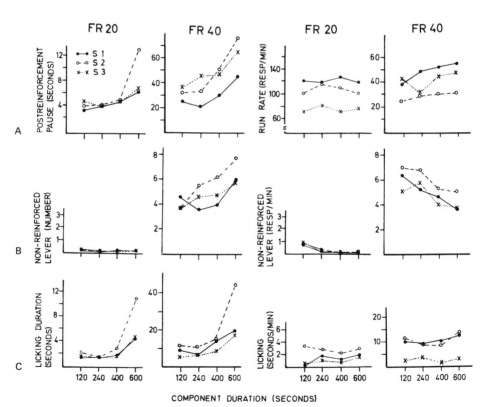

Figure 4.1. Response interactions as a function of the component duration of a *mult* FR 10 FR 40 schedule. **A.** FR postreinforcement pauses and run times. **B.** Nonreinforced responses on alternate lever. **C.** Collateral licking. Data are means from the last five sessions.

Discussion

The differentiation in the operant response pattern across components was clearly associated with a differentiation in the pattern of the recorded collateral responses. The longer postreinforcement pauses under FR 40 were associated with longer durations of licking the empty sucrose delivery tube plus a higher frequency of responses on the nonfunctional lever (Figure 4.1). This finding is in agreement with several previous reports showing an increased postreinforcement pause (Ferster and Skinner, 1957; Felton and Lyon, 1966) and/or an increased duration of collateral responding (Schaeffer and Diehl, 1966; Hutchinson et al., 1968; Flory, 1969; Carlisle, 1971) with increasing FR size. In the present experiment, the duration of collateral licking systematically increased in each component along with the increases in postreinforcement pauses as a function of the manipulated component duration. Thus, postreinforcement pauses and the associated collateral responses may expand not only when the FR size is increased, but also when stimuli enclosing FR schedules are increased in duration.

Apparently, operant as well as collateral responses may change rate and pattern as a function of changes in a *single* independent variable (component duration in this experiment). More broadly, the experiment suggests that multiple schedules generate local interactions among concurrently available responses in *each* schedule component.

Positive Contrast and Collateral Responses (Experiment II)*

Typically, response interactions in multiple schedules refer only to sequential changes in one response across the successive components. The traditional example is that an operant response rate may decrease under the EXT component and increase under the VI component when a simple VI or a *mult* VI VI is changed to *mult* VI EXT (Reynolds, 1961b). The results from Experiment I suggest, however, that concurrent interactions may also occur between the operant response and collateral responses within each component of the multiple schedule.

Collateral responses have occasionally been recorded, but not typically related to operant responses, in the analysis of multiple schedule effects. Some available evidence indicates that collateral responses, such as attack, schedule escape, wheel running, and wing flapping, may occur almost exclusively under the EXT component of various multiple schedules, including *mult* CRF EXT, *mult* FI EXT, and *mult* VI EXT (Skinner and Morse, 1957; Azrin et al., 1966; Catania, 1966; Terrace, 1966, 1971; Rilling et al., 1969, 1973; Rilling and Caplan, 1973). Likewise, collateral attack, mirror pecking, and unreinforced lever

* Experiment was conducted at the University of Copenhagen, from January to December 1974, and reported by I. Iversen (1975a). The author thanks Mrs. E. Nielsen for her assistance during the experiment.

pressing may occur most frequently in the component with the lower operant response rate in *mult* FR FR (Keehn and Bratbak, 1967; Flory, 1969; Cohen and Looney, 1973; Iversen, 1975b). In all the above schedules, a high rate of collateral responding was then associated with a low rate of operant responding and a low rate of collateral responding was associated with a high rate of operant responding. The pattern of still other collateral responses, however, may be highly dependent upon, and indeed reversed by schedule manipulations. Thus, collateral drinking primarily occurs under the EXT component of *mult* CRF EXT (Keehn and Colotla, 1971) but under the VI component of *mult* VI EXT (Jacquet, 1972). Similarly, collateral responses directed toward discriminative stimuli signaling schedule components occur primarily under the VI component of *mult* VI EXT (Keller, 1974).

Quite recently a few experiments have purposely manipulated collateral responses in multiple schedules. In a study by Allen and Porter (1975), access to collateral drinking was prevented in one component of *mult* FI FI. The drinking rate increased in the unchanged component, but unfortunately no data were provided on possible simultaneous changes in the operant response rate. Similarly, Rilling and Caplan (1973) reported that collateral attack responses were more frequent under EXT and lower under VI of *mult* VI EXT relative to simple VI. Again the concomitant changes in operant response rates were not presented. Rilling and Caplan did note, however, that the changes in the rate of collateral attack precluded an analysis of operant responding because the attack response "competed with and lowered" the rate of VI responding. In a subsequent study, Rilling and Caplan (1975) accordingly excluded attack responses from the VI component to prevent competition with the operant response. When a simple VI was changed to *mult* VI EXT, the operant rate increased under VI for four of seven subjects, but decreased or remained unchanged for the remaining three subjects. According to Rilling and Caplan, the latter three subjects showed an increase of competing preattack responses under VI which may have prevented positive operant contrast.

Keller (1974), Schwartz (1975), and Spealman (1976) recorded operant responses on one key as well as collateral responses directed toward the component stimuli of the multiple schedule. The overall rate of the operant response either did not increase (Schwartz, 1975), or actually decreased (Keller, 1974; Spealman, 1976) with the simultaneous emergence of competing stimulus-directed responses during the VI component of a *mult* VI EXT schedule. Spealman (1976) further reported that the rates of the operant and the stimulus-directed responses were increasing and decreasing functions, respectively, of the component durations of the *mult* VI EXT schedule. The interactions in Spealman's experiment were also more local, with an initial low rate of the operant response (in the first 3 sec of each VI component) associated with an initial high frequency of stimulus-directed responses.

Across experiments, the data provide some indication that specific collateral responses change rate during multiple schedules. The *inverse* relationships between the operant and collateral response rates within components particularly invite examination of possible causal relationships between response rate changes in multiple schedules. Such response interdependencies suggest that a functional analysis of sequential interactions might be incomplete by neglecting collateral response changes systematically associated with the schedule manipulations. By and large, relevant interactions between operant and collateral responses in multiple schedules have often been sidestepped by selectively recording only the collateral response changes or only the operant response changes. The extensive interactions between concurrently occurring responses reported in this volume would indicate that changes in collateral responses may perhaps participate in the formation of operant response changes. The rate of collateral responding in multiple schedules may then effectively prevent or promote changes in the operant response which are described as positive and negative behavioral contrast.

Experiment II

The purpose of this experiment was to investigate systematically the relationship between operant responses and collateral responses during a typical multiple schedule manipulation, a change from simple VI to *mult* VI EXT.

Initially, three naive male Wistar albino rats were reduced to 80% of their free-feeding body weights and trained in a general apparatus consisting of a response lever and a food cup mounted on one side of a running wheel. The wheel was 33.0 cm in diameter, and the running surface consisted of 15.5-cm long metal bars spaced every 8.5 mm. Four magnets mounted equidistant on the circumference of the wheel could activate two reed relays spaced 9.0 cm apart on the supporting base of the running wheel. The wheel could turn in both directions. A modified relay served as a brake to the wheel. A $3.0 \times 2.0 \times 1.0$ cm metal food cup was mounted on the right side, 1.0 cm above the running surface. Small holes in the bottom of the food cup prevented accumulation of pellet dust. A 3.0×3.0 cm flat metal lever was mounted with the right edge 4.5 cm from the left edge of the food cup. The lever was also 1.0 cm above the surface of the running wheel. A lever press was recorded as a 3.0-mm depression with a force greater than 10 g. Since lever pressing and wheel running were topographically different and incompatible responses, each response was recorded in duration rather than frequency (Premack, 1965).

The duration of each response was recorded as the number of 0.5-sec periods with one or more instances of that response (Dunham, 1972; and Experiment VI, Chapter 3, this volume). Each quarter revolution of the wheel constituted a response provided both reed relays had been activated in a given 0.5-sec period. Thus, running was only recorded when the wheel was rotated at a minimal speed of 9.0 cm/0.5 sec along the circumference (10.8m/min).

Throughout the experiment, lever pressing was reinforced on a VI 1-min schedule in the presence of a houselight. The reinforcer was one 45-mg food pellet and a session was terminated after 42 min. The running wheel was locked before and after the session.

The first question posed was simply as follows: What will happen to collateral wheel running during the establishment of behavioral contrast for operant responding? After pretraining, lever pressing was maintained on VI 1 min for 15 sessions with free access to wheel running (Phase A). The VI for lever pressing was then changed to *mult* VI EXT with strictly alternating 3-min components (Phase B). The houselight was on during VI and off during EXT.

This change from VI to *mult* VI EXT produced the data presented in Figure 4.2. For all rats, the probability of lever pressing decreased under EXT and increased under VI compared to the simple VI. Wheel running simultaneously increased under EXT and decreased under VI. The wheel-running probability thus changed in a direction opposite to the lever-pressing probability for each component of the *mult* VI EXT. The data were then directly replicated with the schedule changed back to VI (Phase C), and then to *mult* VI EXT again (Phase D).

The increased lever-pressing probability under VI, along with the decreased probability under EXT, is an example of positive contrast for an operant response (Reynolds, 1961b). The simultaneously decreased probability of collateral wheel running under VI and increased probability under EXT would be an example of negative behavioral contrast for a collateral response. These opposing contrast effects for operant and collateral responses appear to have at least some generality, since Rand (1977) recently reported that certain collateral responses in pigeons increased under EXT and decreased under VI along with the typical reverse changes for the operant response. Positive contrast for an operant response may thus be obtained along with negative contrast for a specific collateral response.

The response changes associated with the schedule changes from simple VI to *mult* VI EXT invite the following questions: (1) Did the changing probability of collateral responding influence the probability of operant responding, or (2) did the change in operant responding influence the collateral responding? The same questions may be posed for each component of the multiple schedule. The possible relations between collateral and operant responding were therefore examined by manipulating access to collateral wheel running across experimental phases.

When the wheel was locked under EXT in Phase E, the wheel-running probability of course decreased immediately to zero under EXT; but wheel running simultaneously increased under VI, with a concurrent decrease in lever pressing (Figure 4.2). The lever-pressing and wheel-running probabilities under VI were now comparable to the data obtained with simple VI in Phase C. The increase in lever pressing that previously occurred with the change from VI to *mult* VI EXT was thus counteracted by only allowing wheel running under VI. Hence, positive contrast for the operant response was effectively prevented by manipulating access to the collateral response. This effect was clearly under experimental control, since lever-pressing and wheel-running probabilities returned to the contrast patterns when wheel running was again possible throughout a session (Phase F compared to Phase D).

Again the data are consistent with recent reports. Allen and Porter (1975) showed that preventing access to collateral water drinking under one component of a multiple schedule for food reinforcement increased the duration of

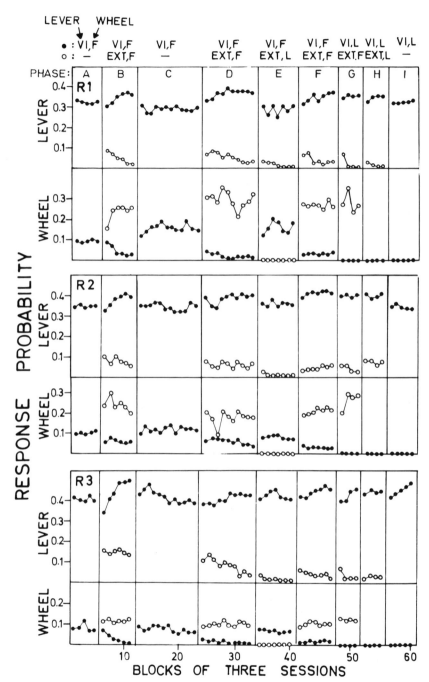

Figure 4.2. Relationships between lever-pressing and wheel-running probabilities in three-session blocks for each rat and experimental phase. Experimental conditions are indicated at the top of each column. The schedule for lever pressing was either VI or EXT and the wheel was free (F) or locked (L) in each schedule component.

drinking under the second component. The available data seem to suggest that reducing the probability of a collateral response in one component may result in an increase in the probability of the same collateral response in a second component.

More minute interactions between lever pressing and wheel running are shown in representative event recorder segments in Figure 4.3 and clearly con-

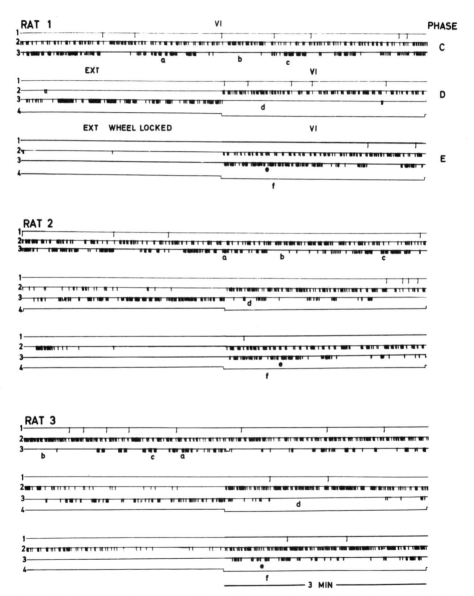

Figure 4.3. Event recorder segments of operant lever pressing and collateral wheel running from Phases C, D, and E for each of three rats. 1, pellet; 2, lever; 3, wheel running; 4, stimulus.

firm the relationships described in Figure 4.2. With VI (Phase C), lever pressing bursts regularly alternated with wheel running (a). Periods with a high lever-pressing density were associated with an absence or infrequent wheel running bursts (b). Conversely, a relatively low lever-pressing density was associated with frequent wheel-running bursts (c). With *mult* VI EXT in Phase D, the frequent alternation between lever pressing and wheel running was now replaced by a more infrequent alternation, largely under control of the component stimuli. At the onset of the VI component, lever pressing emerged and wheel running ceased, whereas onset of the EXT component produced a reverse pattern, with a cessation of lever pressing and emergence of wheel running. The pattern of lever pressing under the VI component now resembled the pattern during VI alone (Phase C), with wheel running either absent or infrequent (d, compare to b). Finally, with wheel running prevented under EXT (Phase E), alternation between lever-pressing and wheel-running bursts returned in the VI component (e) as with the VI in Phase C. Wheel-running bursts, however, were largely confined to the first half of the VI component (f). IRT in lever pressing concomitantly tended to be longer during the first half of the VI component.

Summing up at this point, the critical feature of this experiment was that prevention of wheel running under EXT (Phase E) resulted in an increase in wheel-running probability under VI, which in turn resulted in a concurrent decrease in lever-pressing probability under VI and prevention of contrast. However, this change in lever pressing under VI might be attributed to the simultaneous changes in wheel running under VI, or EXT. This possibility was further analyzed by preventing wheel running under VI (Phase G) and then under EXT (Phase H). The results were clear: lever pressing under VI was unaffected by the gross changes in wheel running under EXT if wheel running was also prevented under VI (Figure 4.2).

In combination, the lever-pressing probability under VI appeared to be directly dependent upon the concurrent probability of wheel running within the same VI component. Yet, an increase in wheel running under VI was produced by preventing wheel running under EXT. Therefore, the changes in VI lever pressing were also indirectly dependent upon the wheel-running probability under EXT. The experimental manipulations thus indicate that positive contrast may be prevented by allowing a specific collateral response to occur only concurrently with the operant response under VI.

The present experiment did not directly assess the possible influence of collateral wheel running on the course of extinction of the operant response under EXT. The results tentatively suggest, however, that a low probability of the operant response under EXT may not be increased when the probability of the concurrently occurring collateral wheel-running response is decreased to zero (Phase E). Therefore, collateral wheel running under EXT did not seem to be responsible for the maintained low probability of the operant response under EXT; rather, the decreased probability of the extinguished operant response allowed for an increase in the probability of wheel running.

The changing interrelations in the VI component from one phase to the next are shown in Figure 4.4. Phase-to-phase changes in lever-pressing probability

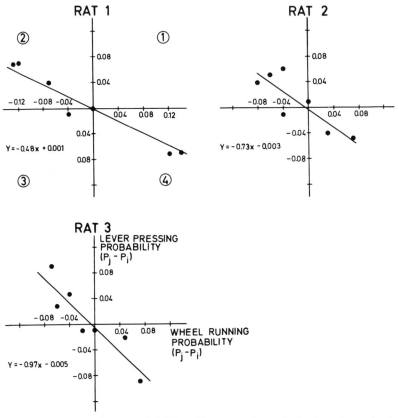

Figure 4.4. Changes in the probabilities of lever pressing and wheel running under the VI component across successive phases of the experiment. Positive and negative values indicate increased and decreased probabilities, respectively. Data represent the differences in response probabilities for the last five sessions of each successive phase. Regression lines were calculated by the method of least squares. (Data are not presented for probability changes from Phase G to Phase I with the wheel locked.)

are plotted on the ordinate and changes in wheel running are plotted on the abscissa. An increase in lever pressing was clearly associated with a decrease in wheel running (data in the second quadrant), and a decrease in lever-pressing was associated with an increase in wheel-running (data in the fourth quadrant). For each rat, the intercept of the regression lines was close to zero, and the lines had a negative slope. Overall, the numerical changes (independent of sign) in the probability of wheel running exceeded or equaled the changes in the probability of lever pressing.

Inverse relations between lever-pressing and wheel-running probabilities were also obtained under EXT in Phases B and D. For all rats, the numerical change in the probability of wheel running was much smaller than the simultaneous change in the probability of lever pressing (Figure 4.2). Under EXT, the change in wheel-running thus fell short of the simultaneous change in lever pressing. In subsequent phases, the lever-pressing probability remained low under EXT across low or high probabilities of wheel running resulting from manipulations of access to run. The results therefore indicate that the decreased probability of the operant response under EXT allowed for the concurrent increase in the probability of wheel running, rather than vice versa.

Discussion

These results are immediately relevant to recent descriptions of collateral responses during multiple schedules. The probability changes in wheel running are analogous to probability changes in collateral attack (Rilling and Caplan, 1973) and collateral turning motions (Rand, 1977). Rilling and Caplan (1975) observed that specific components of collateral attack interfered with and prevented an increased probability of operant responding under VI of *mult* VI EXT. In agreement with the present data, Keller (1974), Schwartz (1975), and Spealman (1976) reported that an increase in operant response rate under VI may not be obtained when concurrent stimulus-directed responses are simultaneously generated predominantly under VI in *mult* VI EXT.

The available data are in agreement that an increased probability of operant responding under VI may be (1) *prevented* when a collateral response can only occur under VI, or (2) *produced* by a decrease in the probability of a collateral response under VI. In combination, positive contrast may not occur when competing responses occur exclusively or predominantly under VI.

We previously posed the question of how a change in the operant response probability in one component may affect the probability of the same operant in succeeding schedule components. Although tentative, the results suggest that this effect is mediated by collateral responses, or more specifically that positive contrast may result from a decreased probability of a collateral response under VI with the schedule change to *mult* VI EXT. At least for wheel running investigated in the present experiment, the relatively unrestricted opportunity to run in the wheel under EXT may decrease the wheel-running probability under VI when running is relatively more constrained by the operant response. Such a displacement of a collateral response away from VI and into EXT would increase the available time for the operant response under VI, resulting in positive contrast. Further, positive contrast was effectively counteracted by locking the wheel under EXT and thereby preventing displacement of collateral wheel running. Wheel running was thus restricted to the VI component and competed with and decreased the probability of the reinforced operant. Operant response interactions across multiple schedule components may then be related to interactions between concurrently available responses within *each* schedule component. Displacement and/or differential generation of collateral responses across schedule components would seem to provide at least some of the possible means by which a manipulation in one schedule component may affect responding in alternate schedule components.

Multi-response Interactions and Local
Behavioral Contrast (Experiment III)*

A much debated issue is whether positive contrast is related to a decreased probability of operant responses or operant reinforcement in an adjacent component (Dunham, 1968; Freeman, 1972). An extensively used experimental strategy has been either to decrease the operant response probability in one component while maintaining a constant reinforcement rate, or to decrease the reinforcement rate while maintaining a near zero probability of the operant response in that component. In common, both manipulations entail a low operant probability in the manipulated component. The purpose of Experiment III was to attempt a complementary design: (1) to decrease the reinforcement rate in one component while maintaining a relatively high operant response probability in that component, and (2) to decrease the operant response probability to zero while maintaining a zero reinforcement rate.

A second purpose was to analyze local changes for both operant and collateral responses. The experiment purposely used an operant response with an above zero baseline probability—wheel running in rats. Wheel running was simply reinforced on VI, and food cup activity, grooming, and exploration were recorded simultaneously as collateral responses.

Three naive Spraque-Dawley rats, maintained at 80% of their free-feeding body weights, were given daily sessions with reinforcement of wheel running by 45-mg food pellets. The apparatus described in Experiment II was also used in this experiment. Physical contact and activity within 0.1 cm of the food cup was recorded with a modified body-capacitance sensitivity system. Grooming and exploration were recorded manually for the two last sessions of each experimental phase by a button being pressed for each response. The rats were viewed from above through a one-way window in the side of the sound-attenuating chamber by means of mirror arrangements. Grooming was recorded when a rat scratched or licked his body. Exploration was recorded whenever a rat was standing up or sniffing the surface or walls of the running wheel. A slow "wheel-walking" response frequently occurred with sniffing the bars of the wheel. However, wheel running was only recorded when the circumferential speed of the turning wheel was above 15.0 cm/sec. Wheel running, food cup activity, grooming, and exploration were recorded in duration. Pulses from a continuously operating recycling timer (time base 0.6 sec) were counted as long as the recording device was activated for each each response. The frequency of changeover responses or switching between the recorded responses was also recorded.

After pretraining, wheel running was reinforced on VI 1 min for 16 sessions (Phase A). The houselight was on during the 42-min sessions, and the wheel was locked before and after each session. In Phase B, the VI was changed to a *mult* VI EXT with strictly alternating 3-min components (20 sessions). The

* Experiment was conducted at the University of Zurich, from February to April 1975, supported by the European Brain and Behavior Society. The author thanks Dr. J. P. Huston for the use of his laboratory facilities.

houselight was on during VI and flickered with on–off periods of 0.3 sec under EXT. The flickering houselight in EXT was accompanied by a clicking sound from the relay controlling the houselight. In Phase C, the schedule remained *mult* VI EXT as in Phase B, but the wheel was locked under EXT (10 sessions). In Phase D, response-independent pellets were delivered under VT 1 min in the component with the locked wheel (the former EXT component; 10 sessions). The schedule was thus *mult* VI VT, with the wheel locked under VT. Finally, in Phase E, wheel running was again maintained on VI throughout a session (6 sessions).

Discussion

Overall Contrast

The results suggest that an increase in the average probability of operant responding in one component (positive contrast) may be partially related to the operant response probability in the adjacent component. Operant wheel running first increased under VI in *mult* VI EXT when the response probability was experimentally decreased to zero under EXT (Figure 4.5). Furthermore, this positive contrast remained apparent when the reinforcement rate was again increased in the adjacent component with VT but the response probability was maintained at zero. A marked decrease in operant responding in one component thus may override a decrease in the reinforcement rate in the production of positive contrast. Indeed, within the procedures used in this experiment, a decreased rate of reinforcement in one component was not necessary for positive contrast.

The present data closely parallel the findings of a previous report using wheel running as the operant response with *mult* VR VR (D. R. Williams, 1965). Previous reports also agree in showing a diminished positive contrast in *mult* VI EXT when the probability of the operant response is only moderately decreased under EXT (Mackintosh et al., 1972; Halliday and Boakes, 1974).

The results of this experiment seem to fit with a model of contrast emphasizing interactions between concurrently occurring responses in each schedule component. The results of Experiment II suggested that positive contrast is associated with displacement of a collateral response that previously occurred in the VI component. Such displacement of a collateral response from VI to EXT would also appear to involve a low operant response probability under EXT. This possibility was tested by purposely manipulating the operant probability under EXT.

Exploration did not shift out of the VI component and positive contrast was not obtained when the operant response still occurred at a moderate probability in the EXT component (Phase B) (Figure 4.5). Exploration first decreased under VI when the operant response probability under EXT was manipulated to zero, allowing for a further increase in exploration under EXT (Phase C). This displacement of exploration, and the accompanying positive contrast for operant wheel running, were clearly maintained in spite of an increased reinforcement rate in the adjacent component conditional upon a maintained zero operant probability (Phase D). The low operant probability under the adjacent

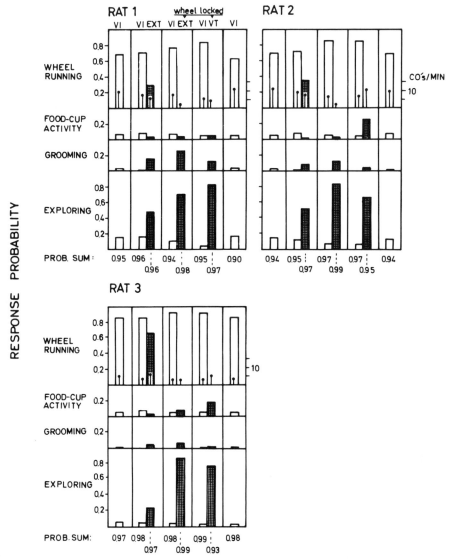

Figure 4.5. Probabilities of four responses for each rat and experimental phase. Sums of the probabilities are shown below each column. Changeover rates between responses are inserted in the columns for wheel running. Data are means obtained during successive 3-min periods for Phases A and E, and during the 3-min components for Phases B, C, and D. White bars—VI; stippled bars—EXT or VT.

component would therefore seem to be one of the variables controlling the component shift of collateral responses, which in turn affects the operant response under the VI component.

In addition to the operant contrast effects and displacement of exploration, changes in grooming and food cup activity under the adjacent component were also related to both the operant response and the reinforcement rate manipulations. Thus, grooming increased under EXT when the operant response was decreased in spite of a maintained zero rate of reinforcement (Phases B to C). However, grooming decreased in the adjacent component when the associated schedule was changed from EXT to VT with a maintained zero probability of the operant response (Phase D). Food cup activity was primarily "tied" to the schedule components with reinforcement. At the same time, however, the probability of food cup activity was also dependent upon the simultaneous operant response probability; that is, for rats 2 and 3, food cup activity occurred at a relatively higher probability in the component with a zero operant probability when reinforcement rate was equal in the two components (Phase D).

The shifting response changes across components and phases entailed changes in an additional set of responses—changeovers between the recorded responses. The rate of changeover responses under VI components was roughly inversely related to the probability of operant responding (Figure 4.5). Furthermore, the summed probability of wheel running, food cup activity, grooming, and exploration appeared to approach 1.0 as the rate of changeover responses decreased toward zero (Figure 4.5). Changes in the summed probability across phases may also be plotted against changes in the changeover rate (Figure 4.6). The summed probability increased for decreasing changeover rates and decreased for increasing changeover rates. Therefore, although an attempt was made to record and account for all responses, the summed probabilities did not quite total 1.0. However, such "pausing" in recorded responses was systematically related to the additional response of changing over among the recorded responses.

This finding is immediately relevant to the analysis of classical conditioning presented in Chapter 6. The over- and underestimation of the probability of one response from the probability of concurrent responses was gradually diminished as more responses were included in the analysis. Clearly, accuracy in

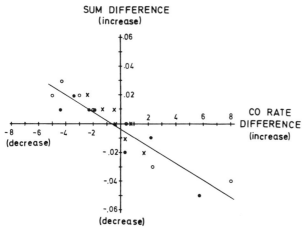

Figure 4.6. Changes in the summed probability of all responses plotted against alterations in changeover rate for each phase, schedule component, and rat. The regression line was determined by the method of least squares. Black circles, rat 1; white circles, rat 2; x, rat 3.

prediction of behavioral changes is greatly augmented by the additional recording of all concurrently occurring responses.

Local Contrast

In recent years, the analysis of positive behavioral contrast has become concerned with the more minute response changes within components of multiple schedules. Thus, operant responding may gradually decrease within the temporal limits of one schedule component that is followed by a second component associated with a relatively lower reinforcement rate (local behavioral contrast; Boneau and Axelrod, 1962; Catania and Gill, 1964; Nevin and Shettleworth, 1966; Terrace, 1966; Bernheim and Williams, 1967; Staddon, 1969; Gonzalez and Champlin, 1974).

To this point the concurrent response analysis has revealed that overall contrast appears to be related to a simultaneous and opposing behavioral contrast for collateral responding. In an extension of this analysis, a significant question arises: How does local contrast for operant responding relate to collateral responding?

Figure 4.7 presents an analysis of the recorded responses in successive 15-sec intervals within each multiple schedule component for Phases B, C, and D. The local probability of operant wheel running initially increased and then gradually decreased within the VI component of *mult* VI EXT for rats 1 and 2 (Phases B and C). This finding is clearly in accord with the results from the previous experiments. However, in some experiments with apparently similar procedures, the pattern of local contrast may be reversed—there may be an initial decrease in the operant probability followed by a gradual increase within VI (Ferster, 1958; Buck et al., 1975). Local positive contrast may also occur in the absence of overall positive contrast, as in Phase B; this finding is confirmed by recent data (Gutman and Minor, 1976; B. A. Williams, 1976). In addition, overall positive contrast may occur without local contrast, as the local operant response probability was relatively constant within the VI component of the *mult* VI VT schedule (Phase D). Consequently, local positive contrast may be obtained with or without overall positive contrast, and vice versa.

We suspect that within-component or local operant contrast is intimately associated with opposing local contrast effects for collateral responses. The local distribution of exploration, and to some extent food cup activity, in the VI component was thus inversely related to the distribution of the operant response for the two subjects with local positive contrast for the operant response (rats 1 and 2). Hence, local positive contrast for operant responding is clearly associated with negative local contrast for one or more collateral responses. Of particular interest is the effect of the introduction of response-independent reinforcement into the component with the wheel locked (Phase D). The local probabilities of food cup activity and exploration then became fairly constant within the VI component, as did the corresponding local operant probability. Therefore, the reverse relationship between contrast for operant and collateral responding in one component appears to be under the control of reinforcement factors in the adjacent component. In agreement with this conclusion, B. A.

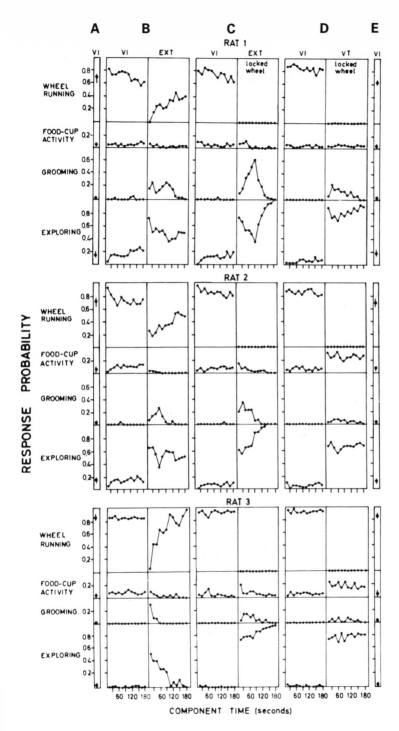

Figure 4.7. Local interactions between wheel running, food cup activity, grooming, and exploration in successive 15-sec intervals within each schedule component in Phases B, C, and D. Means and absolute ranges of the local probabilities for Phases A and E (VI alone) are shown in the left-hand and right-hand columns, respectively.

Williams (1976) has found that the distribution of operant responding in one component may depend upon the temporal location of reinforcement in the adjacent component.

Perhaps a relatively unheeded finding is a local negative contrast for the operant response under EXT. In this experiment, the local operant probability initially decreased and then gradually increased under EXT (Phase B). D. R. Williams (1965) found a similarly increasing probability profile for operant wheel running within the component with the lower reinforcement rate (also see Malone, 1976). The collateral response changes were more complex under the components with extinction or response-independent reinforcement. First, local positive contrast appeared for grooming and exploration (and to some extent for food cup activity), along with the local negative contrast for the operant response under EXT (Phase B). Second, the pattern of exploration reversed, from local positive to local negative contrast, when the operant response was decreased to zero under EXT (Phase C). Finally, all local probabilities of collateral responses were relatively constant with equal rates of reinforcement under the two schedule components.

Little doubt, the present findings only begin to explore how responding in one schedule component is affected by events in a temporally adjacent component. However, the available data do demonstrate continuous associations between local changes in operant and collateral responses. Moreover, the specific response patterns were modifiable by environmental manipulations. The close response interrelationships suggest that a single-response analysis is an insufficient description of multiple schedule effects; rather, the apparent simultaneous changes in local patterns of operant and collateral responses within and across multiple schedule components seem to argue for a multiresponse analysis.

Concluding Comments

This series of experiments seems to provide considerable evidence for an extension of the concurrent response analysis to encompass sequential operant schedules. More specifically, alterations in the probabilities of collateral responses systematically affect the operant response probabilities in multiple schedules. Foremost, perhaps, a particular interaction—positive contrast—may be directly dependent upon differentiation of specific collateral responses across the multiple schedule components.

The findings generally agree with several previous experiments but appear to be incongruent with some previous theoretical accounts of positive contrast. The principles and predictions of the theories might then be analyzed in terms of the available data.

A direct relationship between positive contrast for operant responding and collateral wheel running (Experiment II) seems to suggest that alterations in specific collateral responses may at least override the effect of differential reinforcement rates. Further, in Experiment III, positive contrast was not obtained with EXT in the adjacent component until the probability of the operant response was also reduced to zero. In addition, positive operant contrast was maintained by equal rates of reinforcement across components, conditional upon the absence of the operant response in the adjacent component. The present results thus firmly support previous suggestions that changes in reinforcement rate in an adjacent component are neither necessary nor sufficient for positive operant contrast. However, local contrast effects are more supportive of a reinforcement interpretation. Local positive contrast was obtained with a zero reinforcement rate in the adjacent component but was not clearly apparent with equal reinforcement rates across components. Therefore, local contrast may be related to reinforcement rate under an adjacent component. However, in a recent experiment (B. A. Williams, 1976) local positive contrast systematically depended upon the temporal pattern rather than the overall reinforcement rate under an adjacent component. The pattern of reinforcement within components may then be one of the variables controlling the close associations between local contrast effects for operant and collateral responses.

Positive operant contrast has been said to come about when one schedule is relatively more preferred than the schedule in an adjacent component (Bloomfield, 1969; Premack, 1969). The present data are not easily compared to the preference account because preference among schedule components was not directly assessed in the present experiments. Extrapolating from previous experiments, VI components would in general be expected to be preferred to EXT components (Findley, 1958; Beale and Winton, 1970). However, positive contrast was more dependent upon the pattern of collateral wheel running than upon the schedule components per se with *mult* VI EXT (Experiment II). Therefore, the results may agree with previous findings that relatively less preference for an adjacent component may not be sufficient for positive contrast. More formally, the preference account rests upon the validity of the assumption that relative response rates in choice situations measure preference.

If positive operant contrast is dependent upon aversiveness generated by emission of nonreinforced responses (errors), then the extent of positive contrast may be assumed to depend upon the probability of nonreinforced responses (Terrace, 1966). However, in Experiment III positive contrast was in fact only obtained when the operant response probability was decreased to zero under EXT. Moreover, in Experiment II positive contrast was dependent upon the distribution of collateral wheel running, given the same low probability of operant responding under EXT.

The present findings are consistent with reports of collateral response such as wing flapping, aggression, and schedule escape generated by contrast procedures. Such responses have been offered as "measures" of aversiveness or frustration generated under an adjacent component in association with positive operant contrast (Terrace, 1971, 1972; Rilling and Caplan, 1973; Rilling et al., 1973). Nevertheless, a single collateral response, taken out of the collective behavioral context, is not unequivocally associated with positive contrast. In Experiment III, for example, the increased probability of grooming under EXT was not necessarily associated with positive operant contrast. Similarly, Experiment II found that positive operant contrast was not covariant with collateral wheel running under EXT. The present results thus agree with previous experiments (e.g., Terrace, 1971; Coughlin, 1973; Rilling and Caplan, 1973) that individual collateral responses are not easily employed as indicants of aversiveness or frustration processes taking place between independent and dependent variables; rather, collateral responses seem to be collectively interrelated with operant responses and may actively *participate* in the development of positive operant contrast.

The response additivity model holds that positive operant contrast results when stimulus-directed responses, generated by differential reinforcement rates across schedule components, add to the operant response by activating the operant manipulandum. However, positive contrast was obtained in the present experiments without the discriminative stimuli located on the operant manipulandum, and with equal reinforcement rates in the schedule components.

The present data agree better with a second aspect of response additivity—that positive contrast may *not* occur when stimulus responses are directed toward a second manipulandum. Experiments by Keller (1974), Schwartz (1975), and Spealman (1976) clearly show extensive interactions between operant responses and topographically different stimulus-directed responses. These findings are consistent with Experiment II in that an increase in collateral wheel running during VI (produced by preventing wheel running in the adjacent component with EXT) may decrease the concurrent probability of the operant response and prevent positive contrast. Rilling and Caplan (1975) similarly found that positive operant contrast may be prevented when the procedures generate collateral attack responses concurrently with the operant response in VI of *mult* VI EXT. Concurrent responses generated within one schedule component may then compete with (or actually subtract from) the operant response in that component and thereby block any operant response probability. Thus, although positive contrast may not invariably result from an addition of stimulus-directed responses to the operant manipulandum, the dislocation of the discriminative stimuli away from the operant manipulandum may generate topographically different responses that compete with and prevent positive operant contrast.

A Response–Displacement Model of Positive Contrast?

The experimental results might suggest a novel model emphasizing the displacement of collateral responses in contrast experiments. Experiment II in particular showed that positive contrast was associated with displacement of collateral wheel running across schedule components. Positive operant contrast was then effectively eliminated by prevention of the displacement of collateral wheel running across the different components.

Experiment III suggested a similar mechanism, but only more weakly. A moderate decrease in operant wheel running under EXT allowed some displacement of collateral grooming, but the displacement of grooming was numerically small and did not significantly affect the concurrent probability of the operant response under VI. Similarly, exploration was clearly displaced into the EXT component, allowing for positive contrast for operant responding, only when the competing operant wheel running was prevented under EXT. In combination, the interactions suggest that a decreased operant probability under one component may allow for displacement of some collateral responses toward that component and away from an alternate component with a relatively higher probability of operant responding. As a result, the operant response may further increase in the alternate component because of the reduced probability of collateral responses. To speak loosely, a given collateral response may be displaced from one to another component when the time available for responding is relatively less restricted during the second component.

In the present experiments, a prerequisite for displacement of collateral responses from one component to a second seemed to be a decrease in operant responding during the second component. This is clearly a limiting point for an eventual general model of contrast favoring displacement of collateral responses. First, previous experiments have shown that positive contrast may occur when the operant probability is not appreciably decreased under an adjacent component, as with delayed reinforcement (Wilkie, 1971; Richards, 1972). Second, positive contrast may not occur in spite of a decreased operant probability under an adjacent component, as with certain procedures of errorless discrimination training (Terrace, 1963), response-independent reinforcement (Halliday and Boakes, 1971) or after drug injections or brain lesions (Bloomfield, 1972; Henke et al., 1972). Therefore, compared across experiments, the mean decrease in operant responses in an adjacent component appears to be neither necessary nor sufficient for positive contrast (also Marcucella, 1976).

The available evidence on multiple schedules thus prevents response displacement as yet another global formulation of the sequential interactions found in all experiments. The present experiments do, however, indicate some conditions under which collateral responses in one schedule component may affect the response patterns in a second component, and thereby influence the operant response within the second component. More firmly, the experiments establish that operant and collateral responses concurrently interact under *each* component of multiple schedules. This analysis may generalize, at least potentially, across different topographies of collateral responses and also across the more familiar interactions reported for multiple schedules. An analysis of response interactions seems to provide a worthwhile methodology applicable to prospective investigations of multiple schedules.

Collateral Responses in Multiple Schedules

Collateral responses may simply be defined as not-explicitly reinforced responses that concurrently occur with the specifically reinforced response. Collateral responses may be divided into subcategories, depending upon their relationship to the experimental parameters and the operant response.

One category is responses that have an above zero baseline probability prior to the introduction of conditioning procedures. Such collateral responses come close to the normally understood "prepotent" responses and may include exploration, grooming, rearing, or wheel running, for example. Prepotent collateral responses appear to be most susceptible to displacement across components of multiple schedules and may shift into the component with the relatively lower restriction or interference from the operant response. On the other hand, when the probability of such collateral responses is experimentally forced to zero in one component, then the same collateral response may shift into a second component and in turn restrict or reduce the operant response. The particular pattern shifts and local changes would necessarily be dependent upon specific parameters and the characteristics of the operant response. In Experiment III, for example, collateral exploration reversed from positive to negative local contrast when the operant responding was decreased to zero in the same component. In addition, the distribution of grooming was lowered and flattened by equalizing the reinforcement rates in the two schedule components. Significantly, displacement of prepotent collateral responses originating from a change in the operant probability in one component may in turn influence the operant response in a temporally remote schedule component.

A second category would be the collateral responses specifically induced by the operant reinforcement procedures. Collateral responses that increase from a low or zero baseline probability have also been called *adjunctive* or *schedule-induced* responses. The category includes a variety of response topographies, including water drinking, attack, mirror pecking, and schedule-escape responses (Falk, 1971). Such schedule induced responses can be further subdivided, according to whether they occur primarily in the schedule component with reinforcer delivery or the component without reinforcer delivery. Attack, wing flapping, and schedule-escape responses generally occur during components with relatively lower reinforcement rates (Azrin et al., 1966; Terrace, 1966, 1971; Rilling et al., 1969). On the other hand, specific components of induced responses may be common to both extinction and reinforcement components. Thus Rilling and Caplan (1975) found that attack responses under EXT generated preattack responses under VI. Water drinking may also occur in either the EXT component or the reinforcement component depending upon specific procedures (compare Keehn and Colotla, 1971; Jacquet, 1972).

A third category, somewhat resembling the second, is collateral responses generated by the reinforcement procedures but more explicitly "tied" to the components with reinforcer delivery. This class may include sniffing and licking at reinforcer delivery systems. Stimulus-directed responses would appear as "tied" only to schedule components with reinforcement (Schwartz and Gamzu, 1977). As already mentioned, stimulus-directed responses may effectively increase or decrease the probability of operant responses depending upon whether they are directed toward or away from the operant manipulandum.

Conclusion

In conclusion, subcategories and labels applied to collateral responses are clearly related to procedures rather than a priori arguments over inherent response properties or values. The same physical response may be operant or collateral and may enter different subcategories and interactions depending upon specific parameters. *Collateral responses,* especially in multiple schedules, is not a useful generic term allowing global generalizations to all similarly labeled responses. The fact that a particular subcategory of collateral responses is critically involved with operant responses in one procedural setting does not necessarily suggest that the same collateral response is similarly involved in different procedures. Simply, a specific variable may be neither necessary nor sufficient for positive operant contrast in all experimental contexts. The distribution of operant responses within different parametric contexts may very well involve different subcategories of collateral responses, which could effectively limit explanatory generalizations. The more concrete conclusion then is that collateral response patterns might be more carefully analyzed in relation to operant changes in multiple schedules.

References

Allen, J. D., and Porter, J. H.: Demonstration of behavioral contrast with adjunctive drinking. *Physiol. Behav.,* **15,** 511–515, 1975.

Azrin, N. H., Hutchinson, R. R., and Hake, D. F.: Extinction-induced aggression. *J. Exp. Anal. Behav.,* **9,** 191–204, 1966.

Beale, I. L., and Winton, A. S. W.: Inhibitory control in concurrent schedules. *J. Exp. Anal. Behav.,* **14,** 133–137, 1970.

Beecroft, R. S.: Within-session behavioral contrast? *Psychonomic Sci.,* **17,** 286–287, 1969.

Bernheim, J. W., and Williams, D. R.: Time-dependent contrast effects in a multiple schedule of food reinforcement. *J. Exp. Anal. Behav.,* **10,** 243–249, 1967.

Bloomfield, T. M.: Behavioral contrast and relative reinforcement frequency in two multiple schedules. *J. Exp. Anal. Behav.,* **10,** 151–158, 1967.

Bloomfield, T. M.: Behavioral contrast and the peak shift. In, R. M. Gilbert and N. S. Sutherland (eds.): *Animal Discrimination Learning.* London and New York, Academic Press, 1969.

Bloomfield, T. M.: Contrast and inhibition in discrimination learning by the pigeon: analysis through drug effects. *Learning Motivation,* **3,** 162–178, 1972.

Boakes, R. A.: Frequency of houselight interruption as a dimension for inhibitory generalization testing. *Psychonomic Sci.,* **26,** 249–251, 1972.

Boneau, C. A., and Axelrod, S.: Work decrement and reminiscence in pigeon operant conditioning. *J. Exp. Psychol.,* **64,** 352–354, 1962.

Bradshaw, C. W.: Behavioral contrast in albino rats. *Psychol. Rep.,* **37,** 287–291, 1975.

Bradshaw, C. M., Szabadi, E., and Bevan, P.: Behaviour of rats in multiple schedules of response-contingent and response-independent food presentation. *Q. J. Exp. Psychol.,* **30,** 133–139, 1978.

Brownstein, A. J., and Hughes, R. G.: The role of response suppression in behavioral contrast: signalled reinforcement. *Psychonomic Sci.,* **18,** 50–52, 1970.

Brownstein, A. J., and Newsom, C.: Behavioral contrast in multiple schedules with equal reinforcement rates. *Psychonomic Sci.,* **18,** 25–26, 1970.

Buck, S. L., Rothstein, B., and Williams, B. A.: A re-examination of local contrast in multiple schedules. *J. Exp. Anal. Behav.,* **24,** 291–301, 1975.

Carlisle, H. J.: Fixed-ratio polydipsia: termal effects of drinking, pausing, and responding. *J. Comp. Physiol. Psychol.,* **75,** 10–22, 1971.

Catania, A. C.: Concurrent operants. In, W. K. Honig (ed.): *Operant Behavior: Areas of Research and Application.* New York, Appleton-Century-Crofts, 1966.

Catania, A. C.: Self-inhibiting effects of reinforcement. *J. Exp. Anal. Behav.,* **19,** 517–526, 1973.

Catania, A. C., and Gill, C. A.: Inhibition and behavioral contrast. *Psychonomic Sci.*, **1**, 257–258, 1964.

Chitwood, P. R., and Griffin, P.: The effects of response prevention via operandum removal in the S⁻ of a tonal discrimination. *Psychonomic Sci.*, **27**, 37–38, 1972.

Coates, T. J.: The differential effects of punishment and extinction on behavioral contrast. *Psychonomic Sci.*, **27**, 146–148, 1972.

Cohen, P. S., and Looney, T. A.: Schedule-induced mirror responding in the pigeon. *J. Exp. Anal. Behav.*, **19**, 395–408, 1973.

Coughlin, R. C.: Timeout from a stimulus correlated with the extinction component of a multiple schedule. *Learning Motivation*, **4**, 294–304, 1973.

Dunham, P. J.: Contrasted conditions of reinforcement: a selective critique. *Psychol. Bull.*, **69**, 295–315, 1968.

Dunham, P. J.: Some effects of punishment upon unpunished responding. *J. Exp. Anal. Behav.*, **17**, 443–450, 1972.

Falk, J. L.: The nature and determinants of adjunctive behavior. *Physiol. Behav.*, **6**, 577–588, 1971.

Farthing, G. W.: Behavioral contrast in pigeons learning an auditory discrimination. *Bull. Psychonomic Soc.*, **6**, 123–125, 1975.

Felton, M., and Lyon, D. O.: The post-reinforcement pause. *J. Exp. Anal. Behav.*, **9**, 131–134, 1966.

Ferster, C. B.: Control of behavior in chimpanzees and pigeons by time-out from positive reinforcement. *Psychol. Monogr.*, **72**, 461, 1958.

Ferster, C. B., and Skinner, B. F.: *Schedules of Reinforcement*. New York, Appleton-Century-Crofts, 1957.

Findley, J. D.: Preference and switching under concurrent scheduling. *J. Exp. Anal. Behav.*, **1**, 123–144, 1958.

Flory, R. F.: Attack behavior in a multiple fixed-ratio schedule of reinforcement. *Psychonomic Sci.*, **16**, 156–157, 1969.

Freeman, B. J.: Behavioral contrast: reinforcement frequency or response suppression? *Psychol. Bull.*, **75**, 347–356, 1971.

Friedman, H., and Guttman, N.: Further analysis of the various effects of discrimination training on stimulus generalization gradients. In, D. I. Mostofsky (ed.): *Stimulus Generalization*. Stanford, Calif., Stanford University Press, 1965.

Gaffan, D.: Inhibitory gradients and behavioral contrast in rats with lesions of the fornix. *Physiol. Behav.*, **11**, 215–220, 1973.

Gamzu, E., and Schwartz, B.: The maintenance of key pecking by stimulus-contingent and response-independent food presentation. *J. Exp. Anal. Behav.*, **19**, 65–72, 1973.

Gonzalez, R. C., and Champlin, G.: Positive behavioral contrast, negative simultaneous contrast and their relation to frustration in pigeons. *J. Comp. Physiol. Psychol.*, **87**, 173–187, 1974.

Gutman, A.: Positive contrast, negative induction, and inhibitory stimulus control in the rat. *J. Exp. Anal. Behav.*, **27**, 219–233, 1977.

Gutman, A., and Minor, T.: Local positive behavioral contrast in the rat. *Psychol. Record*, **26**, 349–354, 1976.

Gutman, A., Sutterer, J. R., and Brush, F. R.: Positive and negative behavioral contrast in the rat. *J. Exp. Anal. Behav.*, **23**, 377–383, 1975.

Halliday, M. S., and Boakes, R. A.: Behavioral contrast and response independent reinforcement. *J. Exp. Anal. Behav.*, **16**, 429–434, 1971.

Halliday, M. S., and Boakes, R. A.: Discrimination involving response-independent reinforcement: implications for behavioral contrast. In, R. A. Boakes and M. S. Halliday (eds.): *Inhibition and Learning*. London and New York, Academic Press, 1972.

Halliday, M. S., and Boakes, R. A.: Behavioral contrast without response-rate reduction. *J. Exp. Anal. Behav.*, **22**, 453–462, 1974.

Hemmes, N. S.: Behavioral contrast in pigeons depends upon the operant. *J. Comp. Physiol. Psychol.*, **85**, 171–178, 1973.

Henke, P. G.: Septal lesions and aversive nonreward. *Physiol. Behav.*, **17**, 483–488, 1976.

Henke, P. G., Allen, J. D., and Davison, C.: Effect of lesions in the amygdala on behavioral contrast. *Physiol. Behav.*, **8**, 173–176, 1972.

Herrnstein, R. J.: On the law of effect. *J. Exp. Anal. Behav.*, **13**, 243–266, 1970.

Hughes, R. G.: Probability of signalled reinforcement in multiple variable-interval schedules. *Psychonomic Sci.*, **22**, 57–59, 1971.

Hutchinson, R. R., Azrin, N. H., and Hunt, G. M.: Attack produced by intermittent reinforcement of a concurrent operant response. *J. Exp. Anal. Behav.*, **11**, 489–495, 1968.

Iversen, I. H.: Behavioral contrast and collateral behavior. Paper presented at the Fourth Scandinavian Meeting on Physiological Psychology. Oslo, May 1975a.

Iversen, I. H.: Concurrent responses during multiple schedules in rats. *Scand. J. Psychol.*, **16**, 49–54, 1975b.

Jacquet, Y. F.: Schedule-induced licking during multiple schedules. *J. Exp. Anal. Behav.*, **17**, 413–423, 1972.

Keehn, J. D., and Bratbak, R. B.: Limitations on environmental control of multiple schedule fixed-ratio behavior. *J. Exp. Anal. Behav.*, **10**, 185–190, 1967.

Keehn, J. D., and Colotla, V. A.: Stimulus and subject control of schedule-induced drinking. *J. Exp. Anal. Behav.*, **16**, 257–262, 1971.

Keller, K.: The role of elicited responding in behavioral contrast. *J. Exp. Anal. Behav.*, **21**, 249–257, 1974.

Lander, D. G.: Stimulus control following response reduction with signalled reinforcement. *Psychonomic Sci.*, **23**, 365–367, 1971.

Mackintosh, N. J., Little, L., and Lord, J.: Some determinants of behavioral contrast in pigeons and rats. *Learning Motivation*, **3**, 148–161, 1972.

Malone, J. C.: Local contrast and Pavlovian induction. *J. Exp. Anal. Behav.*, **26**, 425–440, 1976.

Marcucella, H.: Signalled reinforcement and multiple schedules. *J. Exp. Anal. Behav.*, **26**, 199–206, 1976.

Nevin, J. A.: Differential reinforcement and stimulus control of not responding. *J. Exp. Anal. Behav.*, **11**, 715–726, 1968.

Nevin, J. A., and Shettleworth, S. J.: An analysis of contrast effects in multiple schedules. *J. Exp. Anal. Behav.*, **9**, 305–315, 1966.

Premack, D.: Reinforcement theory. In, D. Levine (ed.): *Nebraska Symposium on Motivation.* Lincoln, University of Nebraska Press, 1965.

Premack, D.: On some boundary conditions of contrast. In, J. T. Tapp (ed.): *Reinforcement and Behavior.* New York, Academic Press, 1969.

Rand, J. F.: Behaviors observed during S⁻ in a simple discrimination learning task. *J. Exp. Anal. Behav.*, **27**, 103–117, 1977.

Redford, M. E., and Perkins, C. C.: The role of autopecking in behavioral contrast. *J. Exp. Anal. Behav.*, **21**, 145–150, 1974.

Reynolds, G. S.: An analysis of interactions in a multiple schedule. *J. Exp. Anal. Behav.*, **4**, 107–117, 1961a.

Reynolds, G. S.: Behavioral contrast. *J. Exp. Anal. Behav.*, **4**, 57–71, 1961b.

Reynolds, G. S.: Relativity of response rate and reinforcement frequency in a multiple schedule. *J. Exp. Anal. Behav.*, **4**, 179–184, 1961c.

Richards, R. W.: Reinforcement delay: some effects on behavioral contrast. *J. Exp. Anal. Behav.*, **17**, 381–394, 1972.

Rilling, M.: Stimulus control and inhibitory processes. In, W. K. Honig and J. E. R. Staddon (eds.): *Handbook of Operant Behavior.* Englewood Cliffs, New Jersey, Prentice-Hall, 1977.

Rilling, M., and Caplan, H. J.: Extinction-induced aggression during errorless discrimination learning. *J. Exp. Anal. Behav.*, **20**, 85–92, 1973.

Rilling, M., and Caplan, H. J.: Frequency of reinforcement as a determinant of extinction-induced aggression during errorless discrimination learning. *J. Exp. Anal. Behav.*, **23**, 121–129, 1975.

Rilling, M., Askew, H. R., Ahlskog, J. E., and Kramer, T. J.: Aversive properties of the negative stimulus in a successive discrimination. *J. Exp. Anal. Behav.*, **12**, 917–932, 1969.

Rilling, M., Kramer, T. J., and Richards, R. W.: Aversive properties of the negative stimulus during learning with and without errors. *Learning Motivation*, **4**, 1–10, 1973.

Sadowsky, S.: Behavioral contrast and timeout, blackout, or extinction as the negative condition. *J. Exp. Anal. Behav.*, **19**, 499–507, 1973.

Schaeffer, R. W., and Diehl, J. C.: Collateral water drinking in rats maintained on FR food reinforcement schedules. *Psychonomic Sci., 4,* 257–258, 1966.

Schwartz, B.: Discriminative stimulus location as a determinant of positive and negative behavioral
contrast in the pigeon. *J. Exp. Anal. Behav., 23,* 167–176, 1975.

Schwartz, B., and Gamzu, E.: Pavlovian control of operant behavior. In, W. K. Honig and J. E. R.
Staddon (eds.): *Handbook of Operant Behavior.* Englewood Cliffs, New Jersey, Prentice-Hall,
1977.

Schwartz, B., Hamilton, B., and Silberberg, A.: Behavioral contrast in the pigeon: a study of the
duration of key pecking maintained on multiple schedules of reinforcement. *J. Exp. Anal.
Behav., 24,* 199–206, 1975.

Skinner, B. F., and Morse, W. H.: Concurrent activity under fixed-interval reinforcement. *J.
Comp. Physiol. Psychol., 50,* 279–281, 1957.

Spealman, R. D.: Interactions in multiple schedules: the role of the stimulus-reinforcer contingency. *J. Exp. Anal. Behav., 26,* 79–93, 1976.

Staddon, J. E. R.: Multiple fixed-interval schedules: transient contrast and temporal inhibition. *J.
Exp. Anal. Behav., 12,* 583–590, 1969.

Terrace, H. S.: Discrimination learning with and without "errors." *J. Exp. Anal. Behav., 6,* 1–27,
1963.

Terrace, H. S.: Stimulus control. In, W. K. Honig (ed.): *Operant Behavior: Areas of Research and
Application.* New York, Appleton-Century-Crofts, 1966.

Terrace, H. S.: Escape from S⁻. *Learning Motivation, 2,* 148–163, 1971.

Terrace, H. S.: Conditioned inhibition in successive discrimination learning. In, R. A. Boakes and
M. S. Halliday (eds.): *Inhibition and Learning.* London, Academic Press, 1972.

Vieth, A., and Rilling, M.: Comparison of time-out and extinction as determinants of behavioral
contrast: an analysis of sequential effects. *Psychonomic Sci., 27,* 281–282, 1972.

Wilkie, D. M.: Delayed reinforcement in a multiple schedule. *J. Exp. Anal. Behav., 16,* 233–239,
1971.

Wilkie, D. M.: Signalled reinforcement in multiple and concurrent schedules. *J. Exp. Anal. Behav.,
20,* 29–36, 1973.

Wilkie, D. M.: Behavioral contrast produced by a signalled decrease in local rate of reinforcement.
Learning Motivation, 8, 182–193, 1977.

Williams, B. A.: Behavioral contrast as a function of the temporal location of reinforcement. *J.
Exp. Anal. Behav., 26,* 57–64, 1976.

Williams, D. R.: Negative induction in instrumental behavior reinforced by central stimulation.
Psychonomic Sci., 2, 341–342, 1965.

Chapter 5

Collateral Responses with Simple Schedules

Iver H. Iversen

Reinforced Responses Interacting with Collateral Responses

In the original formulation of an experimental analysis of behavior, Skinner (1938) laid out the principal problem to be the establishment of laws for individual responses (reflexes). Skinner hastened to add that the remaining part of the field was "the interaction of separate reflexes" (1938, p. 46). Models favoring competition among behaviors, however, have not been particularly attractive, which is somewhat surprising, given the awareness among the first experimental analysts of such a phenomenon. Initially, experimental subjects were merely positioned on a table or in an open box with stimuli and objects delivered to the subjects more or less by hand. The investigatory reflexes elicited by even slight noise, odor, light, or temperature changes were well known to "inhibit" the conditioned reflexes. Thus, behavior competition was a serious everyday problem, which in fact must have prevented or at best delayed collection of replicable data. Thus, Pavlov wrote:

> In our old laboratory the neglect to provide against external stimuli often led to a curious complication when I visited some of my co-workers. Having by himself established a new conditioned reflex, working in the room with the dog, the experimenter would invite me for a demonstration, and then everything would go wrong and he would be unable to show anything at all. It was I who presented the extra stimulus: the investigatory reflex was immediately brought into play: the dog gazed at me, and smelled at me, and of course this was sufficient to inhibit every recently established reflex. (Pavlov; 1927, p. 45)

Eventually subjects and experimenters were situated in separate rooms with stimuli and objects delivered by more remote control. Skinner pleaded for a similar control in the establishment of laws of individual reflexes: "a first precaution is the removal of stimuli which elicit other reflexes . . . Not all such stimuli can be removed, but a nearly maximal isolation can be achieved by conducting the experiments in a sound-proof, dark, smooth-walled, and well-ventilated room'' (1938, p. 55).

Until recent times, these arguments were not markedly altered. Thus, in the introductory remarks to a first handbook of operant behavior, Honig wrote:

> In operant work, control of the environment facilitates the concentration upon one kind of response by removing the opportunity for strong competing behaviors. While psychology is the science of behavior, it is naive to believe that ''all'' the behaviors in a situation must be observed and recorded (Honig, 1966, p. 7).

Experimental equipment has been held tightly closed with an automatic record of only the response required for reinforcer delivery. Although the investigated single response was not really believed to occur in a behavioral vacuum, ''other'' behaviors were assumed to remain constant or at best be homogeneously distributed between occurrences of the reference response. In the past two decades, however, several reports have described significant changes in various behaviors occurring with singly reinforced responses.

After observation of behaving organisms, Breland and Breland (1961) thus reported several examples of how ''instinctive'' behaviors intrude and interfere with particular conditioned responses. The simple response of merely drinking water after food reward has recently received considerable attention, but other behaviors have also been found to occur regularly with responses reinforced on various schedules, the so-called adjunctive or schedule-induced behaviors (Falk, 1969, 1971; Staddon and Simmelhag, 1971; Segal, 1972).

Moreover, adjunctive or collateral responses do not occur haphazardly within reinforcement schedules; their rates and patterns seem to vary systematically with manipulated schedule parameters. Even in a simple environment with only ''one'' experimental parameter, several topographically different behaviors may change rate and pattern simultaneously. Thus, an experimental enclosure that excludes extraneous stimuli does not guarantee an elimination or ''stabilization'' of competing behaviors. Perhaps collateral responses significantly participate in the formation or patterning of the reinforced operant response.

Recently several reports have provided simultaneous recordings of collateral responses and reinforced responses. For example, the rate of a reinforced response and the rate of collateral licking may change in opposite directions after brain damage (Wayner and Greenberg, 1972), drug injections (Wuttke and Innis, 1972), ambient temperature changes (Carlisle, 1973), or changes in response contingencies (Dunham, 1971; Iversen, 1975b). Such reports have occasionally been received with some contempt and have been described as ''chicken and egg'' experiments. What affects what, the reinforced response or the collateral response? However, if a particular problem of ''causality'' between collateral and reinforced responses is apparent within one operant schedule, then similar problems must exist in similar applications.

Kuhn (1970) argues that a science develops in accordance with paradigm shifts. A paradigm shift occurs when a "new" or hitherto insufficiently emphasized variable proves to be a powerful determinant of familiar findings. Previous methodological strategies and theoretical models must then be revised to accommodate the new functional relationships. For example, the discovery of x-rays by Roentgen in 1895 led to a change in the apparatus previously used in radiation studies. In the words of Kuhn:

> Though x-rays were not prohibited by established theory, they violated deeply entrenched expectations. Those expectations, I suggest, were implicit in the design and interpretation of established laboratory procedures. By the 1890's cathode ray equipment was widely deployed in numerous European laboratories. If Roentgen's apparatus had produced x-rays, then a number of other experimentalists must for some time have been producing those rays without knowing it. Perhaps those rays, which might well have other unacknowledged sources too, were implicated in behavior previously explained without reference to them. At the very least, several sorts of long familiar apparatus would in the future have to be shielded with lead. Previously completed work on normal projects would now have to be done again because earlier scientists had failed to recognize and control a relevant variable. (Kuhn, 1970, p. 59)

A novel behavioral paradigm might recognize competition among behaviors as an important principle that should not be excluded from experimental evaluation. Consequently, behavior would not be viewed in isolation but within a behavioral context.

Inverse raltionships among simultaneously available behaviors have often been seen as only indirect competition. For example, Hull suggested:

> If the two stimulating situations are presented simultaneously or in close succession in such a way that the acts of striving for one preclude the simultaneous performance of the acts involved in striving for the other, there arises a competition within the body of the organism and that reaction potential which is momentarily greater mediates the corresponding reaction. (Hall, 1952, p. 331)

Another interpretation offered that proprioceptive stimuli from one response become a signal for nonreinforcement for other responses, and thereby exert conditioned inhibitory influences on other responses (Berlyne, 1960). With respect to conditioned inhibition, Hearst wrote:

> In my opinion, some but by no means all of the decrements produced by CIs [conditioned inhibitory stimuli] can be attributed to the development of specific motor responses that compete with or are antagonistic to the measured CR [conditioned response]. In addition to this specific source of response reduction, CIs probably also evoke more general expectancies or emotional states that mediate CR decrement. (Hearst, 1972, p. 21)

Direct competition among responses however, has been considered in specific as well as general explanations of behavior. Admittedly, behavioral models emphasizing response competition have most often been more or less provocative discourses (Guthrie, 1935) without specific recordings and analysis of competing behaviors. The heuristic character of competing response models is perhaps responsible for the diverse references to responses that concurrently occur with a recorded response. Such responses are thus said to be adjunctive,

agitated, alternate, antagonistic, anticipatory, catalyzing, collateral, conflicting, displaced, emotional, extraneous, irrelevant, intercurrent, interfering, in-
terim, intervening, mediating, schedule-induced, or superstitious.

Most recently, Schoenfeld and associates have developed a theoretical treatment that emphasizes not only the temporal relationships between responses
and events, but also the fact that recorded responses are embedded in a "behavioral stream" (e.g., Schoenfeld and Farmer, 1970). In a further development, at least one contemporary competing response model has explicitly for-
mulated a program for a multiresponse methodology. Thus Dunham (1971,
1972) demonstrated that prevention of one response may increase the probability of a concurrent response. Dunham suggested that changes in one response
may be proportional to changes in concurrent responses, so that each specific
response occurs in a fixed proportion of the available time for that response.

Of equal interest, several experiments suggested that the patterning of responses reinforced on DRL schedules may be closely dependent upon the simultaneous pattern of specific collateral responses (Hodos et al., 1962; Laties
et al., 1965; Laties et al., 1969). In addition, collateral responses have been
manipulated in FI, FR, and VI schedules with a resulting alteration in the rate
and pattern of reinforced responding (Skinner and Morse, 1957; Clark, 1962;
Segal and Bandt, 1966; Wayner and Greenberg, 1972; Gilbert, 1974; Colotla
and Keehn, 1975; Cook and Singer, 1976; Iversen, 1976). Thus the patterning of
reinforced responding appears to be related to collateral response characteristics in addition to schedule variables.

The purpose of the following experiments was to systematically amplify the
previous analysis of response interactions within simple reinforcement schedules. More inductively, the experiments described in the preceding chapters
predict that reinforced and collateral responses are also mutually dependent in
simple schedules. The present experiments therefore were undertaken to provide a quantitative analysis of the molecular patterns and interactions between
reinforced and collateral responses.

Pattern Reciprocity Between FR Responding and
Collateral Licking (Experiments I and II)*

With periodic schedules of reinforcement, periods of inactivity typically appear
after reinforcer delivery. These so-called postreinforcement pauses have been
the subject of extensive investigation and explanation (Killeen, 1975). Under
FR schedules, the postreinforcement pause has been manipulated by parameters such as ratio size, reinforcer deprivation, reinforcer size, drugs, and by
adding time-out, shock, or conditioned reinforcers during the ratio (Ferster and
Skinner, 1957; Dardano and Sauerbrunn, 1964; Findley and Brady, 1965;
Boren, 1966; Felton and Lyon, 1966; Powell, 1968, 1969; Barowsky and Mintz).

---

    * Experiments were conducted at the University of Copenhagen, from October 1971 to March
1972, and reported by I. Iversen (1973, 1975a).

A variety of collateral responses, including attack, escape, mirror pecking, water drinking, and wheel running, have now been recorded under FR as well as FI schedules (Falk, 1971; Staddon and Simmelhag, 1971; Segal, 1972; Cohen and Looney, 1973) and often reveal closer relationships between the patterns of reinforced and collateral responses.

Experiment I

In Experiment I (Iversen, 1975a), the FR response pattern was thus clearly associated with the patterning of a particular collateral licking response. Pressing one lever by rats was reinforced with a 20% sucrose solution on FR 40, and responses on a second lever were reinforced on FR 20 in the next component of a multiple schedule. The components alternated every 3 min independent of responding.

Figure 5.1 shows sample event records of lever pressing, licking the sucrose delivery tube, and sucrose delivery for four successive components of the multiple schedule for one rat. Similar records were obtained for two other rats. The postreinforcement pauses in lever pressing were clearly longer under FR 40 than under FR 20, which agrees with previous reports that FR pauses are an increasing function of the FR size (Ferster and Skinner, 1957; Felton and Lyon, 1966). In both schedule components, licking the sucrose delivery tube occurred during consumption of the reinforcer, but also frequently extended well past sucrose delivery. Such lick bursts were considerably longer following FR 40 reinforcement than following FR 20 reinforcement. This differentiation of collateral licking is consistent with previous reports that the duration of specific collateral responses is an increasing function of the FR size (Schaeffer and Diehl, 1966; Hutchinson et al., 1968; Flory, 1969; Carlisle, 1971). Figure 5.1 also reveals that collateral licking alternated with presses on the other (nonreinforced) lever only under FR 40. Quite simply, the data demonstrate reciprocal relations between reinforced and collateral responses. Similar interrelations between collateral attack and FR pauses were reported by Huston and Desisto (1971). In addition, Carlisle (1973) found relatively longer FR pauses in association with bursts of collateral grooming.

Experiment II

The precise relationship between FR pauses and bursts of collateral licking was next examined as a function of the FR size (Iversen, 1973). Lever pressing by rats was maintained with a 20% sucrose solution delivered on a progression of FR schedules (FR 1 to FR 30). Figure 5.2 shows scatter plots between *individual* pauses and lick bursts after reinforcer delivery for each FR size for one rat. Similar data were obtained for two other rats. The FR pause and duration of collateral licking were clearly increasing functions of the response requirement. For all FR sizes, relatively short lick bursts were associated with short pauses, and relatively long lick bursts were correspondingly associated with long pauses. Between 85% and 95% of all data points fall close to the line of equal-

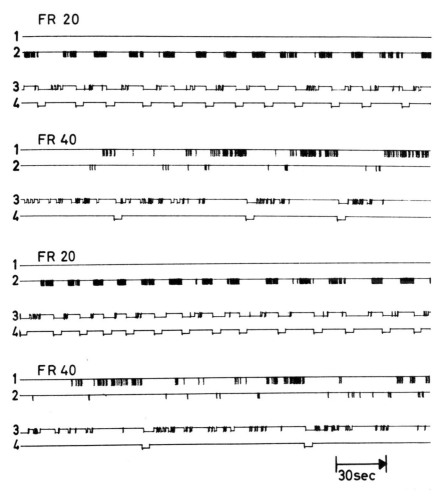

Figure 5.1. Response interactions shown as event records from four successive schedule changes for one rat. In one component, lever A responding was reinforced with a sucrose solution on FR 20 and lever B responding was not reinforced. In the second component, lever B responding was reinforced on FR 40 and lever A responding was not reinforced. 1, lever B; 2, lever A; 3, licking; 4, sucrose. Adapted from Iversen: *Scand. J. Psychol.*, **16**, 49–54, 1975.

ity. Relatively long pauses occasionally occurred, however, without a concomitant long lick burst. Visual observation indicated that these long interruptions in lever pressing were associated with grooming, sniffing, biting of grill bars, jumping, etc.

Discussion

These two experiments show that the postreinforcement pause in FR responding expands in close association with increased durations of a specific collateral

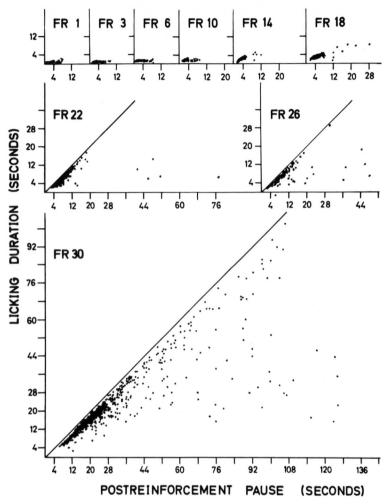

Figure 5.2.   Relationship between collateral licking and FR pausing for each FR size. Each data point show pause duration and licking for an individual pause. Data are presented for the last two sessions of each FR size from FR 1 to FR 26 (98 pauses) and for the last 10 sessions of FR 30 (490 pauses).

response. A molecular analysis especially suggests that each individual FR pause is closely associated with bursts of a specific collateral response across different FR sizes. Therefore, *isolated* causal relationships between ratio size and FR pause, on the one hand, and between the ratio size and collateral responding, on the other hand, cannot be determined unequivocally.

The present results then raise the following questions: How are FR pauses related to bursts of collateral responses. Does the collateral response lengthen the pause or does the pause permit the appearance of the collateral response, or are both perhaps separately affected by FR size?

Pattern Dependency Between FR Responding and
Collateral Licking (Experiment III)*

If collateral responses affect the operantly reinforced response, then the operant response must be *dependent* upon the collateral response as well as upon the explicit schedule contingencies. Some previous experiments purposely manipulated collateral response characteristics and found that the overall rate of reinforced responding may be inversely related to the overall rate or duration of collateral water drinking (Clark, 1962; Segal and Bandt, 1966; Wayner and Greenberg, 1972).

Experiment III

Experiment III (Iversen, 1976) further analyzed interrelations between patterns of reinforced and collateral responses by specifically manipulating the duration of collateral licking. The experiment also sought to determine whether physical compatibility is necessary for interactions between reinforced responses and collateral licking by positioning the drinking tube close to the response lever. Rats were reduced to 80% of their free-feeding body weights, and lever pressing was then reinforced with 45-mg food pellets on FR schedules. The FR was 60, 60, 90, and 40 for rats 1, 4, 7, and 8, respectively. The duration of licking from a freely accessible drinking tube 2.5 cm above the lever was first increased by sweetening the water (to a 2.5% sucrose solution) and next decreased by emptying the bottle.

Licking and lever pressing could easily occur simultaneously, as shown in Figure 5.3 for rat 1. The lever was continuously held down with the left front paw during a lick burst after pellet delivery. For all rats, the lever pressing rate was inversely related to the licking duration (Table 5.1). The data thus show a functional relationship between duration of collateral licking and operant responding. Changes in collateral licking evidently can modify operant responding.

Discussion

Sample cumulative records (Figure 5.4) indicate that the postreinforcement pauses (PRP) in lever pressing were (1) shortest when the bottle was empty, (2) intermediate when the bottle contained water, and (3) longest when the bottle contained the sucrose solution. The local lever-pressing rate preceding pellet delivery (i.e., the run rate) was relatively constant for each rat for all bottle conditions. The inverse relationship between overall lever-pressing rate and licking duration (Table 5.1) thus is obtained because the lever pressing pause is directly related to the licking duration.

The relationships between lick bursts and individual pauses and between

---

* Experiment was conducted at the University of Copenhagen, from October to December 1972, and reported by I. Iversen (1973).

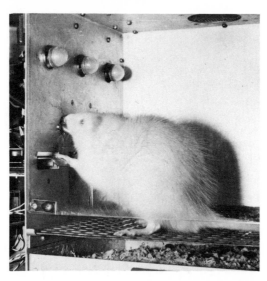

Figure 5.3. Rat 1 lever pressing and licking the drinking tube simultaneously. The lever is continuously held down during a lick burst after pellet delivery. Adapted from Iversen: *Psychol. Record,* **26,** 399–413, 1976.

licking and individual run times are further analyzed in Figure 5.5 for each rat. Individual pauses again were long for long licking durations but short for short licking durations for all bottle conditions. The pause approached the lick bursts for 85% to 90% of all individual pauses for all rats in spite of different pause durations across rats.

Table 5.1   Medians over the means of overall licking duration, response rate, reinforcer rate, postreinforcement pauses (PRP), licking durations for PRP, run times (Run), and licking durations for runs of last 10 sessions

Rat no.	Bottle condition	Licking duration (sec/min)	Response rate (resp/min)	Reinforcer rate (reinf/min)	PRP (sec)	Licking for PRP (sec)	Run (sec)	Licking for Run (sec)
1	empty	6.0	108.0	1.80	12.5	1.5	16.7	1.8
	water	24.0	60.0	1.00	30.8	18.0	30.1	5.3
	sucrose	33.5	33.0	0.55	82.4	50.1	46.6	12.2
4	empty	0.0	67.8	1.13	14.8	0.0	23.4	0.0
	water	16.5	58.6	0.98	35.5	17.7	22.8	0.0
	sucrose	21.0	40.8	0.68	51.4	26.9	24.1	1.3
7	empty	0.0	144.0	1.60	7.0	0.0	25.1	0.0
	water	2.4	130.2	1.45	7.5	1.4	27.2	0.6
	sucrose	14.4	88.2	0.98	34.6	13.1	30.2	1.1
8	empty	9.0	69.0	1.75	16.2	3.1	17.0	3.0
	water	28.2	48.0	1.20	26.8	20.8	20.3	7.8
	sucrose	37.8	40.2	1.01	30.3	23.7	29.4	16.9

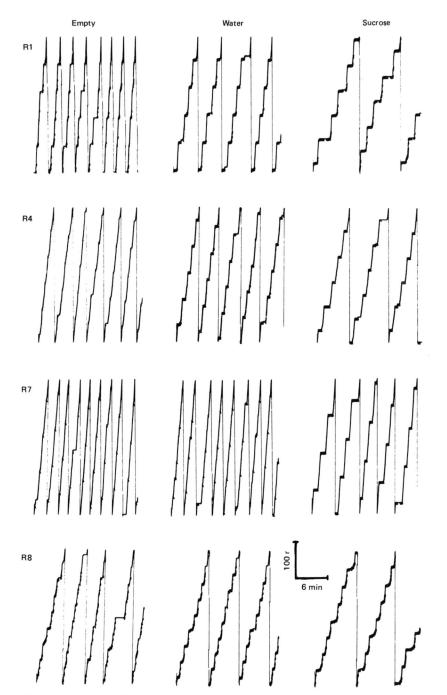

Figure 5.4.   Relationship between licking and FR responding in segments of cumulative records from the last sessions with each bottle condition. The pen was deflected downward by licks and pellet deliveries. From Iversen: *Psychol. Record,* **26,** 399–413, 1976.

The same close correlation was obtained during the ratio run for rats 1 and 8 in the water and sucrose conditions: a very low lever-pressing rate was frequently accompanied by prolonged licking after pellet delivery. Since the fourth lever press defined onset of the run time, all subsequent licking was assigned to the run rather than to the pause. For rats 1 and 8, very brief lick bursts also occurred simultaneously with the high local lever-pressing rate during the run period. For rats 4 and 7, licking after pellet delivery was only infrequently accompanied by lever pressing, and the high run rate was only infrequently accompanied by licking.

The mean pause and lick durations are given in Table 5.1. For all rats, the pauses and run times followed the respective licking durations. Other behaviors, such as grooming and exploration, were also observed with lever pressing and licking throughout the experiment. Consequently, long pauses or run times were recorded when grooming or exploration behaviors occurred for relatively long bursts. The relatively long pauses and run times without similarly long lick durations were included in the calculation of mean durations presented in Table 5.1. Hence the pause considerably exceeded the lick duration for mean comparisons (Table 5.1) but approached the lick duration for most comparisons of individual pauses and lick bursts (Figure 5.5). Because of these additional responses, the differences between the run time and the corresponding lick duration were similarly longer for mean comparisons than for individual comparisons.

These mutual interactions between lever pressing, licking, and other behaviors are more clearly illustrated in Figure 5.6. The event records were obtained with access to water. Food tray entry was recorded by a switch attached to the door to the food tray. Standing, grooming, and exploration (walking around, biting or sniffing grill bars, and sniffing corners or walls) were recorded by observers who depressed approrpiate keys for as long as the responses occurred. Licking after pellet delivery was clearly associated with the pause in lever pressing (A). Note that licking occurred infrequently after pellet delivery for rat 7 (compare to Figures 5.4 and 5.5), and the lever-pressing pause was therefore typically short (B). Prolonged pauses occurred when standing, grooming, or exploration followed the lick burst (C and D). The high lever-pressing rate preceding pellet delivery was rarely interrupted by long bursts of either licking, food tray entry, standing, grooming, or exploration (E). However, brief licks occasionally occurred along with the high rate of lever pressing for rats 1 and 8 (F) (compare to Figure 5.5). A high lever-pressing rate was also associated with frequent brief openings of the food tray floor (G).

Pattern Interdependence Between FR Responding and Collateral Licking (Experiment IV)*

Thus so far, the data argue that collateral licking may participate in the formation of the PRP in FR responding. The question then arises as to whether an

* Experiment was conducted at the University of Copenhagen, from January to December 1974, and reported by I. Iversen (1977a).

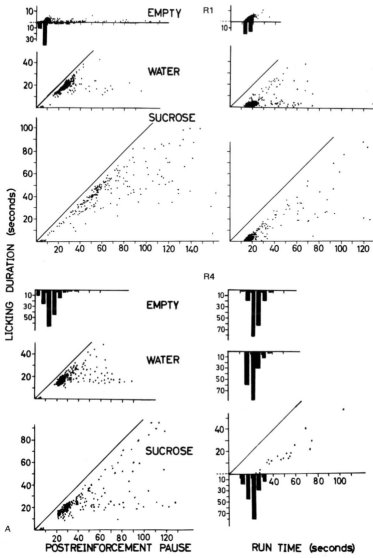

Figure 5.5.   Scatter plots of licking duration during individual FR pauses and during individual FR runs for each of four rats. Frequency distributions of pauses and run times without collateral licking are given in (inverted) histograms. Data are presented for the last 200 ratio runs in each experimental condition. Adapted from Iversen: *Psychol. Record,* **26,** 399–413, 1976.

experimental dislocation of collateral licking into the FR run period might produce a simultaneous dislocation of the pause of FR responding. Simply, will the FR pause go with the burst of collateral licking? Experiment IV addressed two questions. First, how is the FR response pattern affected by different locations of collateral licking within the FR schedule? Second, how is a burst of collateral licking affected by the location within the FR schedule? The experiment also

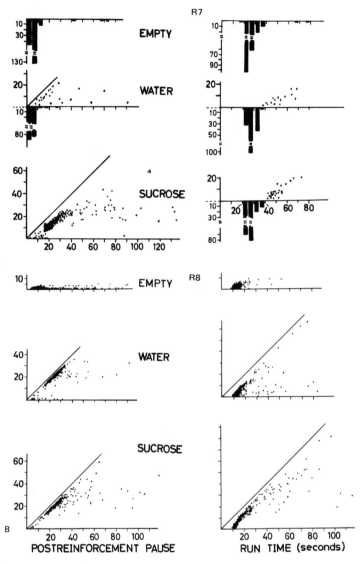

Figure 5.5. (*Continued*)

incorporated an analysis of food cup contact in relation to FR responding and licking.

Experiment IVA

As the operant response, lever pressing by albino rats produced 45-mg food pellets on a FR 60 schedule. The rats were experimentally naive and were maintained at 80% of their free-feeding body weights. The apparatus was the

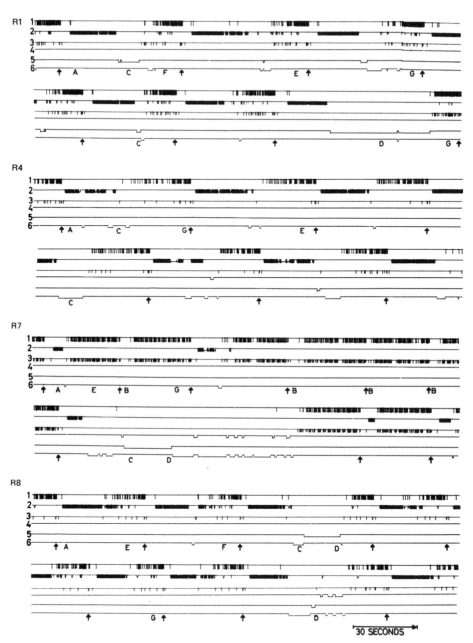

Figure 5.6. Event recorder segments illustrating mutual response interactions between lever pressing (1), licking (2), opening the food tray door (3), standing (4), grooming (5), and exploration (6). Pellet deliveries are indicated by arrows. From Iversen: *Psychol. Record,* **26,** 399–413, 1976.

same as that described in Experiment II, Chapter 4, and included a response lever, a retractable drinking tube, and a food cup. The running wheel was locked throughout the experiment. The drinking tube was located 1.5 cm above and 2.5 cm to the right of the lever; licking and lever pressing, and licking and food cup contact were thus physically compatible response pairs. Licking and food cup contact were recorded by separate drinkometer circuits.

The location of collateral licking was manipulated by inserting the drinking tube at different locations within the FR schedule. For example, the drinking tube was positioned between pellet delivery and the 20th lever press (0–20) or between the 5th lever press and the 25th lever press (5–25). All experimental conditions are given in Table 5.2. Free access to drinking is designated as the 0–60 condition. The drinking probe was presented once for each interreinforcement interval, except in Phase H, in which the tube was continuously retracted.

The experimental manipulations established elaborate discriminative control over collateral licking, which in turn systematically affected the entire pattern of concurrent FR responding.

First, presentation of the drinking probe prompted a changeover to licking and an interruption of lever pressing. When the probe was presented right after pellet delivery, the response patterns were indistinguishable from free access to drinking—a lick burst after pellet delivery and a subsequent changeover to a high rate of lever pressing until the next pellet delivery. The dislocation of the drinking burst into the run period entirely modified this typical "break and run" pattern of FR responding. The PRP contracted, and a second pause appeared in the run period at the exact location of the drinking probe. The duration of licking and the associated pause in lever pressing were parametrically dependent upon the within-run location of the drinking probe. Figure 5.7 presents the relationships between the drink burst, the concomitant pause in lever pressing, and the duration of food cup contact during pauses as functions of the serial location of drinking probes.

Each of the three response measures were decreasing functions of the number of lever presses since pellet delivery. Almost identical pause and lick durations were obtained, with concurrent zero durations of food cup contact, when

Table 5.2   Experimental phases in Experiment IVA

Phase	Probe location	Sessions
A	0–60	8
B	0–20	6
C	20–40	10
D	0–20	3
E	40–60	10
F	0–20	3
G	5–25	10
H	no probe	3
I	0–60	3
J	55–60	10
K	0–60	3

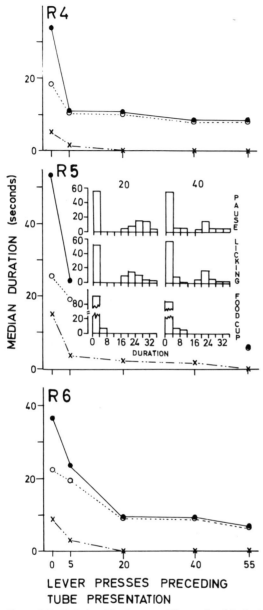

Figure 5.7. Relationships between FR pausing (black circles), licking (white circles), and food cup contact (X) during drinking probes as a function of FR responses preceding tube presentation. FR pause was defined from tube presentation to the second lever press after tube presentation. Data are from the last three sessions under each condition. Inserted histograms for rat 5 illustrate the bimodal response distributions when the probe was preceded by 20 or 40 lever presses.

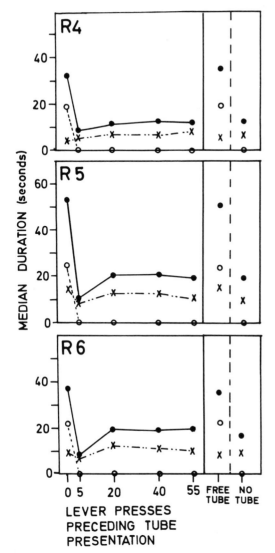

Figure 5.8. Relationships between the postreinforcement pause (black circles), licking (white circles), and food cup contact (X) as a function of lever presses preceding tube presentation. Data are also shown for phases with the tube freely accessible and with the tube absent. Data are from the last three sessions of each phase.

20 or more lever presses preceded the probe. For rat 5, pause and lick bursts were bimodally distributed for the 20 to 40 and the 40 to 60 probes. Median calculations were therefore not representative and are not presented. Instead, histograms showing the exact distribution of pause, lick burst, and food cup contact are inserted in Figure 5.7 for the 20 to 40 and 40 to 60 probes.

With little doubt, the well-known "break and run" pattern of FR responding may be modified by simply altering the collateral response characteristics. The "break and run" pattern was fractionated into a dual pause and run pattern, with licking restricted within the run period: a brief pause associated with food cup contact, a run of FR responses until presentation of the probe, a second pause concomitant with licking, and then the last run of FR responding until the next pellet delivery.

The manipulation of probe location not only affected the response pattern during the probe, but also changed the patterns in the interprobe intervals. The FR PRP (from pellet delivery to the second lever press) was thus shorter with the drinking probe only available within the run period than with freely accessible drinking (Figure 5.8). The data therefore replicate Experiment III, which also found that the FR PRP is shortened when collateral licking is prevented after pellet delivery. However, the shortest pauses were obtained with the 5 to 25 probe. This probe early within the FR run had a clearly facilitating effect upon FR responding compared to later or no probe presentations. Access to collateral licking apparently not only has a suppressive effect upon FR responding *during* the probe, but may also have a facilitating effect upon FR responding *preceding* the probe.

The response interactions can also be followed in the event records in Figure 5.9. In general, these more "on the spot" response alternations confirm the impressions revealed by the overall data. Note, for example, the typical FR response pattern with the tube continuously accessible (0 to 60) and the segmented FR pattern with pausing dislocated into the run period by collateral licking (e.g., 20 to 40). The relatively brief PRPs with the 5 to 25 probe are also clearly apparent along with the increased run times for the long lick bursts.

One outstanding feature is the very brief bursts of licks regularly and rapidly alternating with the high rate of FR responding if the probe was scheduled during the ratio run. The event strips provide some indication that the run time was shorter (and hence the FR run rate higher) when the tube was not presented. Evidently, even these brief lick bursts also suppressed FR responding to some extent. Figure 5.10 presents a high-speed event record of lever pressing and licks during two FR runs with free access to drinking. Licks occurred in clusters of two or three tube contacts and the IRT in lever pressing tended to be longer when licks occurred. Note that licks only rarely occurred in strict simultaneity with a lever press (a).

Experiment IVB

This experiment merely elaborated the experimental analysis to include a systematic replication with response-independent probes presented for fixed 10-sec periods. Probes were distributed on a VT schedule with a mean of 1 min (the individual interprobe intervals were 20, 36, 56, 76, and 96 sec). Probes could therefore occur more than once within individual interreinforcement intervals of the FR schedule. Experiment IVB was scheduled for six sessions between Phases H and I in Experiment IVA.

This systematic replication is described in Figure 5.11. The lick burst remained at the maximal value of 10 sec for all probes for rat 4, but decreased as

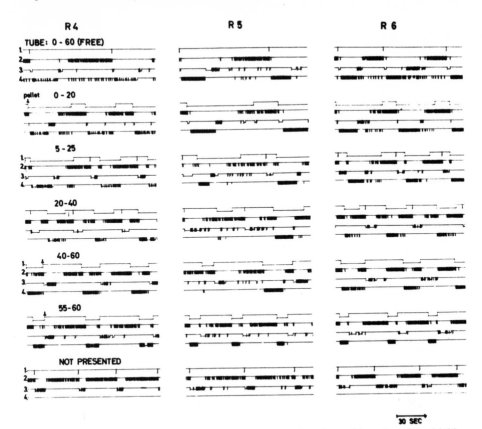

Figure 5.9. Sample event records showing response interactions for each location of the drinking tube. Numbers refer to drinking probe location (20–40, for example, refers to the presentation of the drinking tube between the 20th and the 40th lever press since last pellet delivery). Brief deflections of pen 1 indicate pellet delivery and extended deflections indicate drinking probes. However, pen 1 was not continuously deflected when the drinking tube was continuously accessible (0–60). 1, pellet delivery or tube presentation; 2, lever pressing; 3, food cup contact; 4, licking.

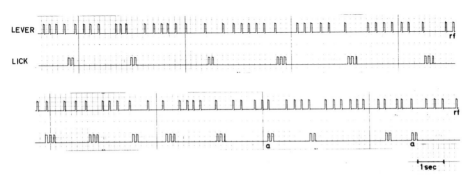

Figure 5.10. High-speed event records of licking linked to lever pressing. Records show the last 40 lever presses of two FR runs terminating in reinforcement (rf). The lower record was selectively chosen to show temporal overlap between a lever press and a lick (a).

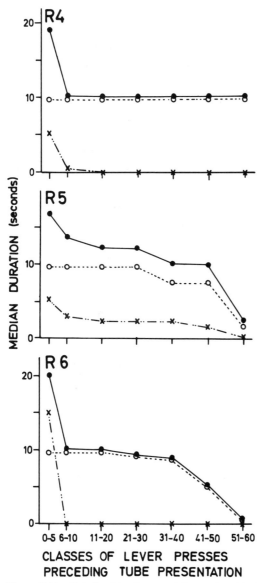

Figure 5.11.   Relationships between FR pausing (black circles), licking (white circles), and food cup contact (X) as a function of the number of lever presses preceding tube presentation.

the probe occurred later in the run period for rats 5 and 6. The duration of food cup contact was zero for rats 4 and 6, and the lever-pressing pause therefore exceeded the lick burst by not more than approximately 0.5 sec for probes in the run period. For rat 5, the pause in lever pressing exceeded the lick burst by an amount that closely approximated the added duration of food cup contact. The pause in lever pressing then approached the sum of the durations of licking

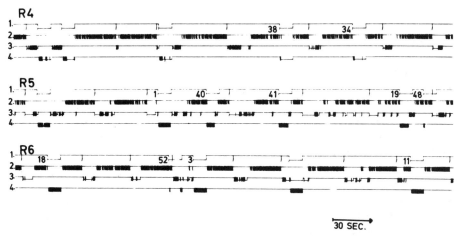

Figure 5.12. Event records showing response interactions when tube presentation occurred for 10 sec independent of lever pressing. Inserted numbers refer to the number of lever presses emitted prior to tube presentations. Brief deflections of pen 1 indicate pellet deliveries and extended deflections indicate tube presentations. Pen 1 deflected upward for pellet deliveries during tube presentation. 1, pellet delivery or tube presentation; 2, lever pressing; 3, food cup contact; 4, licking.

and food cup contact. However, for rat 6 the summed durations of licking and food cup contact exceeded the pause in lever pressing in the first class (0 to 5). This resulted from the occasional emission of both licking and food cup contact.

Similar to the findings in Experiment IVA, drinking probes also affected the response pattern during the interprobe intervals, with a facilitating effect upon lever pressing in the absence of licking. The lever pressing rates with no access to drinking (Phase H in Experiment IVA) were 79.9, 66.6, and 83.7 responses/min for rats 4, 5, and 6, respectively. The rates of lever pressing for interprobe intervals in Experiment IVB were 92.3, 85.7, and 124.1 responses/min for rats 4, 5, and 6, respectively. The lever-pressing rate in the absence of licking was thus clearly higher with the response-independent probes relative to sessions with no access to drinking.

The event records in Figure 5.12 graphically confirm the overall interactions with an interruption of FR responding by licking during drinking probes.

Discussion

The patterning of FR responding was directly affected by the manipulated pattern of collateral licking. The PRP decreased and a "new" pause appeared during the run by simply displacing the burst of collateral licking to the run period. The location of FR pauses may thus be determined by the location of collateral licking, with FR pauses whenever and wherever bursts of licking are emitted. At the same time, the licking burst is functionally determined by the location within the FR schedule. Because licking was physically compatible with both lever pressing and food cup contact, the data further confirm the suggestion that physical incompatibility is not necessary for response competition.

Some previous data would seem to be especially relevant to the present results. Using similar procedures, Flory and O'Boyle (1972) and Gilbert (1974) established that collateral licking may occur at interreinforcement locations other than the postreinforcement period. Gilbert (1974), in addition, found that the overall rate of FI responding increased when collateral licking was transferred from the postreinforcement period to later in the FI. Collateral licking was also changed by the FI response and increased at any given location when the FI response was prevented.

The present experiment further establishes such reciprocal interactions between collateral responses such as food cup contact and licking. The food cup contact was very brief after pellet delivery if licking occurred at that location. However, if licking was restricted to the run period, then food cup contact increased after pellet delivery. Recently, Penney and Schull (1977) reported a similar reciprocal relationship between collateral water drinking and wheel running in rats responding on FI schedules. In the present experiments, however, food cup contact did not expand to entirely replace licking. Ator (1976) similarly found that collateral attack and escape responses are not interchangeable.

The tactic of manipulating experimental events during the run period has been discussed by several investigators. Boren (1961), for example, reported that the probability of a changeover to a second response during a discrete-trial procedure was a decreasing function of the number of FR responses preceding trial presentation. Lyon (1964) also found that suppression during a preshock stimulus was a decreasing function of the number of FR responses emitted since reinforcer delivery. In combination, the data suggest that a variety of discrete events may disrupt an FR response as a function of the relative location within the scheduled interreinforcement intervals.

The discrete-trial methodology has the experimental advantage of establishing elaborate discriminative control over collateral responding. A changeover from either FR responding or food cup contact to collateral licking was especially under the discriminative control of the drinking probe in the present schedules. Since response preference may be expressed in terms of changeovers from one response to another (Skinner, 1950), the results indicate that a collateral response may be momentarily preferred relative to a concurrently reinforced response. This preference analysis is also consistent with the finding by Premack (1971) and Timberlake and Allison (1974) that a momentarily more probable response may reinforce a momentarily less probable response.

In agreement with this formulation, collateral responses can be shown to function as a reinforcer when contingent upon an additional response. Azrin et al. (1965) thus demonstrated that squirrel monkeys would perform a chain-pulling response to produce an object that could be attacked. Rats may similarly respond on a lever to produce access to collateral licking during intermittent food presentation (Falk, 1966; also see Cole and Parker, 1971). In the present experiment, the FR response was facilitated by the scheduled access to collateral licking when the drinking probe was contingent upon a low number of FR responses (Experiment IVA). This facilitation was also apparent when access to collateral licking was independent of FR responding (Experiment IVB). Note that the same event that suppressed FR responses during probes also facilitated the FR response during interprobe intervals. The establishment of discriminative control of collateral responding may thus additionally establish a reinforcement operation that can effectively alter response patterns.

Finally, we should note some semantic problems in the generalization that two physically compatible responses may compete. Food cup contact, for example appeared to comprise a broad class of different response topographies such as sniffing, licking, or gnawing the cup, touching the cup during pellet retrieval, or passively holding the cup during licking. Many of these responses involved orientation of the head to the cup (sniffing, licking, gnawing, and pellet retrieval) and were clearly incompatible with and reciprocally related to tube licking. In this case, topographically different responses activated the same manipulandum and were recorded as the same physical response. However, the different response topographies defined as one response class may not necessarily enter the same relationship with a second response class. Essentially, mere activation of a response manipulandum may not be sufficient to identify the associated response topography. A generalization involving a given response class may therefore not hold for all members of the class. Instead, a more precise statement would be that sniffing, gnawing, or licking the food cup may be reciprocally related to tube licking, whereas holding the food cup more clearly accompanied than competed with licking.

Routine observations may also reveal different topographies of recorded "licking", including tongue, nose, and paw contact. The extended burst of licking after pellet delivery clearly occurred as tongue contact whereas licking linked with lever pressing consisted mainly of nose contacts during rapid up and down movements of the head accompanying the high rate of lever pressing (the tube was only 2.5 cm from the lever and nose contact was especially compatible with lever pressing). A recent analysis similarly indicated that drinking tube contacts occur in two distinct patterns and topographies in a tandem FI schedule (McLeod and Gollub, 1976). Tube contact occurred in a long burst after pellet delivery, and paw rather than tongue contact apparently occurred linked with FI responding.

In conclusion, our precision in description and generalizations would seem to require an equal precision in the analysis of different response topographies entering the same overall response class.

Pauses and Collateral Responses with Reinforcement Omission (Experiment V)*

The purpose of Experiment V was to extend the response-response relationship to a research area in which changes in pauses are critical; the point of interest is the frustration effect (FE) (Amsel and Roussel, 1952). The *FE* histori-

---

* Experiments VA and B were conducted at the University of Copenhagen, from June to December 1974, and reported by I. Iversen (1977A). Experiment VC was conducted at the University of Zurich, in February 1975, and reported by I. Iversen (1977B).

cally refers to an increase in running speed in the second alley of a double runway on those occasions in which reward is omitted in the first goal box. A similar effect can be found in a free-operant situation, in which a response rate maintained on an intermittent schedule may increase following the occasional omission of reinforcement (Staddon and Innis, 1966; Zimmerman, 1971). The rate increase in the free-operant situation has been shown to be due mainly to a shorter pause after reinforcement omission (Staddon and Innis, 1969; McMillan, 1971) rather than to an increased local rate (Dews, 1966).

The implication of response interactions for the frustration effect was first aroused by an equipment failure. In a preliminary experiment, lever pressing by rats was maintained by food pellets on a FR 50 with water freely available. Very brief PRPs suddenly appeared during an otherwise stable baseline of long pauses associated with bursts of licking. An inspection of the apparatus revealed that the pellet feeder had become defective in such a way that it either operated with pellet delivery (as it should), operated without pellet delivery, or did not operate at all. Since these different events appeared to have different effects on lever pressing and licking, the malfunctioning of the feeder was put under experimental control and a brief experiment was conducted.

The FR 50 was maintained continuously, and ordinary pellet delivery consisted of three events: operation of the pellet feeder, pellet arrival in the food tray, and a 0.5-sec illumination of the food tray. For two sessions, 25% of the

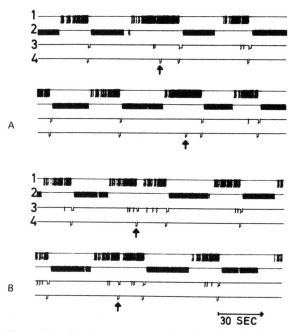

Figure 5.13. Sample event records showing effect of reinforcement omission upon lever pressing, licking, and food tray entry. **A.** Feeder illumination only. **B.** Feeder illumination and feeder operation. Arrows indicate pellet omission. 1, lever pressing; 2, licking; 3, food tray entry; 4, pellet delivery.

pellet deliveries were replaced with only illumination of the food tray, and for two subsequent sessions, with illumination of the food tray and operation of the feeder without pellet delivery.

Figure 5.13 shows event record segments for one rat. Similar records were obtained for two other rats. The rate of lever pressing remained high when the food tray was only lit (arrows in record A). A changeover from lever pressing to a brief food tray entry, and an immediate changeover back to lever pressing, occurred when the food tray was lit and the feeder operated without pellet delivery (arrows in record B). With pellets also delivered, the changeover to food tray entry was followed by licking and a pause in lever pressing. The tentative results demonstrate that the typical pause in FR responding may be eliminated when scheduled events do not control a changeover to a concurrent response (no food tray entry), may be brief when the events control a brief changeover to a concurrent response (food tray entry), and may be long when the schedule controls long bursts or sequences of concurrent responses (both food tray entry and licking).

A concurrent reponse analysis would suggest that part or all of the frustration effect may be related to alterations in the patterning of specific collateral responses by changes in the events surrounding reinforcement omission. The frustration effect of a decreased pause in reinforced behavior may thus result from the decreased duration or virtual absence of collateral behaviors.

In the following three brief experiments, occasional reinforcement omission and prevention of selected portions of the collateral behaviors were investigated in a within-session design.

Experiment VA

The first experiment (VA) compared the frustration effect to the effect of prevention of collateral licking after regular reinforcement. The rats and apparatus were the same as in Experiment IV, with lever pressing reinforced on FR 60. Pellet delivery with the drinking tube retracted, only feeder operation with the tube present, and only feeder operation with the tube retracted were each scheduled three times in mixed order for each session. Normal pellet delivery with the drinking tube present was in effect for the remaining completions of the FR requirement. In the appropriate conditions, the tube was retracted 0.5 sec after feeder operation and was first presented at the next feeder operation. The operations necessary for prevention of pellet delivery were performed manually by the investigator. The soft and flexible rubber tube from the feeder to the food cup was silently disconnected during the run period preceding feeder operation without pellet delivery. The tube was reconnected during the next run period. In no case was lever pressing disrupted during this operation. A predetermined sequence of events was followed during sessions to avoid any bias in the manual scheduling of feeder operations without pellet delivery. Experiment VA was scheduled for six sessions of 25 min each after the last phase of Experiment IVA.

All feeder operations produced a changeover from lever pressing to food cup

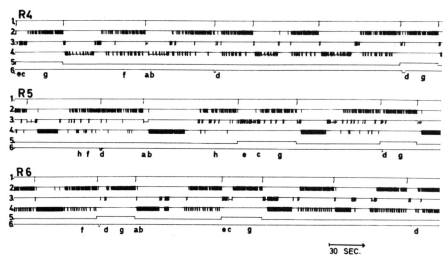

Figure 5.14. Event records showing effects of reinforcement omission and withdrawal of the drinking tube. 1, pellet delivery; 2, lever pressing; 3, food cup contact; 4, licking; 5, tube presentation; 6, empty feeder.

contact (a in Figure 5.14). If the drinking tube was available, a second changeover to licking rapidly followed pellet delivery (b). Pellet delivery with the tube retracted produced a longer burst of food cup contact, but the lever-pressing pause was much shorter than with the additional collateral licking (c). Again, FR pauses were clearly shortened by prevention of collateral licking. After feeder operations without pellet delivery, the burst of food cup contact was very brief and the burst of licking was entirely absent, leading to a very brief lever-pressing pause (d) (the omission effect). Both food cup contact and the lever-pressing pause were longer after pellet delivery with the tube retracted relative to feeder operations with no pellet delivery (e).

Licking during the run period was, however, differently related to reinforcement omission. Licking occurred in brief bursts in rapid alternation with the high local rate of lever pressing (f) after pellet delivery as well as after reinforcement omission. The reinforcement omission thus removed the extended lick burst that normally follows pellet delivery but did not affect the brief lick bursts in alternation with lever pressing. The high rate of lever pressing tended to be slightly increased if the tube was retracted (g).

In summary, the FR pause was equally brief after reinforcement omission or after prevention of collateral licking with regular reinforcement. Reinforcement omission differentially affected the licking pattern during the FR pause and run periods.

Experiment VB

The second experiment (VB) investigated the relationship between extinction of FR responding and collateral licking. Extinction was first scheduled with the drinking tube continuously available (after Phase K in Experiment IVA), and then scheduled again with the drinking tube presented randomly for 10-sec periods (after Experiment IVB). Feeder operation occurred during the extinction sessions, but food pellets were not delivered.

Figure 5.15 presents event records for rat 4 during the extinction session with the drinking tube continuously accessible. Similar records were obtained for rats 5 and 6. The usual licking burst was absent after the first two feeder operations, which made the FR pause very brief (a and b). Subsequently, longer bursts of food cup contact and longer pauses occurred after feeder operations (c). Licking still occurred in brief bursts, alternating with the high lever-pressing rate preceding feeder operations (d). The frequency of brief lick bursts

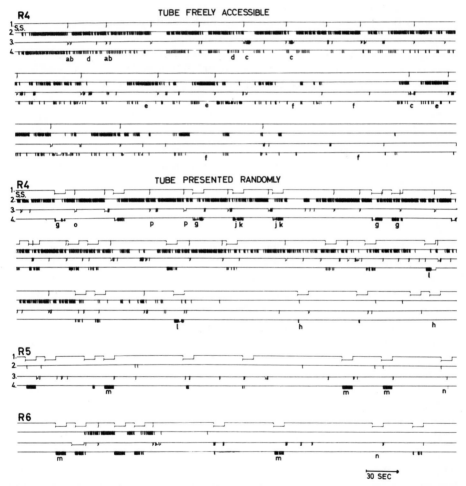

Figure 5.15 Response interactions during FR extinction with the drinking tube present or with random presentation of the tube for fixed 10-sec periods for rat 4. Records are also shown for rats 5 and 6 after lever pressing was extinguished to a low rate. 1, empty feeder/tube presentation; 2, lever pressing; 3, food cup contact; 4, licking; SS, session start.

during the run period, however, rapidly decreased and the *local* rate of lever pressing was concurrently increased during the extinction session (e). Gradually, longer periods without lever pressing, licking, and food cup contact regularly appeared between bursts of lever pressing (f). These periods were associated with unrecorded behaviors such as grooming and exploration. Thus, FR extinction initiates with brief FR pauses in association with the absence of the extended bursts of licking after regular reinforcement.

The relationship between collateral licking and FR extinction was somewhat different when the drinking tube was presented randomly. Event records are shown in three segments for rat 4 in Figure 5.15. Segments are also shown after lever pressing was extinguished for rats 5 and 6. The drinking probe controlled an immediate changeover to licking when presented early (g) but not late in the extinction session (h). Although licking occurred irregularly rather than in an extended burst throughout the probe (j) and alternated with bursts of lever pressing (k), extended bursts of licking did appear when lever pressing was markedly decreased (l). For rats 5 and 6, licking occurred in a long burst in some (m) but not all (n) drinking probes, even after complete extinction of lever pressing. Thus the discriminative control over licking by tube presentation was quite powerful in these experiments.

This experiment shows that the extended bursts of collateral licking may depend upon the absence or presence of controlling stimuli; that is, bursts of licking controlled by pellet delivery were eliminated by FR extinction, whereas licking continued to occur when under the discriminative control of the drinking probe.

Experiment VC

The last experiment (VC) examined the response interactions in a schedule using response-independent reinforcers. Water drinking, food cup contact, exploration, and grooming were recorded when food pellets were merely delivered every minute (FT 1 min) for 14 sessions. Two rats were maintained at 80% of their free-feeding body weights. The apparatus was the same as in Experiment IV and the wheel was locked throughout all sessions. Tube licking and food cup contact were recorded automatically, and exploration (sniffing, climbing in the locked wheel, and standing on hind legs) and grooming (scratching and licking of the body) were recorded by the experimenter pressing appropriate keys for as long as the behaviors occurred. Experimental manipulations were as in Experiment VA, except that the condition with the tube withdrawn after pellet omission was not included.

Figure 5.16 shows the data for one rat. After pellet omission, licking remained at zero probability and food-cup contact did not decrease to zero, which is a reversed pattern relative to pellet delivery accompanied by collateral licking. The reinforcement omission also altered the distribution of exploration and grooming within the FT schedule, with both responses occurring earlier in the interval than after pellet delivery with licking. The exploration probability was therefore increased overall, whereas the grooming probability quickly resumed to zero and was decreased overall. Essentially similar response distribu-

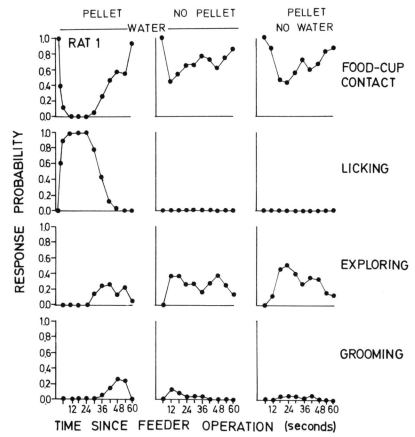

Figure 5.16. Mean response probabilities for rat 1 during successive 6-sec intervals since feeder operation for each experimental condition. Food cup contact and licking probabilities are also shown for the first three 2-sec intervals of the pellet plus water condition. From Iversen: *Physiol. Behav.* **18**, 535–537, 1977.

tions were obtained when the drinking tube was removed and licking prevented after ordinary pellet delivery.

The effect of reinforcement omission therefore again resembles the effect of prevention of the licking burst after regular reinforcement.

Discussion

The reinforcement omission effect now appears to be directly related to simultaneous alterations in the patterning of collateral responses. Allen et al. (1975) and McCoy and Christian (1976) also found an absence of licking and decreased pauses in FI responding after reinforcement omission. In addition, Staddon and Ayres (1975) reported an absence of licking and an increase in food cup approach after omission of response-independent reinforcement on an FT schedule.

The results suggest that the reinforced response pattern produced by reinforcement omission may be simulated after normal reinforcement by experimentally interrupting the sequence of collateral responses. Thus, the pause in FR responding decreased when the burst of licking was prevented after regular reinforcement. A previous significant finding was that licking may be absent after reinforcement omission if lever pressing is simultaneously increased or experimentally prevented (Porter et al., 1975). The absence of licking may thus be a primary effect of reinforcement omission and may be partially a "cause" rather than an exclusive "effect" of the simultaneous probability of other responses.

The present experiments have some implications for a related finding, the FE. The FE of increased response "vigor" after reinforcement omission was originally explained as an active emotional–frustrative motive state created following thwarted reward expectations (Amsel, 1958). A similar explanation was applied to the increased response rates that may be seen during the first minutes of extinction and that has been said to measure the emotion aroused by reinforcement omission (Thompson, 1961). The FE could also result from an absence of short-term satiation or demotivation effects of reinforcer delivery (Seward et al., 1957). By another account reinforcement is considered inhibitory, and omission of reinforcement prevents inhibitory aftereffects and thereby increases the local response rate relative to typical reinforcement (Staddon, 1970; also see Catania and Gill, 1964).

The FE, however, could be examined without reference to intervening concepts. The problem is not simply whether the FE "reflects frustration or inhibition" but exactly how the FE comes about. The accumulating results suggest that the pattern of a reinforced response after reinforcement omission may be related to the patterning of specific collateral responses. The data are thus consistent with previous thoughts that the FE may be related to a decrease in competing responses (Bolles, 1967; Wookey and Strongman, 1974). More precisely, the extent of the omission effect is directly related to the amount of collateral responding under control of the scheduled events. Further, the FE could be closely *simulated* in the absence of reinforcement omission. Simply, reinforced responding may then be increased or decreased to the extent that schedules control the absence or presence of specific collateral responses.

In a traditional account we could say, but are not necessarily forced to do so, that the changed collateral response pattern *mediates* the FE. We would rather argue that reinforcement omission and prevention of collateral licking after regular reinforcement are merely two methods of increasing the probability of reinforced responding—hence the above emphasis that the effect of reinforcement omission is *simulated* by prevention of collateral licking after regular reinforcement.

In Experiments VA and VB, the same collateral licking response occurred in two temporal locations and in two different patterns: a long burst after reinforcement and subsequent brief bursts in rapid alternation with the high rate of FR responding. Rosenblith (1970), Wuttke and Innis (1972), Porter and Kenshalo (1974), and Corfield-Sumner et al. (1977) found licking after reinforcement as well as after brief stimuli in some second-order FI schedules. The cumulative records presented by Rosenblith (1970) and Wuttke and Innis (1972) seem to indicate that licking after brief stimuli was at least partly linked with FI responding. Moreover, data by Segal (1969), Keehn and Colotla (1971), and Allen and Porter (1977) provided some indication that short bursts of licking may alternate with FI responding. Collateral licking may then be differently maintained during the postreinforcement period and the run period. In terms of discriminative control, pellet delivery maintained a long lick burst, whereas FR responding controlled frequent and brief lick bursts. Reinforcement omission or extinction merely remove the event controlling long lick bursts, leaving the brief bursts linked with FR responding. This dualistic control of licking was further evidenced by the presence of relatively long lick bursts during FR rextinction when the discriminative control was changed from pellet delivery to drinking tube presentation. Significantly, this licking apparently was not linked with FR responding since the discriminative control by drinking probes was maintained for some time after FR responding extinguished. Therefore, multiple patterns of collateral responding may be dissociated, dependent upon the selective control of the appropriate discriminative events.

In conclusion, reinforcement omission is a procedure that at least roughly separates different components of collateral responding. One component is the responses that are linked with the reinforced response. The second component is the responses under more direct discriminative control of reinforcer delivery. Removal of the reinforcer then separates the different collateral response components by eliminating only the stimulus control of the collateral response component following reinforcer delivery.

Interresponse Times and
Collateral Responses (Experiment VI)*

A FR schedule provides a relatively clear distinction between pausing and responding by the respective pause and run periods within the interreinforcement interval. Typical FR responding is thus described by a few very long IRTs (the FR pauses) and many very brief IRTs (in the run period). On the other hand, a schedule such as VI generates less dramatic differences between long and short IRTs, with a characteristic mode at intermediate IRTs. If pauses in FR responding can be related to collateral responses, then pauses in VI responding might too.

The relationship between collateral responses and IRTs in VI schedules has been debated over the years. Anger (1956) provided an analysis of IRTs and proposed that collateral responses probably do not mediate IRTs. However, subsequent arguments have proposed that IRTs might be mediated by collateral responses (Shimp, 1969). A very rough distinction has been between whether a subject chooses (1) whether or not to respond at a given time, or (2) how long to wait before emitting the next response (Shimp, 1969, 1973).

* Experiment was conducted at the University of Copenhagen, from January to February 1976.

Our previous results suggest that a particular IRT (the PRP) becomes long if a subject changes over to collateral licking. In fact, knowing that licking occurs at the beginning of the PRP provides some information that the pause will definitely be longer relative to pauses without collateral licking. Essentially, the data suggest that the collateral response at the start of the pause may be a good predictor of pause duration in FR schedules. Perhaps similar predictions would apply for pauses or IRTs in VI schedules. Experiment VI was an attempt to examine such a model of IRTs in VI responding.

Experiment VI

Four experimentally naive Wistar albino rats were maintained at 80% of their free-feeding body weights. The wheel-running equipment was used in this experiment but modified to turn in only one direction (clockwise relative to the panel with the lever and food tray). The drinking tube was not accessible in this experiment, and the hole was covered with a metal plate. Contact with and activity within 2.0 mm of the food cup and the lever were recorded by separate body-capacitance systems. The IRT analysis included eight responses: lever pressing, lever activity, food cup activity, wheel running, exploration, standing, face grooming, and body grooming.

After initial shaping, lever pressing was maintained on VI 1 min for 15 sessions. One 45-mg food pellet was given as reinforcer delivery and each session lasted 30 min.

Examples of the mutual interactions between the responses are shown in Figure 5.17. Wheel running regularly alternated with lever presses for all subjects (a). Most running bursts were of a fairly fixed duration, with the associated IRT in lever pressing also approximately fixed (b). However, if exploration or standing preceded wheel running, then the IRT was relatively longer (c). In addition, relatively brief bursts of wheel running were occasionally interspersed with longer bursts for rats 1 and 3; the associated IRTs were simultaneously relatively short and long, respectively (d). For all rats, a lever press reliably followed a burst of wheel running, but wheel running did not reliably follow a lever press.

The duration of food cup activity was usually shorter than the wheel-running bursts, and the associated IRTs were also less than the IRTs associated with wheel running (e). Prolonged food cup activity was usually obtained after pellet delivery, with the associated IRT simultaneously increased (f). When food cup activity was followed by a changeover to wheel running or exploration, the corresponding IRT was considerably increased (g and h).

More variable interactions were obtained with exploration, which occurred with variable duration and occasionally was followed by standing (i), wheel running (j), or face grooming (k). The associated IRT also varied and were especially long when exploration was followed by standing or grooming.

Activity around the lever obviously occurred with the emission of lever pressing and was usually associated with brief IRTs (l). However, bursts of lever activity occasionally occurred for rat 3 without actual lever pressing, with the associated IRT varying with the burst duration of lever activity (m).

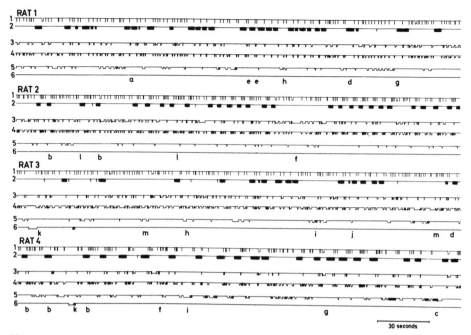

Figure 5.17. Event records showing multiple response interactions. Pellet deliveries are shown as 1-sec deflections of pen 1. Pen 5 is continuously deflected for exploring responses and rapidly pulsed for standing responses. Similarly, pen 6 is continuously deflected for grooming of the face and rapidly pulsed for body grooming. 1, lever/pellet; 2, wheel; 3, food cup activity; 4, lever activity; 5, explore/stand; 6, grooming: body/face.

Overall, different length IRTs appeared to be associated with emission of different collateral responses; the collateral response that occurred right after a lever press thus provided some clue as to the duration of the upcoming IRT.

Relative frequencies of IRTs are given in Figure 5.18 for each rat. The top row gives the conventional calculation of the frequency of a given IRT divided by the number of all IRTs. The subsequent rows give the relative IRT frequencies conditional upon the collateral response that initiated the IRT (the first collateral response within 0.5 sec of the previous lever press). This calculation relates the frequency of a given IRT initiated by a particular collateral response to the frequency of all IRTs initiated by that collateral response.

The IRT distribution without regard to the collateral response was about the same for each rat, with the highest frequencies at relatively short IRTs, and gradually decreasing frequencies for the longer IRTs. In comparison, the distribution of IRTs initiated by lever activity was quite skewed toward relatively brief IRTs. The mean of IRTs initiated by lever activity was much shorter than the mean of all IRTs.

The IRTs initiated by food cup acitivity resembled the overall IRT distribution for all rats. The peak frequency of IRTs initiated by wheel running was skewed toward longer IRTs, with the mean IRT about twice as long as the collective mean for all IRT. (For rat 3, a wheel-running distribution was not ob-

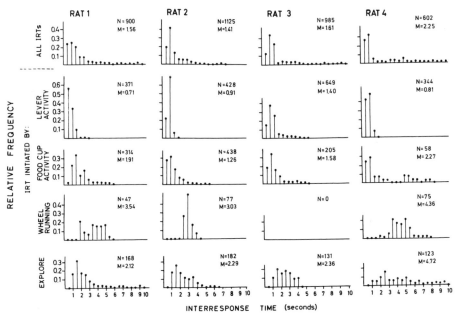

Figure 5.18. Relative frequencies of IRTs. The top distribution includes all IRTs. Each of the subsequent distributions shows the relative frequencies of IRTs initiated by lever activity, food cup activity, wheel running, or exploration. The collateral response initiating an IRT was defined as the response that followed a lever press within 0.5 sec. If lever activity occurred throughout the 0.5-sec period, then the IRT was initiated by lever activity. Data were calculated from event records from the last session. The number (N) of IRT and the mean (M) IRT initiated by that collateral response are shown in each panel.

tained because wheel running never occurred right after a lever press.) Finally, IRTs initiated by exploration were relatively short, but with a gradually decreasing frequency for longer IRTs. The mean IRTs initiated by exploration was therefore higher than the overall mean for all IRTs. Standing and grooming never initiated IRTs.

The mean IRT then changes with different collateral responses. Therefore, the collateral response changed over to provides an estimate of the associated IRT. An IRT calculation based upon the initiating collateral response may thus provide a rather useful tool for a molecular analysis. Simply, a given IRT could be predicted far more accurately by analyzing the initiating collateral response than by knowing only the average of *all* IRT.

The data were also analyzed to determine the probability of a changeover to a lever press conditional upon the momentarily occurring collateral response. The changeover probability within a given bin, conditional upon the particular collateral response, was calculated as follows: within a given bin, the number of times a particular collateral response was followed by a lever press was divided by the total number of times that collateral response occurred in that bin. The calculation of the probability of a changeover to a lever press irrespective of a collateral responding is the ordinary calculation of IRTs per opportunity.

Table 5.3   Rat 1: Probabilities of terminating an IRT within a given bin conditional upon occurring collateral response or irrespective of collateral response

Bin	Irrespective of collateral response	Conditional upon collateral response				
		Lever activity	Food cup activity	Wheel running	Exploring	Standing
0.0–0.5	0.245	0.577	0.131	0.000	0.000	—
0.5–1.0	0.325	0.809	0.408	0.000	0.156	—
1.0–1.5	0.419	1.000	0.677	0.000	0.386	0.200
1.5–2.0	0.277		0.500	0.123	0.359	0.625
2.0–2.5	0.419		0.769	0.228	0.625	0.666
2.5–3.0	0.279		0.666	0.159	0.765	0.000
3.0–3.5	0.288		1.000	0.257	0.250	0.000
3.5–4.0	0.298			0.291	1.000	1.000
4.0–4.5	0.500			0.538		
4.5–5.0	0.750			0.888		
5.0–5.5	0.400			1.000		

The probabilities of terminating IRTs are shown in Tables 5.3 through 5.6. In each table, the first column gives the probability of a lever press as a function of the time since the last lever press irrespective of collateral responding (the ordinary IRTs per opportunity distribution). The subsequent columns show the probability of a lever press conditional upon the collateral response emitted preceding the lever press. (Note that the probability of a lever press conditional upon a collateral response is only defined for actual occurrence of that collateral response in that bin. For example, the probability of a lever press conditional upon standing was not defined for the first bins, because standing never occurred in these bins. In contrast, the probability of lever pressing conditional

Table 5.4   Rat 2: Probabilities of terminating an IRT within a given bin conditional upon occurring collateral response or irrespective of collateral response

Bin	Irrespective of collateral response	Conditional upon collateral response				
		Lever activity	Food cup activity	Wheel running	Exploring	Standing
0.0–0.5	0.200	0.232	0.282	0.000	0.000	—
0.5–1.0	0.525	0.906	0.453	0.000	0.392	—
1.0–1.5	0.371	1.000	0.497	0.005	0.398	0.000
1.5–2.0	0.249		0.412	0.000	0.571	0.000
2.0–2.5	0.327		0.560	0.127	0.700	0.375
2.5–3.0	0.507		0.360	0.429	0.400	0.406
3.0–3.5	0.567		0.500	0.492	0.666	0.333
3.5–4.0	0.600		0.170	0.636	1.000	0.500
4.0–4.5	0.417		0.200	1.000		0.000
4.5–5.0	0.500		1.000			0.000
5.0–5.5	0.500					0.500
5.5–6.0	0.000					0.000
6.0–6.5	0.666					1.000

Table 5.5   Rat 3: Probabilities of terminating an IRT within a given bin conditional upon occurring collateral response or irrespective of collateral response

Bin	Irrespective of collateral response	Conditional upon collateral response				
		Lever activity	Food cup activity	Wheel running	Exploring	Standing
0.0–0.5	0.141	0.166	0.199	—	0.000	—
0.5–1.0	0.397	0.543	0.410	0.000	0.098	—
1.0–1.5	0.466	0.769	0.453	0.025	0.209	0.000
1.5–2.0	0.286	0.676	0.595	0.013	0.222	0.000
2.0–2.5	0.297	0.808	0.666	0.038	0.415	0.180
2.5–3.0	0.314	0.714	0.600	0.147	0.480	0.620
3.0–3.5	0.415	0.857	0.500	0.406	0.333	0.333
3.5–4.0	0.800	1.000	0.000	0.816	0.800	1.000
4.0–4.5	0.818		0.000	1.000	1.000	
4.5–5.0	0.666		1.000			

upon wheel running was zero in the first bins for rat 1 (Table 5.3) because a lever press never occurred in this bin. Note also that the number of bins in each table is less than in Figure 5.18. IRT above 5 or 6 sec were generally few and are not shown.)

Between 0.0 and 1.5 sec (the first three bins) the probability of a lever press conditional upon lever activity was much higher than the probability of a lever press irrespective of the occurring collateral response. The probability of a lever press conditional upon wheel running or exploration was relatively low or

Table 5.6   Rat 4: Probabilities of terminating an IRT within a given bin conditional upon occurring collateral response or irrespective of collateral response

Bin	Irrespective of collateral response	Conditional upon collateral response				
		Lever activity	Food cup activity	Wheel running	Exploring	Standing
0.0–0.5	0.273	0.436	0.241	0.000	0.000	—
0.5–1.0	0.444	0.876	0.415	0.000	0.054	—
1.0–1.5	0.145	1.000	0.267	0.000	0.060	0.000
1.5–2.0	0.087		0.666	0.022	0.110	0.143
2.0–2.5	0.111		0.500	0.011	0.197	0.333
2.5–3.0	0.077		1.000	0.045	0.178	0.000
3.0–3.5	0.155			0.188	0.154	0.250
3.5–4.0	0.183			0.188	0.269	0.276
4.0–4.5	0.177			0.214	0.333	0.100
4.5–5.0	0.352			0.455	0.360	0.143
5.0–5.5	0.316			0.500	0.500	0.500
5.5–6.0	0.128			0.250	0.000	0.333
6.0–6.5	0.215			0.333	0.000	0.500
6.5–7.0	0.121			0.500	1.000	0.000
7.0–7.5	0.207			0.500		1.000
7.5–8.0	0.217			1.000		

zero in the first bins. Therefore, for all rats, a changeover to lever pressing within the first three bins was *far more likely* given lever activity than given wheel running or exploration.

In subsequent bins, the probability of a lever press conditional upon food cup activity was typically higher than the corresponding probability conditional upon either wheel running, exploration, or standing. Simply, the probability of a lever press conditional upon a particular collateral response was substantially different from the probability calculated irrespective of collateral responses. The data were complex however, and might be illustrated by a few examples. For rat 1 (Table 5.3), the probability of a lever press within the 2.5 to 3.0 bin was relatively high given the simultaneous occurrence of either food cup activity or exploration within that bin, but was relatively low given wheel running or standing. For rat 3 (Table 5.5), the lever-pressing probability within the 2.0 to 2.5 bin was relatively high given either lever activity, food cup activity, or exploration, but was low given either wheel running or standing.

Although grooming occurred only rarely, the data were entirely consistent with the analysis in Tables 5.3 to 5.6. Body grooming usually occurred in relatively long bursts for all rats, and then resulted in very long IRTs and a low probability of a changeover to a lever press.

In retrospect, the time since the last lever press *and* the collateral response occurring at any given time yielded a fine-grained estimate of the temporal probability of lever pressing.

Discussion

Pauses in one response apparently depend upon the particular concurrent response engaged at the onset of that pause. Pause termination may then be predicted well by the initiating collateral response rather than the average pause duration. However, the initiating collateral response does not solely determine the total IRT since a changeover from one collateral to a second frequently occurs within an IRT. Consequently, the collateral response occurring at a given time since the IRT onset provides a further clue to the probability of terminating that IRT.

One view holds that the probability of a given response is determined by the stimulus complex at any given moment (Estes, 1950; Bush and Mosteller, 1955). The present data also indicate that the collateral response at IRT onset is a powerful determinant of the IRT distribution. The lever-pressing probability at any given time x since IRT onset would thus depend upon the duration of the initiating collateral response and all subsequent collateral responses. However, at this stage of the sequential analysis, the relationship between IRT termination and collateral responses is perhaps best described as a two-link dependency. The first-order determinant of IRT termination is the collateral response emitted at IRT onset. The second-order determinant is the collateral response emitted at any time x since IRT onset. Clearly, estimates based simply on time per se irrespective of concurrent behaviors would not seem to be equally accurate in the estimation of IRT termination.

The data are more akin to a second model, which holds that the length of an IRT is determined at IRT onset. Shimp (1969) suggested that a subject chooses which IRT to emit rather than whether or not to respond at a given time. The present data would further argue that a particular IRT is probably more of a consequence than a "cause" of the collateral response emitted during the IRT. Shimp (1969) originally suggested that the subject chooses which "mediating behavioral chain to initiate," and the IRT then follows as a consequence of the collateral response selected at IRT onset. Reynolds and McLeod (1970) also suggested that relatively brief IRTs may be associated with one mode of collateral responses (such as standing in front of the response key), whereas relatively long IRTs may be associated with different modes of collateral responses (such as exploring and grooming).

The present data certainly agrees with the view that the examination of molecular behavior patterns is required for a comprehensive behavioral analysis. In support of this argument, Gray (1976) reported differential stimulus control of different IRT lengths of DRL responding during generalization testing, while at the same time stimulus control was obscured by averaging different IRT lengths. Also the results from Experiment VIII in Chapter 3 clearly showed that a response latency may be predicted on the basis of the concurrent response occurring at latency onset. The progressive development of the analysis of response sequences and patterns would emphasize a more conditional approach including the collateral responses that initiate IRTs or latencies.

From whatever perspective, the accruing data strongly indicate that the operant IRT is closely related to collateral responses. Fundamentally, one "choice" occurs when the subject changes over to a collateral response at IRT onset; the next "choice" occurs with the changeover from a collateral response to terminate the IRT. This analysis is consistent with the view that preference or "choice" is the changeover from one response to another (Skinner, 1950).

Concluding Comments

Patterns of responses maintained by simple operant conditioning seem to be systematically interrelated with collateral response characteristics. The response interactions generalized across many different procedures and consistently replicated the behavioral interactions reported with concurrent operant schedules and multiple schedules, as well as classical–operant combinations. Clearly, the present results strengthen the argument that "other" collateral responses may affect reinforced responses and hence serve as independent variables.

The results are first of all consistent with many recent reports of interactions between reinforced and collateral responses within simple operant conditioning (Clark, 1962; Segal and Bandt, 1966; Laties et al., 1969; Dunham, 1971; Wayner and Greenberg, 1972; Cohen and Looney, 1973; Gilbert, 1974; Colotla and Keehn, 1975; Cook and Singer, 1976; Anderson and Shettleworth, 1977).

In particular, the present results are in close accord with the recent emphasis on response competition as penetrating many conditioning procedures. Wong (1977), for example, suggested a "behavioral field approach" of combining naturalistic observation and experimentation. According to Wong, learning and extinction may be viewed as representing narrowing and broadening of the behavioral field that surrounds the instrumental response. Ray and Brown (1975), Anderson and Shettleworth (1977), Rand (1977), and Staddon (1977) have suggested a similar study of the behavioral interrelationships in conditioning situations. The mutual reinforcement of consistent data within and across laboratories supports the generalization that collateral responses may be fundamental determinants within conditioning procedures.

Response interactions have also been of some advantage to applied research areas such as the study of physiological and pharmacological processes. Changes in reinforced behavior after central nervous system lesions, for example, are clearly associated with changes in specific collateral responses (Slonaker and Hothersall, 1972; Wayner and Greenberg, 1972). Ellen et al. (1977) also suggested that such lesion-induced changes might be critically affected by competing behaviors hitherto unexamined. In the field of behavioral pharmacology there is a growing emphasis on the incorporation of concurrent behaviors into the functional analysis of pharmacological agents (Wuttke and Innis, 1972; Smith and Clark, 1975; Wallace and Singer, 1976; Sanger, 1977).

Our stress on increased attention to interacting responses also ties in with recent considerations that simple operant schedules may be viewed as concurrent schedules (Herrnstein, 1970, 1974). Similarly, Staddon (1977) considers reinforced responses to be in a reciprocal relationship with other behaviors. These models, however, consider response interactions as coming about by means of changes in underlying reinforcement values or behavioral states. This emphasis would retain rather molar constructs where response averages are either synonymous or isomorphic with the explanatory values and states. The many experimental findings in this and previous chapters in turn argue that molecular interactions are also important, and in fact appear to be rather systematic and controllable. The more specific implications of interacting response patterns will be discussed next.

One critical feature of these interactions is that the same collateral response may both reinforce and inhibit the ongoing operant response. Collateral licking thus suppressed FR responding during the drinking probe but facilitated responding in the absence of the probe, provided that access to drinking was scheduled early in the FR run or response independently. The reinforcing and suppressive effects of changeovers to collateral responses hence refer to separate effects within different temporal intervals and describe the sequential effects of operant–collateral pairings or the concurrent effects of simultaneous access to operant and collateral responses. Changeovers to collateral responses may then be arranged to serve both as sequential reinforcers or concurrent inhibitors of operant responding. Consequently, collateral responses do not compete "because" they are reinforcers, since competition and reinforcement describe different response interactions in different temporal intervals.

The present experiments were primarily concerned with the relationships between pausing in reinforced responding and concurrent emission of collateral responses. Postreinforcement pause (PRP) describes the pause between reinforcer delivery and the beginning of the run period of responding. This usage was intended to be descriptive. Recently, the term *PRP* was characterized as a "misnomer" because the pause is considered to be largely a function of the upcoming ratio size or run time (Griffiths and Thompson, 1973). Neuringer and Schneider (1968) and Barowsky and Mintz (1975) reported that the PRP was increased by inserting time-out periods to lengthen the run time of FR responding. In the present experiments, the PRP was altered by either manipulating the duration of collateral licking during the pause, without changing the run time, or by increasing the run time by inserting a drinking probe within the run period (Experiment IVA). In this case, however, the PRP was *decreased* by *lengthening* the run time. So increasing the run time by time-out is apparently not functionally equivalent to lengthening the run time by inserting collateral licking. These findings suggest that the PRP depends upon other parameters in addition to the run time [also see Dardano and Sauerbrunn (1964), Findley and Brady (1965) and Boren (1961) for manipulations of the PRP by alterations in the run period of FR responding.] In summary, the PRP appears to be critically dependent upon the particular events occurring during the run period as well as during the PRP, rather than only upon the duration of the run period per se.

Of equal interest, pausing in FR responding is not invariably located immediately after reinforcement; rather, multiple pauses may be effected by locating experimental events, such as drinking probes, during the run period. Such pauses seem to be associated with different response interactions, with pauses after pellet delivery associated with food-cup contact and pauses during the run period associated with drinking. The exact location of the experimental probe further determines the relative duration of each of these pauses. Pauses in simple FR schedules may thus be fruitfully considered to be multiplicatively determined.

Different pause terminologies have been suggested to reflect the different functional relations: pause after reinforcement, postrun pause, prerun pause, and between-run pause (e.g., Griffiths and Thompson, 1973). The descriptive term *PRP* seems at least to serve the purpose of referring to the location of a pause after reinforcement as opposed to a pause within the run period.

In any case, the present experiments amplify the variety of functional relations between bursts of collateral responses and FR pauses. The manipulated access to a collateral response was a precise predictor of the simultaneous pause in the ongoing operant response. The opposite interpretation, that the FR pause predicts the simultaneous duration of a particular collateral response, however, provides a much less clear-cut account. One particular collateral response is not clearly assessed in retrospect from a particular pause, since a pause may be generated by various collateral responses and changeovers between them, which is not evidenced by the operant pause per se. However, the operant pause is more immediately known at the moment of the changeover to one or another collateral response. Therefore, pausing or absence of one response does not invariably discriminate between the occurrence of one or more collateral responses. More clearly, the data show that the absence of an operant response is not associated with a homogeneous distribution of interchangeable collateral responses.

The relationship between pauses and collateral responses, however, is not merely a one-way interaction. The interdependence between reinforced and collateral responses was probably more clearly apparent in Experiment IV, in which collateral licking served both as an independent and a dependent variable. The present results would then be misread to suggest that *all* pauses in reinforced responding are *caused* by collateral responses. The observed mutual interdependencies among end terms jeopardize the fixing of simple causative relations among overt behaviors as well as physiological responses (Horridge, 1969).

The analysis offered in Part II was originally initiated by observations of an inverse relationship between one reinforced and one other concurrently available but nonreinforced response (Iversen, 1973). The experimental analysis quickly becomes problematic when more than one or two responses are recorded. However, recording only one response does not so much prevent as avoid the analytic problems. For example, the addition of an LH contingency to a VI schedule not only increased the rate of VI responding, but also decreased the rate of collateral licking and decreased the rate of VI reinforcement (Iversen, 1975b). If only the VI response had been recorded, the interpretation would have been superficially straightforward—the LH contingency presumably reinforced IRTs shorter than the LH duration. Had only the licking response been recorded, the interpretation could have been that the LH reduced either the reinforcement rate or the opportunity for adventitious reinforcement of licking. However, with both responses recognized, the increase in VI responding may be interpreted as responsible for the decrease in licking, and vice versa. The analysis was complicated by the fact that only two responses were recorded and would have been even more complicated by incorporating still more responses.

The now more firmly established relationship between collateral and reinforced responses recognizes the possibility that an independent variable might have an indirect effect brought about by means of affected collateral responses. For example, a particular brain lesion might directly affect the pattern of a particular collateral response and thereby change the pattern of the reinforced response (Wayner and Greenberg, 1972). Conversely, yet another lesion might directly affect the reinforced response and only indirectly affect collateral responses. The analysis would be complicated, but necessarily so since the basic question remains unsolved by recording only one response of theoretical interest.

Clearly, a functional relationship can be established between an independent variable and a dependent variable without any concern for the molecular nuances of the relationship. However, a science has been said to progress when a once established relationship is subdivided into evermore detailed functional relationships (Kuhn, 1970). A previous suggestion by Findley thus pointed out that "the way to increase our understanding of behavior is not to analyze a particular bit of behavior exhaustively, but rather to complicate the sample of be-havior under investigation as rapidly as good experimental and technological procedure permit'' (1962, p. 114). Various recording devices are now available for the simultaneous monitoring and recording of several behaviors. The pres-ent series of experiments suggests that the analysis of such behavioral interac-tions may provide a fruitful starting point for a more comprehensive analysis of previously established laboratory facts.

A long tradition in the experimental analysis of behavior has favored overall averages sampled over minutes, hours, or days as dependent variables, with fre-quent arguments that behavior is better represented at molar than molecular levels. Molar averages are easy to deal with. They smoothly fit hand in hand with theoretical constructs in a simple one on one fashion (motive up–response up, motive down–response down). This straight isomorphism between con-struct and molar behavior does not, however, strike the observer of performing animals as being particularly useful. A subject emits one response and then soon another, but at which moment is the underlying conceptual determinant in force? Molecular changes in behavior have been rendered ''chaotic'' and not consistent with theory, and eventually have been disregarded as data. How-ever, an experimental analysis must eventually cope with precisely such molec-ular behavior patterns, especially since averages obviously are made up of mo-lecular changes. Consider a previous argument that molecular patterns are not important because a molar measure may remain unchanged in spite of altera-tions in molecular patterns. We may reverse the argument: if the molecular pat-tern changes but the molar pattern does not, then the molar pattern is not suffi-ciently sensitive or relevant to the experimental manipulation. Molecular changes are significant, and worthy of study in and of themselves, in spite of the possibility that they may have no effect on an overall molar measure.

Molecular interactions of this nature are perhaps best illustrated by the last experiment in this series. The distribution of operant IRTs was related to differ-ent collateral responses initiating each IRT. Essentially, the collateral response initiating an IRT proved to be a powerful determinant of the duration of the IRT. Knowledge of the collateral response and the previous distribution of cor-responding IRTs yields a prediction of the ensuing IRT duration.

The ongoing collateral response at any given moment also provides informa-tion on the immediate probability of terminating the IRT. Collateral responses such as lever activity and food cup activity, which occurred in relatively short bursts, allow the prediction that the probability of IRT termination is relatively high. Wheel running, exploration, standing, and grooming, however, which occur in relatively long bursts, all indicate a much lower probability of IRT ter-mination. The collateral response at any given time therefore provides defini-tive information on the characteristic distribution of operant behavior in time.

Overall, the results are entirely consistent with the more general conclusion from previous chapters that scheduled events ''inhibit'' one response to the ex-tent that they control emission of concurrent responses. A significant step in the control and prediction of response probability at a given time is therefore provided by incorporation of concurrent responses into the behavioral analysis. The precise control of molecular response patterns might then be well within the domain of operant conditioning and analysis.

References

Allen, J. D., and Porter, J. H.: Sources of control over schedule-induced drinking produced by second-order schedules of reinforcement. *Physiol. Behav., 18*, 853–863, 1977.

Allen, J. D., Porter, J. H., and Arazie, R.: Schedule-induced drinking as a function of percentage reinforcement. *J. Exp. Analy. Behav., 23*, 223–232, 1975.

Amsel, A.: The role of frustrative nonreward in noncontinuous reward situations. *Psychol. Bull., 55*, 102–119, 1958.

Amsel, A., and Roussel, J.: Motivational properties of frustration: I. Effect on a running response of the addition of frustration to the motivational complex. *J. Exp. Psychol., 43*, 363–368, 1952.

Anderson, M. C., and Shettleworth, S. J.: Behavioral adaptation to fixed-interval and fixed-time food delivery in golden hamsters. *J. Exp. Anal. Behav., 27*, 33–49, 1977.

Anger, D.: The dependence of interresponse times upon the relative reinforcement of different interresponse times. *J. Exp. Psychol., 52*, 145–161, 1956.

Ator, N.: Interchangeability of mirror attack and response-produced time out in pigeons. *Paper presented at the meeting of the Americal Psychological Association,* Washington, D. C., September 1976.

Azrin, N. H., Hutchinson, R. R., and McLaughlin, R.: The opportunity for aggression as an operant reinforcer during aversive stimulation. *J. Exp. Anal. Behav., 8*, 171–180, 1965.

Barowsky, E. I., and Mintz, D. E.: The effects of time-out locus during fixed-ratio reinforcement. *Bull. Psychonomic Soc., 5*, 137–140, 1975.

Berlyne, D. E.: *Conflict, Arousal, and Curiosity.* New York, McGraw-Hill, 1960.

Bolles, R. C.: *Theory of Motivation.* New York, Harper & Row, 1967.

Boren, J. J.: Stimulus probes of the fixed ratio run. Paper presented at Eastern Psychological Association, Philadelphia, 1961.

Boren, J. J.: The study of drugs with operant techniques. In, W. K. Honig (ed.): *Operant Behavior: Areas of Research and Application.* New York, Appleton-Century-Crofts, 1966.

Breland, K., and Breland, M.: The misbehavior of organisms. *Am. Psychol., 16*, 681–684, 1961.

Bush, R. R., and Mosteller, F.: *Stochastic Models for Learning.* New York, Wiley, 1955.

Carlisle, H. J.: Fixed-ratio polydipsia: termal effects of drinking, pausing, and responding. *J. Comp. Physiol. Psychol., 75*, 10–22, 1971.

Carlisle, H. J.: Schedule-induced polydipsia: effects of water termperature, ambient temperature, and hypothalamic cooling. *J. Comp. Physiol. Psychol., 83*, 208–220, 1973.

Catania, A. C., and Gill, C. A.: Inhibition and behavioral contrast. *Psychonomic Sci., 1*, 257–258, 1964.

Clark, F. C.: Some observations on the adventitious reinforcement of drinking under food reinforcement. *J. Exp. Anal. Behav., 5*, 61–63, 1962.

Cohen, P. S., and Looney, T. A.: Schedule-induced mirror responding in the pigeon. *J. Exp. Anal. Behav., 19*, 395–408, 1973.

Cole, J. M., and Parker, B. K.: Schedule-induced aggression: access to an attackable target bird as a positive reinforcer. *Psychonomic Sci., 22*, 33–35, 1971.

Colotla, V. A., and Keehn, J. D.: Effects of reinforcer-pellet composition on schedule-induced polydipsia with alcohol, water, and saccharin. *Psychol. Record, 25*, 91–98, 1975.

Cook, P., and Singer, G.: Effects of stimulus displacement on adjunctive behavior. *Physiol. Behav., 16*, 79–82, 1976.

Corfield-Sumner, P. K., Blackman, D. E., and Stainer, G.: Polydipsia induced in rats by second-order schedules of reinforcement. *J. Exp. Anal. Behav., 27*, 265–273, 1977.

Dardano, J. F., and Sauerbrunn, D.: Selective punishment of fixed-ratio performance. *J. Exp. Anal. Behav., 7*, 255–260, 1964.

Dews, P. B.: The effect of multiple S^Δ periods on responding on a fixed-interval schedule: V. Effect of periods of complete darkness and of occasional omissions of food presentations. *J. Exp. Anal. Behav.*, **9**, 573–578, 1966.

Dunham, P. J.: Punishment: method and theory. *Psychol. Rev.*, **78**, 58–70, 1971.

Dunham, P. J.: Some effects of punishment upon unpunished responding. *J. Exp. Anal. Behav.*, **17**, 443–450, 1972.

Ellen, P., Gillenwater, G., and Richardson, W. K.: Extinction responding by septal and normal rats following acquisition under four schedules of reinforcement. *Physiol. Behav.*, **18**, 609–615, 1977.

Estes, W. K.: Toward a statistical theory of learning. *Psychol. Rev.*, **57**, 94–107, 1950.

Falk, J. L.: The motivational properties of schedule-induced polydipsia. *J. Exp. Anal. Behav.*, **9**, 19–25, 1966.

Falk, J. L.: Conditions producing psychogenic polydipsia in animals. *Ann. N. Y. Acad. Sci.*, **157**, 569–593, 1969.

Falk, J. L.: The nature and determinants of adjunctive behavior. *Physiol. Behav.*, **6**, 577–588, 1971.

Felton, M., and Lyon, D. O.: The post-reinforcement pause. *J. Exp. Anal. Behav.*, **9**, 131–134, 1966.

Ferster, C. B., and Skinner, B. F.: *Schedules of Reinforcement*. New York, Appleton-Century-Crofts, 1957.

Findley, J. D.: An experimental outline for building and exploring multi-operant behavior repertoires. *J. Exp. Anal. Behav.*, **5**, 113–166, 1962.

Findley, J. D., and Brady, J. V.: Facilitation of large ratio performance by use of conditioned reinforcement. *J. Exp. Anal. Behav.*, **8**, 125–129, 1965.

Flory, R. K.: Attack behavior in a multiple fixed-ratio schedule of reinforcement. *Psychonomic Sci.*, **16**, 15615—157, 1969.

Flory, R. K., and O'Boyle, M. K.: The effect of limited water availability on schedule-induced polydipsia. *Physiol. Behav.*, **8**, 147–149, 1972.

Gilbert, R. M.: Ubiquity of schedule-induced polydipsia. *J. Exp. Anal. Behav.*, **21**, 277–284, 1974.

Gray, V. A.: Stimulus control of differential-reinforcement of low-rate responding. *J. Exp. Anal. Behav.*, **25**, 199–207, 1976.

Griffiths, R. R., and Thompson, T.: The post-reinforcement pause: a misnomer. *Psychol. Record*, **23**, 229–235, 1973.

Guthrie, E. R.: *The Psychology of Learning*. New York, Harper, 1935.

Hearst, E.: Some persistent problems in the analysis of conditioned inhibition. In, R. A. Boakes and M. S. Halliday (ed.): *Inhibition and Learning*. London and New York, Academic Press, 1972.

Herrnstein, R. J.: On the law of effect. *J. Exp. Anal. Behav.*, **13**, 243–266, 1970.

Herrnstein, R. J.: Formal properties of the matching law. *J. Exp. Anal. Behav.*, **21**, 159–164, 1974.

Hodos, W., Ross, G. S., and Brady, J. V.: Complex response patterns during temporally spaced responding. *J. Exp. Anal. Behav.*, **5**, 473–479, 1962.

Honig, W. K.: Introductory remarks. In, W. K. Honig (ed.): *Operant Behavior: Areas of Research and Application*. New York, Appleton-Century-Crofts, 1966.

Horridge, G. A.: The interpretation of behavior in terms of interneurons. In, M. A. B. Brazier (ed.): *The Interneuron*. Los Angeles, University of California Press, 1969.

Hull, C. L.: *A Behavior System*. New Haven, Yale University Press, 1952.

Huston, J. P., and Desisto, M. J.: Interspecies aggression during fixed-ratio hypothalamic self-stimulation in rats. *Physiol. Behav.*, **7**, 353–357, 1971.

Hutchinson, R. R., Azrin, N. H., and Hunt, G. M.: Attack produced by intermittent reinforcement of a concurrent operant response. *J. Exp. Anal. Behav.*, **11**, 489–495, 1968.

Iversen, I. H.: Interactions between reinforced and non-reinforced responses. Paper presented at the Third Scandinavian Meeting on Physiological Psychology, Copenhagen, May 1973.

Iversen, I. H.: Concurrent responses during multiple schedules in rats. *Scand. J. Psychol.*, **16**, 49–54, 1975a.

Iversen, I. H.: Interactions between lever pressing and collateral drinking during VI with limited hold. *Psychol. Record*, **25**, 47–50, 1975b.

Iversen, I. H.: Interactions between reinforced responses and collateral responses. *Psychol. Record*, **26**, 399–413, 1976.

Iversen, I. H.: Behavioral pauses and their relation to concurrent behaviors. Paper presented at the Easter Conference of the English Experimental Analysis of Behavior Group. Exeter, March 1977a.

Iversen, I. H.: Reinforcement omission and schedule-induced drinking in a response-independent schedule in rats. *Physiol. Behav.,* **18,** 535–537, 1977b.

Keehn, J. D., and Colotla, V. A.: Schedule-induced drinking as a function of interpellet interval. *Psychonomic Sci.,* **23,** 69–71, 1971.

Killeen, P.: On the temporal control of behavior. *Psychol. Rev.,* **82,** 89–115, 1975.

Kuhn, T. S.: *The Structure of Scientific Revolutions. International Encyclopedia of Unified Science,* vol. 2, No. 2, 2nd ed. Chicago, University of Chicago Press, 1970.

Laties, V. G., Weiss, B., Clark, R. L., and Reynolds, M. D.: Overt "mediating" behavior during temporally spaced responding. *J. Exp. Anal. Behav.,* **8,** 107–116, 1965.

Laties, V. G., Weiss, B., and Weiss, A. B.: Further observations on overt "mediating" behavior and the discrimination of time. *J. Exp. Anal. Behav.,* **12,** 43–57, 1969.

Lyon, D. O.: Some notes on conditioned suppression and reinforcement schedules. *J. Exp. Anal. Behav.,* **7,** 289–291, 1964.

McCoy, J. F., and Christian, W. P.: Schedule-induced drinking and reinforcement omission. *Physiol. Behav.,* **17,** 537–539, 1976.

McLeod, D. R., and Gollub, L. R.: An analysis of rats' drinking-tube contacts under tandem and fixed-interval schedules of food presentation. *J. Exp. Anal. Behav.,* **25,** 361–370, 1976.

McMillan, J. C.: Percentage reinforcement of fixed-ratio and variable-interval performances. *J. Exp. Anal. Behav.,* **15,** 297–302, 1971.

Neuringer, A. J., and Schneider, B. A.: Separating the effects of interreinforcement time and number of interreinforcement responses. *J. Exp. Anal. Behav.,* **11,** 661–667, 1968.

Pavlov, I. P.: *Conditioned Reflexes* (Translated by G. V. Anrep). London, Oxford, 1927 (Reprinted, New York, Dover, 1960).

Penney, J., and Schull, J.: Functional differentiation of adjunctive drinking and wheel running in rats. *Anim. Learning Behav.,* **5,** 272–280, 1977.

Porter, J. H., and Kenshalo, D. R.: Schedule-induced drinking following omission of reinforcement in the rhesus monkey. *Physiol. Behav.,* **12,** 1075–1077, 1974.

Porter, J. H., Arazie, R., Holbrook, J. W., Cheek, M. S., and Allen, J. D.: Effects of variable and fixed second-order schedules on schedule-induced polydipsia in the rat. *Physiol. Behav.,* **14,** 143–149, 1975.

Powell, R. W.: The effect of small sequential changes in fixed-ratio size upon the post-reinforcement pause. *J. Exp. Anal. Behav.,* **11,** 589–593, 1968.

Powell, R. W.: The effect of reinforcement magnitude upon responding under fixed-ratio schedules. *J. Exp. Anal. Behav.,* **12,** 605–608, 1969.

Premack, D.: Catching up with common sense or two sides of a generalization: reinforcement and punishment. In, R. Glaser (ed.): *The Nature of Reinforcement.* New York, Academic Press, 1971.

Rand, J. F.: Behaviors observed during S⁻ in a simple discrimination learning task. *J. Exp. Anal. Behav.,* **27,** 103–117, 1977.

Ray, R. D., and Brown, D. A.: A systems approach to behavior. *Psychol. Record,* **25,** 459–478, 1975.

Reynolds, G. S., and McLeod, A.: On the theory of interresponse-time reinforcement. In, G. H. Bower (ed.): *The Psychology of Learning and Motivation.* New York, Academic Press, 1970.

Rosenblith, J. Z.: Polydipsia induced in the rat by a second-order schedule. *J. Exp. Anal. Behav.,* **14,** 139–144, 1970.

Sanger, D.: Schedule-induced drinking of chlordiazepoxide solutions by rats. *Pharmacol. Biochem. Behav.,* **7,** 1–6, 1977.

Schaeffer, R. W., and Diehl, J. C.: Collateral water drinking in rats maintained on FR food reinforcement schedules. *Psychonomic Sci.,* **4,** 257–258, 1966.

Schoenfeld, W. N., and Farmer, J.: Reinforcement schedules and the "behavior stream." In, W. N. Schoenfeld (ed.): *The Theory of Reinforcement Schedules.* New York, Appleton-Century-Crofts, 1970.

Segal, E. F.: Transformation of polydipsic drinking into operant drinking: A paradigm? *Psychonomic Sci.,* **16,** 133–135, 1969.

Segal, E. F.: Induction and the provenance of operants. In, R. M. Gilbert and J. R. Millenson (eds.): *Reinforcement: Behavioral Analysis.* New York, Academic Press, 1972.

Segal, E. F., and Bandt, W. M.: Influence of collateral water drinking on bar pressing under complex reinforcement contingencies. *Psychonomic Sci.,* **4,** 377–378, 1966.

Seward, J. P., Pereboom, A. C., Butler, B., and Jones, R. B.: The role of prefeeding in an apparent frustration effect. *J. Exp. Psychol.,* **54,** 445–450, 1957.

Shimp, C. P.: Optimal behavior in free-operant experiments. *Psychol. Rev.,* **76,** 97–112, 1969.

Shimp, C. P.: Synthetic variable-interval schedules of reinforcement. *J. Exp. Anal. Behav.,* **19,** 311–330, 1973.

Skinner, B. F.: *The Behavior of Organisms,* New York, Appleton-Century-Crofts, 1938.

Skinner, B. F.: Are theories of learning necessary? *Psychol. Rev.,* **57,** 193–216, 1950.

Skinner, B. F., and Morse, W. H.: Concurrent activity under fixed-interval reinforcement. *J. Comp. Physiol. Psychol.,* **50,** 279–281, 1957.

Slonaker, R. L., and Hothersall, D.: Collateral behaviors and the DRL deficit of rats with septal lesions. *J. Comp. Physiol. Psychol.,* **80,** 91–96, 1972.

Smith, J. B., and Clark, F. C.: Effects of *d*-amphetamine, chlorpromazine, and chlordiazepoxide on intercurrent behavior during spaced-responding schedules. *J. Exp. Anal. Behav.,* **24,** 241–248, 1975.

Staddon, J. E. R.: Temporal effects of reinforcement: a negative "frustration" effect. *Learning Motivation,* **1,** 227–247, 1970.

Staddon, J. E. R.: Schedule-induced behavior. In, W. K. Honig and J. E. R. Staddon (eds.): *Handbook of Operant Behavior.* Englewood Cliffs, New Jersey: Prentice-Hall, 1977.

Staddon, J. E. R., and Ayres, S. L.: Sequential and temporal properties of behavior induced by a schedule of periodic food delivery. *Behaviour,* **54,** 26–49, 1975.

Staddon, J. E. R., and Innis, N. K.: An effect analogous to "frustration" on interval reinforcement schedules. *Psychonomic Sci.,* **4,** 287–288, 1966.

Staddon, J. E. R., and Innis, N. K.: Reinforcement omission on fixed-interval schedules. *J. Exp. Anal. Behav.,* **12,** 689–700, 1969.

Staddon, J. E. R., and Simmelhag, V. L.: The "superstition" experiment: a reexamination of its implications for the principles of adaptive behavior. *Psychol. Rev.,* **78,** 3–43, 1971.

Thompson, T.: Effect of chlorpromazine on "aggressive" responding in the rat. *J. Comp. Physiol. Psychol.,* **54,** 398–400, 1961.

Timberlake, W., and Allison, J.: Response deprivation: an empirical approach to instrumental performance. *Psychol. Rev.,* **81,** 146–164, 1974.

Wallace, M., and Singer, G.: Schedule-induced behavior: a review of its generality, determinants and pharmacological data. *Pharmacol. Biochem. Behav.,* **5,** 483–490, 1976.

Wayner, M. J., and Greenberg, I.: Effects of septal lesions on palatability modulation and schedule-induced behavior. *Physiol. Behav.,* **9,** 663–665, 1972.

Wong, P. T.: A behavioral field approach to instrumental learning in the rat: I. Partial reinforcement effects and sex differences. *Anim. Learning Behavior,* **5,** 5–13, 1977.

Wookey, P. E., and Strongman, K. T.: Reward shift and general activity in the rat. *Br. J. Psychol.,* **65,** 103–110, 1974.

Wuttke, W., and Innis, N. K.: Drug effects upon behavior induced by second-order shcedules of reinforcement: the relevance of ethological analysis. In, R. M. Gilbert and J. D. Keehn (eds.): *Schedule Effects: Drugs, Drinking, and Aggression.* Toronto, University of Toronto Press, 1972.

Zimmerman, D. W.: Rate changes after unscheduled omission and presentation of reinforcement. *J. Exp. Anal. Behav.,* **15,** 261–270, 1971.

CLASSICAL CONDITIONING PROCEDURES

Chapter 6

Response Patterning in Classical Conditioning

Wendon W. Henton

Review of Conditioning and Competing Responses

This chapter describes an initial extension of the concurrent responses–concurrent schedules analysis to include standard and not so standard classical conditioning procedures. Classical conditioning surely enjoys an extensive history within experimental psychology, with precursor associationistic formulations apparent throughout the history of philosophy and metaphysics (e.g., Descartes, Locke, Hobbes, J. S. Mill, etc.; excellent reviews by Jones, 1952; Boring, 1957). The physiology and psychology of reflexive behavior separated from the philosophy of mentalistic associations with the early work on unconditioned reflexes by Sherrington (1906) and Sechenov (1935; also Creed et al., 1932). The extraordinary accomplishment of Pavlov was the systematic elaboration of the unconditioned reflex model (unconditioned stimulus—unconditioned response) into the now familiar model of conditioned reflexes (conditioned stimulus–conditioned response; unconditioned stimulus–unconditioned response). The conditioned or acquired reflexes were optimistically offered as factual alternatives to "the fantastic speculations as to the existence of any possible subjective state in the animal which may be conjectured on analogy with ourselves" (Pavlov, 1927, p. 161). As noted by Razran (1957), the Pavlovian conception of conditioned reflexes was pointedly aimed at scrapping the mentalistic states and faculties then serving as explanations of behavior. Although Pavlov's repeated warnings (Pavlov, 1906, 1927, 1932) against philosophical explanations are frequently ignored by Western psychologists, the Sherringtonian reflex model remains the basic analytic unit for classical conditioning by Soviet and Eastern European investigators (Konorski, 1948, 1967; Bykov, 1958; Sokolov, 1960).

In only brief review, a CR is acquired when a "neutral" stimulus (CS) is

paired with the presentation of a second stimulus that invariably elicits a specific response (UCS–UCR). Several pairings of the CS with the UCS–UCR result in the elicitation of a CR during the previously ineffective CS. Responses
recorded as conditioned reflexes include salivation, heart rate, respiration, leg
flexion, eyeblink, and many other responses elicited by unconditioned stimuli
such as food (alimentary conditioning) or electric shock (defensive conditioning) (review by Osgood, 1953). The CR has been variously described as identical with the UCR, a fractional component of the UCR, or a preparatory response adjusting the organism for UCS onset (Kimble, 1961).

Classical conditioning may be arbitrarily divided into excitatory and inhibitory procedures. In general, *excitatory conditioning* refers to procedures that
increase the frequency or intensity of the CR. Among the more common excitatory procedures are (1) *simultaneous conditioning,* in which the onset of the CS
is immediately followed by the UCS, (2) *delay conditioning,* in which the onset
of the CS is followed by the UCS only after a specific temporal interval, (3)
trace conditioning, in which both CS onset and offset precede UCS onset, and
(4) *compound conditioning,* in which two CS are combined and followed by the
UCS. *Inhibitory conditioning* refers to a withholding or diminution of a reference response, and therefore occurs within the context of previous excitatory
conditioning. Inhibitory procedures are subdivided into *internal inhibition,*
which refers to an acquired or conditioned withholding of the CR, and *external
inhibition,* which refers to the elicitation of inborn, unconditioned reflexes that
are antagonistic to the CR. The gradual acquisition of internal inhibition occurs
(1) during the initial portion of relatively long CS–UCS delay conditioning (inhibition of delay) (2) when the CS is no longer paired with the UCS, (inhibition
of extinction) of (3) when a CS paired with a UCS is occasionally combined
with a second neutral stimulus, but the two-stimulus complex is never followed
by the UCS (differential or conditioned inhibition). Unconditioned inhibition
immediately occurs when a novel stimulus is (1) superimposed upon an excitatory conditioning procedure and the reference CR is diminished (external inhibition) or (2) superimposed upon an internal inhibition procedure and the reference inhibition of the CR is disrupted (inhibition of inhibition, or
disinhibition).

Although classical conditioning is occasionally described as a simple method
of conditioning involuntary and stupid behaviors, Pavlov described a multitude
of variables that would modify the probability of the CR. Fundamental requirements were that the subject be alert and healthy, and that the to-be-conditioned
stimulus be presented prior to the UCS, overlap the UCS, and be neither "too
strong nor too weak" (Pavlov, 1927). The fourth point concerning the intensity
of the CS introduced a fundamental interaction that substantially complicates
the analysis of classical conditioned reflexes. Virtually all "neutral" or to-be-
conditioned stimuli are not in fact neutral but are UCSs in their own right.

The initial presentation of a novel stimulus unconditionally elicits an orienting reflex toward the stimulus source (Pavlov, 1927). The unconditioned orienting reflex is an integrated set of reactions (receptor orientation, somatomo-

tor responses, and changes in respiration, electroencephalogram, galvanic skin response, and cardiovascular responses) that are biologically adaptative and exclude or inhibit all other reflex systems (Sokolov, 1960, 1963). With repetitive stimulation, the stimulus-orienting reflex is replaced by the adaptation reflex. With CS–UCS pairings, however, the orienting reflex is replaced by conditioned reflexes (Bykov, 1958) or is transformed into a conditioned orienting reflex (Biriukov, 1958). Yet, an intense "neutral" stimulus unconditionally elicits defense reflexes that never adapt and are antagonistic to the development of conditioned reflexes during subsequent CS–UCS pairings. The interplay of stimulus-orienting, adaptation, and defense reflexes with conditioned reflexes has become a major element in the analysis of classically conditioned effects (review by Razran, 1961). "Simple" classical conditioning thus results in a multifaceted interaction between unconditioned orienting, adaptation, and defense reactions elicited by the CS, conditioned orienting and consummatory reactions generated by CS–UCS pairings, and unconditioned reactions elicited by the UCS.

Undoubtedly, a most comprehensive analysis of orienting reflexes has been provided by Sokolov and associates (Sokolov, 1958, 1959, 1960, 1963), resulting in a detailed Pavlovian model of perception and attention (reviews by Lynn, 1966; Graham, 1973). Sokolov emphasized that orienting reflexes actually embrace two distinct reactions: a narrowly defined unconditioned orienting to stimulus novelty, resulting in a nonspecific "tuning" of sensory analysers, and a conditioned reflex chain of investigatory and exploratory behaviors. Similarly, Biriukov (1958) described the orienting reflex as a complex unconditioned–conditioned reaction consisting of two phases: an unconditioned reflex that rapidly dissipates with stimulus repetition, overlaid by a conditioned orienting reaction to the CS that is "practically unextinguishable". The latter conditioned component is approximately analogous to the approach and contact responses toward the CS described by Pavlov. Orienting and investigatory responses toward stimuli paired with reinforcers had not been described in the Western literature, with the notable early exception of Zener (1937), until quite recently. Patton and Rudy (1967), for example, reported an increased frequency of approach toward a light paired with delivery of water to rats. The approach or "autoshaping" responses toward stimuli paired with response-independent reinforcers have also been described by Brown and Jenkins (1968), Williams and Williams (1969), among many others (review by Schwartz and Gamzu, 1977).

Pavlovian conditioning is complicated still further by the multiple response or polyeffector nature of all conditioned and unconditioned reflexes. "It is essential to realize that each of these two reflexes—the alimentary reflex and the mild defense reflex to rejectable substances—consists of two distinct components, a motor and a secretory" (Pavlov, 1927, p. 17). In a similar manner, we have just seen that orienting and exploratory reflexes are also described as polyeffector reactions with both autonomic and skeletal components.

One of the most detailed treatments of the interactions between polyeffector reflexes is the analysis by Konorski (1967). In the Konorski system, classical conditioning involves not one but two unconditioned reflexes elicited by the UCS, described as consummatory reflexes and drive (or preparatory) reflexes. Therefore, a stimulus paired with a UCS will generate two corresponding sets of conditioned consummatory and conditioned drive responses. At this point, classical conditioning is an interaction between four different reflexes (conditioned and unconditioned consummatory responses, conditioned and unconditioned drive responses). Next, each unconditioned reflex is opposed by an antagonistic reflex. The opposing sets of consummatory versus anticonsummatory reflxes and drive versus antidrive reflexes are somewhat analogous to the "on" and "off" neural systems responding to the presence and absence of stimulation (Hartline, 1938). For example, preparatory drive reflexes, such as "hunger," consist of motor activity, sensitivity to stimuli, and arousal of the sympathetic autonomic system, whereas the antidrive or "satiation" reflexes involve the opposite reactions of general motor relaxation and parasympathetic activation. A still further complication is that the conditioning environment also includes stimuli paired with the anticonsummatory and antidrive reflexes and will necessarily result in the acquisition of conditioned anticonsummatory and conditioned antidrive reflexes. Thus, Konorski reports that classical conditioning is a complex interweaving of eight different polyeffector reflexes (conditioned and unconditioned consummatory reflexes versus conditioned and unconditioned anticonsummatory reflexes, plus conditioned and unconditioned drive reflexes versus conditioned and unconditioned antidrive reflexes). Classical conditioning might then be only deceptively simple and may result in a literal mosaic of distinct sets of covert and overt responses continuously interacting with other conditioned and unconditioned reflex systems.

A different view of classical conditioning, however, had become common to Western theories of psychology. A traditional belief among American psychologists, for example, holds that classical conditioning only involves covert responses, not skeletal responses (Skinner, 1937; Mowrer, 1960). The covert–overt and autonomic–skeletal distinctions have generated a variety of two-process theories proposing that classical conditioning generates states, expectancies, motivations, etc. (Mowrer, 1960; Solomon and Turner, 1962). In general, state theories propose that the sensory link mediates perception, the efferent link controls responses, and an intermediate connecting link serves internal states of emotion and motivation (Arnold, 1969). The mediational interpretations frequently propose that these internal states are indexed by autonomic measures and motivate or energize skeletal responses (reviews by Rescorla and Solomon, 1967; Black, 1971). Furthermore, the effects of classically conditioned motives and expectances are determined solely by the characteristics of the central state and should not be attributed to interactions between conditioned skeletal responses (Seligman et al., 1971). The classical conditioning of internal states remains the prevalent view among contemporary theorists and continues to generate substantial experimental research (e.g., Prokasy, 1965; Black and Prokasy, 1972).

Given the extensive and occasionally argumentative history of classical conditioning, the extension of the concurrent response analyses to include conditioned reflexes should be decidedly easy and simply involve some days collating previous data, followed by a straightforward analysis of the reported results. The initial impression, however, is incorrect. The behavioral data unfortunately do not exist in the previous American literature, with the particular exceptions of Wendt (1936), Zener (1937), Bindra and Palfai (1967), and Palfai and Cornell (1968). On one hand, central state interpretations have relegated overt behaviors to minor and trivial roles in the analysis of classically conditioned motivational processes. At best, skeletal responses are only used as indirect measures of covert, unrecordable states. In general, skeletal responses are viewed as a nuisance, to be literally eliminated with curare or figuratively eliminated by deductive logic and control procedures. The mediational view has thus tended to become a self-fulfilling argument, with the lack of empirical data on overt behaviors in turn bolstering the proposition that classically conditioned effects are uniquely due to covert states. Within the central state interpretations, recording and analyzing skeletal behaviors during classical conditioning would be little more than a fool's errand, as our critics delightedly inform us.

The mediational interpretations however, are not free of criticism. Arnold noted that "over and over again, it is said that emotion motivates; but hardly ever does anyone come out and say unambiguously just how this is done" (1969, p. 1041). In a critical review, Black (1971) similarly concluded that the simplified view of classical conditioning common to two-process theories may be inadequate and may provoke erroneous conclusions. The reluctant conclusions of Black, Myer (1971), and other investigators (Brady et al., 1969; Hineline, 1973) are rather similar to previous critiques of Anohkin, Biriukov, and other Russian investigators. Anohkin (1958), for example, pointedly criticized the fractionalization of polyeffector reflexes into seemingly independent components, with the resultant erroneous interpretation that one covert component mediates other covert or overt components. Rather, Anohkin insisted that reflexes are integrated, holistic sets of overt and covert responses collectively elicited and conditioned by the CS–UCS pairings. Moreover, Pavlov irremediably rejected emotions, motivations, and other "fantastic states" as metaphysical faculties. Instead, "playfulness," "fear," "anger," and other "states" were viewed as nothing more nor less than reflexes, not psychological states intervening between stimuli and responses. Konorski's (1967) system is similarly rich in the use of state and drive terminology such as "hunger" and "fear." Konorski, however, clearly defined states and drives as polyeffector reflexes, not disembodied mental processes ambiguously energizing locomotor activities. The interaction between reflex systems may thus be an interaction between one set of covert and overt responses and a second set of covert and overt responses, rather than a mediation of skeletal behaviors by covert responses.

On the other hand, the quantitative analysis of overt behaviors is also unavailable in the Russian classical conditioning literature, but for different reasons. Initially, Russian investigators tended to follow Pavlov's earlier description of skeletal responses as essentially important but difficult to quantify relative to autonomic responses. In addition, Brozek (1963) previously noted that Soviet psychology is occasionally weak in the quantitative analysis of data. With occasional exceptions (e.g., Bykov, 1958), the Russian investigators remain predominantly biased toward qualitative or observational analysis rather than automated behavioral measurements. The Russian literature dating back to Pavlov, however, is replete with brief, qualitative descriptions of the interactions between skeletal responses in classical conditioning. Pavlov described the pitting of one reflex against a second reflex, as in the suppression of restless escape behaviors ("the freedom reflex") by an increase in the motor and secretory responses of appetitive conditioned reflexes ("the hunger reflexes") (Pavlov, 1927, pp. 11–12). The pitting of one reflex against a second is in fact a "concurrent reflex" analysis. Similarly, Pavlov (1927) described the disruption of alimentary reflexes by orienting reflexes (pp. 44–45), the disruption of defensive reflexes by alimentary reflexes (pp. 29–30), the augmentation of conditioned reflexes by the addition of similar conditioned reflexes (p. 79), and the augmentation of extinguished reflexes by the addition of orienting reflexes (pp. 62–67). At a behavioral level, the interactions described by Pavlov provide perhaps the earliest account of the inhibition and facilitation effects of concurrent responses.

One exception to the suppression of one reflex by the excitation of a second competing reflex was raised by Pavlov's account of internal inhibition as an antagonism between excitatory and inhibitory processes. The inhibitory processes were localized in the center of the inhibitory CS, with an irradiation of inhibition spreading outward across the cortex. As described by Konorski and other investigators, the Pavlovian assumption of internal inhibition may not be consistent with more recent physiological and behavioral evidence. Konorski concluded that the "inhibitory CR is no more and no less inhibitory that the excitatory food CR," and that the theoretical terms of "internal inhibition" and "inhibitory CR" should be abandoned as inadequate (1967, p. 327). Instead, the inhibition of one reflex is always a consequence of the concurrent excitation of a second reflex system. Specifically, the inhibition of all motor acts is a result of the excitation of antagonistic reflexes (Konorski, 1972).

Anohkin (1958, 1968) has similarly proposed an "exclusion principle" based upon the dominant interpretation of Ukhtomsky (1954). The principle of exclusion proposes that the organism cannot simultaneously combine two or three sets of reflexes: "Every holistic activity of the organism has a tendency to be the only one present at a given time and to exclude all other acts" (Anohkin, 1958, p. 4). For Anohkin, complimentary inhibition is the first and foremost interaction between reflexes. Special exceptions to the exclusion principle are the summation or enhancement of one reflex by a second reflex, and the transformation of a current reflex by latent or previously conditioned reflexes. A concurrent response analysis would therefore seem to be not only applicable but already qualitatively applied to classically conditioned reflexes (also see Ukhtomsky, 1954; Kupalov, 1955; Russell, 1966).

Simple Classical Conditioning (Experiment I)*

The first group of experiments was designed to analyze the behavioral interactions previously observed within standard classical conditioning procedures (e.g., Zener, 1937), but used the more quantitative methods described by Bykov (1958), Bindra and Palfai (1967), and Palfai and Cornell (1968). Initially, Wendt (1936) reported that external inhibition, internal inhibition, inhibition of extinction, and inhibition of delay were all examples of a redirection of activity into other response systems, a "competition between reaction systems." Competing responses that inhibited food-retrieval responses of monkeys were relative specific to individual subjects and included retreat to the back of the cage, repetitive circling of the cage, climbing and hanging responses, etc. Wendt concluded that all inhibitory effects were more appropriately described as the reciprocal or complimentary inhibition produced by the elicitation of more dominant behaviors. Excitatory classical conditioning effects were then described by Zener (1937). A bell was sounded for 25 sec, with the response-independent delivery of food into a pan at the 15th sec.

> After conditioning, the dog may look at either the bell or the food pan during the entire delay period. A few of the older, long-trained and stable dogs may look at the bell immediately and continuously until the food drops or until a second or two before. . . More frequent, however, are transitional cases in which the bell is first fixated, for varying number of seconds, and then the food pan for the remainder of the delay period. More frequent still is oscillation between bell and food pan. Occasionally there may be 6 or more successive glances from bell to food pan and back during the interval. (Zener, 1937, pp. 390–391)

Still more pronounced orienting and approach behaviors were observed when the restraints of the conditioning harness were removed from the subjects. During extinction, Zener, like Wendt, reported a decrease in positive approach responses and a corresponding increase in restless movements and negative responses away from the food pan. Zener noted that the conditioned orienting responses to the CS were neither identical with nor components of the UCR elicited by the food UCS, and were therefore inconsistent with the traditional stimulus substitution or S-S contiguity conception of classical conditioning. Zener instead proposed a sign–urge interpretation, in which a perceptual reorganization of the psychological field interacts with tension systems to release activity toward or away from signified goals.

More recently, Bykov (1958) measured the time spent in orienting reflexes elicited by the CS (motor and respiratory responses) and conditioned reactions elicited by CS–UCS pairings (motor and secretory responses) during appetitive conditioning with dogs. The simple presentation of a 15-sec novel stimulus initially elicited prolonged orienting behaviors accompanied by a complete inhibition of all other responses. Stimulus orienting progressively decreased over subsequent trials, with a resumption of ongoing activities throughout the re-

* Experiments were conducted by W. Henton, Washington, D. C., from December 1974 to April 1975.

mainder of the stimulus duration. Classical conditioning with the stimulus paired with a food UCS again increased orienting reflexes to 12 to 15 sec, with a virtually zero duration of conditioned consummatory reflexes throughout the first six trials. The conditioned food reflexes then systematically increased to nearly 14 sec/trial, with a reduction of CS orienting reflexes to approximately 1 sec over conditioning trials. Bykov further reported that differential classical conditioning generated a complex, three-stage interaction between orienting and conditioned reflexes within and across the positive CS paired with food and a negative CS explicitly unpaired with food. Within all Pavlovian procedures, Bykov found a continuous interaction between CS orienting and conditioned consummatory reflexes, with concomitant inhibition as the "root of the struggle" between the reflex systems.

The pattern of activity during defensive as well as appetitive classical conditioning has been described by Bindra and Palfai (1967) and Palfai and Cornell (1968). Briefly, perambulation and grooming decreased and freezing increased during a stimulus previously paired with shock. On the other hand, a CS paired with food resulted in decreased grooming and a slight increase in perambulation with an unchanged duration of sitting responses. Bindra and Palfai (1967) suggested that the basic effects of appetitive and defensive conditioning were an increase in specific environment-orienting and environment-rejecting behaviors, respectively, with compensatory changes in other response categories. The environment-orienting and -rejecting behaviors were in turn proposed to result from a central motive state (Bindra, 1969, 1974).

The specific purpose of the present studies was to further quantify the behavioral interactions in Pavlovian conditioning by combining the analysis of CS and UCS orienting behaviors described by Zener and Bykov with the analysis of general activity reported by Bindra and associates. The time spent in individual responses was recorded when unrestrained rats were exposed to various appetitive classical conditioning procedures. The absolute duration of each response was measured during a 10-sec CS, either a red light or a white light, and during the immediately preceding control period. The number of recorded responses was dependent upon the specific experimental procedure and progressively increased from three to seven behavioral categories across successive phases of the study. (A preliminary analysis of the present experiments was reported by Henton, 1976.)

A standard Lehigh-Valley rodent test chamber was used as the conditioning apparatus. A red jewel lamp mounted on the left side of the response panel served as CS 1, and a white lamp mounted on the right side of the panel served as CS 2 or as a neutral stimulus. Food cup 1 and food cup 2 were placed on the grid floor and attached to the front wall, 10.1 cm from the left and right cage walls, respectively. Each food cup was 3.8 × 2.5 × 1.3 cm. The two food cups were separated by a Plexiglas divider (6.4 × 0.6 × 6.4 cm) in order to more easily identify the separate orienting and approach responses to each food cup. Feeder 1 and feeder 2 were balanced to deliver single 45-mg rat food pellets into the respective food cups with an approximate latency of 0.3 sec. The back wall of the chamber was painted flat black to reduce reflected light from the CS. The chamber was placed in a semidarkened room and diffusely illuminated by approximately 25 foot-candles of ambient lighting.

The time spent in selected behaviors was recorded by the method described by Bindra and Palfai (1967) and Palfai and Cornell (1968). Each subject was observed through the right Plexiglas wall of the chamber, and the duration of each behavior was measured by completing individual electronic circuits connected to a 0.33-sec recycling timer. The separate circuits were activated by touching a stylus to metal contacts on a recording sheet. This stylus device was used rather than microswitches to eliminate the mechanical latency of switch closure. Behaviors recorded in different phases of the experiment were approach of the head within 3.8 cm of (1) stimulus 1, (2) food cup 1, (3) stimulus 2, or (4) food cup 2, plus collateral behaviors of (5) standing up on hind legs, and (6) sniffing the grid floor/sawdust waste tray (Nadel, 1968). In addition, the time spent away from the stimuli and food cups was separately recorded as time spent in the back half of the chamber. The configuration of the data-recording contacts approximated the physical location of the lights, food cups, floor, and ceiling of the subject's chamber. This relative distribution was an attempt to balance the unrecorded time spent by the subject changing over from one to another behavior by a corresponding time spent by the observer changing over from one to another recording contact. The number of 0.33-sec time units spent in each behavior was separately accumulated on individual counters for the 10-sec pre-CS (control) period and the 10-sec CS–UCS interval of each trial. All trials were initiated by the observer, but with a 5-sec delay to prevent biasing or selection of the data sample during the pre-CS period. The subjects received five conditioning trials per 30-min session, with irregular intertrial intervals varying between 5 sec and 20 min.

Delay Conditioning (Experiment IA)

The purpose of the first study was to record the relative durations of CS orienting and UCS approach responses as a replication of the Zener and Bykov experiments. In addition, standing in the back of the chamber away from the CS and UCS was recorded in each session. The study was actually divided into three phases: general habituation to the experimental chamber (5 sessions), food hopper or UCS training (5 sessions), and delay classical conditioning (10 sessions). The time spent in each behavior and experimental phase is shown in Figure 6.1. The ordinate gives the temporal probability expressed as the absolute fraction of each second allocated to each behavioral class. In the general habituation sessions, the subjects were simply placed in the chamber, and the three behaviors were recorded during five 10-sec sample periods. Orienting to both the unilluminated red light and the empty food tray was virtually zero for each subject. The time spent in the back of the chamber varied between 300 and 650 millisec/sec within and across subjects.

During the UCS training sessions, each 10-sec sample period was ended with the delivery of a single food pellet. The unsignaled delivery of the UCS increased the responses to the food cup, with a range of 75 to 300 millisec/sec for

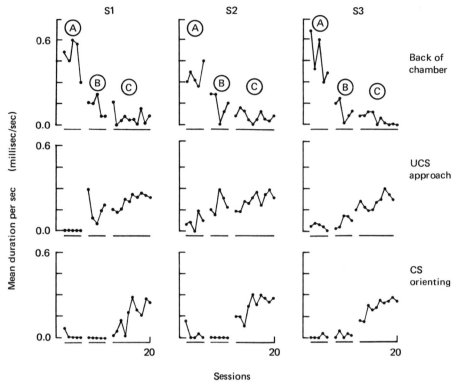

Figure 6.1. Response patterns during habituation to apparatus (A), UCS training (B), and CS–UCS pairings (C). Each column gives the data for a different subject, and each row gives the mean time spent in the back of the chamber, in UCS approach responses, or in CS orienting responses. Each data point is the mean of five trials per session.

subjects 1 and 2, and 30 to 90 millisec/sec for subject 3. The increase in approach behaviors was relatively specific to the food cup and did not generalize to increased orienting to other environmental features. The duration of orienting to the unilluminated red light, for example, remained at approximately zero for each subject. The UCS training, however, did substantially reduce the time spent in the back of the chamber from perhaps 50% to approximately 15% of the session time. This altered distribution is somewhat surprising, in that the food hopper procedure is also a standard ''UCS only'' control procedure used in classical conditioning, with typical reports of no effects of unsignaled UCS presentation (review by Kimble, 1961). The decreased time spent in the back of the chamber and the increased duration of food cup responses seem to be conditioned effects and may facilitate the subsequent effects of CS–UCS pairings.

The subjects were then trained with delay classical conditioning in each of the next 10 sessions, a total of 50 trials. The classical conditioning consisted of the red light CS presented throughout the 10-sec interval preceding UCS delivery. The three behaviors were also recorded during a 10-sec pre-CS or control period immediately preceding CS onset. During the CS–UCS interval, ori-

enting to the CS systematically increased across sessions, stabilizing at approximately 200 to 300 millisec/sec over the final 25 conditioning trials. UCS approach responses also ranged between 200 and 300 millisec/sec over the last 5
sessions. Relative to the previous UCS only training, however, the UCS responses were only slightly increased, whereas the CS orienting responses were
more substantially increased for each subject. The time spent in the back of the
chamber was generally less than 100 millisec/sec throughout the classical conditioning sessions. We should also point out that the total duration of the three
recorded responses sum to 450 to 500 millisec/sec, or approximately 45% to
50% of the CS. The remaining portion of the CS duration was allocated to
changing over from one recorded behavior to another, as well as unrecorded
collateral behaviors of sniffing the grid floor and standing up on hind legs previously described by Nadel (1968).

The primary conditioning effect was thus a sustained increase in CS orienting over successive trials, as reported by Zener (1937; also see Brown and
Jenkins, 1968), rather than the biphasic increase and decrease in CS responses
described by Bykov (1958). For each subject, 1- to 3-sec bursts of stimulus orienting alternated with equally brief bursts of preparatory UCS responses; that
is, neither CS nor UCS responses were positively accelerated during the 10-sec
CS. The regular oscillation between responses has been characterized by Zener
as the most frequent behavioral pattern during classical conditioning. However, Zener further noted that the duration of UCS responses could be increased, with a virtual elimination of CS orienting responses, by additional procedural manipulations. Although the parameters are far from clear, the
divergent patterns of high and low rates of CS orienting reported by Western
and Russian investigators might then be dependent upon additional constraints
and procedural nuances (also see Konorski, 1967).

External Inhibition (Experiment IB)

The orienting–investigatory reflexes to novel stimuli were initially described by
Pavlov as the "what is it" reflex. The phasic elicitation and extinction of stimulus-orienting reflexes have been described in some detail by Bykov (1958). Pavlov and all subsequent investigators have consistently reported the transient inhibition of other conditioned reflexes by the superimposed elicitation of
orienting to novel stimuli (i.e., external inhibition). If complimentary interdependence of reflexes is the Pavlovian mechanism of external inhibition, then we
might anticipate a reciprocal, quantitative interaction between conditioned responses and imposed orienting responses during external inhibition procedures. The first purpose of the present study was to record these interactions
when a novel stimulus was superimposed upon CS–UCS pairings. The second
purpose was to expand the number of recorded behaviors to include the sniffing
and standing behaviors observed in Experiment IA. The study was conducted
in two phases of 25 trials each, with an external inhibition procedure in Phase A
and a return to the classical conditioning baseline in Phase B.

As before, all behavior in the back of the chamber was merely recorded in

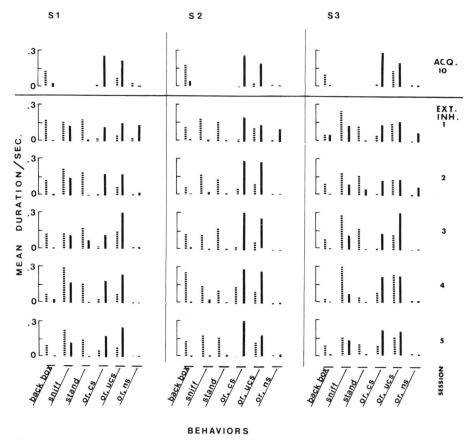

BEHAVIORS

Figure 6.2. External inhibition: distribution of responses during delay conditioning and five subsequent sessions of external inhibition (rows) for each of three subjects (columns). Each histogram gives the mean duration of each response during the 10-sec control interval (hatched bars) and the 10-sec CS–UCS interval (solid bars).

one category. Behaviors in the front half of the chamber were further subdivided into orienting to the CS, approach to the UCS, orienting to the novel stimulus, sniffing the grid floor, and standing or rearing on hind legs. The external inhibition procedure simply consisted of the white (right) light presented as a novel stimulus during the first 5 sec of the 10-sec delay conditioning procedure. Figure 6.2 presents the response profile of each subject during the five sessions of external inhibition. The last session of delay conditioning from Experiment IA is also presented for comparison. Each behavior during the CS and the immediately preceding control period is represented by solid and hatched histograms, respectively, for each subject (columns) and each session (rows) in Figure 6.2. In the first external inhibition session, orienting to the neutral stimulus occurred for approximately 100 millisec/sec during the CS, with a low or zero duration during the control periods. CS orienting and preparatory UCS responses also increased relative to the control periods, but decreased relative to the previous delay conditioning sessions. This relative attenuation of conditioned behaviors during the CS is the external inhibition effect described by Pavlov. Orienting elicited by the novel stimulus quickly habituated and decreased to zero by the second session (subject 2) or the third session (subjects 1 and 3), as previously reported by Bykov. This rapid habituation of orienting to the external inhibitor was paralleled by a progressive increase in CS and/or UCS responses over the first three sessions. The additional behaviors in the back of the chamber or sniffing and standing in the front of the chamber were reduced during the CS relative to pre-CS control rates, as previously observed during simple delay conditioning. Thus, the net effect of superimposed orienting to a novel stimulus was a change in the pattern of CS and UCS responding, rather than a change in the patterning of background collateral responses. The reciprocal interactions between orienting and conditioned responses would be consistent with the reflex antagonism model of external inhibition.

A comparison of the control and CS intervals further suggests that responses elicited by the CS, UCS, or novel stimulus were associated with matching compensatory decreases in the background collateral activities. For example, for

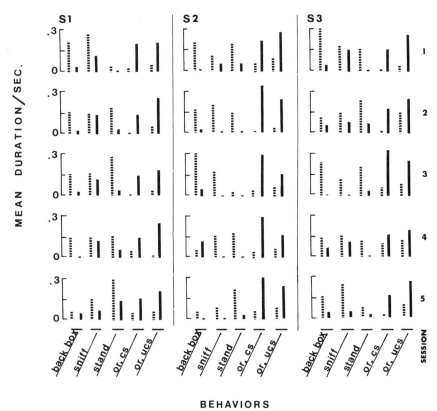

BEHAVIORS

Figure 6.3. Delay conditioning: distribution of collateral and conditioned responses during five successive sessions of delay conditioning with CS 1–UCS 1 pairings. See Figure 6.2 legend.

subject 1 in session five, responses to the CS and the UCS increased a total of 360 millisec/sec compared to the control period, and the collective time spent in all collateral responses decreased 380 millisec/sec (with an unchanged zero duration of responses to the novel stimulus). Figure 6.3 similarly presents the response profiles for each subject during simple delay conditioning in the five baseline sessions of Phase B. The increased durations of conditioned CS and UCS responses were again intimately associated with complimentary decreases in the time spent in other behaviors. To continue the example of subject 1 and session five, the total duration of CS and UCS responses increased 330 millisec/sec and the combined durations of collateral responses decreased 363 millisec/sec during the CS relative to the control interval. The quantitative results simply demonstrate that background activities are inhibited by superimposed CS and UCS responses in the same reciprocal manner that the conditioned responses are themselves externally inhibited by imposed orienting responses.

Extinction (Experiment IC)

The elimination of conditioned behaviors by the repeated presentation of the CS without the UCS is frequently viewed as a prototypical model of internal inhibition. The gradual decrement in responses was described by Pavlov as an interaction between inhibitory and excitatory processes within the CS–UCS bond, rather than as an antagonism toward other conditioned reflexes. The neurophysiological evidence for the internal inhibition model has recently been reviewed by Asratian (1969) and Molnar and Grastyan (1972). Alternatively, other investigators have reported behavioral effects of extinction that do not wholly support the internal inhibition model nor the usual dichotomy of internal versus external inhibition. Konorski (1967), for example, used a repeated acquisition–extinction procedure and found rapid sequential changes in the conditioned responses that are inconsistent with the gradual accumulation of internal inhibition. Wendt (1936) and Zener (1937) also reported qualitative observations of complimentary behavioral interactions during extinction, not a simple decrement in conditioned responses. The present study was an attempt to systematically replicate the observations of Wendt and Zener by measuring the actual time spent in competing behaviors during classically conditioned extinction.

The subjects and delay conditioning procedures of the preceding experiments were used again, with the exception that the 10-sec CS was no longer terminated by the UCS food pellet. Extinction was continued for 10 sessions (50 trials). Figure 6.4 presents the response distributions for each subject during sessions 1, 3, 5, 7, 9, and 10. CS-orienting and UCS approach responses progressively decreased across the successive extinction sessions for all subjects. In general, approach to the UCS food cup appeared to extinguish marginally faster than orienting to the CS. By the seventh session, the response distributions were relatively equivalent during the control and CS intervals, with virtually zero durations of CS and UCS responses. This extinction of condi-

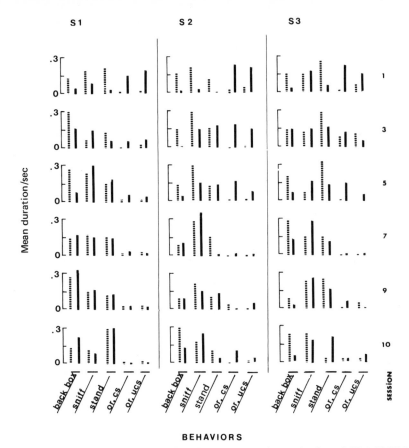

BEHAVIORS

Figure 6.4.   Extinction: distribution of responses during extinction of CS 1–UCS 1 conditioning. See Figure 6.2 legend.

tioned responses was associated with a corresponding increase in the collateral responses during the CS. In the latter sessions, the response interactions were primarily corresponding increases and decreases in the durations of individual collateral responses, rather than the previous interactions between conditioned and collateral behaviors.

The quantitative interactions are especially consistent with the previous observations of complimentary interactions during extinction procedures (Wendt, 1936; Zener, 1937). Extinction procedures thus do not simply inhibit conditioned responses, but instead generate complex, reciprocal interactions involving increasing as well as decreasing response probabilities. Traditionally, extinction has been argued to be only a response decrementing procedure, and therefore would be most consistent with an internal inhibition model of Pavlovian extinction. In turn, the recorded behavioral decrements seemed to obviously oppose external inhibition accounts, which required increments in antagonistic behaviors. Wendt, however, insisted that a simple behavioral decrement interpretation is more of an accurate description of limited behavioral analysis than an analysis of the subject's actual behavior. The present results amplify Wendt's concern that CR inhibition should not be generalized as an unbiased description of all behaviors during Pavlovian extinction.

A basic argument against extinction as reciprocal inhibition is the apparent requirement for an acquisition of competing responses in the absence of any acquisition reinforcement procedure. The present results would suggest, however, that the acquisition of additional competing behaviors is not basic to an external inhibition account of extinction. The competing behaviors were in fact intrinsic to the classical conditioning procedure in the form of ongoing collateral responses during the intertrial interval. During acquisition, the ongoing stream of behaviors is disrupted or suppressed by conditioned responses elicited by the CS–UCS pairings (as in Experiments IA and IB). Extinction may only lower the frequency of changing over from ongoing behaviors to previously conditioned responses at CS onset. In this system, extinction may be a passive failure of formerly conditioned responses to inhibit ongoing intertrial interval behaviors, rather than an active inhibition of conditioned responses by the acquisition of still more competing behaviors.

However, as noted by Wendt and throughout this volume, response elimination procedures involve special difficulties in identifying the initial or primal cause of the altered behavioral interactions. On one hand, the initial effect may be a decrement in one overt response allowing increased durations of other behaviors. This decremental interpretation would not necessarily be embarrassing to an internal inhibition model expanded to predict complimentary incremental effects. Alternatively, the first effect may be the extinction of changeover responses, with the high and unchanged rate of ongoing collateral responses mediating the low rates of CR. This latter interpretation would be more akin to the complimentary inhibition account proposed by Konorski (1967, 1972). Moreover, pure instances of internal and external inhibition may only be problematic and perhaps an illusory theoretical dichotomy. In either theoretical case, extinction procedures clearly involve a progression of complex behavioral interactions that seem to be directly amenable to a systematic empirical analysis.

Delay Conditioning plus Inhibition of Extinction (Experiment ID)

One derivative of extinction as only an inhibitory procedure is the proposition that internal inhibition will spread to combine with and reduce the excitation of other reflexive behaviors (Pavlov, 1927). Alternatively, a complimentary response inhibition would deny a generalized suppression by a superimposed extinguished CS, and instead propose that any disruption of the reference reflex is related to specific competing responses maintained by the extinction procedure. In the present experiment, the extinquished CS 1 used in Experiment IC was superimposed upon a delay conditioning baseline. The fundamental question was whether the inhibition of extinction would generalize to decrement the

time spent in all other behaviors or would differentially suppress baseline responses by eliciting antagonistic behaviors.

Initially, CS 2 (the white, right light) was illuminated for 10 sec and paired
with UCS 2 (delivery of one food pellet into food cup 2). Next, the previously
extinguished CS 1 (the red, left light of Experiment IC) was also illuminated
throughout the 10-sec CS 2–UCS 2 delay interval. Each experimental phase
lasted 10 sessions, with 5 trials per session. Recorded responses were orienting
and approach to CS 1, CS 2, UCS 1, UCS 2, standing up, or floor sniffing in
the front half of the chamber, and the collective time spent in the back of the
chamber.

Figure 6.5 presents the mean duration of each response during the acquisition of CS 2–UCS 2 delay conditioning. Orienting to CS 2 and approach to UCS
2 increased over the initial sessions and stabilized at approximate asymptotic
levels by the fifth acquisition session for all subjects. Relative to the intertrial
control periods, the increments in CS 2–UCS 2 behaviors were associated with
compensatory decrements in the time spent sniffing, standing, or in the back of

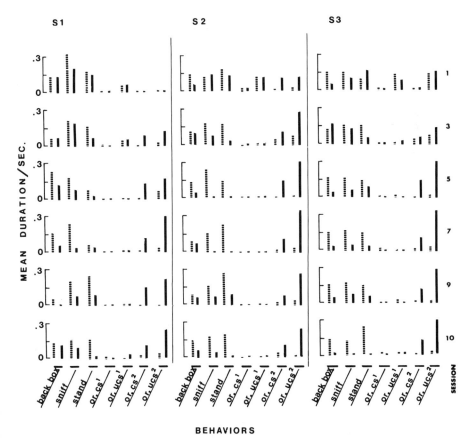

BEHAVIORS

Figure 6.5. Delay conditioning with CS 2–UCS 2: distribution of responses during the acquisition
of 10-sec delay conditioning using CS 2–UCS 2 pairings. See Figure 6.2 legend.

the chamber. For each subject, the final response pattern stabilized more rapidly during this CS 2–UCS 2 conditioning than during the original CS 1–UCS 1 conditioning in Experiment IA. However, CS orienting was markedly less than UCS approach responses in the present study, in contrast to the regular oscillation and approximately equal durations of CS and UCS responses with the CS 1–UCS 1 pairings in Experiment IA. This change to a predominance of UCS responses is analogous to the patterns described by Bykov (1958) and reported for "high hunger states" by Zener (1937).

In addition, the present CS 2–UCS 2 pairings also induced a transient increase in the extinguished approach responses to the UCS 1 food cup (sessions 1 to 3). The UCS 1 responses not only were elicited by the onset of CS 2, but also increased during the intertrial control periods. The increments in UCS 1 responses within sessions 1 to 3 were followed by a return to the near zero, extinguished baselines by session 5 for each subject. In contrast, responses to the unilluminated former CS 1 remained at unchanged zero duration throughout the CS 2–UCS 2 conditioning. This transient "spontaneous recovery" of previously extinguished reflexes was noted by Pavlov when his subjects were returned to the conditioning chamber or exposed to unsignaled delivery of the former UCS. The increased UCS 1 responses may be related to the spontaneous recovery phenomenon, especially since the UCS 2 food pellets were identical to the former UCS 1 and perhaps were functionally unsignaled during the early CS 2–UCS 2 pairings.

Second, the usual definition of excitatory conditioning as only response-incrementing techniques also seems to be somewhat inaccurate. The disruption of normal activities by a CS previously paired with shock was described by Bindra and Palfai (1967), with the proposal that the response disruption may be identical to the conditioned suppression of operant responses by superimposed classical conditioning (Brady and Hunt, 1955). This disruption or suppression

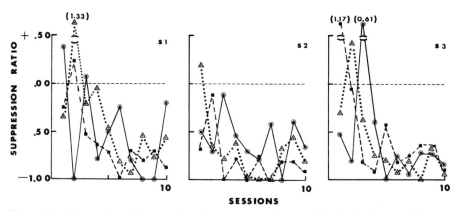

Figure 6.6. Suppression of three collateral responses during appetitive Pavlovian conditioning of three subjects. Each data point is the percent change in response duration during the CS relative to the control period (Hunt et al., 1952). Complete response suppression is −1.00. Each data point is the mean of five trials per session. Circled points indicate back of box; triangles: sniffing; solid squares: standing up.

of each collateral response is given in Figure 6.6, expressed as a ratio of the response times during the control period (i.e., the "inflection" ratio of Hunt et al., 1952; also see Chapter 1, this volume). With the apparent exceptions of sessions 1 to 3, the probability of each response was clearly decreased during the CS. The magnitude of disruption was relatively variable across sessions and response classes. Experimenter-imposed events, such as CS–UCS pairings, may then result in the disruption of the subject's current behavior as well as the acquisition of additional behaviors. The apparent interactions between collateral behaviors and CS 2–UCS 2 responses argue that excitatory conditioning, like inhibitory conditioning, may be a mixed amalgam of incremental and decremental effects.

The further effects of adding the previously extinguished CS 1 are described in Figure 6.7. The behavioral changes were quite marginal and were limited to a transient increase in CS 1 and UCS 1 responses for subject 3 and, to a lesser extent, subject 1. The small increments in orienting and approach to CS 1 and UCS 1 resulted in equally small decrements in both CS 2 and UCS 2 responses. The final response patterns over the latter sessions were limited to the usual

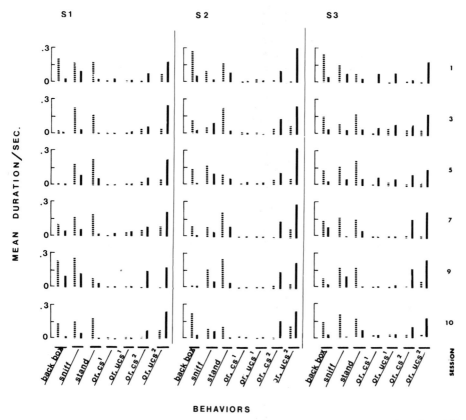

BEHAVIORS

Figure 6.7. Superimposed inhibition of extinction: mean duration of responses during CS 2–UCS 2 delay conditioning when combined with previously extinquished CS 1. See Figure 6.2 legend.

interactions between the three collateral behaviors and CS 2–UCS 2 responses and were indistinquishable from the response patterns during the previous delay conditioning sessions for each subject. The effects of an extinquished CS upon Pavlovian baselines are apparently marginal and temporary and may be dependent upon the spontaneous recovery of formerly extinguished responses.

The marginal effects of the inhibitory CS 1, however, provide only an inverted description of the more robust stimulus overshadowing effects described by Pavlov. That is, CS 1 and CS 2 were simultaneously presented and terminated by the same UCS food pellet, yet orienting responses were consistently elicited only by CS 2, not CS 1, throughout the 50 compound-stimulus conditioning trials. Pavlov (1927) described similar procedures that resulted in responses predominantly conditioned to one stimulus element rather than equally conditioned to both elements of a compound CS. The asymmetrical stimulus–response bias may be dependent upon a variety of variables and has been extensively described by Wagner and Rescorla (1972) and Kamin (1969). Similar to most tests of conditioned inhibition, the inhibitory procedure in the present study was a compound classical conditioning method combining two stimuli with divergent conditioning histories. The slight inhibitory effects of CS 1 could be equally well described as an overshadowing of CS 1 by CS 2 during the compound trials. The biased responding within each compound trial is consistent with the overshadowing effects usually assessed by separate test trials with each CS element (Kamin, 1969; Rescorla and Wagner, 1972; Wagner and Rescorla, 1972). Inhibition by an imposed CS and overshadowing by the baseline CS might then be opposing results defining the continuum of possible interactions between the different responses elicited by each CS element.

Delay Conditioning: Replication (Experiment IE)

Sidman's review of scientific research methods (1960) described a variety of experimental techniques to establish the generality and reliability of empirical relationships. A systematic replication procedure was adopted throughout the present experiments, for example, and the collective results suggest that behavioral interactions commonly occur over a wide range of classical conditioning situations. The reliability of experimental findings may also be assessed by a second technique of direct replication, or duplication of previous procedures. The purpose of the last study was to use the direct replication method to further examine the internal consistency and reliability of the observed response patterns. The 10-sec delay conditioning of Experiment IA was repeated, but with the collateral responses as well as CS and UCS responses recorded during each trial. Figure 6.8 presents the duration of each response during the five CS 1–UCS 1 trials of sessions 1, 3, 5, 7, 9, and 10. In session 1, CS orienting and UCS approach increased up to 140 millisec/sec relative to intertrial control rates. The CS 1–UCS 1 pairings also generated a transient increase in approach responses to the empty UCS 2 food cup (subjects 1 and 2) or to the unilluminated CS 2 (subject 3) used in the previous study. Similar to the original conditioning in Experiment IA, CS 1 and UCS 1 responses again increased to asymptotic levels over successive conditioning sessions, with a further inhibition of collat-

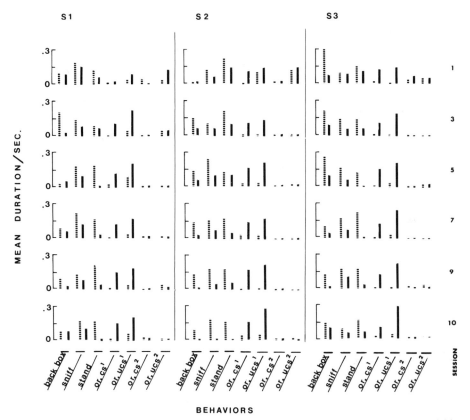

Figure 6.8. Reacquisition of delay conditioning: distribution of responses during the reacquisition of delay conditioning with the previously extinguished CS 1 paired with UCS 1. See Figure 6.2 legend.

eral responses and an unchanged zero duration of CS 2 and UCS 2 responses. For each subject, the time allocated to UCS 1 responses was consistently greater than the time spent in CS 1 orienting responses. These results substantially replicate the behavioral patterns observed in the comparable delay conditioning in Experiment IA, using CS 1–UCS 1 pairings, and Experiment ID, using CS 2–UCS 2 pairings. Moreover, many experiments in the present series are in fact direct or systematic replications of the conditioning effects described by previous investigators (Wendt, 1936; Zener, 1937; Palfai and Cornell, 1968). The data within and across replications strongly suggests that classical conditioning methods consistently elicit broad changes in the distribution and temporal integration of mutually antagonistic response systems (Anohkin, 1958; Konorski, 1967).

Summary

From the outset, a major finding of the concurrent responses analysis has been the seemingly intimate relationships between the probability of any given response and the concurrent probabilities of other respondents, operants, and collateral behaviors in the subject's repertoire (Brady and Hunt, 1955; Henton and Brady, 1970; Henton, 1972; Henton and Iversen, 1973; Iversen, 1975). We have noted throughout the present experiment, for example, that the absolute duration of any one response is closely associated with complimentary alterations in the obtained durations of other responses. The conditional probability of one response upon the simultaneous probabilities of concurrent responses might then be used to formally describe the behavioral patterns generated by conditioning schedules:

$$\text{Time } Rs_{a,...,n(\text{CS})} = \text{Time } Rs_{a,...,n(\text{pre}-\text{CS})} = 1000 \text{ millisec/sec.} \tag{1}$$

This descriptive equation represents the exhaustive case, when the total time of all recorded responses (Rs $a, \cdots n$) equals the total available time during the CS and the pre-CS control intervals. The absolute time spent in any given response may be partialed out of the total response time, yielding

$$R_{a(\text{CS})} = R_{a(\text{pre-CS})} + Rs_{b,...,n(\text{pre-CS})} - Rs_{b,...,n(\text{CS})} \tag{2}$$

or

$$R_{a(\text{CS})} - R_{a(\text{pre-CS})} = -[Rs_{b,...,n(\text{CS})} - Rs_{b,...,n(\text{pre-CS})}] \tag{3}$$

Equation 2 specifies that the time spent in any response a during the CS is dependent upon the base duration of that response during the pre-CS and the concurrent changes in the durations of all other responses $b, \cdots, n$. Equation 3 suggests that any alteration in the duration of a single response a will exactly balance the collective changes in all other responses over the two time samples.

Unfortunately, the equations must be immediately scrapped and are little more than concise descriptions of our long-sought goal of complete behavioral analysis. Contemporary experimental techniques most frequently record only one response, accounting for a few hundred milliseconds per second. The present procedures are only slightly less removed from the ideal; and recorded seven responses summing to no more than 700 millisec/sec. Equation 1 may be reformulated, however, to describe more realistically our current capabilities by replacing the equal symbol with an approximation. Equation 1 would then recognize our less than complete behavioral analysis and propose that the actually recorded durations during the CS could only approximate the actually recorded response durations during the pre-CS. The accuracy of the approximation would be systematically increased as more and more responses are analyzed and the total durations approach 1000 millisec/sec in each time interval. More simply, the accuracy of behavioral analyses is directly dependent upon recording all relevant behaviors that are present, rather than conjectured responses that are nevertheless absent. Alternatively, the inaccuracy of the approximation is the discrepancy between the summed durations recorded during the CS and the pre-CS time samples. Similarly, Equations 2 and 3 could be rewritten as approximations to propose that the recorded changes in one response will approximately balance the simultaneous changes in other recorded responses.

Figure 6.9 presents a comparison of the obtained duration of each response during the CS in Experiment IE relative to the duration expected by Equation 3. The data for each subject in Figure 6.9 correspond to the results presented in Figure 6.8. The obtained durations during the CS closely approximated the net changes in the concurrent probabilities of other responses for each subject. The maximal discrepancy between calculated and obtained durations ranged from an underestimation of 87 millisec/sec (subject 2, session 2, not shown) to an overestimation of 100 millisec/sec (subject 3, sessions 1 and 3). In general, the error was greater during the acquisition of new behavioral patterns in the initial sessions than for the stabilized response patterns within the final sessions. The mean error for each of the final five sessions ranged from -60 to $+13$, -75 to $+13$, and -33 to $+47$ millisec/sec for subjects 1, 2, and 3, respectively. The quantitative interactions thus quite firmly describe a substantial interdependence in the temporal patterning of concurrent responses. Indeed, a literal application of the response interaction analysis rather accurately describes the

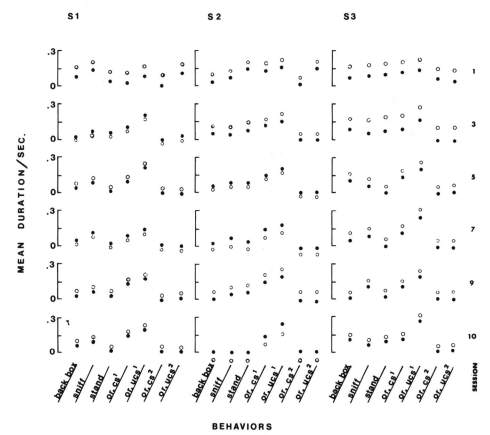

Figure 6.9. Obtained duration of each response during the CS (filled circles) compared to expected duration (open circles). Expected duration is the complement of the summed changes in all other responses. Each data point is the mean of five delay conditioning trials per session.

absolute duration of each of seven recorded responses within and across individual sessions and subjects, with a maximum error of about 100 millisec/sec. Moreover, the accuracy was neither generated by massive statistical averaging nor numerous statistical assumptions.

The individual analysis of each session and subject was limited to a comparison of five 10-sec pre-CS periods with five 10-sec CS–UCS intervals, or a total of two 50-sec samples. Presumably, sophisticated statistical treatments across a large number of trials or sessions would create at least the appearance of greater precision. Second, the analysis describes the duration of collateral and conditioned responses with equivalent accuracy. This result suggests that the quantitative analysis is relatively free of underlying assumptions concerning the emitted, elicited, or adjunctive nature of individual responses; that is, the concurrent responses analysis is behaviorally atheoretical as well as statistically nonparametric, and thus equally applicable to various combinations of operants, respondents, and collateral behaviors. Such an equivalence principle, however, is only a more formal restatement of the empirical generality of response interactions previously noted within various operant conditioning procedures (Part II) and classical–operant combinations (Part I).

Although gratifyingly accurate, we should nevertheless hope that the present analysis may be further improved by more complete data recording. As noted above, the seven responses recorded in the present procedures accounted for perhaps 700 millisec/sec, with a resultant discrepancy between available and obtained response durations of at least 300 millisec/sec. This discrepancy is in fact the so-called behavioral pause and is the magnitude of error within a concurrent response analysis. The error in Equation 3 reduces to the discrepancy between the amount of behavior analyzed during the pre-CS and CS intervals. This bias may be illustrated with the two sets of data presented in Table 6.1. For the data from session 8, the total response times during the CS and the pre-CS are equal. Therefore, the changes in the absolute duration of any arbitrary response would precisely equal the net change in the remaining six responses. On the other hand, the response times during the pre-CS summed to 55 millisec/sec more than the CS response times for the data from session 9 (Table 6.1). As a result of the recording discrepancy, a change in any one response cannot precisely balance the net change in the other recorded responses. Thus, the relationship between any given response and recorded concurrent responses would necessarily be in error by 55 millisec/sec (the "behavioral pause"). This recording of different amounts of behavior in two time samples is the usual disproof of complimentary behavioral changes. Yet, the apparent deviation from true reciprocity is a constant, dependent upon the total amount of behavior recorded, and not a variable dependent upon the specific characteristics of any response. The divergent response totals are a direct consequence of the failure to analyze behavior during 432 millisec/sec of the pre-CS but 487 millisec/sec of the CS.

A behavioral analysis may then be unintentionally altered by yet unanalyzed behaviors such as grooming, immobility, etc., as well as the inherent differences within the set of required changeover responses. For example, the

Table 6.1   Relative changes in response duration (millisec/sec): subject 2

Responses	Pre-CS	CS	Net change	Change other responses	Deviation from exact reciprocity
Session 8					
Back of Chamber	330	26	− 304	304	0
Front of Chamber					
Sniffing	140	33	− 107	107	0
Standing	60	66	6	− 6	0
Orient CS 1	0	178	178	− 178	0
Orient UCS 1	90	317	227	− 227	0
Orient CS 2	0	0	0	0	0
Orient UCS 2	0	0	0	0	0
Total	620	620			
Session 9					
Back of Chamber	139	20	− 119	64	55
Front of Chamber					
Sniffing	191	66	− 125	70	55
Standing	205	59	− 146	91	55
Orient CS 1	20	151	131	− 186	55
Orient UCS 1	13	217	204	− 259	55
Orient CS 2	0	0	0	0	55
Orient UCS 2	0	0	0	0	55
Total	568	513			

change-over time from spatially separated responses (such as standing in the back of the chamber to CS orienting in the front of the chamber) is substantially greater than the changeover time between spatially close responses (such as orienting to the CS and approach to the neighboring UCS). The unrecorded durations and patterns of changeover responses therefore should affect the distribution of reference responses. Thus, the absolute duration of a recorded response is determined by alterations in any and all concurrent responses, independent of whether the behaviors happen to be recorded by the experimenter.

Equating inaccuracy with unrecorded events is admittedly a begging of assumptions, no matter how logically derived. The same point may be empirically derived, however, by analyzing the successive higher order relationships between specifically recorded responses. Figure 6.10 presents the relative increments in one response during the CS compared to the simultaneous changes in one response, or the combined changes in two, three, and four concurrently available responses. Figure 6.10A shows that the increase in UCS responses cannot be fully explained by simultaneous changes in the time spent in the back of the chamber. For each subject, the time in the back of the chamber generally underestimates the concurrent changes in UCS responses. The seeming absence of any close relationship might then be logically generalized to suggest a comparable lack of association with all other responses. Alternatively, the ap-

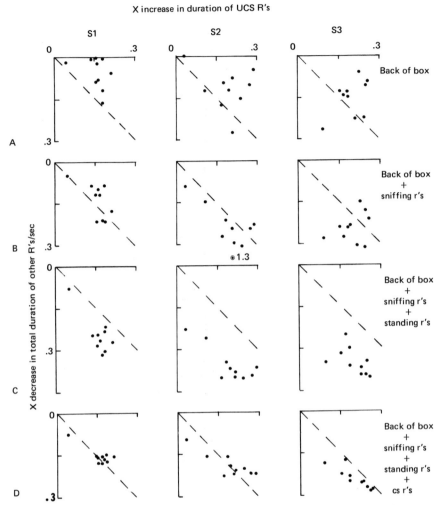

Figure 6.10. Changes in UCS responses relative to the simultaneous changes in other responses. **A.** Change in 1 response. **B.** Net change in 2 concurrent responses. **C.** Net change in 3 concurrent responses. **D.** Net change in 4 concurrent responses. Each data point is the mean of 5 trials for each of 10 delay conditioning sessions.

parent discrepancy may be a failure to describe other relevant responses. The underestimation of UCS response durations is substantially altered by expanding the analysis to include a second response (Figure 6.10B) and a third response (Figure 6.10C). The collective changes in the three collateral responses would then result in an overestimation of UCS responses for each subject. Again, the relationship between responses might be offered as a disproof of behavioral interactions, or merely a failure to record actual behaviors.

A further expansion of the analysis to include CS orienting responses would yield the close relationship between responses in Figure 6.10D. Conversely, responses to CS 2 and UCS 2 were at virtually zero durations throughout both the pre-CS and the CS for each subject, as shown in Figure 6.8. The absence of interactions involving CS 2 and UCS 2 responses therefore do not alter the obtained response relationships and were not included in Figure 6.10. That is, the potential behaviors that do not occur during an experiment could be listed ad infinitum but are quite irrelevant to the actual response patterns generated by particular conditioning schedules. In each case, the discrepancy within arbitrary comparisons is systematically related to unanalyzed occurrences of actual behavior, and thus is systematically eliminated by the additional analysis of concurrent responses. A more complete description of classical conditioned effects might then be profitably based upon a comprehensive analysis of behavioral patterns, rather than an isolated analysis of individual responses abstracted out of the behavioral matrix.

Concurrent Classical Conditioning (Experiments II, III, and IV)*

Some years ago, we summarized our data in a 16-fold table comparing classical and operant procedures superimposed upon other classical or operant conditioning baselines (Henton and Iversen, 1973). In the case of classical conditioning, clearly similar response patterns occur when (1) classical conditioning is superimposed upon an operant baseline, or (2) operant procedures are superimposed upon a classical conditioning baseline (Chapter 2, this volume). The purpose of the final set of experiments was to offer a preliminary analysis of the third and remaining combination, classical conditioning superimposed upon classical conditioning.

The concurrent classical conditioning methods used in Experiment II are described in Figure 6.11. Initially, all subjects were trained with CS 1 and UCS 1

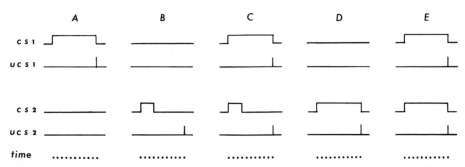

Figure 6.11. Classical conditioning used in Phases A to E of Experiment II. **A.** Delay conditioning with CS 1–UCS 1. **B.** Trace conditioning with CS 2–UCS 2. **C.** Concurrent delay–trace conditioning. **D.** Delay conditioniing with CS2–UCS 2. **E.** Concurrent delay–delay conditioning. Top to bottom traces: onset of CS 1, UCS 1, CS 2, UCS 2, and time in 1-sec intervals, respectively.

* Experiments were conducted by W. Henton, Washington, D. C., from May 1975 to June 1976.

in a simple delay conditioning procedure (Phase A), then with CS 2 and UCS 2 in a trace conditioning procedure (Phase B), and finally with the delay and trace conditioning components combined into a concurrent schedule (Phase C, concurrent delay–trace conditioning). Next, the CS 2–UCS 2 trace conditioning was altered to simple delay conditioning (Phase D), which was later superimposed upon the CS 1–UCS 1 delay conditioning (Phase E, concurrent delay–delay conditioning). The concurrent delay–trace schedules of Phase C and the concurrent delay–delay schedules of Phase E are thus related to traditional compound stimulus procedures, but with the addition that each CS element is individually terminated by an independent UCS.

Concurrent Delay–Trace Conditioning (Experiments IIA,B, and C)

Three experimentally naive Long-Evans rats were trained in a three-phase experiment, each phase consisting of 5 trials in each of 10 sessions. The apparatus and data recording methods described in Experiment I were used throughout the present study. In Phase A, the left, red light (CS 1) was presented for 10 sec and immediately terminated by one food pellet delivered into food cup 1 (UCS 1). In Phase B, the right, white light (CS 2) was illuminated for 3 sec, followed by a 7-sec interval, and then the delivery of one food pellet into food cup 2 (UCS 2). In Phase C, the onsets of the 10-sec CS 1 and the 3-sec CS 2 were simultaneous; both UCS 1 and UCS 2 were delivered 10 sec after CS onset.

The duration of CS orienting and UCS approach responses for the acquisition of CS 1–UCS 1 delay conditioning is shown in Figure 6.12A, CS 2–UCS 2 trace conditioning in Figure 6.12B, and concurrent delay-trace conditioning in Figure 6.12C. The delay conditioning in Phase A generated the typical increase in CS 1 and UCS 1 responses across sessions, as described in Experiment I. In contrast, the trace conditioning in Phase B resulted in lower response durations for all subjects. Also, the relative proportions of CS orienting and UCS approach responses were variable across subjects, with CS 2 orienting most probable for subject 1, UCS 2 approach responses most probable for subject 3, and a more intermixed response pattern for subject 2. Trace conditioning therefore seems to support lower frequencies and shorter durations of both CS orienting and UCS approach responses compared to simple delay conditioning. The lowered probability of conditioned UCS consummatory responses has frequently been noted in trace conditioning by Pavlov and many other workers. Although tentative, the present results imply that CS orienting is also sharply reduced in trace conditioning relative to delay procedures.

The concurrent conditioning in Phase C elicited slightly different interactions between the delay and trace conditioned responses across subjects. For subject 1, CS 1 and UCS 1 responses were clearly inhibited relative to the previous delay conditioning baselines of Phase A, while CS 2 and UCS 2 responses were less disrupted relative to the trace conditioning baselines of Phase B. For subjects 2 and 3, however, the concurrent procedures resulted in a more mutual inhibition of the CS 1–UCS 1 and CS 2–UCS 2 responses relative to the previous baselines. The trace conditioned responses were slightly more affected

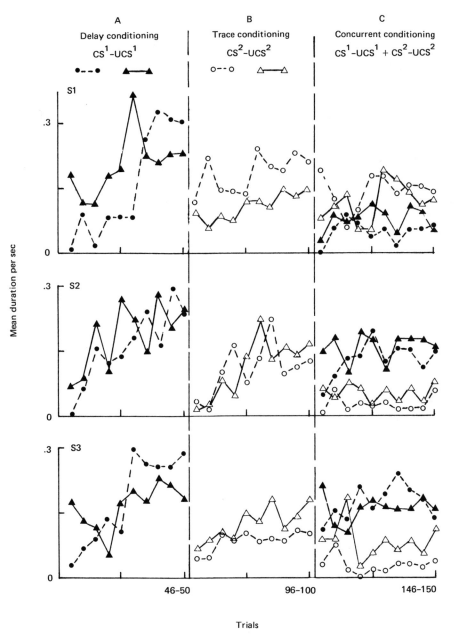

Figure 6.12. Mean duration of CS orienting and UCS approach responses. **A.** CS 1–UCS 1 delay conditioning. **B.** CS 2–UCS 2 trace conditioning. **C.** Concurrent delay (CS 1–UCS 1)–trace (CS 2–UCS 2) conditioning. Each row gives the data for a different subject, and each data point is the mean of five trials.

than the delay conditioned responses for both of these subjects. For all subjects, CS orienting tended to be more disrupted than UCS approach responses within each component of the concurrent schedules. In all comparisons, response durations were unequally distributed between CS 1 and CS 2 responses, between UCS 1 and UCS 2 responses, and between the collective time spent in delay conditioned CS 1–UCS 1 responses and trace conditioned CS 2–UCS 2 responses. The unequal distributions of concurrent responses therefore did not "match" the equal rates of obtained UCS reinforcers and would not support a response–reinforcer matching theory for concurrent classical conditioning schedules.

Response profiles for delay, trace, and concurrent delay–trace schedules are given in Figure 6.13. As in Experiment IA, the delay procedure increased CS 1 and UCS 1 responding, with a concomitant inhibition of the three collateral responses relative to control periods. In a like fashion, the trace conditioning increased CS 2 and UCS 2 responses with simultaneous decrements in collateral responding. The responses elicited by CS 1 and UCS 1 were markedly attenuated by the concurrent conditioning in Phase C compared to the delay conditioning in Phase A. Similarly, the conditioned increments in CS 2 and UCS 2 responses were attenuated during the concurrent conditioning relative to the previous trace conditioning in Phase B. The three collateral responses, however, were approximately equally suppressed during the concurrent CSs as during the previous baseline phases for each subject. Thus, the concurrent

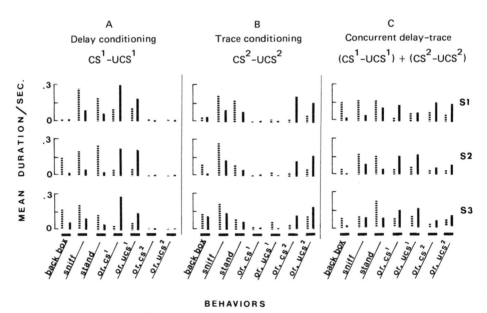

Figure 6.13. Response distribution during control and CS–UCS intervals. **A.** Last session of delay conditioning. **B.** Last session of trace conditioning. **C.** Last session of concurrent delay–trace conditioning. See Figure 6.2 legend.

schedule did not result in an additive inhibition of collateral responses, but a mutual inhibition of delay and trace conditioned responses.

Parallel interactions were also observed during the intertrial interval, with corresponding interactions between the two sets of CS orienting and UCS approach responses. Initially, CS 1 and UCS 1 responses were most probable during the control intervals of the delay conditioning in Phase A, but CS 2 and UCS 2 responses were more frequent during the control intervals of the trace conditioning in Phase B. Combining the two sets of responses resulted in lower frequencies of each response during the control intervals of the concurrent schedules relative to the previous baselines. Concurrent classical–classical conditioning therefore systematically alters the characteristic response pattern of each schedule component, with both subtle and obvious pattern changes throughout the conditioning sessions.

Concurrent Delay–Delay Conditioning (Experiments IID,E)

The CS 2–UCS 2 procedure was changed to a simple 10-sec delay conditioning for the next 10 sessions (Phase D), which was in turn superimposed upon the 10-sec CS 1–UCS 1 delay conditioning baseline (Phase E). The effects of this concurrent delay–delay conditioning are described in Figure 6.14. The last four sessions of the previous concurrent delay–trace conditioning are also presented for comparison in Figure 6.14A. The schedule change to simple delay conditioning in Phase D resulted in an immediate increase in orienting to CS 2 for each subject. Responses to UCS 2 also increased, but more gradually, across the 10 CS 2–UCS 2 delay conditioning sessions. The proportion of CS orienting and UCS approach responses over the final sessions closely replicated the relative response distributions during the comparable CS 1–UCS 1 delay conditioning in Phase A, with subjects 1 and 3 spending more time in CS orienting, and subject 2 spending marginally more time in UCS approach responses.

Combining the two delay components into a concurrent schedule again generated different interaction patterns across subjects. For subjects 1 and 2, the delay–delay conditioned patterns were relatively comparable to the interactions with the delay–trace schedules of Phase C (comparison of Figures 6.14C and 6.14A). Subject 1 spent relatively more time responding to the CS 2–UCS 2 component, whereas subject 2 responded more to the CS 1–UCS 1 component. For subject 3, however, orienting to CS 2 was clearly greated during delay–delay conditioning than delay–trace conditioning. This predominance of CS 2 responses resulted in a further inhibition of concurrent CS 1 and UCS 1 responses.

A more detailed analysis of the individual response profiles is presented in Figure 6.15 for the last session of concurrent delay–delay conditioning (Figure 6.15B) compared to the last session of concurrent delay–trace conditioning (Figure 6.15A). For all subjects, response times were asymmetrically distributed across the two delay conditioning components, and again did not correspond to the matched parameters and obtained rates of UCS reinforcers. The relative distributions of both CS and UCS responses therefore do not simply

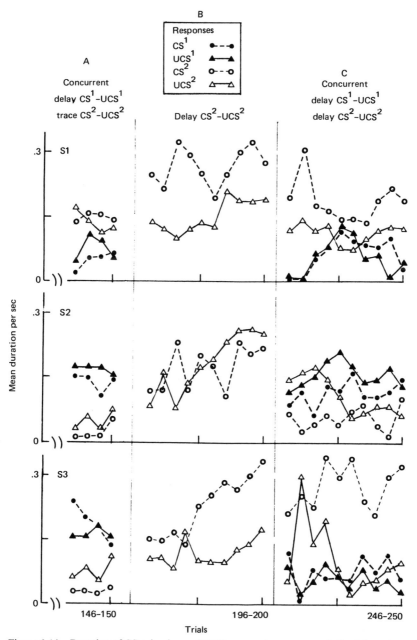

Figure 6.14. Duration of CS orienting and UCS approach responses. **A.** Last 4 sessions of concurrent delay–trace conditioning. **B.** Next 10 sessions of simple delay conditioning. **C.** Next 10 sessions of concurrent delay–delay conditioning. Each row gives data for a different subject.

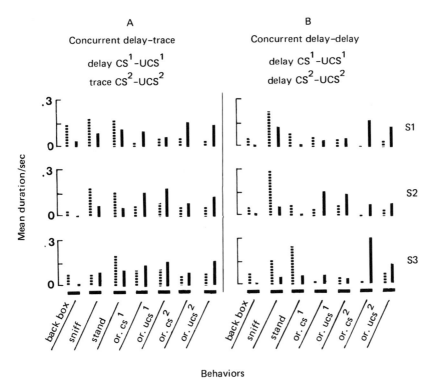

Figure 6.15. Response distribution during control and CS–UCS intervals. **A.** Last session of concurrent delay–trace conditioning. **B.** Last session of concurrent delay–delay conditioning. Each row gives the data for a different subject.

reflect the relative strength of the UCS. The response patterns seem to be more adequately described as the complimentary inhibition of concurrent responses, in the reciprocal inhibition model, rather than reinforcer inhibition, in the reinforcer value model.

The idiosyncratic patterns of responding across subjects emphasize that a uniform experimenter manipulation does not necessarily result in a uniform conditioned effect. Individual differences, although commonly reported in the operant literature, are frequently washed out in the averaging of classical conditioning data over groups of subjects. Instead, individual differences may be as common in respondent as in operant conditioning, with the effects of a given environmental manipulation importantly conditional and constrained by distinct interaction patterns within the response matrix.

The obtained deviation from exact complimentary response interaction is presented in Figure 6.16 for each subject, phase, and session of Experiment II. Each data point represents the discrepancy between the recorded response durations during the CS and control intervals. The deviation from exact reciprocity was relatively equal within and across the various experimental phases, with similar deviations obtained with delay conditioning (Phases A and D),

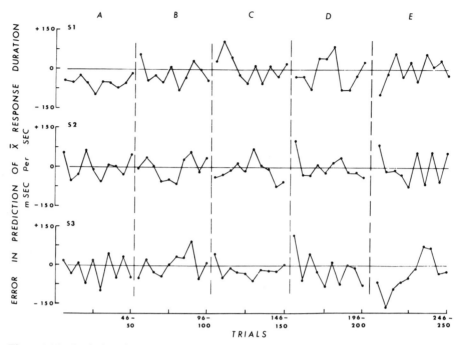

Figure 6.16.   Deviation of responses during the CS from true complementary interactions for each session of each phase of Experiment II. Each data point is the difference between obtained response durations and the exact complement of all changes in other recorded responses in milliseconds per second. Each data point is the mean of five trials.

trace conditioning (Phase B), and the more complex schedules of delay–trace conditioning (Phase C) and delay–delay conditioning (Phase E). The difference between obtained and expected response durations was less than 100 millisec/sec for 146 of the 150 session means in Figure 6.16. (The exceptions are subject 1, Phase E, session 1; subject 2, Phase D, session 1; and subject 3, Phase D, session 1 and Phase E, session 2.) The balancing pattern of simultaneous response probabilities clearly suggests an interdependence rather than an independence of concurrent responses in a variety of classical conditioning procedures. In summary, the quantitative nature of the present results affirm the previous competing response and complimentary inhibition interpretations of classical conditioned effects (Zener, 1937; Anohkin, 1958; Konorski, 1967).

Concurrent Delay–Delay Conditioning: Systematic Replication (Experiment III)

To some extent, the final behavior patterns noted in the previous study could have been influenced by the sequential order of the delay and trace conditioning components across the successive experimental phases. The purpose of the present experiment was to replicate the effects of concurrent delay–delay conditioning with four additional subjects by using slightly different procedures.

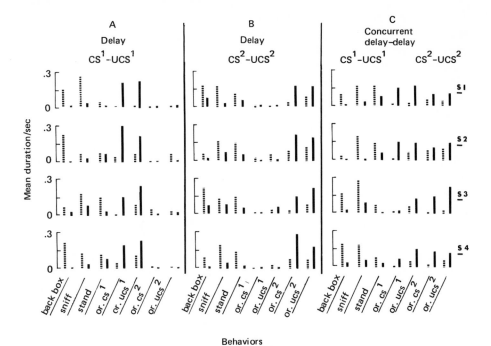

Behaviors

Figure 6.17. Replication of response distributions. **A.** Simple CS 1–UCS 1 delay conditioning. **B.** Simple CS 2–UCS 2 delay conditioning. **C.** Concurrent delay–delay conditioning. Each row gives the data for a different subject. See Figure 6.2 legend.

Each 30-min session was initially divided into two equal parts, with one block of five trials using CS 1–UCS 1 pairings and a second block of five trials using CS 2–UCS 2 pairings. In each case, a simple 10-sec delay procedure was used, with intertrial intervals ranging between 20 sec and 10 min. The sequential order of conditioning trials was alternated within daily sessions. The two delay conditioning components were then simultaneously scheduled in 10 additional sessions in Phase B, with 10 trials scheduled at intervals ranging between 20 sec and 5 min.

The initial acquisition and terminal pattern of delay conditioned responses were qualitatively comparable to the data described in previous studies in this section. Figure 6.17 presents a summary comparison of the response profiles during the last session of CS 1–UCS 1 delay conditioning (Figure 6.17A), CS 2–UCS 2 delay conditioning (Figure 6.17B), and concurrent delay–delay conditioning (Figure 6.17C). For a given subject, the response distributions were quite similar within each of the two delay conditioning components. The CS 1–UCS 1 pairings and the CS 2–UCS 2 pairings elicited virtually equal durations of CS orienting and UCS approach responses for subject 1. In contrast, subject 2 spent marginally more time in CS orienting, and subject 3 spent marginally more time in UCS approach responses in each of the separate delay conditioning components. The single exception is that subject 4 spent relatively more time in food cup approach responses in the CS 1–UCS 1 pairings, but more time in CS orienting in the CS 2–UCS 2 pairings. For all subjects, responses in the back of the chamber or sniffing and standing in the front of the chamber were inhibited during the CS relative to the control intervals.

The distribution of responses within the concurrent conditioning phase were consistent within individual subjects but again variable cross subjects, as in the preceding Experiment II. CS 1–UCS 1 responses were most common for subject 1, CS 2–UCS 2 responses were most common for subject 3, and there was a more intermixed distribution across the two conditioning components for subjects 2 and 4. As before, the concurrent delay–delay procedure did not result in an increased suppression of the collateral responses relative to previous baselines, but instead generated reciprocal decrements in the CS and UCS responses conditioned within each component. As one example, CS 1 plus UCS 1 responses by subject 4 decreased a total of 252 millisec/sec during the concurrent CSs compared to the previous CS 1–UCS 1 delay conditioning, with an approximately balancing increase of 235 millisec/sec in CS 2 and UCS 2 responses (comparison of bottom rows of Figures 6.17A and 6.17C). Relative to the CS 2–UCS 2 delay conditioning, CS 2 plus UCS 2 responses decreased a total of 228 millisec/sec during the concurrent CSs, with a simultaneous increase of 211 millisec/sec in CS 1 and UCS 1 responses (bottom row of Figure 6.17B versus 6.17C). Substantially similar patterns of mutual increments and decrements in concurrent responses were obtained with subjects 1, 2, and 3. The interlocking distributions of responses, both within and across conditioning components, systematically replicate the patterns obtained with the delay–delay conditioning in Experiment II. The complimentary inhibition of responses, relative to both control periods and previous baselines, would be yet again consistent with the suggestion that overt responses are disrupted to the degree that other behaviors are increased.

Concurrent Trace–Trace Conditioning (Experiment IV)

Given concurrent delay–delay and delay–trace conditioning, one last experiment remains—an experiment to examine concurrent trace–trace classical conditioning. The next study therefore examined the concurrent response patterns when two separately established trace conditioning procedures were scheduled simultaneously. The study was also designed with several additional and secondary purposes.

The data analysis to this point has involved an interaction analysis of seven responses manually recorded by the investigator. This procedure introduces two attendant problems. First, such observation procedures are open to observer bias, with at least the potential for selectively recording and misrecording data. The problem is not immediately solved by electronic instrumentation, however, since data displayed on counters and recorders can also be easily selected and misreported. For this reason, sciences rich in theory and inference such as psychology especially require cross-laboratory verification of experimental results. Indeed, the traditional defense against continuing prejudicial experimental descriptions has been the success or failure of direct and systematic replication by the scientific community. We can only note here that the present observer recordings are fundamentally consistent with the previous results obtained in other laboratories (e.g., Zener, 1937; Konorski, 1967, 1972; Patton and Rudy, 1967; Palfai and Cornell, 1968), and we can only expect that the results will also be consistent with future experimental findings.

A second problem of observer recordings is the time required daily to conduct one study at the expense of other experimenter activities. This is, if you will, a competing response analysis of the experimental behavior of the investigator rather than the subject and is more immediately solved by automated data recording. The secondary purpose of the experiment was then to instrument the classical conditioning chamber and thereby attenuate the potential problem of observer bias and reduce the experimental time devoted to data recording.

The conditioning chamber was rebuilt with transparent Plexiglas, with light-sensitive photocells (Archer 276-176, 1.3 cm diameter) placed 2.5 cm immediately above each CS and each UCS food cup. A directional lamp holder was fashioned from a miniature in-line phone jack and surgically fixed to the midline of the subject's skull. A white 12-V minilamp was attached to the screw base of the phone jack, with the forward intensity set to activate each photocell when the subject was within 5.0 cm and facing the corresponding CS or food cup. To minimize light reflection within the chamber, the front wall was painted flat black, except for a 1 cm^2 area in front of each photocell, and the entire back wall was also blackened. The side walls remained transparent for observation of the subjects with a closed-circuit television camera. To avoid masking of the CSs by the white directional light, CS 1 and CS 2 were changed respectively to yellow and green jewel lamps that blinked on and off 6 times/sec. A 5 × 5 matrix of photocells was placed beneath the Plexiglas floor to record downward orientation of the head, approximating the previous manually recorded floor sniffing responses. Standing up on hind legs was also recorded as the relative position of a counterbalanced arm connected to the wires and lamp mounted on the subject's skull. Standing responses were defined as the vertical position of the subject's head 12.5 cm or more above the floor. However, the time spent in the back half of the chamber was not separately recorded in the present study. The experiment thus additionally served as a systematic replication of the previous experiments by using an automated apparatus and six rather than seven recorded response categories. [Blough (1977) has recently reported a similar although reverse technique for recording stimulus-orienting behaviors. In the Blough apparatus, a single photocell is mounted on the subject and various light sources are placed within the environment, with the coincidence of photocell activation matched to the unique flicker rate of each stimulus by an on-line computer.]

Three experimentally naive Long-Evans rats were initially trained with separate 10-trial blocks of CS 1–UCS 1 pairings and CS 2–UCS 2 pairings within each session. A 10-sec delay procedure was used in each block of trials during the first five sessions (Phase A), but was then altered to trace conditioning for 10 additional baseline conditioning sessions (Phase B). Trace conditioning consisted of a 5-sec CS, followed by a 5-sec trace interval, and then the response-independent delivery of one food pellet into the appropriate food cup. The 50 trials of Phase A and the 100 trials of Phase B with each conditioning component thus served as an automated replication of simple delay conditioning and simple trace conditioning. The response distributions during the last sessions of delay conditioning are given in Figure 6.18A and those of trace conditioning are described in Figure 6.18B for subjects 1, 2, and 3.

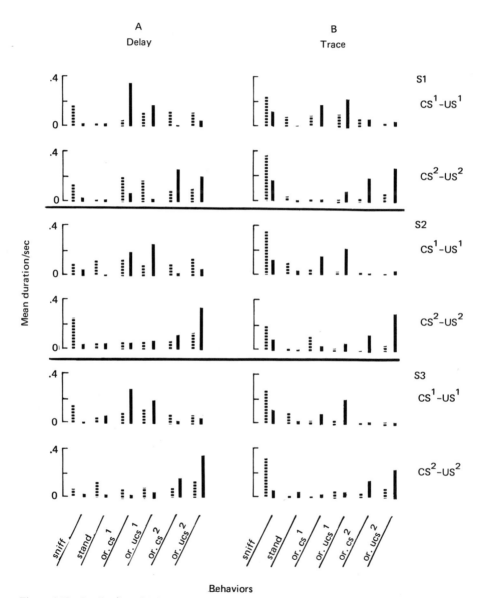

Figure 6.18. Replication of delay and trace conditioning using automated apparatus. **A.** Delay conditioning. **B.** Trace conditioning. Each pair of rows shows data for different subject. See Figure 6.2 legend.

Subjects 1 and 2 developed a consistent pattern of responses across both delay conditioning components, with relatively more CS orienting in each component for subject 1 and relatively more UCS approach responses for subject 2. In comparison, subject 3 spent more time in CS orienting responses within the CS 1–UCS 1 pairings but more time in UCS approach responses within the CS 2–UCS 2 pairings. This comparison of response patterns across different subjects is quite similar to the individual distributions of delay conditioned responses manually recorded in the previous experiments (e.g., Figure 6.17).

With the trace conditioning, UCS responses were consistently more probable than CS orienting in each component for all subjects. The relatively greater probability of UCS responses was independent of whether CS responses or UCS responses had been more probable during the previous delay conditioning of each subject. Also, the combined durations of conditioned CS and UCS responses were somewhat decreased during trace conditioning relative to the comparable durations in the delay conditioning phase. As a consequence, floor sniffing was somewhat increased during the trace pairings compared to the previous delay procedure; that is, floor sniffing was relatively more suppressed by the higher durations of delay conditioned responses and relatively less suppressed by the lower durations of trace conditioned responses.

(Standing responses were at relatively low durations during the intertrial interval as well as during the CS–UCS interval of the trace conditioning for all subjects. This low probability of standing responses during the intertrial interval is not in agreement with the probabilities recorded in all previous experiments. A session by session examination of the data revealed that standing initially occurred at relatively long durations in the first two or three delay conditioning sessions, with mean durations ranging up to 289, 476, and 323 millisec/sec for subjects 1, 2, and 3, respectively. These mean durations decreased to no more than 83 millisec/sec during the latter trace conditioning sessions. Perhaps one possibility is that the lamp holder and attached wires, the smooth Plexiglas floor, or some other equipment modification might have reduced the probability of standing responses over successive sessions, although this now remains only a speculation.)

In the final Phase C, the trace conditioned CS 1–UCS 1 responses and the trace conditioned CS 2–UCS 2 responses were concurrently scheduled for 10 sessions. The concurrent trace–trace conditioning consisted of 10 trials per session, with intertrial intervals ranging between 20 sec and 5 min. Figure 6.19 presents the response distributions during the control and CS intervals for concurrent sessions 1, 3, 5, 7, 9, and 10 for each subject. The simultaneous presentation of the two trace components produced distinctive response increments and decrements for each subject. The concurrent procedure resulted in a mutual inhibition of all conditioned responses for subject 1, with responding to each CS and each UCS decreased relative to the previous individual baselines. The response patterns were more asymmetric for subjects 2 and 3, with a differential inhibition of the behaviors within one of the two trace conditioning components. Initially, for subject 2, the CS 2–UCS 2 responses were relatively unchanged compared to simple trace conditioning, with a concurrent suppression of CS 1 and UCS 1 responses. A transition to a reversed interaction began with

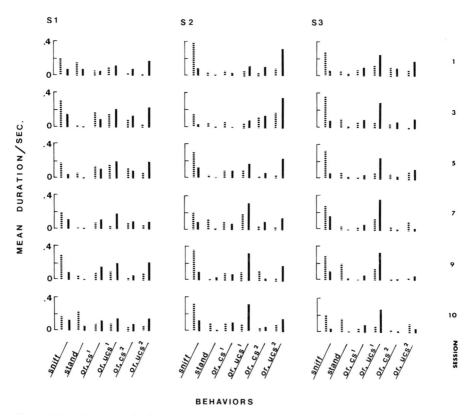

Figure 6.19. Response distributions during concurrent trace–trace classical conditioning. Columns give data for individual subjects and rows give data for different sessions. See Figure 6.2 legend.

session 5, with a resultant predominance of CS 1–UCS 1 responses and inhibition of the formerly dominant CS 2–UCS 2 responses across the final sessions. A similar pattern of differential responding to CS 1 and UCS 1 occurred consistently throughout all concurrent sessions for subject 3. For each subject, UCS approach responses remained relatively more frequent that the corresponding CS orienting responses within each component, independent of the overall distribution between the two components. The relative increments and decrements in any one response during the CS–UCS interval were counterbalanced by reciprocal changes in one or more concurrent responses to within 100 millisec/sec for 104 of the 120 blocks of trials throughout the study.

The interactions recorded electronically in the present trace–trace conditioning thus systematically replicate the asymmetric distributions of responses across components in the previous delay–delay and delay–trace conditioning. Apparently, all types of concurrent classical conditioning tend to differentially inhibit conditioned responses in one component, conditional upon relative and reciprocal increments in other conditioned responses maintained by the concurrent component.

Lastly, an Esterline-Angus strip chart recorder was added to the equipment for this experiment, and we might appropriately end this chapter with a more molecular trial by trial analysis of the responses within concurrent classical conditioning. Figure 6.20 presents the temporal pattern of concurrent responses within selected trials for subject 2. The records in Figure 6.20A are from the last session with isolated CS 1–UCS 1 pairings and CS 2–UCS 2 pairings. In each simple trace conditioning procedure, floor sniffing intermittently occurred throughout the pre-CS control interval, with occasional orienting to the unilluminated CS or approach to the empty UCS food cup. The onset of the trace CS elicited immediate if relatively brief orientation to the appropriate CS, followed by a changeover to the corresponding UCS food cup. Offset of the 5-sec CS and the beginning of the 5-sec trace interval frequently elicited a changeover to a concurrent response, such as orienting to the unilluminated CS 2 in the trace interval of the CS 1–UCS 1 component, or approach to the empty UCS 1 food cup during the CS 2–UCS 2 trace interval. Preparatory responses

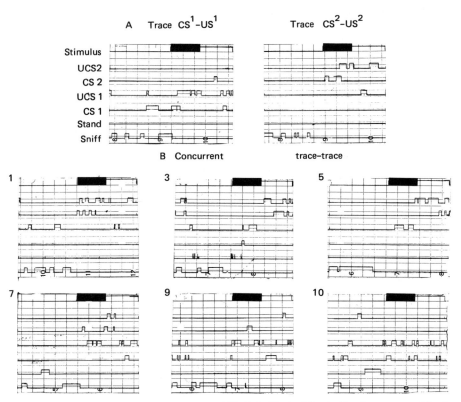

Figure 6.20. Concurrent response patterns within individual trials. **A.** Simple trace conditioning with CS 1–UCS 1 and CS 2–UCS 2 pairings. **B.** Concurrent trace–trace conditioning from sessions 1, 3, 5, 7, 9, and 10. Individual tracings within each strip chart are, from top to bottom, (1) onset of the 5-sec CS plus the 5-sec trace interval; (2) UCS 2 approach responses; (3) CS 2 orienting responses; (4) UCS 1 approach responses; (5) CS 1 orienting responses; (6) standing on hind legs; and (7) sniffing/orienting toward the floor.

to the appropriate UCS food cup were the most frequently elicited response throughout the last 2 or 3 sec of the trace interval of each component.

Concurrent trace–trace conditioning generated the response patterns shown in Figure 6.20B. The successive changes and pattern transitions described in the previous figure for subject 2 are also apparent in the individual trials taken from sessions 1, 3, 5, 7, 9, and 10. The concurrent CSs initially elicited responses within the CS 2–UCS 2 component, with a low or zero concurrent probability of CS 1 and UCS 1 responses. This response pattern mainly consisted of rapid alternation between brief bursts of CS 2 orienting and UCS 2 approach responses. Over subsequent sessions, onset of the two CSs progressively elicited more and more responses to the CS 1–UCS 1 component, with a growing inhibition of the formerly dominant CS 2–UCS 2 responses. The temporal patterning in the latter concurrent trials was then similar to the interactions with simple CS 1–UCS 1 trace conditioning, virtually as if the CS 2–UCS 2 component had not been concurrently scheduled. In the final sessions, preparatory UCS 1 responses were most frequent during both the CS and the subsequent trace intervals, with occasional changeovers to CS 1 responses but a continuing inhibition of the concurrent CS 2–UCS 2 responses. Additionally, the collateral responses of floor sniffing and standing that occurred during the intertrial interval were also suppressed to near zero probabilities during the CS–UCS interval. Similar interactions between the six recorded responses were obtained for subjects 1 and 3.

Summary

The reciprocal frequencies and patterns of responses within concurrent classical conditioning share some common characteristics with the behavioral patterns in concurrent classical–operant conditioning (Part I). In each case, the set of responses controlled by a classical conditioning component is markedly altered by the additional set of responses maintained by the concurrent component, independent of whether that alternate component is a classical or an operant conditioning procedure. The changes in any one response seem to be dependent upon the actual elicitation or emission of concurrent responses and occur in both the presence and absence of any specifically delivered reinforcer. Indeed, the local and averaged response probabilities are frequently asymmetric across components with equated rates of reinforcers in concurrent delay–delay conditioning, concurrent delay–trace conditioning, and concurrent trace–trace conditioning. The data therefore suggest that the obtained response patterns do not simply reflect the value of the reinforcer or the valence of a state isomorphic with reinforcer value. All too frequently such discrepancies are resolved by argument for the primacy of the assumed explanatory state and the irrelevancy of peripheral responses in classical conditioning. An uncomfortable relationship between explanation and observation may be differently resolved, however, by appealing to the primacy of observed events and the irrelevancy of assumed causality. Although starting from different perspectives, we can at least agree with Holland's recent concerns that the relationship between assumed associative states and conditioned responses "may well be looser than is usually assumed" and may reflect "differences in the nature of responding, which were perhaps unrelated to the strength of association" (Holland, 1977, p. 102).

The results of concurrent schedules involving one or more classical conditioning components are also consistent with the response interactions obtained when two operant conditioning procedures are concurrently scheduled (Part II). The combined results again indicate that the effects of concurrent schedules are related to actual probabilities of concurrent responses instead of molar states or predispositions to respond. This dissociation of actual from potential functional relationships is most readily apparent in the analysis of local probabilities and trial to trial response patterns. The resultant pattern analysis of concurrently available responses is then at least broadly consistent with the principle that similar response interactions may, or indeed must, occur in concurrent classical–classical schedules, classical–operant schedules, and operant–operant schedules.

Concurrent classical conditioning is then but one of many procedures that simultaneously control the rates and patterns of interacting sets of responses. As in Konorski's system, the experimental evidence suggests that even "simple" classical conditioning procedures may be viewed as temporally concurrent schedules of experimental events, with the CS and associated responses variously combined with a UCS and associated preparatory or consummatory responses, and the entire lot imposed upon ongoing behaviors maintained by still other environmental variables. Such an analysis is not far removed from the suggestion that even "simple" operant schedules also have many of the functional properties of concurrent schedules controlling reinforced, collateral, and ongoing behaviors. This response pattern analysis of both classical and operant conditioning has therefore been both the title and substance of this volume.

Response patterns as basic characteristics of conditioning schedules unfortunately run headlong into the prevalent belief that overt responses are irrelevant to the analysis of schedule effects. The supposedly trivial and irrelevant nature of response interactions is especially entrenched in classical conditioning—so much so that many authors insist that overt conditioned responses are of little interest and useless to the "proper" interpretation of Pavlovian conditioning. In reply, however, Razran (1965) some years ago pointed out that American interpretations are not necessarily consistent with the analysis of Pavlov and subsequent Russian investigators. Razran's thesis was that Pavlovian principles were frequently altered and revised to suit the needs of then dominant American theory ("passing Pavlov through Hull's wringer"), with current theories being ideological revisions of still previous revisions of Pavlov. The debate over skeletal responses in classical conditioning is one such case. The initial reporting in the American literature of motor and skeletal responses directed to the CS (Zener, 1937; Patton and Rudy, 1967) plausibly argued for an elimination of the autonomic–skeletal distinction between classical and operant conditioning, and, more recently, some reconsideration of whether such overt responses violate stimulus substitution theory of classical conditioning (e.g., Mackintosh, 1974). In contrast, Russian investigators have all along insisted upon overt responses as one of the integral components of conditioned reflexes, and the reporting of skeletal responses therefore did not require the overthrow or revision of Pavlovian theory. Furthermore, many East European and Russian investigators deny that sustained CS orienting ("autoshaping") responses are conditioned reflexes, and therefore do not require any redefinition of stimulus substitution. Konorski (1967), for example, described the maintenance of CS-directed responses as the adventitious instrumental reinforcement of orienting reflexes by the delivery of the UCS reinforcer. Although such adventitious reinforcement effects were initially dismissed by American authors, more recent studies have implicated response–reinforcer contingencies in the maintenance of CS-directed responses (Wessells, 1974; Deich and Wasserman, 1977). Ironically then, Western psychologists have argued that CS autoshaping responses are true examples of Pavlovian conditioning principles, yet Pavlovian investigators argue that such responses may be examples of instrumental or Skinnerian conditioning.

A more fundamental distinction, however, is that Pavlovian analysis is not restricted to the examination of cognitive states or autonomic responses, and is certainly not based on the assumption that skeletal responses are irrelevant to the study of classical conditioning. Indeed, overt responses may be seen to be a part of rather than a threat to Pavlovian analysis. Bykov (1958), for example, insisted that motor responses are especially advantageous to the study of the dynamic interactions between orienting–exploratory reactions and conditioned consummatory reflexes, and their mutual interactions with still other activities which serve as the background to conditioned reflexes. The interactions between CS orienting responses, UCS approach responses, and ongoing intertrial interval behaviors in the present series of experiments then firmly commit us to a similar view of overt responses as fundamental rather than trivial characteristics of classical conditioning.

We therefore have good reason to believe that concurrent response patterns may be used to some advantage in the analysis of Pavlovian conditioning. More particularly, the response patterns verify a central principle offered by a broad spectrum of previous researchers. A common thread shared by investigators from Anohkin to Zener has been the analysis of response interactions, and has been summarized with a simple clarity by Konorski: "Inhibition of the maladaptive motor acts occurs owing to excitation of neurons eliciting antagonistic motor acts" (1972, p. 354). The present concurrent response analysis of classical conditioning, as our previous analyses of other schedules, is therefore neither new nor unique, but simply fits within a more extensive context of previous work.

We would surely be remiss, however, if we at all implied that a concurrent response analysis is finished or complete at this point. The examination of response patterns has too often been foreclosed by denials of skeletal behaviors in classical conditioning to be yet complete. Moreover, Anohkin (1958) has set out three general types of interactions between polyeffector reflexes: conflict or mutual exclusion, assimilation, and transformation of one reflex by another. The data presently in hand are primarily concerned with the first and most common type of interaction between overt responses. The latter two interactions of assimilation and transformation may well be involved in summation and facilitation of overt responses, and are especially in need of laboratory investigation. Furthermore, the concomitant relationships between covert and overt responses are not yet understood, nor are the higher order relationships between sets of covert–overt responses interacting with other polyeffector response sets. Currently, we can only prejudicially guess whether skeletal, autonomic, endocrine, and cardiovascular response patterns are intrinsically fixed or are composed of interacting yet separable (Brady, 1971) or dissociable (Black, 1972) responses influenced by myriad variables and contingencies. The recent work by Powell and associates, Obrist, and other investigators is fortunately directed toward this much needed analysis (Obrist et al., 1970; Howard et al., 1974; Powell and Joseph, 1974; Powell et al., 1976).

Still more demanding and difficult is the eventual analysis of sequential as well as concurrent response patterns. The large but finite number of concurrent interactions is enormously expanded when the analysis is extended to the sequential permutations of responses ordered across time. Such a detailed analysis of response chains and sequences has now been initiated by Ray, whose timely report (Ray, 1977) is an elegant example of sequential analysis of overt responses in Pavlovian conditioning. Additional examples of response sequences in classical conditioning are presented in Figure 6.20. Moreover, these sequential changes do not differ notably from the sequential changeovers between responses in operant conditioning schedules (Part II) or classical–operant combinations (Part I). Again, our argument is not that cognitive-based theory cannot accurately specify response patterning, but only that explanations of behavior should do so. We must then conclude, perhaps reluctantly, that concurrent and sequential pattern analyses are only beginning rather than finishing, but nevertheless offer the promisory note of a more complete understanding of conditioning and behavior.

References

Anohkin, P. K.: The role of the orienting–exploratory reflex in the formation of the conditioned reflex. In, L. G. Voronin, A. N. Leontiev, A. R. Luria, E. N. Sokolov, and O. S. Vinogradova (eds.): *Orienting Reflex and Exploratory Behavior.* Moscow, Academy of Pedagogical Sciences, 1958.

Anohkin, P. K.: *The Biology and Neurophysiology of the Conditioned Reflex.* Moscow, Medihsina, 1968.

Arnold, M. B.: Emotion, motivation and the limbic system. *Ann. N. Y. Acad. Sci., 159,* 1041–1056, 1969.

Asratian, E. A.: Mechanism and localization of conditioned inhibition. *Acta Biol. Exp. 29,* 271–291, 1969.

Bindra, D.: A unified interpretation of emotion and motivation. *Ann. N. Y. Acad. Sci., 159,* 1071–1083, 1969.

Bindra, D.: A motivational view of learning, performance, and behavior modification. *Psychol. Rev., 81,* 199–214, 1974.

Bindra, D., and Palfai, T.: Nature of positive and negative incentive motivational effects on general activity. *J. Comp. Physiol. Psychol.,* **63,** 288–297, 1967.

Biriukov, D. A.: On the nature of the orienting reaction. In, L. G. Voronin, A. N. Leontiev, A. R. Luria, E. N. Sokolov, and O. S. Vinogradova (eds.): *Orienting Reflex and Exploratory Behavior.* Moscow, Academy of Pedagogical Sciences, 1958.

Black, A. H.: Autonomic aversive conditioning in infrahuman subjects. In, R. F. Brush (ed.): *Aversive Conditioning and Learning.* New York, Academic Press, 1971.

Black, A. H.: The operant conditioning of central nervous system electrical activity. In, G. H. Bower (ed.): *The Psychology of Learning and Motivation.* New York, Academic Press, 1972.

Black, A. H., and Prokasy, W. F. (eds.): *Classical Conditioning II.* New York, Appleton-Century-Crofts, 1972.

Blough, D. S.: Visual search in the pigeon: hunt and peck method. *Science,* **196,** 1013–1014, 1977.

Boring, E. G.: *A History of Experimental Psychology.* New York, Appleton-Century-Crofts, 1957.

Brady, J. V.: Emotion revisited. *J. Psychiatr. Res.,* **8,** 363–384, 1971.

Brady, J. V., and Hunt, H. F.: An experimental approach to the analysis of emotional behavior. *J. Psychol.,* **40,** 313–325, 1955.

Brady, J. V., Kelly, D. D., and Plumlee, L.: Autonomic and behavioral responses of the rhesus monkey to emotional conditioning. *Ann. N. Y. Acad. Sci.,* **150,** 959–975, 1969.

Brown, P. L., and Jenkins, H. M.: Auto-shaping of the pigeon's key peck. *J. Exp. Anal. Behav.,* **11,** 1–8, 1968.

Brozek, J.: Soviet psychology. Appendix B in M. N. Marx and W. A. Hillix: *Systems and Theories in Psychology.* New York, McGraw-Hill, 1963.

Brozek, J.: Recent developments in Soviet psychology. *Annu. Rev. Psychol.,* **15,** 493–594, 1964.

Bykov, V. D.: On the dynamics of the orienting–exploratory reaction during the formation of positive and inhibitory conditioned reflexes and their alterations. In, L. G. Voronin, A. N. Leontiev, A. R. Luria, E. N. Sokolov, and O. S. Vinogradova (eds.): *Orienting Reflex and Exploratory Behavior.* Moscow, Academy of Pedagogical Sciences, 1958.

Creed, R. S., Denny-Brown, D., Eccles, J. C., Lidell, E. G. T., and Sherrington, C. S.: *Reflex Activity of the Spinal Cord.* London, Oxford University Press, 1932.

Deich, J. D., and Wasserman, E. A.: Rate and temporal pattern of key pecking under autoshaping and omission schedules of reinforcement. *J. Exp. Anal. Behav.,* **27,** 399–405, 1977.

Graham, F.: Habituation and dishabituation of responses inneverated by the autonomic nervous system. In, H. V. S. Peeke and M. J. Hertz (eds.): *Habituation,* vol. 1. New York, Academic Press, 1973.

Hartline, H. K.: The response of single optic nerve fibers of the vertebrate eye to illumination of the retina. *Am. J. Physiol.,* **121,** 400–415, 1938.

Henton, W. W.: Avoidance response rates during a pre-food stimulus in monkeys. *J. Exp. Anal. Behav.,* **17,** 269–275, 1972.

Henton, W. W.: Concurrent response patterns in simple and concurrent classical conditioning following exposure to microwave radiation. Paper read at Southeastern Psychological Association, New Orleans, March 1976.

Henton, W. W., and Brady, J. V.: Operant acceleration during a pre-reward stimulus. *J. Exp. Anal. Behav.,* **13,** 205–209, 1970.

Henton, W. W., and Iversen, I. H.: Concurrent response rates during pre-event stimuli. Paper read at the Easter Conference, Cambridge, March 1973.

Hineline, P. N.: Varied approaches to aversion: a review of aversive conditioning and learning. *J. Exp. Anal. Behav.,* **19,** 531–540, 1973.

Holland, P. C.: Conditioned stimulus as a determinant of the form of the Pavlovian conditioned response. *J. Exp. Psychol.* [*Anim. Behav. Processes*], **3,** 77–104, 1977.

Howard, J. L., Obrist, P. A., Gaebelein, C. J., and Galosy, R. A.: Multiple somatic measures and heart rate during classical aversive conditioning in the cat. *J. Comp. Physiol. Psychol.,* **87,** 228–236, 1974.

Hunt, H. F., Jernberg, P., and Brady, J. V.: The effect of electroconvulsive shock (ECS) on a conditioned emotional response: the effect of post-ECS extinction on the reappearance of the response. *J. Comp. Physiol. Psychol.,* **45,** 589–599, 1952.

Iversen, I. H.: Reciprocal response interactions in concurrent variable interval and discrete trial fixed ratio schedules. *Scand. J. Psychol., 16,* 280–284, 1975.

Jones, W. T.: *A History of Western Philosophy.* New York, Harcourt, Brace, 1952.

Kamin, L. J.: Predictability, surprise, attention and conditioning. In, B. A. Campbell and R. M. Church (eds.): *Punishment and Aversive Behavior.* New York, Appleton-Century-Crofts, 1969.

Kimble, G. A.: *Hilgard and Marquis' Conditioning and Learning.* New York, Appleton-Century-Crofts, 1961.

Konorski, J.: *Conditioned Reflexes and Neuron Organization.* London, Cambridge University Press, 1948.

Konorski, J.: *Integrative Activity of the Brain.* Chicago, University of Chicago Press, 1967.

Konorski, J.: Some ideas concerning physiological mechanisms of so-called internal inhibition. In, R. A. Boakes and M. S. Halliday (eds.): *Inhibition and Learning.* New York, Academic Press, 1972.

Kupalov, P. S.: General results of the study of cerebral inhibition. *Zh. Vyssh. Nerv. Deiat., 5,* 157–172, 1955.

Lynn, R.: *Attention, Arousal and the Orientation Reaction.* London, Pergamon Press, 1966.

Mackintosh, N. J.: *The Psychology of Animal Learning.* New York, Academic Press, 1974.

Molnar, P., and Grastyan, E.: The significance of inhibition in motivation and reinforcement. In, R. A. Boakes and M. S. Halliday (eds.): *Inhibition and Learning.* New York, Academic Press, 1972.

Mowrer, O. H.: *Learning Theory and Behavior.* New York, Wiley, 1960.

Myer, J. S.: Some effects of noncontingent aversive stimulation. In, R. F. Brush (ed.): *Aversive Conditioning and Learning.* New York, Academic Press, 1971.

Nadel, L.: Dorsal and ventral hippocampal lesions and behavior. *Physiol. Behav., 3,* 891–900, 1968.

Obrist, P. A., Webb, R. A., Sutterer, J. R., and Holland, J. L.: The cardiac–somatic relationship: some reformulations. *Psychophysiology, 6,* 569–587, 1970.

Osgood, C. E.: *Method and Theory in Experimental Psychology.* New York, Oxford University Press, 1953.

Palfai, T., and Cornell, J. M.: Effect of drugs on consolidation of classically conditioned fear. *J. Comp. Physiol. Psychol., 66,* 584–589, 1968.

Patton, R. L., and Rudy, J. W.: Orienting during classical conditoning: acquired vs. unconditioned responding. *Psychonomic Sci., 7,* 27–28, 1967.

Pavlov, I. P.: Scientific study of the so-called psychical processes in higher animals. Paper read at Charing Cross Medical School, London, 1906, reprinted in W. Dennis (ed.): *Readings in the History of Psychology.* New York, Appleton-Century-Crofts, 1948.

Pavlov, I. P.: *Conditioned Reflexes.* London, Oxford University Press, 1927.

Pavlov, I. P.: The reply of a physiologist to psychologists. *Psychol. Rev., 39,* 91–127, 1932.

Powell, D. A., and Joseph, J. A.: Autonomic–somatic interaction and hippocampal theta activity. *J. Comp. Physiol. Psychol., 87,* 978–986, 1974.

Powell, D. A., Milligan, W. L., and Buchanan, S. L.: Orienting and classical conditioning in the rabbit (Oryctolagus cuniculus): effects of septal lesions. *Physiol. Behav., 17,* 955–962, 1976.

Prokasy, W. F. (ed.): *Classical Conditioning: A Symposium.* New York, Appleton-Century-Crofts, 1965.

Ray, R. D.: Psychology experiments as interbehavioral systems—a case study from the Soviet Union. *Psychol. Record, 2,* 279–306, 1977.

Razran, G.: Recent Russian psychology: 1950–1956. *Contemp. Psychol., 2,* 93–101, 1957.

Razran, G.: The observable unconscious and the inferable conscious in current Soviet psychophysiology: interoceptive conditioning, semantic conditioning, and the orienting reflex. *Psychol. Rev., 68,* 81–147, 1961.

Razran, G.: Russian physiologists' psychology and American experimental psychology: a historical and a systematic collation and a look into the future. *Psychol. Bull., 63,* 42–64, 1965.

Rescorla, R. A., and Solomon, R.: Two-process learning theory: relationships between Pavlovian conditioning and instrumental learning. *Psychol. Rev., 74,* 151–182, 1967.

Rescorla, R. A., and Wagner, A. R.: A theory of Pavlovian conditioning: variations in the effectiveness of reinforcement and nonreinforcement. In, A. H. Black and W. F. Prokasy (eds.): *Classical Conditioning II*. New York, Appleton-Century-Crofts, 1972.

Russell, R. W.: Biochemical substrates of behavior. In, R. W. Russell (ed.): *Frontiers in Physiological Psychology*. New York, Academic Press, 1966.

Schwartz, B., and Gamzu, E.: Pavlovian control of operant behavior: an analysis of autoshaping and of interactions between multiple schedules of reinforcement. In, W. K. Honig and J. E. R. Staddon (eds.): *Handbook of Operant Behavior*. Englewood Cliffs, New Jersey: Prentice-Hall, 1977.

Sechenov, I.: *Selected Works*. Moscow, State Publishing Houses, 1935.

Seligman, M. E. P., Maier, S. F., and Solomon, R. L.: Unsignalled and uncontrollable aversive events. In, R. F. Brush (ed.): *Aversive Conditioning and Learning*. New York, Academic Press, 1971.

Sherrington, C. S.: *The Integrative Action of the Nervous System*. New Haven, Yale University Press, 1906.

Sidman, M.: *Tactics of Scientific Research: Evaluating Experimental Data in Psychology*. New York, Basic Books, 1960.

Skinner, B. F.: Two types of conditioned reflex: a reply to Konorski and Miller. *J. Genet. Psychol.*, **16**, 272–279, 1937.

Sokolov, E. N.: The orienting reflex, its structure and mechanisms. In, L. G. Voronin, A. N. Leontiev, A. R. Luria, E. N. Sokolov, and O. S. Vinogradova (eds.): *Orienting Reflex and Exploratory Behavior*. Moscow, Academy of Pedagogical Sciences, 1958.

Sokolov, E. N.: *Orienting Reflex and Problems of the Higher Nervous Activity in Normal and Abnormal Children*. Moscow, Academy of Pedagogical Sciences, 1959.

Sokolov, E. N.: Neuronal models and the orienting influence. In, M. A. B. Brazier (ed.): *Central Nervous System and Behavior*. New York, Josiah Macy, 1960.

Sokolov, E. N.: *Perception and the Conditioned Reflex*. New York, MacMillan, 1963.

Solomon, R. L., and Turner, L. H.: Discriminative classical conditioning in dogs paralyzed by curare can later control discriminative avoidance responses in the normal state. *Psychol. Rev.*, **69**, 202–219, 1962.

Ukhtomsky, A. A.: *Complete* Works, vol. 5. Leningrad, State Publishing, 1954.

Wagner, A. R., and Rescorla, R. A.: Inhibition in Pavlovian conditioning: application of a theory. In, R. S. Boakes and M. S. Halliday (eds.): *Inhibition and Learning*. New York, Academic Press, 1972.

Wendt, G. R.: An interpretation of inhibition of conditioned reflexes as competition between reaction systems. *Psychol. Rev.*, **43**, 258–281, 1936.

Wessells, M. G.: The effects of reinforcement upon the prepecking behaviors of pigeons in the autoshaping experiment. *J. Exp. Anal. Behav.*, **21**, 125–144, 1974.

Williams, D. R., and Williams, H.: Auto-maintenance in the pigeon: sustained pecking despite contingent nonreinforcement. *J. Exp. Anal. Behav.*, **12**, 511–520, 1969.

Zener, K.: The significance of behavior accompanying conditioned salivary secretion for theories of the conditioned response. *Am. J. Psychol.*, **50**, 384–403, 1937.

Index